EUROPEAN HANDE

GERM
RAILWAYS

Part 2. PRIVATE RAILWAYS, PRESERVED LOCOMOTIVES AND MUSEUMS

FIRST EDITION

The complete guide to all Locomotives and
Multiple Units of German Private Railways plus Preserved
Locomotives, Museums and Museum Lines

Brian Garvin and Peter Fox

Published by Platform 5 Publishing Ltd., Wyvern House, Sark Road, Sheffield S2 4HG, England.
Printed in England by Hubbard Print, Dronfield, Sheffield.
ISBN 1 902336 37 2

Above: Ex-DB Class 50 2-10-0 50 2740 leaves Goldhausen with the 13.14 Siershahn–Limburg on 04/10/02 during the "Dampf-Takt über dem Westerwald" Plandampf. **Keith Satterly**

Front cover: A Vossloh type MaK1700BB loco owned by Angel Trains Cargo shunting at Grosskorbetha (MaK 1001212/2003) in 2003 on hire to InfraLeuna Infrastruktur und Service GmbH. **Philip Wormald**

Back cover top: The Freiberger Eisenbahn Gesellschaft has three Regioshuttle units for the service from Freiberg to Holzhau. VT3.03 is seen with the 15.34 Freiberg–Holzhau on 16/05/02. **Peter Fox**

Back cover bottom: The Lössnitzgrundbahn between Radebeul Ost and Radeburg has recently been sold to BVO Bahn GmbH. The enthusiasts' organisation "Traditionsbahn Radebeul" operate vintage trains over this route using preserved Meyer 99 1539-8 which carries its original livery and number of 132, despite having been "reconstructed" in the 1960s. The loco has been altered in some respects to look like an original Sachsen IV K, e.g. it has riveted tank sides. **Peter Fox**

CONTENTS

Above: On the Inselbahn Langeoog, locos 2 and 4 top-and-tail a set of multi-coloured coaches between Langeoog Bahnhof and the ferry terminal on 04/07/02. **Brian Garvin**

FOREWORD

Welcome to this first edition of German Railways Part 2 which covers private railways and operators, preserved locomotives and museums. The changes in Germany in recent years mean that today almost anywhere on the DB Network it is possible to find privately owned locomotives working trains over the main lines. This book is designed to help you identify those locomotives and the railways to which they belong.

The starting point has been those railways listed as belonging to the Verband Deutscher Verkehrsunternehmen (VDV) and enlarged to include others that the authors consider of interest (e.g. track contractors).

Because some of the preserved railway operators have become fully fledged operators (having a safety case etc) it has been decided to include all the museums and museum lines in this book as well as the lists of preserved locomotives. These lists have been expanded to include private lines' locomotives.

The format of the private railway section is different to that of the DB book. Only summary details of locomotives are shown but these details include the works numbers – often vital in identifying locomotives that have changed owners several times.

The compiling of this book has been difficult with changes taking place each week. The task started in 2000 but the period since then has been one of continuous change! The data is basically up to date to the end of 2003 with a few 2004 items added. Any errors or omissions should be brought to the notice of the authors who hope there are not too many! (As the book went into the final production stage several private operators became insolvent. They are still listed in this book as they have been part of the scene for the last few years and readers might like to have a record of their stock).

It is hoped that this book will answer many questions about the private lines and their locations and encourage more journeys off the beaten track in Germany.

INTRODUCTION

BACKGROUND

Railway fans from the UK often went to Germany via the Harwich–Hook of Holland route and entered Germany via Bad Bentheim. At this very first town in Germany some private railway shunting locomotives could be seen with the logo *BE* on them – *Bentheimer Eisenbahn*. But how many more such lines were there? The answer is many. For many years they were in decline but are now having a renaissance.

Latterly the private railways in Germany have been known as the "Nichtbundeseigene Eisenbahnen" – literally "non-state-owned railways" i.e. private lines. Germany has always had private railways the format of which was laid down by law. Besides the state run lines other railways were built as feeder lines or simple railways connecting some local communities. There were four main types:

Nebenbahnen: Standard gauge secondary railways normally with a top speed of 50 km/h. Some of the state railway's secondary lines were called Nebenbahnen as they came into this category.

Kreisbahnen/Lokalbahnen: These could be of 1435 mm, 1000 mm or 750 mm gauge but with a lower speed than Nebenbahnen.

Kleinbahnen: In addition to the above gauges a Kleinbahn could be of 600 mm gauge.

Examples of some railway names are:

Augsburger Localbahn	AL
Bentheimer Eisenbahn	BE
Rügensche Kleinbahn	RüKB
Dürener Kreisbahn	DKB
Hohenzollerische Landesbahn	HzL
Nebenbahn Nürtingen–Neuffen	NN

Note that each railway company has its own official abbreviation.

Until a few years ago the number of private railways was declining but this has changed now because of regionalisation and open access arrangements brought about by European Union legislation.

Regionalisation. Local passenger train service levels have always been decided by local authorities and run by DB. The change in railway legislation and the need for savings allowed the local authorities to tender for the supply of rail passenger services. It was found that DB prices were quite high compared to new local operators. Consequently local operators have taken over passenger trains in many areas that were once run by DB.

Open Access. The European Union has directed that track and signalling should be accounted for separately to show the costs of operating railways against roads. Consequently in several countries "Track Authorities" have been set up. The precise manner varies between countries but the result is that in the EU there should be open access for any train company to run trains over the railway networks.

Train Operators. The changes mentioned above have led to a surge in new operators both passenger and freight. In the latter category the freight operators can be sub-divided into commercial freight operators and track contractors – the latter hauling their own equipment and supplies around the national network. All locomotives and rolling stock have to conform to certain norms laid down by the Eisenbahnbundesamt (EBA – see later). The growth in the number of operators has meant a booming market in second hand locomotives. These operators have snapped up redundant locomotives being thwarted for a while by DB. Many got hold of locomotives that had been sold to preservation groups who were glad to have the cash (the loco after all is still available to preserve later) or imported locomotives that had "grandfather" rights on the DB. In this category come Polish ST44, CD 781 which were the same as DB class 220 (ex-DR). These could not be refused an operating licence as the safety case already existed!

Contractors and Dealers. The growth in the private sector has led to the creation of smaller back up organisations and quite a few entrepreneurs. Track renewal contractors have mushroomed with more and more track work being contracted out. Locomotive dealers have emerged who are quite adept at finding spare locomotives should someone be short. This has led to locomotives being imported as previously mentioned. Not to be outdone the major manufacturers have seen the opportunities and have set up hire fleets for short term hire for particular flows. In a case of "if you cannot beat them join them" the DB diesel overhaul works at Stendal (DB Regio) started selling or hiring out reconditioned Class 202 diesels before being taken over by Alstom. However under the new regime the work continues with ex-DB 212s also being overhauled and hired out or even sold.

Eisenbahn Bundesamt. This organisation is where the German Railways differ from the UK. The track authority in Germany is DB Netz. It owns the tracks and provides the signalling and signallers etc. However the safety case for the equipment is done by the EBA which has a supervisory role. Locomotives and rolling stock in Germany must comply with certain laid down safety and operating criteria (e.g. being fitted with Indusi, proper braking systems etc.). Imported locomotives have to meet these criteria and the locomotives will be inspected to ensure they do. DB itself has to get its locomotives and rolling stock passed by the EBA and each locomotive, unit or carriage will have stamped into the frame somewhere its EBA authorisation number. On new locomotives only the prototypes will be fully inspected and once agreed to run authority is granted for a fleet of similar locomotives etc. Should there be an incident where EBA standards have not been complied with there will be severe penalties.

Industrial Railways. These operate to different standards and locomotives are not normally allowed on to DB tracks. Usually they can work into exchange sidings only. Some industrial operators have always had special concessions for running over part of DB (Auf DB Gleis zugelassen); in particular this applies to industrial operators in the Ruhr area where firms would take traffic from a mine to a steelworks which would include a short section of DB track. A few of these railways have been included as their locomotives are often to be seen when passing through the Ruhr area.

▲ Städtische Eisenbahn Krefeld (StEK) No. D IV (type G1206) at Gladbeck West on 17/08/04.

▼ RAG Bahn und Hafen Betrieb has a large fleet of locos including four Mak type G2000 leased from Angel Trains. No. 904 stands at Duisburg Wedau on the same date as above.

Philip Wormald (2)

▲ 185CL007 is a Bombardier Class 185 operated by rail4chem. It is seen on a container train at Grosskorbetha on 21/05/02. **Brian Garvin**

▼ Siemens Dispolok ES 64 U2-025 working for the Karsdorfer Eisenbahn Gesellschaft (KEG) waits as Grosskorbetha on 06/08/03. **Philip Wormald**

USING THIS BOOK

The style used is that of some German publications from the 1980s and 1990s which the authors have been used to referring to when visiting Germany. The lists are in railway company order of the abbreviation. When visiting a particular railway normally the line's own rolling stock will be seen. However with open access and hire fleets certain locomotives work all over Germany. Having some idea of the train operator will obviously help but if a locomotive is not listed then please consult the hire fleets of Angel Trains Cargo, Bombardier Transportation, Siemens Dispolok, Vossloh or some of the smaller companies that lease their locomotives e.g. Rent a Rail. Some of the hire locomotives do not carry a running number the only identification is the works number. If the train is passing at speed then there is an obvious problem in identification!

Note: Names are shown in italics.

LOCOMOTIVE FLEETS

The locomotive fleets are a very mixed lot as one would expect from numerous private railways. However many locomotives on the different lines are of the same basic type. To meet the needs of the private railways all major German manufacturers produced some standard models most of these being types not in use on the main lines. In the 1970s the Bundesverband Deutscher Eisenbahnen decided on a series of standard diesel locomotives for use on private lines. Perhaps one manufacturer that should be mentioned in particular is MaK, later Siemens FT and now Vossloh. It has built hundreds of locomotives for industry and private railways none of which types were built for DB. The MaK B-B single cab diesel now totals more than 1000 examples with the type being continually refined to meet customer needs. This locomotive type has found itself on to several national railway systems such as NS (Class 6400) and Belgian Railways (Class 7700).

Classification of Locomotives

In the lists the locomotives are referred to by their manufacturer's classification such as G1200BB, MG530C etc or by their DB classification when ex-main line. The classification system is quite simple but does seem to vary from builder to builder; consequently some classifications are still not explained.

In the example of a MaK G1200BB this is broken down as follows:

G	=	Gelenkwelle – cardan shaft
1200	=	1200 horse power
BB	=	B-B wheel arrangement.

A Deutz MG530C is :

M	=	Mittellok i.e. mid horsepower range 300–800 h.p.
G	=	Gelenkwelle – cardan shaft
530	=	530 horse power
C	=	Three axles

Some Deutz descriptions also have an additional suffix of E or M denoting Endführerhaus (end cab) or Mittelführerhaus (middle or centre cab).

V100

Many of these locomotives appear in the lists. Some are ex-DB V100 and shown as V100DB or even ex-DR type machines shown as V100DR or by their DB/DR class number. Others are shown as V100.4 or V100.5. These are the LEW class descriptions. V100.4 are basically DR Class 293 later 298 whilst V100.5 are ex-DR Class 710. However it will be noted that, for example, 201201 is shown as a V100.4. This is because the locomotive has been rebuilt for private use to the V100.4 standard. The power of these locomotives varies considerably. Some locomotives have retained their original engines whilst others passing through the Adtranz/Bombardier or ALS works have been fitted with new Caterpillar engines. The information on which locomotives have received new engines is not easy to obtain as overhauls are done in so many places according to the wishes of the owners.

1. LOCOMOTIVE & RAILCAR BUILDERS & TYPES

1.1. LOCOMOTIVES

The private railways in Germany have many and varied locomotives but they are of several basic types. Details follow of the principle types with explanations of some of the abbreviations used to describe them. They are listed in builder or railway company order.

ALLRAD RANGIERTECHNIK GMBH, HEILIGENHAUS, GERMANY.

A rather recent addition to the names of locomotive builders, having only started production about 1970; just a few locomotives on private lines but others exist in industrial service.

TYPE: Cargolok DH440

Built: 1997
Engine: Deutz BF8M1015 (Water Cooled) 400 kW
Transmission: Hydraulic
Maximum Tractive Effort: up to 155 kN
Wheel Diameter:
Train Heating: None.

Weight in Full Working Order: 56 tonnes
Length Over Buffers: 10.9 m
Maximum Speed: 50 km/h

CKD PRAHA, CZECHOSLOVAKIA

Just a few locomotives from this builder and as would be expected they are in the eastern area and basically the same as DR type V75/CSD T435.
Built: 1962 onwards
Engine: 6S310DR of 551 kW
Maximum Tractive Effort:
Wheel Diameter: 1000 mm
Train Heating: Nil

Transmission: Electric
Weight in Full Working Order: 61 tonnes
Length Over Buffers: 12.56 m
Maximum Speed: 60 km/h

CRAIOVA – ELECTROPUTERE, CRAIOVA, ROMANIA

This Romanian builder supplied many locomotives to eastern European countries but not to the former DDR. However its 060DA model was in Poland as Class ST43 and as such had been passed for working into Germany on cross-border services. When open access came along lots of locomotives were spare in Romania and KEG saw the opportunity to acquire some.
The 060DA is a Swiss design with a Sulzer engine and has been built under licence in Romania from the 1960s and exported to many countries. Details are given for the standard model

TYPE: CFR 060DA later Class 60.

Built: 1965–1982
Engine: Sulzer 12 LDA 28 of 1544 kW
Maximum Tractive Effort: 314 kN
Wheel Diameter: 1100 mm
Train Heating: Nil

Transmission: Electric
Weight in Full Working Order: 116 tonnes
Length Over Buffers: 17.40 m
Maximum Speed: 100 km/h

DSB MY DIESELS

This is another class that had clearance for running into Germany so when open access came along these Nohab built GM locomotives were eagerly south after; being GMs they just keep on going! 10 locomotives came to Germany following electrification of lines in Denmark.

Built: 1954–1965
Engine: GM 16-567C of 1433 kW
Maximum Tractive Effort: 235 kN
Wheel Diameter: 1016 mm
Train Heating: (Steam, when built)

Builder: Nohab/GM, Tröllhattan, Sweden.
Transmission: Electric
Weight in Full Working Order: 101.6 tonnes
Length Over Buffers: 18.9 m
Maximum Speed: 133 km/h

▲ Spitzke Logistik (SLG) V100SP002 (ex-DR 202 547) stabled at Maschen Yard on 02/06/02.

▼ ITL Eisenbahngesellschaft is a company which works engineering and freight trains. It has three ex DR Class 118 (later 228) diesel-hydraulics.118 001 (ex-228 119) is seen working a ballast train through Erfurt.   **Brian Garvin (2)**

▲ Westfälische Almetalbahn (WAB) has three of these "Taiga Trommel" Russian-built diesel-electrics (DR Class 120 later 220), although none of them were ever DR locos. This one, No. 26, is seen on shed at Altenbeken.

▼ The WAB also owns 11 ex-DR Class 142 electric locos bought from Switzerland. Ex 477 911 and others are lined up at Altenbeken shed. **Brian Garvin (2)**

GMEINDER

A well known builder of shunting locomotives having built may Köfs and a variety of other types for industrial and private lines. The classification system used by Gmeinder is quite straightforward e.g. D35B where D = diesel, 35 = 350 h.p. and B = 2 axles.

TYPE D25B

Engine: Mercedes Benz OM424 of 180–200 kW
Maximum Tractive Effort:
Wheel Diameter: 850 mm
Train Heating: None

Transmission: Hydraulic
Weight in Full Working Order: 32 tonnes
Length Over Buffers: 7.040 m
Maximum Speed: 50 km/h

TYPE D100BB

Engine: MTU 12V4000 R20
Maximum Tractive Effort:
Wheel Diameter: 1000 mm
Train Heating: None

Transmission: Hydraulic
Weight in Full Working Order: 64–100 tonnes
Length Over Buffers: 12.4 m
Maximum Speed: 40–110 km/h

TYPE D65BB

Engine: of 480–750 kW
Maximum Tractive Effort:
Wheel Diameter: 950 mm
Train Heating: None

Transmission: Hydraulic
Weight in Full Working Order: 56–68 tonnes
Length Over Buffers: 10.240 m
Maximum Speed: 70 km/h

HENSCHEL/ADTRANZ/BOMBARDIER

Henschel was not only a builder of main line types it also had many of its own designs that were used on private lines and in industry. As with other builders the type code is easily explained. DH or DE stands for a Diesel Hydraulic or Diesel Electric locomotive; however, the addition of the letter G (Gelenkwellen) to DH denotes a carden shaft drive so no coupling rods. The figures once again denote horsepower or later kilowatt rating followed by a code for the wheel arrangement. The letter A indicates Akkumulator or battery whilst ED is electro-diesel.

TYPE DHG700C

Engine: MTU 6V396 TC12
Maximum Tractive Effort:
Wheel Diameter:
Train Heating: None

Transmission: Hydraulic L3r4U2
Weight in Full Working Order: 47 tonnes
Length Over Buffers:
Maximum Speed: 58 km/h

TYPE DHG1000BB

Engine: MTU 12V396 TC12
Maximum Tractive Effort:
Wheel Diameter:
Train Heating:

Transmission: Hydraulic
Weight in Full Working Order: 44 tonnes
Length Over Buffers:
Maximum Speed: 90 km/h

JUNG

Another builder that contributed to main line loco construction but also developed its own types for private and industrial use. The Jung Classification is slightly different with types coded R30B. R42C etc. As most types were hydraulic and diesel, the prefix R denotes a *Rangier* or shunting locomotive; horsepower and wheel arrangement codes then follow.

TYPE R42C

Engine:
Maximum Tractive Effort:
Wheel Diameter:
Train Heating:

Transmission: Hydraulic
Weight in Full Working Order: 36–48 tonnes
Length Over Buffers: 3.40 m
Maximum Speed:

KHD

This firm built many locos for the main line but these are virtually insignificant compared to those built for industry, private railways and export. The Deutz type classification was different from other builders e.g. KS225B, MS650D, DG2000CCM. K = Klein (small, 28-300 hp) but a second K = Kette (chain); S = stangen (coupling rods) M = Mittel (middle range 300-800 hp) but D = Drehgestell (bogie). The figures denote horsepower whilst the suffix letter/s denotes the number of axles with an additional E denoting end cab, M – middle cab!

TYPE KG275B

Engine: Deutz BA12L714
Maximum Tractive Effort:
Length Over Buffers: 8.03 m

Transmission: Hydraulic, Voith L213
Weight in Full Working Order: 32–36 tonnes
Maximum Speed: 28.5 km/h

TYPE MG530C

Engine: Deutz T8M625 of 530 h.p.
Maximum Tractive Effort:
Length Over Buffers: 9.88 m

Transmission: Hydraulic, Voith L37Ab
Weight in Full Working Order: 48–60 tonnes
Maximum Speed: 60 km/h

TYPE DG1200BBM

Engine: BT12M625 of 1200 h.p.
Maximum Tractive Effort:
Length Over Buffers: 13.30 m

Transmission: Hydraulic, Voith L306r
Weight in Full Working Order: 68–80 tonnes
Maximum Speed: 70 km/h

KRAUSS MAFFEI

This well known München locomotive builder had its own range of locomotive types for private and industrial line use.

TYPE MH05C

Engine: MTU 6V396TC12 or 13 of 500 kW
Maximum Tractive Effort:
Wheel Diameter:
Train Heating: Not fitted

Transmission: Voith Hydraulic
Weight in Full Working Order: 60–65 tonnes
Length Over Buffers: 9.860 m
Maximum Speed: 40 km/h

LKM

LKM is the former Orenstein & Koppel works that ended up being in East Germany and thus became state controlled and given a new name. It carried on the O&K tradition by building lots of small diesel locomotives for industry but also entered the main line scene being involved in the DR diesel programme. Some locomotives are described by their DR designation where these types had main line equivalents but sometimes abbreviations are used such as V10B where V = Verbrennungslok, 10 = 100 hp and B = 2 axles.

LUGANSK

This builder is represented by two main types – the M62 and TE109 or DB 230, 231, 232. The M62 was built by Lugansk first for Hungary and the Hungarian classification has stuck as a class type. The locomotive was in East Germany as class 120 (later 220), Poland as ST44, Czechoslovakia as 781 as well as in other countries. However it is Poland and the Czech Republic that hasveprovided locomotives for the German private railways with the Polish ones easily identified by their large headlights. The M62 specification is given under DB in this section whilst the 232 type details are in Part 1.

Mak/VSFT/VOSSLOH.

MaK, now Vossloh Locomotives is perhaps the builder most associated with the private lines. Besides building many locomotives for DB MaK had its own line of locomotive types for the private and industrial lines. In the recent past MaK was taken over by Krupp, then Siemens and then Vossloh. It is under the Vossloh period that terrific growth has taken place with over 150 locomotives being built per year now compared to 40–50 just a few years ago. It is not possible to describe every type of MaK locomotive type in use so a few main examples are shown. If we take the standard BB diesel hydraulic with an off centre cab this has grown from G1100BB through G1202, G1203, G1204, G1205, G1206 G1300, G1600 models and now the G1700! Basically all these types derive from the models built for DB such as V100 and V90 but the design has been constantly revised and improved. Many MaK types are in use on the private lines and readers must surely be aware that MaK types are now on the Austrian, Belgian, French, Netherlands and

▲ OME 0005 is an example of a Bombardier "Talent" unit. It is seen stabled at Neubrandenburg in
August 2000.   **Ray Smith**

▼ The Siemens "RegioSprinter" pre-dated the "Desiro" fleet. Vogtlandbahn VT45 is one which is
modified for street-running in Zwickau and is seen at the town centre terminus on 21/05/02.
                                                                                  Brian Garvin

▲ The LINT41 is designed by Linke-Hofmann-Busch, now owned by Alstom. Mecklenburg Bahn 701 waits to depart from Schwerin on 05/04/04 with the 16.56 to Parchim.   **Peter Fox**

▼ The Stadler GTW 2/6 is an odd design with the engine contained in a central "pod". BLE 509107 is seen at Hungen on 29/05/02 with the 09.35 to Beienheim.   **Keith Fender**

Swiss Railways. The G2000 type when it came out was a surprise with end cabs but not across the whole width of the locomotive allowing access to the side panels. Later versions have been built with a full width cab especially for countries where an assistant driver is used.

TYPE G50BB, G1100BB*

Engine: MaK 6M282A of 626 kw. 850 h.p. or 6M282AK of 810 kW/1100 h.p.*
Transmission: Hydraulic, Voith.

Maximum Tractive Effort:	**Weight in Full Working Order:** 68 – 80 tonnes
Wheel Diameter: 1000 mm	**Length Over Buffers:** 12.200 m
Train Heating: Not fitted	**Maximum Speed:** 36–60 km/h

TYPE G1206BB

Engine: MTU 16V396TC14 of 1570 kW, MTU 12V4000R20 of 1570 kW or Caterpillar 3512 B DI-TA of 1500 kW
Transmission: Hydraulic, Voith.

Maximum Tractive Effort:	**Weight in Full Working Order:** 90/87.3 tonnes
Wheel Diameter: 1000 mm	**Length Over Buffers:** 14.700 m–15.300 m
Train Heating: Not fitted	**Maximum Speed:** 80–100 km/h

TYPE MaK 1700

Engine: MTU 12V4000R20 of 1500 kW or CAT 3512 B-HD of 1700 kW
Transmission: Hydraulic

Maximum Tractive Effort:	**Weight in Full Working Order:** 87/80 tonnes
Wheel Diameter: 1000 mm	**Length Over Buffers:** 14.7 m or 15.2 m
Train Heating: Not Fitted	**Maximum Speed:** 100 km/h

TYPE G 2000

Engine: CAT 3516 B-HD of 2240 kW or MTU 20V4000 R42 of 2700 kW
Transmission: Hydraulic

Maximum Tractive Effort:	**Weight in Full Working Order:** 87.3 or 90 tonnes
Wheel Diameter: 1000 mm	**Length Over Buffers:** 17.4 m
Train Heating: Not fitted	**Maximum Speed:** 120 km/h

O&K ORENSTEIN & KOPPEL

O&K produced many diesel shunting locomotives. It took a good hand in production for the DB with Köfs and also provided many locomotives to private and industrial lines. After World War II all O&K diesels were produced at the company's Dortmund plant. The Berlin plant became LKM in DDR times.

SCHÖMA

This is a well known builder of industrial locomotives with just a few types getting on private lines.

SIEMENS

The main locomotives from Siemens are standard types used by Siemens Dispolok. The ES64U2 is basically the ÖBB class 1116 or DB 182. Similarly ES64F4 is DB class 189 whilst the Eurorunner (ER) type is the same as ÖBB class 2016. Details of the DB classes can be found in part 1 whilst those for the Eurorunner appear below:

TYPE ER20

Engine: MTU 16V4000 R41 of 2000 kW	**Transmission:** Electric
Maximum Tractive Effort: 235 kN	**Weight in Full Working Order:** 80 tonnes
Wheel Diameter:	**Length Over Buffers:** 19.275 m
Train Heating: Electric	**Maximum Speed:** 140 km/h

WINDHOFF

The Windhoff factory is in Rheine and produced many types of small diesel shunting locomotives for private and industrial use. It was an early supplier of remotely controlled locomotives of both diesel and battery electric types.

1.2. RAILCARS

DUEWAG

Predominately a carriage and tramcar builder, this company is now part of the Siemens empire. It continues to thrive on these products but has also produced diesel railcars for the emerging private operators starting off with the Regio Sprinter and going on to what is now the DB class 642 *"DESIRO"*.

TYPE: REGIO SPRINTER
Built: 1995–1998
Builder Siemens-Duewag
Engine: 2 MAN D2865 LU3 of 198 kW   **Transmission:** Mechanical
Length Over Couplings: 24.8 m   **Weight:** 49.2 tonnes
Accommodation: –/74   **Maximum Speed:** 100 km/h

DWA

This builder emerged from the old DDR production lines and had specialised in supplying carriages to the DR and the Soviet Union. After unification it produced its own lightweight railcar but the type has not been taken up in any large numbers. Later DWA was taken over by Bombardier who decided to abandon the DWA railcars.

TYPE: LVT/S
Built:
Length Over Couplings: 16.54 m   **Weight:** 23 tonnes
Accommodation: –/64 (5)   **Maximum Speed:** 120 km/h

TALBOT

Although appearing as Talbot this firm is now part of the Bombardier group. Before being taken over by Bombardier Talbot had great success with its *TALENT* railcars (**Ta**lbots **Le**ichter **N**ahverkehrs **T**riebwagen).
Typical specifications can be found in Part 1 as DB has these railcars as classes 643 and 644.

WAGGON UNION

This builder was a big supplier of trams and railcars and produced the so called standard private line railcar in the 1980s known as the NE81. It also produced the follow on design with the Regio Shuttle before being taken over by Adtranz. In the process the firm was moved to a new site at Pankow and later was bought by Stadler Rail and now trades as Stadler Pankow. Details of typical Regio Shuttle specifications can be found in Part 1 as DB type 650. Basic details of the NE 81 units follows:
Built: 1981–1994
Engine: 2 MAN D2566 MTUE of 199 kW or 2 MAN D2866 LUE of 250 kW
Length Over Couplings: 23.89 m   **Weight:** 39–46 tonnes
Maximum Speed: 80–90 km/h   **Accommodation:** –/78

1.3. DB & DR TYPES

Naturally many former DB and DR main line and shunting locomotives have ended up in service with private railways. Many are just as they were on DB/DR but some V100 and 232s have been rebuilt with more modern engines of varying power. Once open access really got going some builders diverted locos intended for DB to private operators e.g. 145CL which are exactly the same as DB locos. For technical details of DB/DR types that are still in use on the main line see Part 1. Older types are listed below.

1.3.1. ELECTRIC

CLASSES 109 & 142*   Bo-Bo
Built: 1962–76 for DR.
Builder: LEW
One Hour Rating: 2920 kW.   **Weight**: 82 tonnes.
Wheel Diameter: 1350 mm.   **Length over Buffers**: 16.26 m
Maximum Tractive Effort: 209 (245*) kN.   **Maximum Speed** 120 (100*) km/h.
Electric Brake: Rheostatic (Class 142 only).

1.3.2. DIESEL

CLASS 211   B-B
Built: 1958–1963 for DB.
Builders: MaK, Jung, Deutz, Henschel, Krauss Maffei, Esslingen.
Engine: MTU MD 12V538 TA, MB 12V493TZ or MB 12V652 TZ of 820 kW or 1005 kW.
Transmission: Hydraulic
Maximum Tractive Effort: 183 kN   **Weight in Full Working Order**: 62 tonnes
Wheel Diameter: 950 mm   **Length Over Buffers**: 12.10 m
Train Heating: Steam.   **Maximum Speed**: 100 km/h

CLASS 220 DR (formerly 120)   Co-Co
Built: 1966–84 for DR.
Builder: Lugansk.
Engine: 1470 kW.   **Transmission**: Electric
Maximum Tractive Effort: 373 kN   **Weight in Full Working Order**: 116 tonnes
Wheel Diameter: 1050 mm.   **Length Over Buffers**: 17.55 m
Train Heating: None.   **Maximum Speed**: 100 km/h

CLASS 220 DB   B-B
Built: 1953–1963 for DB.
Builder: Krauss Maffei, MaK.
Engine: MTU MB12V493TZ of 820 kW.
Transmission: Hydraulic
Weight in Full Working Order: 73.5–81 tonnes
Wheel Diameter: 950 mm.   **Length Over Buffers**: 18.47 m.
Train Heating: Steam.   **Maximum Speed**: 140 km/h

CLASS 221   B-B
Built: 1962–1965 for DB.
Builder: Krauss Maffei.
Engine: MTU MB12V652TA. of 1000 kW.
Transmission: Hydraulic
Weight in Full Working Order: 78–79.5 tonnes
Wheel Diameter: 950 mm.   **Length Over Buffers**: 18.44 m.
Train Heating: Steam.   **Maximum Speed**: 140 km/h

CLASS 228 (formerly DR 118)   B-B (228.1/5) or C-C (228.2/6)
Built: 1962–1970 for DR.
Builder: LKM.
Engine: 2 x 736 kW (2 x 883 kW Class 228.6).   **Transmission**: Hydraulic.

Maximum Tractive Effort:
Weight in Full Working Order: 78 tonnes (228.1/5), 90 tonnes (228.2/6)
Wheel Diameter: 1000 mm.   **Length Over Buffers:** 19.46 m
Train Heating: Steam.   **Maximum Speed:** 120 km/h

CLASS 230 (formerly DR 130)   Co-Co

For details see Class 232 except:
Weight in Full Working Order: 120 tonnes   **Maximum Speed:** 100 km/h

CLASS V320   C-C

Built: 1962
Builder: Henschel
Engine: 2 x 1400 kW   **Transmission:** Hydraulic
Maximum Tractive Effort: 36.4 kN   **Weight in Full Working Order:** 121.4 tonnes
Wheel Diameter: 1100 mm   **Length Over Buffers:** 23.0 m
Train Heating: (Steam when built)   **Maximum Speed:** 160 km/h

1.3.3. DIESEL RAILBUS

CLASS 796 DRB   A-A

Railbuses with normal couplings and buffers. Some were converted to one-person operation and classified 796.

Built: 1955–62 for DB.   **Transmission:** Mechanical.
Builder: Uerdingen, MAN, WMD.   **Weight in Full Working Order:** 27 tonnes
Engine: 2 x 112 kW.   **Length Over Buffers:** 13.95 m.
Accommodation: –/56 1T.   **Maximum Speed:** 90 km/h

ACKNOWLEDGEMENTS

Brian Garvin has collected data over many years and consulted many books and magazines. In recent times the Internet has become a valuable source of information but care has to be taken using this medium. The following books have been consulted and provided background information

Railway Holiday in Northern Germany (David & Charles 1965)
Die Privatbahnen in der Bundesrepublik Deutschland (Eisenbahn Kurier 1984)
NE90, NE92 – Die Triebfahrzeuge der Deutschen Privatbahn (Schweers & Wall)
Jahrbuch Schienenverkehr – various issues
Verband Deutscher Verkehrsunternehmen Jahrbuch – 2000, 2002 issues
Die Kleinbahn (Zeunert)

The following magazines have been consulted and all report developments on the private lines: Bahn Report, Der Schienenbus, Drehscheibe, Eisenbahn Kurier, Eisenbahn Revue International, LOK-Report, Lokrundschau, Bulletin (The magazine of the Locomotive Club of Great Britain), Today's Railways.

Websites. The following websites can be recommended for information on developments:
www.railfan.de – compiled by Georg Ringler and excellent.
www.lok-report.de – the website of the German Magazine – updated virtually daily.
www.drehscheibe-online.de – forum pages very useful and good links.
www.museumslok.de – the website of Jürgen Utecht – useful lists and updated regularly
www.privat-bahn.de – the website of Alexander Bückle – useful lists and a museum line update each month.
www.v100-online.de – the website of Dieter Römshild concentrating on the DR V100

Thanks must also be passed on to all those many correspondents who over the years have sent to me details of their tours and visits. Thanks everyone.

Brian Garvin

2. NARROW GAUGE RAILWAYS OF THE DEUTSCHE REICHSBAHN (DR)

At the time of the union of the two Germanys the DR had a number of narrow gauge railways which were still operated by steam locomotives. The survival of these lines was generally due to the poor condition of the highway infrastructure with the use of steam being due to lack of funds for new diesel locomotives. All of the lines which were extant in 1990 are still operating, all now under "private" ownership. The word "private" is stated with quotation marks since the shareholders of many of these companies tend to be the various local authorities in the area concerned. The two lines around Dresden have just been sold to BVO Bahn GmbH, the owner of the Fichtelbergbahn and have some finance from the Verkehrsverbund Oberelbe (Oberelbe transport union – the German equivalent of a British Passenger Transport Executive). These are:

- Radebeul Ost–Radeburg, now known as the Lössnitzgrundbahn
- Freital Hainsberg–Kurort Kipsdorf, now known as the Weisseritztalbahn. This line is at present closed due to the 2002 floods.

All remaining lines in normal service are of 750 mm gauge which was the standard for narrow gauge lines in Sachsen (Saxony), except for the Harz network which is metre gauge and the Mollibahn which is 900 mm gauge. There are also a number of preservation ventures.

These listings show the complete classes for convenience and are duplicated in the main private railway and museum sections of this book.

Lines still open as public railways

1. Cranzahl–Kurort Oberwiesenthal.

Now known as the Fichtelbergbahn, this line runs from Cranzahl on the line from Flöha to Vejprty (CD) as far as Kurort Oberwiesenthal, the highest town in Sachsen. The fleet consists entirely of 2-10-2T locos. The line is operated by BVO Bahn, BVO being the local bus company.

2. Radebeul Ost–Radeburg.

This line runs from Radebeul Ost in the Dresden suburbs to Radeburg along a valley known as the Lössnitzgrund and is now known as the Lössnitzgrundbahn. There is a major tourist destination half-way along at Moritzburg where there is a moated castle which was once Augustus der Starke's hunting lodge.

3. Freital Hainsberg–Kurort Kipsdorf.

This line runs from Freital to Kipsdorf and has some very scenic parts including the lake at Malter. Unfortunately it is at present closed due to the disastrous floods of 2002.

4. Zittau–Kurort Oybin/Kurort Jonsdorf.

This line runs into the hills from Zittau near the Czech/Polish border to a junction station at Bertsdorf where the two branches diverge. There is a small workshop here with the main depot being at Zittau. Empty stock crosses the station square to get from the depot to the narrow-gauge station.

5. Oschatz–Mügeln–Kemmlitz.

This line is the odd one out of all the Sachsen lines as it was a freight-only line at German unification. Pairs of Sachsen type IVK Meyers were employed carrying standard gauge wagons on transporters. This traffic has now ceased but a passenger service has been reintroduced and for a time this was partly steam–hauled. One of the line's former Meyers has now been restored to working order with one being stored and one having been hired to Ludger Guttwein owner of the museum at Prora on Rügen.

6. The Rügensche Kleinbahn

This 750 mm gauge line runs from Putbus to Göhren on the Baltic Sea island of Rügen. It is the remnant of a much larger system and has its own distinctive loco classes as well as three of the standard 2-10-2Ts, two of which were transferred from Sachsen in DR days with the other having been bought since. This line is marketed as "Rasender Roland" (Racing Roland).

7. The Molli

This line runs between Bad Doberan and Kühlungsborn on the Baltic coast. It has the unusual gauge of 900 mm.

8. Harzer Schmalspurbahnen (1000 mm gauge)

Perhaps the most famous of the East German narrow-gauge lines, the HSB is now a thriving concern. It consists of three separate lines as follows:

• The Harzquerbahn which runs from Wernigerode to Nordhausen.
• The Brockenbahn which runs from Drei Annen Hohne on the Harzquerbahn to Brocken.
• The Selketalbahn. This is a network of lines from Gernrode to Hasselfelde with a branch from Alexisbad to Harzgerode and another one from Stiege to Eisfelder Talmühle where connection is made with the Harzquerbahn.

For a time (from 1961 to 1983) the Selketalbahn was closed between Güntersberge and Stiege, the missing section having been removed by the Soviet Union as war reparations. The line from Gernrode to Harzgerode and Güntersberge was operated by the remaining Mallets whilst the line from Eisfelder Talmühle to Hasselfelde was operated as part of the Harzquerbahn. The Selketalbahn is due to be extended from Gernrode to Quedlinburg the town centre of which is a world heritage site.

The HSB has a fleet of powerful 2-10-2T locomotives plus a solitary 2-6-2T and two 0-6-0Ts. There are also four Mallets, three of which were built in the 19th century. Normal services on the line from Wernigerode to Brocken are worked by the 2-10-2T locos, whilst the Selketalbahn has one daily steam diagram, normally the 2-6-2T 99 6001. The rest of the services on the Selketalbahn plus most trains on the Harzquerbahn are diesel railcars. However there is an additional steam diagram from Gernrode on Fridays and Saturdays in summer, normally Mallet 99 5906 and there are two return steam workings in summer on the Harzquerbahn, one from Nordhausen to Brocken and one from Wernigerode to Eisfelder Talmühle. The Mallets which used to work the Selketalbahn were vacuum-braked but have been fitted with air brakes since privatisation and are now used on specials and charter trains.

Mention should also be made of the diesel fleet. The HSB has five C-C "coathanger" locos which were converted by the DR from standard gauge Class 110 B–Bs. Ten of these were converted, the plan being to replace steam locos, but five have now been sold with the five remaining used for shunting, works trains, snow plough and e.c.s. duties. The HSB also obtained some second–hand railcars from the Inselbahn Langeoog and has bought a small fleet of new railcars. In addition, dual-mode Siemens Combino trams are now running through from the Nordhausen tram network to Ilfeld under diesel power.

Preserved lines

There are two preserved 750 mm gauge lines in Sachsen, the Pressnitztalbahn and the Museumsbahn Schönheide. Both these lines operate Sachsen IV K Meyers. In addition the "Öchslebahn" at Ochsenhausen in Baden-Württemburg operates two ex-Sachsen locos. Details will be found in the "Museums and Museum Lines" section of this book.

NUMBERING SYSTEMS

The locomotives have had three numbering systems (four in the case of the original Sachsen locos). The three systems are as follows:

The original DR system. Consists of the number "99" plus a serial number, e.g. 99 741.

The DR computer system. Consists of the number "99" plus a serial number plus a computer check digit. The serial number is the same as the original with the addition of an extra digit in front of a 3-digit number e.g. 99 1741-0.

The DB AG computer system. Consists of the number "099" plus a serial number plus a computer check digit. The serial number is different from the original e.g. 099 725-4 is the DB number of the loco which was originally 99 741 and later 99 1741-0.

Although DB computer numbers were allocated to the Harz locos, the line was privatised before they could be applied. Other lines all used the new DB numbers, but these have now been abandoned on all lines. BVO Bahn, Oberwiesenthal and SOEG have reverted to the original DR numbers but other lines generally use the DR computer numbers. Please note if inspecting a stored loco that the numbers stamped on the rods are likely to be the original ones.

LOCOMOTIVES & RAILCARS

Note: In the following lists, only ex-DR/DB ocos are generally shown. Certain railways have acquired various diesel shunters from various places recently, but these are not shown.

900 mm GAUGE LOCOMOTIVES (Mollibahn)

CLASS 99.32   2-8-2T (1'D1'h2t)

These smart 2-8-2Ts were built in 1932 to replace old locos.

Built: 1932.
Builder: O&K.
Driving Wheel Dia.: 1100 mm.
Length over Buffers: 10.60 m.
Max. Speed: 50 km/h.

Gauge: 900 mm.
Boiler Pressure: 14 bar.
Weight: 43.68 tonnes.
Cylinders: (2) 380 x 550 mm.

DR.	DR (c)	DB	Build details
99 321	99 2321-0	099 901-1	O&K 12400/1932
99 322	99 2322-8	099 902-9	O&K 12401/1932
99 323	99 2323-6	099 903-7	O&K 12402/1932

CLASS 99.33   0-8-0T (Dh2t)

These locos were built for the Wismut AG industrial concern and came to the DR in 1961. They are normally used on works trains.

Built: 1950.
Builder: LKM.
Driving Wheel Dia.: 800 mm.
Length over Buffers: 8.86 m.
Max. Speed: 35 km/h.

Gauge: 900 mm.
Boiler Pressure: 14 bar.
Weight: 32.4 tonnes.
Cylinders: (2) 370 x 400 mm.

Wismut AG.	DR No.	DR (c)	DB No.	Build details
22	99 331	99 2331-9	099 904-5	LKM 30011/1991
44	99 332	99 2332-7	099 905-2 (plinthed)	LKM 30013/1991

750 mm GAUGE LOCOMOTIVES

KSStEB Class IV K   MEYER   0-4-4-0T (BBn4vt)

The KSStEB's best known locomotive is the "IV K" Meyer. This is a four-cylinder compound in which the two sets of cylinders face each other. Most of the existing locos were built new at RAW Görlitz in the 1960s, but were classed as rebuilds for accounting purposes and retain their original identities. The ones in original condition are marked with an asterisk.

Built: 1899–1921.
Builder: Hartmann.
Driving Wheel Dia.: 760 mm.
Length over Buffers: 9.00 m.
Max. Speed: 30 km/h.

Gauge: 750 mm.
Boiler Pressure: 15 bar.
Weight: 27.4-29.6 tonnes.
Cylinders: (4) 2 high pressure: 240 x 380 mm.
       2 low pressure: 370 x 380 mm.

KKStEB	DR	DR (c)	DB	Location	Build details
108	99 516	99 1516-6		Museumsbahn Schönheide	Hart 1779/1892
127	99 534	99 1534-9		Gemeinde Geyer (static exhibit)	Hart 2030/1894
128	99 535*			Verkehrsmuseum Dresden	Hart 2276/1894
132	99 539	99 1539-8	099 701-5	Traditionsbahn Radebeul, Radeburg.	Hart 2381/1899
135	99 542	99 1542-2	099 702-3	Pressnitztalbahn Jöhstadt	Hart 2384/1899
145	99 555	99 1555-4		SOEG Bertsdorf	Hart 3208/1908
151	99 561	99 1561-2	099 703-1	Döllnitzbahn Mügeln	Hart 3214/1909
152	99 562	99 1562-0	099 704-9	DDM Neuenmarkt-Wirsberg	Hart 3218/1909
154	99 564	99 1564-6	099 705-6	DB Museum. Freital Hainsberg	Hart 3217/1909
156	99 566	99 1566-1		Sächsisches EM, Chemnitz-Hilbersdorf	Hart 3219/1909
158	99 568	99 1568-7	099 706-4	Pressnitztalbahn Jöhstadt	Hart 3450/1910
164	99 574	99 1574-5	099 707-2	Döllnitzbahn Mügeln (Z)	Hart 3556/1912
169	99 579*	99 1579-4		Schmalspurmuseum Oberrittersgrün	Hart 3561/1912
171	99 582	99 1582-8	099 708-0	Museumsbahn Schönheide	Hart 3593/1912
173	99 584	99 1584-4	099 709-8	Prora, Rügen	Hart 3596/1912

175	99 585	99 1585-1	099 710-6	Museumsbahn Schönheide	Hart 3597/1912
176	99 586	99 1586-9	099 711-4	Traditionsbahn Radebeul (Z)	Hart 3606/1913
180	99 590	99 1590-1		Pressnitztalbahn Jöhstadt	Hart 3670/1913
184	99 594	99 1594-3		Straupitz	Hart 3714/1914
194	99 604*			DGEG Bochum Dahlhausen	Hart 3792/1914
196	99 606	99 1606-5	099 712-2	DB Museum Nürnberg	Hart 3907/1916
198	99 608	99 1608-1	099 713-0	BVO Freital Hainsberg	Hart 4521/1921

DRG "Nachbau VI K"   0-10-0T (Eh2t)

This class is a development of the KKStEB Class VIk. 47 were built of which 14 were rebuilt in 1963 with new boilers, cabs and motion. 99 716 became a DB loco after the war.

Built: 1927.
Builder: Hartmann.
Driving Wheel Dia.: 800 mm.
Length over Buffers: 8.99 m.
Max. Speed: 30 km/h.

Gauge: 750 mm.
Boiler Pressure: 14 bar.
Weight: 42.25 tonnes.
Cylinders: (2) 430 x 400 mm.

DR	DR (c)	DB	Location	Build details
99 713	99 1713-9	099 720-5	Traditionsbahn Radebeul, Radeburg	Hart 4670/1927
99 715	99 1715-4		Dippoldiswalde	Hart 4672/1927
99 716	99 1716-2		Öchslebahn. Ochsenhausen.	Hart 4673/1927

CLASS 99.73   2-10-2T (1'E1'h2t)

These locomotives introduced in the DRG period were built as a standard locomotive for 750 mm gauge lines but most were concentrated in Sachsen. Active SOEG, Zittau locos were converted to oil firing using light oil (diesel fuel), but all active ones have been converted back to coal firing. Certain locos shown here may now be withdrawn from service.

Built: 1928–33.
Builder: Hartmann.
Driving Wheel Dia.: 800 mm.
Length over Buffers: 10.54 m.
Max. Speed: 30 km/h.

Gauge: 750 mm.
Boiler Pressure: 14 bar.
Weight: 56.7 tonnes.
Cylinders: (2) 450 x 400 mm.

DR	DR (c)	DB	Location	Build details
99 731	99 1731-1	099 722-1	SOEG, Zittau	Hart 4678/1928
99 734	99 1734-5	099 723-9	BVO Freital Hainsberg	Hart 4681/1928
99 735	99 1735-2	099 724-7	SOEG, Zittau	Hart 4682/1928
99 741	99 1741-0	099 725-4	BVO Freital Hainsberg	Hart 4691/1928
99 746	99 1746-9	099 726-2	BVO Freital Hainsberg	BMAG 9535/1929
99 747	99 1747-7	099 727-0	BVO Freital Hainsberg	BMAG 9536/1929
99 749	99 1749-3	099 728-8	SOEG, Zittau	BMAG 9538/1929
99 750	99 1750-1	099 729-6	SOEG, Zittau (Z)	BMAG 9539/1929
99 757	99 1757-6	099 730-4	SOEG, Zittau (Z)	BMAG 10148/1933
99 758	99 1758-4	099 731-2	SOEG, Zittau	BMAG 10149/1933
99 759	99 1759-2	099 732-0	Schmalspurmuseum, Oberrittersgrün	BMAG 10150/1933
99 760	99 1760-0	099 733-8	SOEG, Zittau	BMAG 10151/1933
99 761	99 1761-8	099 734-6	BVO Freital Hainsberg	BMAG 10152/1933
99 762	99 1762-6	099 735-3	BVO Freital Hainsberg	BMAG 10153/1933

CLASS 99.77   2-10-2T (1'E1'h2t)

A post World War II version of the preceding class built by DR to improve the fleet of locomotives on the Sachsen narrow gauge lines. Two locomotives were transferred to the RüKB by the DR and a third was bought by the RüKB after privatisation.

Built: 1952–1957.
Builder: BMAG, LKM.
Driving Wheel Dia.: 800 mm.
Length over Buffers: 10.54 m
Max. Speed: 30 km/h.

Gauge: 750 mm.
Boiler Pressure: 14 bar.
Weight: 58 tonnes.
Cylinders: (2) 450 x 400 mm.

DR	DR (c)	DB	Location	Build details
99 771	99 1771-7	099 736-1	BVO Bahn, Freital Hainsberg	LKM 32010/1952
99 772	99 1772-5	099 737-9	BVO Bahn, Oberwiesenthal	LKM 32011/1952
99 773	99 1773-3	099 738-7	BVO Bahn, Oberwiesenthal	LKM 32012/1952
99 775	99 1775-8	099 739-5	BVO Bahn, Radebeul Ost	LKM 32014/1953

▲ **Öchslebahn.** Sachsen VI K 0-10-0T 99 716 waits to leave Ochsenhausen for Warthausen on 17/08/02.   **Brian Garvin**

▼ **Rügensche Kleinbahn.** 0-8-0WT 53M^h leaves Jagdschloss Granitz with the Today's Railways "Coast & Peaks" special from Göhren to Putbus on 21/06/01.   **Peter Fox**

▲ **Rügensche Kleinbahn.** 2-10-2T 99 782 at Posewald with a Putbus–Göhren train on New Year's Eve 1991. **Steffen Scharf**

▼ **Mollibahn.** 0-8-0T 99 2331-9 works the Today's Railways "Coast & Peaks" special from Ostseebad Kühlungsborn through the streets of Bad Doberan on 20/06/01. This loco is normally only used on works trains. **Peter Fox**

99 776	99 1776-6	099 740-3	BVO Bahn, Oberwiesenthal (Z)	LKM 32015/1953
99 777	99 1777-4	099 741-1	BVO Bahn, Freital Hainsberg	LKM 32016/1953
99 778	99 1778-2	099 742-9	BVO Bahn, Radebeul Ost	LKM 32017/1953
99 779	99 1779-0	099 743-7	BVO Bahn, Radebeul Ost	LKM 32018/1953
99 780	99 1780-8	099 744-5	BVO Bahn, Freital Hainsberg (Z)	LKM 32019/1953
99 781	99 1781-6	099 745-2	DB Museum, Nürnberg	LKM 3202?/1953
99 782	99 1782-4	099 746-0	RüKB, Putbus	LKM 32023/1953
99 783	99 1783-2	099 747-8	RüKB, Putbus	LKM 32024/1953
99 784	99 1784-0	099 748-6	RüKB, Putbus	LKM 32025/1953
99 785	99 1785-7	099 749-4	BVO Bahn, Oberwiesenthal	LKM 32026/1954
99 786	99 1786-5	099 750-2	BVO Bahn, Oberwiesenthal	LKM 32027/1954
99 787	99 1787-3	099 751-0	SOEG, Zittau	LKM 32028/1956
99 788	99 1788-1	099 752-8	Öchslebahn, Ochsenhausen	LKM 32029/1956
99 789	99 1789-9	099 753-6	BVO Bahn, Radebeul Ost	LKM 32030/1956
99 790	99 1790-7	099 754-4	BVO Bahn, Freital Hainsberg	LKM 32031/1956
99 791	99 1791-5	099 755-1	Radebeul Ost. Preserved.	LKM 32032/1956
99 793	99 1793-1	099 756-9	BVO Bahn, Radebeul Ost	LKM 32034/1956
99 794	99 1794-9	099 757-7	BVO Bahn, Oberwiesenthal	LKM 32035/1956

99.4532   0-8-0T (Dn2t)

This locomotive was built for the now closed Wernshausen–Trusetal line. For many years it was used as station/yard pilot at SOEG, Zittau but was then stored. It is now being restored by the line's support group.

Built: 1924.
Builder: O&K.
Driving Wheel Dia.: 750 mm.
Length over Buffers: 6.93 m.
Max. Speed: 25 km/h.

Gauge: 750 mm.
Boiler Pressure: 12 bar.
Weight: 21 tonnes.
Cylinders: (2) 300 x 400 mm.
2 built.

DR	DR (c)	DB	Location	Build details
99 4532	99 4532-0	099 760-1	SOEG Bertsdorf (Z)	O&K 10844/1924

CLASS 99.46   0-8-0WT (Dh2t)

These locos were built new for the Rügensche Kleinbahn and still work on the line. No. 51Mh is preserved and has been bought by Ludger Guttwein and repatriated to Rügen. However his attempt to buy the RüKB failed and its future is not known. Both working examples were repainted in original numbers in original green livery, but 99 4632-8 has been put back into DR livery with DR number.

Built: 1914, 1925.
Builder: Vulcan.
Driving Wheel Dia.: 850 mm.
Length over Buffers: 8.00 m.
Max. Speed: 30 km/h.

Gauge: 750 mm.
Boiler Pressure: 12 bar.
Weight: 24 tonnes.
Cylinders: (2) 350 x 400 mm.
3 built.

RüKB	DR	DR (c)	DB	Location	Build details
51Mh	99 4631	99 4631-0		L. Gutwein, Prora	Vulcan 2896/1913
52Mh	99 4632	99 4632-8	099 770-0	RüKB, Putbus	Vulcan 2951/1914
53Mh	99 4633	99 4633-6	099 771-8	RüKB, Putbus	Vulcan 3851/1925

CLASS 99.48   2-8-0T (1Dh2t)

These locos were built for the Kleinbahnen des Kreises Jerichow, These lines were closed in the 1960s/70s and the locos moved to the RüKB.

Built: 1938.
Builder: Henschel.
Driving Wheel Dia.: 850 mm.
Length over Buffers: 9.44 m.
Max. Speed: 45 km/h.

Gauge: 750 mm.
Boiler Pressure: 13 bar.
Weight: 29.7 tonnes.
Cylinders: (2) 360 x 400 mm.

KJI	DR	DR (c)	DB	Location	Build details
20	99 4801	99 4801-9	099 780-9	RüKB Putbus	Hens 24367/1938
21	99 4802	99 4802-7	099 781-7	RüKB Putbus	Hens 24368/1938

CLASS 199   C

This loco formerly shunted a paper factory at Wilschthal on the remnants of a once large 750 mm gauge system.

Engine: 6KVD14.5SRL of 75 kW.
Maximum Tractive Effort: 42.2 kN.
Driving Wheel Dia: 700 mm.
Max. Speed: 24 km/h.

Transmission: Hydraulic.
Weight in Full Working Order: 16 tonnes.
Length over Buffers: 5.34 m.

DR	Döllnitzbahn	Location	
199 008-4	199 032-4	Döllnitzbahn, Mügeln	LKM 250027/1957

1000 mm GAUGE LOCOMOTIVES (HSB)

CLASS 99.59   MALLET   0-4-4-0T (B'Bn4vt)

Five of these locos were built for the Nordhausen–Wernigeroder Eisenbahn, but 99 5906 is of a different design and was obtained from the Ruhr-Lippe Eisenbahn in 1920. 99 5901/2 are used on special services whilst 99 5903 is stored and 99 5906 works from Gernrode.

Builder: Jung.
Driving Wheel Dia.: 1000 mm.
Length over buffers: 8.875 (9.40*) m.

Boiler Pressure: 14 bar
Weight: 36 tonnes.
Cylinders (4): Two high pressure: 285 x 500 mm
Two low pressure: 425 x 500 mm

NWE No.	DR/HSB No.	Build details	NWE No.	DR/HSB No.	Build details
11	99 5901-6	Jung 258/1897	13	99 5903-2	Jung 345/1898
12	99 5902-4	Jung 261/1897	41	99 5906-5*	Karl 2052/1918

CLASS 99.60   2-6-2T (1'C1'h2t)

Built by Krupp as a prototype standard loco for metre gauge lines this loco became a unique example on the Harz lines. It is first choice for the regular Gernrode steam turn.

Boiler Pressure: 14 bar.
Weight: 47.6 tonnes.
Cylinders: (2): 420 x 500 mm.

Driving Wheel Dia.: 1000 mm.
Length over Buffers: 8.91 m.
Max. Speed: 50 km/h.

NWE No.	DR/HSB No.	Build details
21	99 6001-4	Krupp 1875/1939

CLASS 99.61   0-6-0T (Ch2t (Cn2t*))

These are two small shunting locos. 99 6102 has been restored by the Selketalbahn support group.

Boiler Pressure: 14 bar.
Weight: 32 tonnes.
Cylinders: (2): 400 x 400 mm.

Driving Wheel Dia.: 800 mm.
Length over Buffers: 7.73 m.
Max. Speed: 30 km/h.

NWE No.	DR/HSB No.	Build details
6	99 6101-2	Henschel 22879/1914
7	99 6102-0*	Henschel 22880/1914

CLASS 99.72   2-10-2T (1'E1'h2t)

These big and powerful locomotives are a narrow gauge version of Class 85.99 7222 was one of the three locomotives built for the now closed Eisfeld-Schönbrunn line. It came to Wernigerode from Eisfeld in 1966. The remainder of the class were built after World War II as a modernised version to help out the ageing Mallets on the Schönbrunn and Harz lines. 99 7244-9 is displayed at Hasselfelde, 99 7246-4 is in a shed at Benneckenstein and 99 7247-7 is in the shed at Gernrode and has been donated to the i.G. Selketalbahn.

Boiler Pressure: 14 bar.
Weight: 65.8, 65 tonnes.
Cylinders: (2) 500 x 500 mm.

Driving Wheel Dia.: 1000 mm.
Length over Buffers: 11.73 (11.64*) m.
Max. Speed: 40 km/h.

▲ Standard HSB 2-10-2T 99 7231-6 approaches Drei Annen Hohne with the 14.40 Wernigerode–Brocken on 16/02/01.   **Wilf Carey**

▼ Harz Mallet 99 5901 with a Today's Railways charter special between Hasselfelde and Stiege 03/06/03.   **Peter Fox**

▲ HSB 199 870-7 shunts empty standard gauge stone wagons on transporters at Eisfelder Talmühle on 15/06/98.

▼ New HSB railcar 187 018-7. **Colin Boocock (2)**

DR No.	Later DR/HSB No.	Build details	DR No.	Later DR/HSB No.	Build details
99 222	99 7222-5*	BMAG 9921/1931	99 239	99 7239-9 (Z)	LKM 134 016/1956
99 231	99 7231-6 (Z)	LKM 134 008/1954	99 240	99 7240-7 (Z)	LKM 134 017/1956
99 232	99 7232-4	LKM 134 009/1954	99 241	99 7241-5	LKM 134 018/1956
99 233	99 7233-2 (Z)	LKM 134 010/1954	99 242	99 7242-3	LKM 134 019/1956
99 234	99 7234-0	LKM 134 011/1954	99 243	99 7243-1	LKM 134 020/1956
99 235	99 7235-7	LKM 134 012/1954	99 244	99 7244-9 (Z)	LKM 134 021/1956
99 236	99 7236-5	LKM 134 013/1955	99 245	99 7245-6	LKM 134 022/1956
99 237	99 7237-3	LKM 134 014/1955	99 246	99 7246-4 (Z)	LKM 134 023/1956
99 238	99 7238-1	LKM 134 015/1956	99 247	99 7247-2 (Z)	LKM 134 024/1956

CLASS 199.05 B

These diesel locos were built for the Spreewaldbahn and were transferred to the Harz lines when that line closed in 1983. Both now transferred to the line's support group at Nordhausen.

Engine: 6KVD14.5SRL of 75 kW.
Maximum Tractive Effort: 48 kN.
Driving Wheel Dia: 1000 mm.
Max. Speed: 24 km/h.
Transmission: Mechanical.
Weight in Full Working Order: 16 tonnes.
Length over Buffers: 5.40 m.

| 199 005-0 (Z) | LKM 230352/1964 | 199 006-8 (Z) | LKM 230353/1964 |

CLASS 199.10 B

These are rebuilt standard gauge Class 310 Köfs. 199 011-8 is the Westerntor works shunter.

Engine: 6KVD145 of 92 kW.
Maximum Tractive Effort: 39 kN.
Driving Wheel Dia: 850 mm.
Max. Speed: 30 km/h.
Transmission: Hydraulic.
Weight in Full Working Order: 16–17 tonnes.
Length over Buffers: 6.38 m.

| 199 010-0 (100 325) (Z) | BMAG 10224/1934 | 199 012-6 (100 213) (Z) | BMAG 10164/1933 |
| 199 011-8 (100 639) | Jung 5666/1935 | | |

CLASS 199.3 C

This was the prototype for an export order to Java. After testing on the Harz lines, the loco returned to the builder only to be taken into DR stock in 1969.

Engine: ER6VD1815 of 143 kW.
Maximum Tractive Effort: 48 kN.
Driving Wheel Dia: 900 mm.
Max. Speed: 24 km/h.
Transmission: Hydraulic.
Weight in Full Working Order: 30 tonnes.
Length over Buffers: 8.00 m.

| 199 301-3 (Z) | LKM 263001/1966 |

CLASS 199.8 C-C

These are DR Class 110 B-B diesel locos (DB Class 201) rebuilt by DR in 1988/90 by RAW Stendal for use on the Harz network with new narrow-gauge C-C bogies. Ten were converted but only five remain, as the HSB has decided that all loco-hauled passenger trains will be steam-hauled. The remaining locos are used for shunting, e.c.s., works trains and snowplough duties.

Engine: 736 kW.
Maximum Tractive Effort: 39 kN.
Driving Wheel Dia:
Max. Speed: 50 km/h.
Transmission: Hydraulic.
Weight in Full Working Order: 60 tonnes.
Length over Buffers: 14.24 m.
Train Heating: Steam.

199 861-6 (110 861-2)	LEW 15379/1976	199 874-9 (110 874-5)	LEW 15392/1976
199 871-5 (110 871-1) (Z)	LEW 15389/1976	199 877-2 (110 877-8) (Z)	LEW 16371/1978
199 872-3 (110 872-9)	LEW 15390/1976	199 892-1 (110 892-7)	LEW 16386/1978

187.001 A-1

This old four-wheeled railcar was built for the Gernrode-Harzgerode Eisenbahn and is effectively preserved and available for charter.

Engine: 66 kW.
Length over buffers: 8.600 m.
Wheel diameter: 700 mm.
Transmission: Mechanical.
Weight: 12.5 tonnes.
Maximum Speed: 30 km/h.

GHE   *DR*   *Build details*
T1   187 001-3   Dessau 3046/1933

187.011/013   1A-A1

These railcars were bought from the Inselbahn Langeoog in 1996, having been bought from the Kreis Altenaer Eisenbahn in 1961/2.

Engines: Two of 107 kW.
Transmission: Mechanical.
Accommodation: –/65.
Wheel diameter: 650 mm.

Length over buffers: 16.200 m.
Weight: 28.2 tonnes.
Maximum Speed: 50 km/h.

187 011-2 (IL VT1)   Talbot 97519/1955 | 187 013-8 (IL VT4)   Talbot 97520/1955

187.012   B-B

This railcar was bought from the Inselbahn Langeoog in 1995, having been originally built for the Nebenbahn Zell–Todtnau, sold to the WEG for working Amstetten–Laichingen in 1968, and going to the Inselbahn Langeoog in 1976. It has wooden slatted seats.

Engines: Two of 155 kW.
Transmission: Hydraulic.
Accommodation: –/48.
Wheel diameter: 850 mm.

Length over buffers: 16.130 m.
Weight: 34.2 tonnes.
Maximum Speed: 60 km/h.

187 012-0 (IL VT3)   Fuchs 91071955

187.015   B-2

This is a new prototype railcar bought by the HSB.

Engines: 242 kW.
Transmission: Hydraulic.
Accommodation: –/49 1T.
Wheel diameter: 720 mm.

Length over buffers: 16.050 m.
Weight: 32.0 tonnes.
Maximum Speed: 50 km/h.

187 015-3   DB Wittenberge 1996

187.016–019   B-2

This is the production version of the new railcar.

Engines: 254 kW.
Transmission: Hydraulic.
Accommodation: –/46 1T.
Wheel diameter: 720 mm.

Length over buffers: 17.300 m.
Weight: 30.0 tonnes.
Maximum Speed: 50 km/h.

187 016-1   DB Halberstadt 1999 | 187 018-7   DB Halberstadt 1999
187 017-9   DB Halberstadt 1999 | 187 019-5   DB Halberstadt 1999

187.025   Bo-Bo

This old railcar is now used for works duties.

Engine: 345 kW.
Length over buffers: 15.600 m.
Wheel diameter: 800 mm.

Transmission: Electric.
Weight: 34.5 tonnes.
Maximum Speed: 60 km/h.

NWE   *DR*   *Build details*
T3   187 025-2   Wismar/BBC 1939

CLASS 187.2   COMBINO DUO   Bo-2-Bo TRAM

These dual-mode trams operate over the Nordhausen tramway and the HSB as far as Ilfeld.
Engine: 180 kW.
Transmission: Electric. Four 100 kW traction motors.   **Length over buffers:** 20.040 m.
Accommodation: –/27.   **Weight:** 25.0 tonnes.
Wheel diameter: 800 mm.   **Maximum Speed:** 70 km/h.

187 201-9 | 187 203-5
187 202-7

3. PRIVATE RAILWAYS

AHAUS ALSTÄTTER EISENBAHN AAE

Nordrhein Westfalen

Routes: Ahaus–Alstätte.
Length: 9.3/11.9 km.
EVU Licence: Freight, 10/11/1989.

Depot: Ahaus.
Livery: Red.

This small railway is located close to the Dutch border and is only 9.3 km long being the remnants of the one time Ahaus–Enschede Eisenbahn. It really only services some sidings but its big business is wagon leasing. In recent years this side of the business has grown substantially and the company now owns more than 20,000 wagons. If it had to take them all home it would soon run out of space for them! Its wagons can be seen in traffic all over Europe and it now even has its own UIC number – 68. During the summer months it often runs some tourist trains. AAE now also operates Lunen Süd–Coesfeld–Ahaus on behalf of DB Cargo.

No.	Builder, No. & Year	Type	kW Details	Comments
Alstätter I	Jung 12991/1958	R30C	250 C DH	Preserved 2002. Then sold on.
Alstätter II	LEW 16372/1977	V100-4	1060 B-B DH	Ex 201 878 via Adtranz
Alstätter III	Jung 5494/1934	II	94 4wD	Ex BE D15 ex DB 323 405

ANGELN BAHN, FLENSBURG AB

Flensburg,Schleswig Holstein

Depot: Flensburg.
EVU Licence: Freight and Passenger 04/03/2002.

This company is an offshoot of a local preservation society which has formed a separate company with the aim of finding work for their locos on ballast trains etc. In 2002 AB started working with NVAG with freight trips from Schleswig to Flensburg/Padborg/Kappeln.

No.	Builder, No. & Year	Type	kW Details	Comments
DL 1	Hens 29776/1959	DH240B	150 0-4-0 DH	Ex ZF Schleswig 1
DL 2	LEW 15363/1978	V60D	478 0-8-0 DH	Ex Kabelwerke Schwerin
DL 3	LEW 15373/1976	V60D	478 0-8-0 DH	Ex Kieswerk Langhagen
DL 4	Diema 2351/1960	DVL30		Ex Papierfabrik Stora
DL 101	Lugansk 0161/1967	M62	1470 Co-Co DE	Ex DB 220 027 ex DR

ANKUM-BERSENBRÜCKER EISENBAHN GmbH ABE

Niedersachsen/Bremen

Depot: None.
EVU Licence: Freight and Passenger 26/10/1995.
This is a short line – 5.3 km. which comes under the Verkehrsgesellschaft Osnabrück (VLO) but is served by DB!

ANHALTISCHE BAHN GESELLSCHAFT mbh ABG

Dessau, Sachsen Anhalt

Depot: Dessau
EVU Licence: Freight and Passenger 16/02/2000.

This is a subsidiary of Dessauer Verkehrs und Eisenbahngesellschaft mbH (DVE). It is running passenger trains in the tourist season between Dessau and Wörlitz and has taken over freight moves from DB on the line from Stassfurt to Engeln and sidings at Westerengeln. NB: The line from Dessau damaged in the floods of August 2002 and reopened in Spring 2003 running WSSuO.

No.	Builder, No. & Year	Type	kW Details	Comments
V18 403	LKM 261403/1964	V18B	162 0-4-0 DM	

V22 219	LKM 262219/1970	V22	162	0-4-0 DH	Ex Westerengeln
V22 305	LKM 262305/1971	V22	162	0-4-0 DH	Ex Industrial in Riesa. Now Dessau Works pilot?
V60 030	LEW 11030/1966	V60D	478	0-8-0 DH	Ex Bernburg Zement
V60 162	LKM 270162/1964	V60D	478	0-8-0 DH	Ex Westeregeln
V60 196	LEW 15196/1976	V60D	478	0-8-0 DH	Ex BKW Gustav Sobottka
V60 583	LEW 12583/1970	V60D	478	0-8-0 DH	Ex Solvay Bernberg
670 002	DWA 1.571/2/1998	670	250	1-A DMR	
670 005	DWA 1.571/5/1998	670	250	1-A DMR	
670 006	DWA 1.571/6/1998	670	250	1-A DMR	

AHG GRUPPE (AHG HANDELS & LOGISTIK)   AHG

Gross Gaglow, Brandenburg

EVU Licence: Freight and Passenger 11/07/2000
This is a Lausitz based building contractor that is getting involved in railway infrastructure work having acquired its first locomotive in mid 2001. It is also now working local freight trips from Cottbus.

No.	Builder, Works No. & Year	Type	kW	Details	Comments
01	LEW 11936/1968	V100DR	736	B-B DH	Ex DB 202 298
02		V10B	75	0-4-0 DH	Ex ?
03		V23B	162	0-4-0 DH	Ex ?

ALTONA–KALTENKIRCHEN–NEUMÜNSTER EISENBAHN AG AKN

Hamburg/Schleswig Holstein
Routes: Hamburg Langenfelde–Kaltenkirchen–Neumünster (KBS 137, 65.2 km); Norderstedt Mitte–Ulzburg Süd (KBS 138, 7.8 km); Elmshorn–Barmstedt–Ulzburg (KBS 139, 24.5 km); Tiefstack–Glinde–Hamburg–Bergedorf–Gessthacht

Length: 111.5/270.3 km.
Depots: Kaltenkirchen, Hamburg Billbrook.
Livery: Locos: orange and yellow; Railcars similar but now changing to red and white.
EVU Licence: 15/12/1997. Freight and Passenger

This company has lines north of Hamburg totalling some 120 km and runs a busy commuter service into Hamburg. It is also involved in various freight flows in the Hamburg area. Besides covering the area denoted by its name the company also has lines Ulzburg to Elmshorn and Hamburg-Bergedorf to Geesthacht. It is also involved now wth providing passenger trains over some DB lines in the area (e.g. Neumünster–Heide). Latest traffic figures show 4.6 million journeys (49.5 million passenger km) and 174,000 tonnes of freight. In November 2000 AKN took over the DB Regio passenger service from Heide to Busum (KBS 133) and recently had this contract extended to December 2011. Two more LINT 41 DMUs have been ordered. AKN has taken over the passenger services on KBS 142 Neumünster–Bad Segeberg–Bad Oldesloe under the auspices of a separate company – Nordbahn (q.v.).

No.	Builder, No. & Year	Type	kW	Details	Comments
V2.009	MaK 220022/1954	240B	178	B DH	
V2.016	MaK 800116/1970	G1100BB	808	B-B DH	Billbrook. Sold(Italy)
V2.017	MaK 800167/1972	G1100BB	808	B-B DH	Billbrook
V2.018	MaK 800168/1972	G1100BB	808	B-B DH	Billbrook
V2.019	MaK 800169/1972	G1100BB	808	B-B DH	
V2.021	MaK 1000830/1985	DE1002	1170	Bo-Bo DE	
V2.022	MaK 1000792/1982	DE1002	1170	Bo-Bo DE	Ex TWE V 152
V2.023	MaK 1000794/1982	DE1002	1119	Bo-Bo DE	Ex DB 031 2002.
V2.024	MaK 1000829/1982	DE1002	1119	Bo-Bo DE	Ex DE 032 2002.
(VT2.31 withdrawn and sections used to replace accident damaged units)					
VT2.32	LHB 02/1976	VT2E	2x228	Bo-2-Bo DER	
VT2.33	LHB 03/1976	VT2E	2x228	Bo-2-Bo DER	
VT2.34	LHB 04/1976	VT2E	2x228	Bo-2-Bo DER	
VT2.35	LHB 05/1976	VT2E	2x228	Bo-2-Bo DER	
VT2.36*	LHB 16A/06B/1977/76	VT2E	2x228	Bo-2-Bo DER	Half sets 46/36

VT2.37	LHB 07/1976	VT2E	2x228	Bo-2-Bo DER	
VT2.38*	LHB 08/1976	VT2E	2x228	Bo-2-Bo DER	
VT2.39	LHB 09/1976	VT2E	2x228	Bo-2-Bo DER	
VT2.40	LHB 10/1977	VT2E	2x228	Bo-2-Bo DER	
VT2.41	LHB 11/1977	VT2E	2x228	Bo-2-Bo DER	
VT2.42	LHB 01A/12B/1976–77	VT2E	2x228	Bo-2-Bo DER	Half sets 31/42
VT2.43*	LHB 13/1977	VT2E	2x228	Bo-2-Bo DER	
VT2.44	LHB 14/1977	VT2E	2x228	Bo-2-Bo DER	
VT2.45	LHB 15/1977	VT2E	2x228	Bo-2-Bo DER	
VT2.46	LHB 06A/16B/1976/77	VT2E	2x228	Bo-2-Bo DER	Half sets 36/46
VT2.51	LHB 2.51/1993	VTA	485	Bo-2-Bo DER	
VT2.52	LHB 2.52/1993	VTA	485	Bo-2-Bo DER	
VT2.53	LHB 2.53/1993	VTA	485	Bo-2-Bo DER	
VT2.54	LHB 2.54/1993	VTA	485	Bo-2-Bo DER	
VT2.55	LHB 2.55/1993	VTA	485	Bo-2-Bo DER	
VT2.56	LHB 2.56/1993	VTA	485	Bo-2-Bo DER	
VT2.57	LHB 2,57/1993	VTA	485	Bo-2-Bo DER	
VT2.58	LHB 2.58/1993	VTA	485	Bo-2-Bo DER	
VT2.59	LHB 2.59/1993	VTA	485	Bo-2-Bo DER	
VT2.60	LHB 2.60/1993	VTA	485	Bo-2-Bo DER	
VT2.61	LHB 2.61/1993	VTA	485	Bo-2-Bo DER	
VT2.62	LHB 2.62/1993	VTA	485	Bo-2-Bo DER	
VT2.63	LHB 2.63/1993	VTA	485	Bo-2-Bo DER	
VT2.64	LHB 2.64/1993	VTA	485	Bo-2-Bo DER	
VT2.65	LHB 2.65/1993	VTA	485	Bo-2-Bo DER	
VT2.66	LHB 2.66/1993	VTA	485	Bo-2-Bo DER	
VT2.67	LHB 2.67/1993	VTA	485	Bo-2-Bo DER	
VT2.68	LHB 2.68/1993	VTA	485	Bo-2-Bo DER	Schleswig Holstein
VT2.76	Als /2003	LINT 41			Spare for SHB and NBE
VT3.07	MAN 146595/1962	798	2 x 110		Ex DB 728 001/798 813
VT3.08	Uer 68640/1961	795	110	1A	DMR
VT3.09	Uer 72837/1967	795	110	1A	DMR

Notes: VT3.08 retained for excursions.
• = refurbished set

AUGSBURGER LOCALBAHN GmbH   AL

Bayern

Routes: Local lines around Augsburg.
Depot: Augsburg Ring. (Friedbergstrasse).
Length: 10.4/26.8 km.
Livery: Orange with white bands.
EVU Licence: Freight and Passenger 04/08/1995.

As the name suggests this railways serves local destinations around Augsburg. It is freight only and basically serves the industries in and around Augsburg. It is permitted to operate on to DB Netz and has recently increased its fleet with some modernised DR V100 to work trains of paper from Augsburg to Schongau. In 2003 AL handled 880 000 tonnes of freight.

No.	Builder, No. & Year	Type	kW	Details	Comments
V 22	KM 18326/1956	ML440C	323	C D?	Radio controls
V 23	KM 18327/1956	ML440C	323	C D?	
V 24	KM 18328/1956	ML440C	323	C D?	Radio controls
V 25	KM 18329/1956	ML440C	323	C D?	Radio controls
V 26	KM 18330/1956	ML440C	323	C D?	Radio controls
V 31	Allrad 180/1998	Cargolok	440	B-B DH	
V 41	LEW 14892/1975	V100.4	1060	B-B DH	Ex 201 828
V 42	LEW 16378/1978	V100.4	1060	B-B DH	Ex 201 884
V 43	LEW 16385/1978	V100.4	1060	B-B DH	Ex 199 891
V 44	Adtranz 72580/2000	V100.4	1060	B-B DH	Ex ?
V 45	Adtranz/2001	V100.4	1060	B-B DH	Ex ?

(NB: V41/42/43 rebuilt by Adtranz 1997–1999 and fitted with Indusi, remote radio control and train radio.)

ALLGÄU EXPRESS ALEX
Konstanz, Baden Württemberg

In February 2003 the Bayerische Verkehrsministerium awarded the contract for the replacement Inter Regio service from München to Kempten and Oberstorf to a new consortium "Die Landerbahn". This is a joint venture between Regentalbahn AG and the Euro Thurbo company. The service is now marketed as Allgäu Express or ALEX and commenced on 14/02/2003. 21 carriages were obtained which were modernised or refurbished at PFA Weiden. These are formed into seven coach trains normally formed 1 first, 1 bistro and 5 second class carriages. Locomotives are hired in Euro Runners (a.k.a. ÖBB 2016) from Dispolok (q.v.). The operating base has not been announced at the time this book was prepared.

ALSTOM LOKOMOTIVEN SERVICE ALS
(DB WERK STENDAL)
Stendal, Sachsen Anhalt

If you can't beat them, join them! DB Regio had lots of class 202 diesels spare following branch line closures or introduction of new railcars. Nearly two hundred of these locos were at Stendal works and some were overhauled as part of a hire fleet and given numbers in the 203 series. Below 500 the locos are completely rebuilt and fitted with MTU or CAT engines according to the customers choice. Locos numbered above 500 are straightforward class 202 just freshly overhauled at Stendal. These locos will appear anywhere in the country providing help to any company who needs a loco at short notice–traffic increase, failure of own loco etc. The works is also overhauling locos for outright sale such as 202 487 to EBM.

In 2002 Stendal works was part bought by Alstom in a joint venture with DB. Meanwhile Stendal keeps turning out locos for DB subsidiaries such as DB Bahnbau and to private firms. However it has retained a fleet of locos for itself; these are for hire to customers who need a loco quickly for spot hire or indeed to hire whilst a locomotive is modernised to specific order. Meanwhile DB Cargo has been withdrawing many class 212 locomotives and these have ended up at Stendal. Many are in good condition and consequently some of these have also been hired out!

No.	Builder, No. & Year	Type	kW	Details	Comments
202 001	LEW 14447/1974	V100.	1086	B-B DH	Ex Duisport Rail, ex ALS, ex DB 202 746
203 001	LEW 12858/1971	V100.4	1240	B-B DH	Ex 202 349 – RCN
203 101	LEW 12235/1977	V100.	1050	B-B DH	Ex 202 850 – EBM (Was demloco 203.1)
203 501	LEW 12542/1970	V100.4	883	B-B DH	Ex 202 260 – EfW
203 502	LEW 13522/1972	V100.4	883	B-B DH	Ex 202 483 —MWB
203 503	LEW 14844/1973	V100.4	883	B-B DH	Ex 202 787 – EfW
203 504	LEW 12546/1976	V100.4	883	B-B DH	Ex 202 264 – TLG
203 505	LEW 12835/1971	V100.4	883	B-B DH	Ex 202 326 – UAT
212 045	MaK 1000181/1963	V100	992	B-B DH	EfW
212 054	MaK 1000190/1963	V100	992	B-B DH	HSL
212 189	Jung 13665/1963	V100	992	B-B DH	
212 258	MaK 1000305/1965	V100	992	B-B DH	Press
212 276	MaK 1000323/1965	V100	992	B-B DH	EfW
212 285	MaK 1000332/1965	V100	992	B-B DH	HGB
212 305	MaK 1000352/1966	V100	992	B-B DH	HSL

AmE RAILLOGISTIK GmbH AmE
Wittenberge, Brandenburg

EVU Licence: Freight, 04/03/2002.

This company was formed by several former DB/DR drivers from the Wittenberge area. At first drivers were hired out to any of the emerging freight operators including NeCoss. On 04/03/2002 AmE became a fully fledged EVU for freight traffic but so far has not acquired any locomotives. In early 2003 there were 18 drivers on the books working NeCoss trains from Bremen to Duisburg/ Bebra and Erfurt.

ADAM & MALOWA LOKVERMIETUNGS–GmbH   AML

This firm was set up up early in 2001 to allow the hiring out of locos that could otherwise be spare. It is owned by Uwe Adam (50%), and MaLoWa (37%) and a private person (13%).

No.	Builder, No. & Year	Type	kW Details	Comments
02	LEW 12243/1965	V60D	478 0-8-0 DH	Ex Kali Bischhofferode
05	LKM 280201/1969	V180	1470 C-C DH	Ex Vennbahn ex 228 792
6	LEW 12493/1970	V100	883 B-B DH	Ex AMP6 ex DB 201 211
7	LEW 12244/1965	V60D	478 0-8-0 DH	Ex Kali Südharz 3

AMP BAHNLOGISTIK GmbH   AMP

Thüringen

Depot: Eisenach (old DB depot).

AMP are the initial letters for the names of the owners – Messrs Adam, Müller and Pfotenhauer. This is a new organisation taking advantage of the open access arrangements in Germany. Originally based in Gotha it has recently moved to Eisenach. It uses the skills of displaced railway staff used to former DR locos and hires out former East German types and provides spares for other users. It was established as recently as August 1999. Its locomotives can be found in use by industry and also by track contractors. Uwe Adam has since formed two other companies, AML and UAT (q.v.).

No.	Builder, No. & Year	Type	kW	Details	Comments
1	LEW 18008/1983	V60D	478	0-8-0 DH	Ex IND
2	LEW 15137/1976	V60D	478	0-8-0 DH	Ex IND Furstenwalde
3	LEW 13867/1974	V60D	478	0-8-0 DH	Ex IND Furstenwalde. Sold 2003 to B&S 3
4	LEW 16968/1980	V60D	478	0-8-0 DH	Ex IND Walzwerk Hettstedt
5.1	LKM 262656/1976	V22	162	0-4-0 DH	Ex DWU, Ex BKK Bitterfeld Di 466-22-B2 *MAX*
5.2	LKM 262539/1974	V22	162	0-4-0 DH	Ex EIB 9 *MORITZ*
10 FRED	LKM 251185/1957	N4	66	B DM	Ex Felswerke Oberrohn Lok 2.
228 578	LKM 651078/1965	V180	1470	B-B DH	Ex Falz, Juterbog

VERKEHRSBETRIEBE ACHERN–OTTENHÖFEN
AO (SWEG)

Baden Württemberg

Route: Achern–Ottenhofen (KBS 717)
Length: 10.4 km.
Depot: Ottenhöfen
Livery: Locos blue; Railcars: Orange and white.

This line is part of the SWEG empire (q.v.) and operates the line denoted in the title connecting with DB trains at Achern. Rolling stock is numbered in one common SWEG list and sometimes gets swapped around to cover failures on other lines. The depot at Ottenhöfen is being enlarged to service the Offenburg area Regio Shuttles which are also expected to take over from VT 125 which may be transferred elsewhere. The DGEG operates steam trains on certain weekends in the summer.

No.	Builder, No. & Year	Type	kW Details	Comments
V 100	MaK 1000801/1982	G1203BB735 B-B DH		Remote radio controls
VT 125	WagU 30900/1981	NE 81 2x199 B-B DHR		

ANGEL TRAINS CARGO   ATC

A complicated story! The British leasing company Angel Trains wanted to get into the main European scene. The Rolling Stock Company first got into bed with Vossloh to form Locomotion Service GmbH which was 90% Vossloh and 10% Angel Trains. At about the same time another company was formed – Locomotion Capital Ltd which had the opposite holdings 10% Vossloh and 90% Angel Trains. Locomotion Capital has since developed into Angel Trains Cargo thus bringing the main company name to the fore. Angel Trains Cargo provides the financing for purchase or leasing of locomotives and rolling stock. The leasing arrangements can be short term or up to 15 years in some cases.

It is not intended to show all locomotives owned by Angel Trains Cargo as some are not in Germany (all the SNCF class 461000 were acquired through Angel Trains). There are other examples in Austria (LTE 2150) and Luxembourg.

In the list that follows the electric locomotives are listed in type order and in the case of the diesel locomotives these are then in works number order.

No.	Builder, No. & Year	Type	kW	Details	Last known user
145 CL 005	Adtranz 33843/2001	145	4200	Bo-Bo E	R4C
145 CL 031	Adtranz 33850/2001	145	4200	Bo-Bo E	TXL
145 CL 201	Adtranz 33844/2001	145	4200	Bo-Bo E	RAG
145 CL 202	Adtranz 33845/2001	145	4200	Bo-Bo E	RAG
145 CL 203	Adtranz 33846/2001	145	4200	Bo-Bo E	RAG
145 CL 204	Adtranz 33847/2001	145	4200	Bo-Bo E	RAG
185 CL 004	Bomb 33453/2001	185	4200	Bo-Bo E	R4C
185 CL 005	Bomb 33451/2001	185	4200	Bo-Bo E	R4C
185 CL 006	Bomb 33458/2001	185	4200	Bo-Bo E	R4C
185 CL 007	Bomb 33456/2001	185	4200	Bo-Bo E	R4C
185 CL 008	Bomb 33477/2001	185	4200	Bo-Bo E	RAG (221)
185 CL 009	Bomb 33498/2001	185	4200	Bo-Bo E	RAG (222)
185 510	Bomb 33510/2002	185	5600	Bo-Bo E	TXL
185 511	Bomb 33512/2002	185	5600	Bo-Bo E	TXL
185 512	Bomb 33514/2002	185	5600	Bo-Bo E	TXL
185 513	Bomb 33516/2002	185	5600	Bo-Bo E	TXL
185 514	Bomb 33522/2002	185	5600	Bo-Bo E	TXL
185 515	Bomb 33523/2002	185	5600	Bo-Bo E	NOB/CCL
185 516	Bomb 33529/2002	185	5600	Bo-Bo E	NOB/CCL
185 517	Bomb 33531/2002	185	5600	Bo-Bo E	Believed actually owned by R4C
185 518	Bomb 33533/2002	185	5600	Bo-Bo E	TXL
185 519	Bomb 33535/2002	185	5600	Bo-Bo E	CFL
185 520	Bomb 33544/2003	185	5600	Bo-Bo E	CFL
185 521	Bomb 33581/2003	185	5600	Bo-Bo E	CFL
185 522	Bomb 33596/2003	185	5600	Bo-Bo E	CFL
185 523	Bomb 33601/2003	185	5600	Bo-Bo E	CFL
185 524	Bomb 33614/2003	185	5600	Bo-Bo E	CFL
185 525	Bomb 33592/2003	185	5600	Bo-Bo E	BLS
185 526	Bomb 33618/2003	185	5600	Bo-Bo E	BLS
185 527	Bomb 336. . /2003	185	5600	Bo-Bo E	BLS
185 528	Bomb 33624/2003	185	5600	Bo-Bo E	LTE
185 529	Bomb 33628/2003	185	5600	Bo-Bo E	Contrain
185 530	Bomb 33633/2004	185	5600	Bo-Bo E	Contrain
185 531	Bomb 33630/2004	185	5600	Bo-Bo E	TXL
185 532	Bomb 336. . /2004	185	5600	Bo-Bo E	R4C
185 533	Bomb 33639/2004	185	5600	Bo-Bo E	R4C
185 534	Bomb 336. . /2004	185	5600	Bo-Bo E	
185 535	Bomb 336. . /2004	185	5600	Bo-Bo E	
185 536	Bomb 336. . /2004	185	5600	Bo-Bo E	
Am 842 101	VL 1001461/2003	G1000	1100	B-B DH	SBB Schaffhausen for trips onto DB
Am 842 102	VL 1001463/2003	G1000	1100	B-B DH	SBB Schaffhausen for trips onto DB
V200 001	VSFT 1001021/2000	G1206	1500	B-B DH	BCB
?	VSFT 1001025/2000	G1206	1500	B-B DH	CFL
?	VSFT 1001114/2000	G1206	1500	B-B DH	TXL Emden
116?	VSFT 1001116/2000	G1206	1500	B-B DH	R4C
45	VSFT 1001117/2000	G1206	1500	B-B DH	Unisped
?	VSFT 1001119/2000	G1206	1500	B-B DH	MEG
?	VSFT 1001125/2000	G1206	1500	B-B DH	RAG
?	VSFT 1001127/2001	G1206	1500	B-B DH	NEG
V1001-129	VSFT 1001129/2001	G1206	1500	B-B DH	RBB
V1001-130	VSFT 1001130/2001	G1206	1500	B-B DH	WEG
?	VSFT 1001138/2001	G1206	1500	B-B DH	R4C Hamburg (ex Hoyer)
207?	VSFT 1001207/2002	G1700	1700	B-B DH	NEG
208?	VSFT 1001208/2002	G1700	1700	B-B DH	NEG
?	VSFT 1001212/2003	G1700	1700	B-B DH	NIAG

1702	VSFT 1001214/2003	G1700 1700	B-B DH	VPS	
901	VSFT 1001030/2001	G2000 2240	B-B DH	RAG	
902	VSFT 1001031/2001	G2000 2240	B-B DH	RAG	
903	VSFT 1001032/2001	G2000 2240	B-B DH	RAG	
V1001-033	VSFT 1001033/2001	G2000 2240	B-B DH	WEG	
?	VSFT 1001034/2001	G2000 2240	B-B DH	Shortlines? (NL)	
?	VSFT 1001035/2001	G2000 2240	B-B DH	MEG	
V280.1	VSFT 1001037/2002	G2000 2240	B-B DH	OHE Sp	
V300 001	VSFT 1001038/2002	G2000 2240	B-B DH	BCB	
V1001-039	VSFT 1001039/2002	G2000 2240	B-B DH	Contrain RBG 6	
V1001-041	VSFT 1001041/2002	G2000 2240	B-B DH	Contrain/Pfalzbahn	
V1001-042	VSFT 1001042/2002	G2000 2240	B-B DH	EVB	
V1001-043	VSFT 1001043/2002	G2000 2240	B-B DH	Contrain RBG 7	
?	VSFT 1001325/2003	G2000 2240	B-B DH	Infra Leuna	
V280.2	VSFT 1001326/2003	G2000 2240	B-B DH	OHE Sp	

Note. ATC short term lease locomotives tend not to have a fleet number so it is possible to assume that those such as Unisped 45 or OHE Sp V280.1 are on long term leases and the others are much shorter leases.

Locomotives 185 512/515/516/518 are cleared for Austria; 185 517 is cleared for Switzerland; 185 519-524 are cleared for Luxembourg and Germany; 185 525 is cleared for Austria and Switzerland.

ALBTAL–VERKEHRSGESELLSCHAFT mbH/
VERKEHRSBETRIEBE KARLSRUHE   AVG/VBK
Baden Württemberg

Routes: Karlsruhe–Bad Herrenalb (KBS 710.1, 25.8 km); Ettlingen Stadt–Ettlingen West 2.2 km; Busenbach–Ittersbach (KBS 710.1 14.1 km); Karlsruhe–Hochstetten (710.1, 24.0 km); Bruchsal–Menzingen (KBS 710.3, 19.6 km); Ubstart Orb–Odenheim (KBS 710.3,11 km); Karlsruhe Grötzingen–Eppingen–Heilbronn (KBS 710.4; 66 km). By the end of 2004 AVG will also serve Rastatt–Freudenstadt–Eutingen, Pforzheim–Bad Wildbad–Bad Wildbad Kurpark, Wörth Rathaus–Wörth Badepark, Heilbronn–Öhringen. More units have been ordered.
Length: 103/129.5 km.
Depots: Ettlingen, Bad Herrenalb, Hochstetten, Ittersbach, Menzingen, Eppingen.
Electrical System: 750 V DC and 15 kV AC.
EVU Licence: Freight and Passenger 10/05/1995.

The AVG and VBK are now both owned by the local authority. The network has undergone great changes in recent years. Originally the Albtalbahn was 1000 mm gauge whilst the Karlsruhe tram network was standard gauge. The Albtalbahn was converted to standard gauge and later integrated with the city tramway network, VBK. The big changes came about in the 1990s when a connection was built to the DB. AVG trams then started to run to destinations on the DB network and the "Karlsruhe Model" was born. Now AVG/VBK operate S-Bahn services over DB to Baden-Baden, Bretten, Bruchsal, Gölshausen, Pforzheim, Wörth and more recently to Heilbronn. All the 800 series railcars are dual-voltage for working over DB. The introduction of the new S-Bahn services has been a great success with passenger numbers continuing to climb. The system of trains/trams running along main lines and then into the streets of the cities being served is being followed by other places. Note that four units have also got DB numbers. This dates from the period before open access when DB and AVG shared some costs so that DB provided some units. With open access this was not continued. Various extensions took place in 2003 including Wörth Rathaus–Wörth Baderpark; Pforzheim–Bad Wildbad; Rastatt–Freudenstadt. Other extensions in the pipeline are Freudenstadt Eutingen and Heilbronn to Öhringen. More trams have been ordered. Freight traffic totalled 249 000 tonnes in 2000.

Notes:
551–560 ex 851'–860'. Rebuilt from 6-axle cars 581'–590' in 1990 with panoramic centre sections.
561–570 ex 861'–870'.
571–580 ex 871'–880' .Rebuilt from 6-axle cars 531–540 in 1995.
581–590 ex 521–530.

No.	Builder, No. & Year	Type	kW Details		Comments
80	Rastatt/1930		2 x 47	Bo ER	Staff transport
90	Rastatt/1957		2 x 100	B-B ER	Salon car

452	Essl 25206/1958		2 x 202	B-B D?R	Ex SWEG VT 108
461	Essl 5294/1962	V100	809	B-B DH	Ex DB 211 358
462	MaK 1000802/1982	G1203BB	736	B-B DH	Ex SWEG V 101
463	KM 19819/1976	M500C	390	C DH	Ex Krupp Stahl
464	MaK 1000799/1982	G1203BB	736	B-B DH	Ex VKP V 103
465	MaK 1000387/1966	V100DB	809	B-B DH	Ex DB 213 340 (2001)
466	MaK 1000037/1961	V100DB	809	B-B DH	Ex DB 211 019 (Spares)
467	VSFT 1001132/2001	G1206BB	1500	B-B DH	
468	Essl 5301/1963	V100DB	809	B-B DH	Ex ÖBB 2048 014, DB 211 365
469	VSFT 1001112/2003	G1700	1700	B-B DH	
501	WagU 32638/1983	GT6-80C	2 x 235	B-2-B ER	Owned by VBK.
502	WagU 32639/1983	GT6-80C	2 x 235	B-2-B ER	Owned by VBK.
503	WagU 32640/1983	GT6-80C	2 x 235	B-2-B ER	Owned by VBK.
504	WagU 32641/1983	GT6-80C	2 x 235	B-2-B ER	
505	WagU 32642/1983	GT6-80C	2 x 235	B-2-B ER	
506	WagU 32643/1984	GT6-80C	2 x 235	B-2-B ER	
507	WagU 32644/1984	GT6-80C	2 x 235	B-2-B ER	
508	WagU 32645/1984	GT6-80C	2 x 235	B-2-B ER	
509	WagU 32646/1984	GT6-80C	2 x 235	B-2-B ER	
510	WagU 32647/1984	GT6-80C	2 x 235	B-2-B ER	
511	WagU 32731/1984	GT6-80C	2 x 235	B-2-B ER	
512	WagU 32732/1984	GT6-80C	2 x 235	B-2-B ER	
513	WagU 32733/1984	GT6-80C	2 x 235	B-2-B ER	
514	WagU 32734/1984	GT6-80C	2 x 235	B-2-B ER	
515	WagU 32735/1984	GT6-80C	2 x 235	B-2-B ER	
516	WagU 32736/1984	GT6-80C	2 x 235	B-2-B ER	
517	WagU 32737/1984	GT6-80C	2 x 235	B-2-B ER	
518	WagU 32738/1984	GT6-80C	2 x 235	B-2-B ER	
519	WagU 32739/1984	GT6-80C	2 x 235	B-2-B ER	
520	WagU 32740/1984	GT6-80C	2 x 235	B-2-B ER	Owned by VBK.
551	Duew 37474/1989	GT8-80C	2 x 280	B-2-2-B ER	
552	Duew 37475/1989	GT8-80C	2 x 280	B-2-2-B ER	
553	Duew 37476/1989	GT8-80C	2 x 280	B-2-2-B ER	
554	Duew 37477/1989	GT8-80C	2 x 280	B-2-2-B ER	Owned by VBK.
555	Duew 37478/1989	GT8-80C	2 x 280	B-2-2-B ER	Owned by VBK.
556	Duew 37479/1989	GT8-80C	2 x 280	B-2-2-B ER	Owned by VBK.
557	Duew 37480/1989	GT8-80C	2 x 280	B-2-2-B ER	Owned by VBK.
558	Duew 37481/1989	GT8-80C	2 x 280	B-2-2-B ER	Owned by VBK.
559	Duew 37482/1989	GT8-80C	2 x 280	B-2-2-B ER	Owned by VBK.
560	Duew 37483/1989	GT8-80C	2 x 280	B-2-2-B ER	Owned by VBK.
561	Duew 37713/1991	GT8-80C	2 x 280	B-2-2-B ER	
562	Duew 37714/1991	GT8-80C	2 x 280	B-2-2-B ER	
563	Duew 37715/1991	GT8-80C	2 x 280	B-2-2-B ER	
564	Duew 37716/1991	GT8-80C	2 x 280	B-2-2-B ER	
565	Duew 37717/1991	GT8-80C	2 x 280	B-2-2-B ER	
566	Duew 37718/1991	GT8-80C	2 x 280	B-2-2-B ER	
567	Duew 37719/1991	GT8-80C	2 x 280	B-2-2-B ER	
568	Duew 37720/1991	GT8-80C	2 x 280	B-2-2-B ER	
569	Duew 37721/1991	GT8-80C	2 x 280	B-2-2-B ER	
570	Duew 37722/1991	GT8-80C	2 x 280	B-2-2-B ER	
571	Duew 37304/1987	GT8-80C	2 x 280	B-2-2-B ER	Owned by VBK.
572	Duew 37305/1987	GT8-80C	2 x 280	B-2-2-B ER	Owned by VBK.
573	Duew 37306/1987	GT8-80C	2 x 280	B-2-2-B ER	Owned by VBK.
574	Duew 37307/1987	GT8-80C	2 x 280	B-2-2-B ER	Owned by VBK.
575	Duew 37308/1987	GT8-80C	2 x 280	B-2-2-B ER	Owned by VBK.
576	Duew 37309/1987	GT8-80C	2 x 280	B-2-2-B ER	Owned by VBK.
577	Duew 37310/1987	GT8-80C	2 x 280	B-2-2-B ER	Owned by VBK.
578	Duew 37311/1987	GT8-80C	2 x 280	B-2-2-B ER	Owned by VBK.
579	Duew 37312/1987	GT8-80C	2 x 280	B-2-2-B ER	Owned by VBK.
580	Duew 37313/1987	GT8-80C	2 x 280	B-2-2-B ER	Owned by VBK.
581	Duew 37342/1987	GT8-80C	2 x 280	B-2-2-B ER	Owned by VBK.
582	Duew 37343/1987	GT8-80C	2 x 280	B-2-2-B ER	Owned by VBK.
583	Duew 37344/1987	GT8-80C	2 x 280	B-2-2-B ER	Owned by VBK.
584	Duew 37345/1987	GT8-80C	2 x 280	B-2-2-B ER	Owned by VBK.

585	Duew 37346/1987	GT8-80C	2 x 280	B-2-2-B ER	Owned by VBK.
586	Duew 37347/1987	GT8-80C	2 x 280	B-2-2-B ER	Owned by VBK.
587	Duew 37348/1987	GT8-80C	2 x 280	B-2-2-B ER	Owned by VBK.
588	Duew 37349/1987	GT8-80C	2 x 280	B-2-2-B ER	Owned by VBK.
589	Duew 37350/1987	GT8-80C	2 x 280	B-2-2-B ER	Owned by VBK.
590	Duew 37351/1987	GT8-80C	2 x 280	B-2-2-B ER	Owned by VBK.
801	Duew 37554/1991	GT8-100C/2S	2 x 280	B-2-2-B ER	Owned by VBK.
802	Duew 37555/1991	GT8-100C/2S	2 x 280	B-2-2-B ER	Owned by VBK.
803	Duew 37556/1991	GT8-100C/2S	2 x 280	B-2-2-B ER	Owned by VBK.
804	Duew 37557/1991	GT8-100C/2S	2 x 280	B-2-2-B ER	Owned by VBK.
805	Duew 37558/1991	GT8-100C/2S	2 x 280	B-2-2-B ER	Owned by VBK.
806	Duew 37559/1991	GT8-100C/2S	2 x 280	B-2-2-B ER	Owned by VBK.
807	Duew 37560/1991	GT8-100C/2S	2 x 280	B-2-2-B ER	Owned by VBK.
808	Duew 37561/1991	GT8-100C/2S	2 x 280	B-2-2-B ER	Owned by VBK.
809	Duew 37562/1991	GT8-100C/2S	2 x 280	B-2-2-B ER	Owned by VBK. Fitted with toilet.
810	Duew 37563/1991	GT8-100C/2S	2 x 280	B-2-2-B ER	Owned by VBK. Fitted with toilet.
811	Duew 38048/1994	GT8-100C/2S	2 x 280	B-2-2-B ER	
812	Duew 38049/1994	GT8-100C/2S	2 x 280	B-2-2-B ER	
813	Duew 38050/1994	GT8-100C/2S	2 x 280	B-2-2-B ER	
814	Duew 38051/1994	GT8-100C/2S	2 x 280	B-2-2-B ER	
815	Duew 38052/1994	GT8-100C/2S	2 x 280	B-2-2-B ER	
816	Duew 38053/1994	GT8-100C/2S	2 x 280	B-2-2-B ER	Owned by DB (450 005)
817	Duew 38054/1994	GT8-100C/2S	2 x 280	B-2-2-B ER	Owned by DB (450 001)
819	Duew 38056/1994	GT8-100C/2S	2 x 280	B-2-2-B ER	Owned by DB (450 003)
820	Duew 38057/1994	GT8-100C/2S	2 x 280	B-2-2-B ER	Owned by DB (450 004)
821	Duew 38059/1994	GT8-100C/2S	2 x 280	B-2-2-B ER	Owned by VBK.
822	Duew 38059/1994	GT8-100C/2S	2 x 280	B-2-2-B ER	Owned by VBK.
823	Duew 38060/1994	GT8-100C/2S	2 x 280	B-2-2-B ER	Owned by VBK.
824	Duew 38061/1994	GT8-100C/2S	2 x 280	B-2-2-B ER	Owned by VBK.
825	Duew 38062/1994	GT8-100C/2S	2 x 280	B-2-2-B ER	Owned by VBK.
826	Duew 38063/1994	GT8-100C/2S	2 x 280	B-2-2-B ER	
827	Duew 38064/1994	GT8-100C/2S	2 x 280	B-2-2-B ER	
828	Duew 38065/1994	GT8-100C/2S	2 x 280	B-2-2-B ER	
829	Duew 38066/1994	GT8-100C/2S	2 x 280	B-2-2-B ER	
830	Duew 38067/1994	GT8-100C/2S	2 x 280	B-2-2-B ER	
831	Duew 38359/1995	GT8-100C/2S	2 x 280	B-2-2-B ER	
832	Duew 38360/1995	GT8-100C/2S	2 x 280	B-2-2-B ER	
833	Duew 38361/1995	GT8-100C/2S	2 x 280	B-2-2-B ER	
834	Duew 38362/1995	GT8-100C/2S	2 x 280	B-2-2-B ER	
835	Duew 38363/1995	GT8-100C/2S	2 x 280	B-2-2-B ER	
836	Duew 38364/1995	GT8-100C/2S	2 x 280	B-2-2-B ER	
837	Duew 38602/1997	GT8-100D/2SM	2 x 280	Bo-2-2-Bo ER	"M" denotes a low-floor
838	Duew 38603/1997	GT8-100D/2SM	2 x 280	Bo-2-2-Bo ER	centre section.
839	Duew 38605/1997	GT8-100D/2SM	2 x 280	Bo-2-2-Bo ER	
840	Duew 38606/1997	GT8-100D/2SM	2 x 280	Bo-2-2-Bo ER	
841	Duew 38604/1997	GT8-100D/2SM	2 x 280	Bo-2-2-Bo ER	
842	Duew 38607/1997	GT8-100D/2SM	2 x 280	Bo-2-2-Bo ER	
843	Duew 38608/1997	GT8-100D/2SM	2 x 280	Bo-2-2-Bo ER	
844	Duew 38609/1997	GT8-100D/2SM	2 x 280	Bo-2-2-Bo ER	
845	Duew 38610/1997	GT8-100D/2SM	2 x 280	Bo-2-2-Bo ER	Bistro car. White livery.
846	Duew 38611/1997	GT8-100D/2SM	2 x 280	Bo-2-2-Bo ER	Bistro car. White livery.
847	Duew 38612/1997	GT8-100D/2SM	2 x 280	Bo-2-2-Bo ER	Bistro car. White livery.
848	Duew 38613/1997	GT8-100D/2SM	2 x 280	Bo-2-2-Bo ER	Bistro car. White livery.
849	Duew 38752/1997	GT8-100D/2SM	2 x 280	Bo-2-2-Bo ER	
850	Duew 38753/1997	GT8-100D/2SM	2 x 280	Bo-2-2-Bo ER	
851[II]	Duew 38754/1997	GT8-100D/2SM	2 x 280	Bo-2-2-Bo ER	
852[II]	Duew 38755/1997	GT8-100D/2SM	2 x 280	Bo-2-2-Bo ER	
853[II]	Duew 38756/1997	GT8-100D/2SM	2 x 280	Bo-2-2-Bo ER	
854[II]	Duew 38757/1997	GT8-100D/2SM	2 x 280	Bo-2-2-Bo ER	
855[II]	Duew 38758/1997	GT8-100D/2SM	2 x 280	Bo-2-2-Bo ER	
856[II]	Duew 38759/1997	GT8-100D/2SM	2 x 280	Bo-2-2-Bo ER	
857[II]	Duew 38760/1997	GT8-100D/2SM	2 x 280	Bo-2-2-Bo ER	
858[II]	Duew 38992/1999	GT8-100D/2SM	2 x 280	Bo-2-2-Bo ER	
859[II]	Duew 38993/1999	GT8-100D/2SM	2 x 280	Bo-2-2-Bo ER	

860[II]	Duew	38994/1999	GT8-100D/2SM	2 x 280	Bo-2-2-Bo	ER
861[II]	Duew	38995/1999	GT8-100D/2SM	2 x 280	Bo-2-2-Bo	ER
862[II]	Duew	38996/1999	GT8-100D/2SM	2 x 280	Bo-2-2-Bo	ER
863[II]	Duew	38997/1999	GT8-100D/2SM	2 x 280	Bo-2-2-Bo	ER
864[II]	Duew	38998/1999	GT8-100D/2SM	2 x 280	Bo-2-2-Bo	ER
865[II]	Duew	38999/1999	GT8-100D/2SM	2 x 280	Bo-2-2-Bo	ER
866[II]	Duew	39000/1999	GT8-100D/2SM	2 x 280	Bo-2-2-Bo	ER
867[II]	Duew	39001/1999	GT8-100D/2SM	2 x 280	Bo-2-2-Bo	ER
868[II]	Duew	39002/1999	GT8-100D/2SM	2 x 280	Bo-2-2-Bo	ER
869[II]	Duew	39003/1999	GT8-100D/2SM	2 x 280	Bo-2-2-Bo	ER
870[II]	Duew	39004/1999	GT8-100D/2SM	2 x 280	Bo-2-2-Bo	ER
871[II]	Duew	39005/1999	GT8-100D/2SM	2 x 280	Bo-2-2-Bo	ER
872[II]	Duew	39316/2000	GT8-100D/2SM	2 x 280	Bo-2-2-Bo	ER
873[II]	Duew	39317/2000	GT8-100D/2SM	2 x 280	Bo-2-2-Bo	ER
874[II]	Duew	39318/2000	GT8-100D/2SM	2 x 280	Bo-2-2-Bo	ER
875[II]	Duew	39319/2000	GT8-100D/2SM	2 x 280	Bo-2-2-Bo	ER
876[II]	Duew	39320/2000	GT8-100D/2SM	2 x 280	Bo-2-2-Bo	ER
877[II]	Duew	39321/2000	GT8-100D/2SM	2 x 280	Bo-2-2-Bo	ER
878[II]	Duew	41667/2000	GT8-100D/2SM	2 x 280	Bo-2-2-Bo	ER
879[II]	Duew	41668/2002	GT8-100D/2SM	2 x 280	Bo-2-2-Bo	ER
880[II]	Duew	41669/2002	GT8-100D/2SM	2 x 280	Bo-2-2-Bo	ER
881	Duew	41670/2002	GT8-100D/2SM	2 x 280	Bo-2-2-Bo	ER
882	Duew	41671/2002	GT8-100D/2SM	2 x 280	Bo-2-2-Bo	ER
883	Duew	41672/2002	GT8-100D/2SM	2 x 280	Bo-2-2-Bo	ER
884	Duew	41673/2002	GT8-100D/2SM	2 x 280	Bo-2-2-Bo	ER
885	Duew	41674/2002	GT8-100D/2SM	2 x 280	Bo-2-2-Bo	ER
886	Duew	41675/2002	GT8-100D/2SM	2 x 280	Bo-2-2-Bo	ER
887	Duew	41676/2002	GT8-100D/2SM	2 x 280	Bo-2-2-Bo	ER
888	Duew	41677/2002	GT8-100D/2SM	2 x 280	Bo-2-2-Bo	ER
889	Duew	41678/2002	GT8-100D/2SM	2 x 280	Bo-2-2-Bo	ER
890	Duew	41780/2002	GT8-100D/2SM	2 x 280	Bo-2-2-Bo	ER
891	Duew	41781/2002	GT8-100D/2SM	2 x 280	Bo-2-2-Bo	ER
892	Duew	41782/2002	GT8-100D/2SM	2 x 280	Bo-2-2-Bo	ER
893	Duew	41783/2002	GT8-100D/2SM	2 x 280	Bo-2-2-Bo	ER
894	Duew	41784/2002	GT8-100D/2SM	2 x 280	Bo-2-2-Bo	ER
895	Duew	41785/2002	GT8-100D/2SM	2 x 280	Bo-2-2-Bo	ER
896	Duew	41786/2002	GT8-100D/2SM	2 x 280	Bo-2-2-Bo	ER
897	Duew	41787/2002	GT8-100D/2SM	2 x 280	Bo-2-2-Bo	ER
898	Duew	41788/2002	GT8-100D/2SM	2 x 280	Bo-2-2-Bo	ER
899	Duew	41789/2002	GT8-100D/2SM	2 x 280	Bo-2-2-Bo	ER
900	Duew	42259/2004	GT8-100D/2SM	2 x 280	Bo-2-2-Bo	ER	Fitted with toilet
901	Duew	42260/2004	GT8-100D/2SM	2 x 280	Bo-2-2-Bo	ER	Fitted with toilet
902	Duew	42261/2004	GT8-100D/2SM	2 x 280	Bo-2-2-Bo	ER	Fitted with toilet
903	Duew	42262/2004	GT8-100D/2SM	2 x 280	Bo-2-2-Bo	ER	Fitted with toilet
904	Duew	42263/2004	GT8-100D/2SM	2 x 280	Bo-2-2-Bo	ER	Fitted with toilet
905	Duew	42264/2004	GT8-100D/2SM	2 x 280	Bo-2-2-Bo	ER	Fitted with toilet
906	Duew	. . . . ./2004	GT8-100D/2SM	2 x 280	Bo-2-2-Bo	ER
907	Duew	. . . . ./2004	GT8-100D/2SM	2 x 280	Bo-2-2-Bo	ER
908	Duew	. . . . ./2004	GT8-100D/2SM	2 x 280	Bo-2-2-Bo	ER
909	Duew	. . . . ./2004	GT8-100D/2SM	2 x 280	Bo-2-2-Bo	ER
910	Duew	. . . . ./2004	GT8-100D/2SM	2 x 280	Bo-2-2-Bo	ER
911	Duew	. . . . ./200.	GT8-100D/2SM	2 x 280	Bo-2-2-Bo	ER
912	Duew	. . . . ./200.	GT8-100D/2SM	2 x 280	Bo-2-2-Bo	ER
913	Duew	. . . . ./200.	GT8-100D/2SM	2 x 280	Bo-2-2-Bo	ER
914	Duew	. . . . ./200.	GT8-100D/2SM	2 x 280	Bo-2-2-Bo	ER
915	Duew	. . . . ./200.	GT8-100D/2SM	2 x 280	Bo-2-2-Bo	ER
916	Duew	. . . . ./200.	GT8-100D/2SM	2 x 280	Bo-2-2-Bo	ER
917	Duew	. . . . ./200.	GT8-100D/2SM	2 x 280	Bo-2-2-Bo	ER
918	Duew	. . . . ./200.	GT8-100D/2SM	2 x 280	Bo-2-2-Bo	ER
919	Duew	. . . . ./200.	GT8-100D/2SM	2 x 280	Bo-2-2-Bo	ER
920	Duew	. . . . ./200.	GT8-100D/2SM	2 x 280	Bo-2-2-Bo	ER
921	Duew	. . . . ./200.	GT8-100D/2SM	2 x 280	Bo-2-2-Bo	ER
922	Duew	. . . . ./200.	GT8-100D/2SM	2 x 280	Bo-2-2-Bo	ER

BAHN UND SERVICE GmbH   B&S
Walburg, Hessen

This company is the EIU formed by Eisenbahnfreunde Walburg so that use can be made of their shunting locomotives on ballast trains.

No.	Builder, No. & Year	Type	kW Details	Comments
V60.1	LEW 12670/1970	V60D	478 0-8-0 DH	Ex Kali & Salz, Grasleben
V60.2	LEW 13777/1973	V60D	478 0-8-0 DH	Ex Kali AG Merkers 13
V60.3	LEW 13778/1973	V60D	478 0-8-0 DH	Ex Kali & Salz, Zielitz
Köf 6424	KHD 57282/1959	Kof II	97 4w DH	Ex DB 323 137
Köf 6499	Gm 5133/1959	Kof II	97 4w DH	Ex DB 323 681

BASF AG SERVICE CENTRE RAILWAY   BASF
Ludwigshafen, Rheinland Pfalz

Routes: BASF Factory in Ludwigshafen to various destinations.
Length: -/208.6 km. **Depot:** Ludwigshafen.
EVU Licence: Freight and Passenger 02/07/1996.

BASF (Badische Anilin und Soda Fabrik) has a large chemical works in Ludwigshafen and has some 17 internal user locomotives. It puts about five million tonnes of traffic to rail each year. Open access gave the firm the opportunity to run its own trains which it now does with locos hired from Adtranz. Early in 2001 the BASF main line operations were taken over by Rail4Chem (q.v). The diesels work trains locally between Ludwigshafen and Mannheim Industriehafen but still do a main line turn from Ludwigshafen to Germersheim. In 2002 the diesels started working a train to France handing over to SNCF at Lauterbourg. This runs TThSO, BASF dep. 07.30, Lauterbourg 09.42-10.33, BASF arrive 12.19. During 2003 BASF took back in house the limestone trains from Stromberg to Ludwigshafen previously handled by BGW. This leaves Ludwigshafen at about 07.00 TTho and after loading departs Stromberg at 13.30 getting back to BASF at 17.30.

No.	Builder, No. & Year	Type	kW Details	Comments
1001	LEW 15084/1975	V100.4 1030 B-B DH		Ex 201 812 (FFS) Grüner Klaus
1002	Adtranz 72030/1998	V100.4 1030 B-B DH		(FFS) Heinerle
1003	Adtranz 70110/1999	V100.4 1030 B-B DH		Grune Minna

(There are many more internal user locomotives.)

BAYERN BAHN BETRIEBSGESELLSCHAFT   BBB
Nördlingen, Bayern

Depot: Nördlingen
EVU Licence: 04/04/1995 Freight and Passenger

This organisation is the operating arm of the Bayerisches Eisenbahn Museum in Nördlingen. This EVU has been set up so that trains can be run over the DB Netz lines from Nördlingen to Dombuhl and Guzenhausen for which BBB has now become the EIU for some 90 km of track.

The operating locos are from the Bayerisches Eisenbahn Museum in Nördlingen (e.g. 01 066, E94 192 etc) but two diesel locomotives have been obtained specifically for freight trips.

No.	Builder, No. & Year	Type	kW Details	Comments
V100 1365	Essl 5301/1962	V100	992 B-B DH	Ex VSFT, ex ÖBB 2048 014 ex DB 211 365. (CAT engine)
350 001	Hens 26750/1960		500 6w DH	Ex E-ON power station Anglberg.

BAHNBETRIEBSGESELLSCHAFT STAUDEN mbH   BBG
Augsburg, Bayern

Depot: Augsburg
EVU Licence: Freight and Passenger 03/09/2002.

This is another enthusiasts' group that has formed its own EVU for passenger and freight operations. During 2003 additional passenger trains were needed on the Günzburg – Mindelheim line and DB Regio sub-contracted these trains to BBG Stauden! Early in 2004 BBG was planning to get some extra stock from Austria.

No.	Builder, No. & Year	Type	kW	Details	Comments
5081 561	SGP 78200/1965	VT98	2x110	A-A DMR	Ex ÖBB
VT 05	Essl 23350/1951	Essl	225		Ex RBG VT 03
2143 006	SGP 18344/1966	2143	1114	B-B DH	Ex ÖBB
4030 238	SGP 67866/1970	4030	900	Bo-Bo ER	Ex ÖBB

BAYERN CARGO BAHN   BCB

Holzkirchen, Bayern

Depot: Holzkirchen
EVU Licence: Freight and Passenger 14/03/2002.

This is a Connex Company and an offshoot of BOB Bayern. Freight activities are being sought in Bayern and in 2002 the firm started getting involved in container movements as well as odd freight trips. Actual locos tend to fluctuate according to Connex Cargo demands. In 2003 the BOB was involved in oil train trips at Ingolstadt in connection with HGK and KEG flows.

No.	Builder, No. & Year	Type	kW	Details	Comments
V100 001	LEW 15382/1976	V100	1050	B-B DH	Ex RBB V142 ex DB 201 864
V100 003	LEW 15381/1976	V100	1050	B-B DH	Ex RBB V145, ex HSB 199 863
V200 001	VSFT 1001382/2003	G1206	1500	B-B DH	Owned by Riebel, operated by BCB
V300 001	VSFT 1001038/2000	G2000	2200	B-B DH	Leased from ATC

BENTHEIMER EISENBAHN   BE

Niedersachsen

Routes: Coevorden (NL)–Neuenhaus–Nordhorn–Bad Bentheim–Ochtrup–Brecht
Length: 75.7/97.3 km.
Depots: Nordhorn Süd, Nordhorn, Bad Bentheim.   **Livery:** Red.
EVU Licence: Freight and Passenger 26/10/1995.

British visitors to Germany who used to travel via Hoek van Holland and Hengelo would have spotted BE locos at Bad Benthem. This freight railway is quite interesting being an international operation as it runs into The Netherlands at Coeverden. South of Bad Bentheim the line used to run to Gronau but now terminates at Ochtrup-Brechte. The railway now has a new combined bus and rail depot at Nordhorn Süd but locos can be found stabled at Bad Bentheim Nord, Nordhorn, Laarwald and Coeverden. The BE 211's have workings over DB to Rheine and/or Münster with traffic destined for the WLE whilst in the evening the railway produces a container train for the DB also worked by 211's to the above points. BE handled 570,000 tonnes of freight in 1998. A recent development is that BE has taken over from DB Cargo the trip workings from Rheine to Spelle and Emsdetten.

No.	Builder, No. & Year	Type	kW	Details	Comments
D 1	O&K 26421/1966	Köf III	176	B DH	DB 332 306
D 2	O&K 26341/1964	Köf III	176	B DH	DB 332 103
D 3	Jung 13747/1964	Köf III	176	B DH	DB 332 161
D 4ᴵᴵ	O&K 26458/1969	Köf III	176	B DH	DB 335 099
D 11	Gm 4671/1951	Köf II	94	B DH	DB 323 939 Sold Jan. 2002
D 13	O&K 20975/1938	Köf II	94	B DH	DB 323 970 Preserved
D 15	Jung 5494/1934	Köf II	94	B DH	DB 323 405 To AAE
D 16	Gm 4877/1955	Köf II	94	B DH	DB 323 555
D 17	Jung 13188/1960	Köf II	94	B DH	DB 323 820
D 20	MaK 1000092/1962	V100	940	B-B DH	DB 211 074 Sold via Pacton to EIB
D 21	Deutz 57362/1962	V100	940	B-B DH	DB 211 125
D 22	MaK 800180/1972	G1100BB	809	B-B DH	
D 23	MaK 1000790/1980	G1202BB	1000	B-B DH	*Landkreis Graftschaft Bentheim*
D 24	MaK 1000795/1983	DE1002	1119	Bo-Bo DE	*Neuenhaus-Veldhausen*
D 25	Jung 13472/1962	V100	940	B-B DH	DB 211 345

BAHNGELLSCHAFT WALDHOF AG   BGW

Mannheim, Baden-Württemberg

Routes: Mannheim–Waldhof–Mannheim Sandhofen 4.8 km, Alzey–Kirchheimboladen 19.6 km, Langenlonsheim–Simmern–Morbach 79 km.

Length: 103.4/110.0 km.   **Depot:** Mannheim Sandhofen.
EVU Licence: Freight and Passenger 30/10/1996.

BGW is an operator that had expanded greatly in the last few years. Originally BGW just ran some 5 km of line in Mannheim from Waldhof to Sandhofen serving industries in the area. Then along came open access so in 1995 BGW took over from DB the freight traffic between Alzey and Kirchheimbolanden and later in 1997 took over the line itself! Since then expansion has followed more or less each year with Langenlonsheim–Simmern–Morbach part of the BGW empire and even on to Hermeskeil if any traffic develops on that part of the closed DB network. BGW is understood to be owned by Rhenus Logistik (75%) and RP Eisenbahn (25%). BGW has rapidly become an open access operator working far away from home e.g. rubbish trains between Hildesheim and Helmstedt. It also works freights between Stromberg and Ludwigshafen on behalf of BASF. BGW locos can turn up anywhere working for track contractors. BGW is now also a passenger operator as it is involved with the Eurobahn (q.v.). Note that locos have new numbers in the DH/DE number series but also have an internal BGW number. After expansion in the early years of open access BGW has since contracted and has lost the contract from Hildesheim to OHE.

In late 2002 BGW was operating on a much reduced scale and in its own sidings now uses road-rail Unimogs. The only regular traffic flow, the BASF traffic from Stromberg to Ludwigshafen, transferred to BASF in 2003 leaving BGW back were it started from.

No.	Builder, No. & Year	Type	kW	Details	Comments
DH 280 01	Deutz 57846/1965	V169	1580	B-B DH	BGW 04 ex DB 219 001. To EVB
DE 300 01	Lugansk 0325 /1974	232	2200	Co-Co DE	BGW 05 ex DB 232 103. To EVB
DE 300 02	Lugansk 0248/1974	232	2200	Co-Co DE	BGW 06 ex DB 232 057. To EKO
495	KM 19400/1969	M275B		B D?	Sold 2002.
496	O&K 26281/1964	MB7N		B DH	Withdrawn
802	Gm 5250/1962	D35B	176	B DH	Withdrawn
323 912	KM 15444/1934	Köf	94	B DH	Ex museum? ex DB.To ESG

Note: The DE300 obtained via Kaliningrad and thought now to have new CAT engines. DH280 01 obtained from track contractor in Italy where it was T 1591 and susequently sold to EVB.

BORKUMER KLEINBAHN UND DAMPFSCHIFFART GmbH BK

Borkum, Niedersachsen

Gauge: 900 mm
Routes: Borkum Bhf–Borkum Reede
Length: 7.4/13.0 km.   **Depot:** Borkum Stadtbahnhof.
EVU Licence: Freight and Passenger 24/01/1996.

This 900 mm gauge line on the Ostfriesland island of Borkum connects the harbour with the town. Freight finished in 1968 but the line is very busy in the summer season when steam hauled trains are also run. Note the locomotives have no numbers–only names–how splendid! The line is 7.4 km long (has 3.2 km of double track). The railway carried 775,000 passengers in 1998 and 818,000 in 1999.

No.	Builder, No. & Year	Type	kW	Details	Comments
Emden	Schöma 3222/1970	CFL200DA	169	B DM	Ex Faxe, Denmark
Leer	DWK 551/1934	40		B DM	
Münster	Schöma 1989/1957	82		B DM	
Berlin	Schöma 5342/1993	CFL150DCL	180	B DH	
Hannover	Schöma 5343/1993	CFL150DCL	180	B DH	
Münster	Schöma 5385/1994	CFL150DCL	180	B DH	

BURGENLANDBAHN   BLB

Zeitz, Sachsen Anhalt

This is a joint company formed by DB (70%) and KEG (30%) (q.v.) to operate regional passenger services on local lines.

Routes: Naumburg/Weissenfels–Zeitz (KBS 551, 53.3 km); Naumburg–Artern (KBS 585, 55.5 km); Merseburg–Querfurt (KBS 586, 34.7);Querfurt–Röblingen (KBS 587, 31.0 km); Merseburg–Schafstadt (KBS 588, 12.8 km).
Length: 187.3 km, all DB Netz.   **Depots:** Karsdorf, Zeitz.
EVU Licence: Passenger 22/12/1998.

No.	Builder, No. & Year	Type	kW	Details	Comments	Name
VT3.01	DWA/1999	LVT/S	265	A-1 DMR	DB 672 901	Querfurter Pfingsbursche
VT3.02	DWA/1999	LVT/S	265	A-1 DMR	DB 672 902	Rotkäppchen
VT3.03	DWA/1999	LVT/S	265	A-1 DMR	DB 672 903	
VT3.04	DWA/1999	LVT/S	265	A-1 DMR	DB 672 904	
VT3.05	DWA/1999	LVT/S	265	A-1 DMR	DB 672 905	Stadt Naumburg
VT3.06	DWA/1999	LVT/S	265	A-1 DMR	DB 672 906	
VT3.07	DWA/1999	LVT/S	265	A-1 DMR	DB 672 907	
VT3.08	DWA/1999	LVT/S	265	A-1 DMR	DB 672 908	Kohlebau Deuben
VT3.09	DWA/1999	LVT/S	265	A-1 DMR	DB 672 909	Weissenfelser Schusterjunge
VT3.10	DWA/1999	LVT/S	265	A-1 DMR	DB 672 910	
VT3.11	DWA/1999	LVT/S	265	A-1 DMR	DB 672 911	
VT3.12	DWA/1999	LVT/S	265	A-1 DMR	DB 672 912	Stadt Rossleben
VT3.13	DWA/1999	LVT/S	265	A-1 DMR	DB 672 913	
VT3.14	DWA/1999	LVT/S	265	A-1 DMR	DB 672 914	
VT3.15	DWA/1999	LVT/S	265	A-1 DMR	DB 672 915	
VT3.16	DWA/1999	LVT/S	265	A-1 DMR	DB 672 916	Burgerlandkreis
VT3.17	DWA/1999	LVT/S	265	A-1 DMR	DB 672 917	Erben Luther
VT3.18	DWA/1999	LVT/S	265	A-1 DMR	DB 672 918	

BUTZBACH–LICHER EISENBAHN AG   BLE

Hessen
Routes: Butzbach Ost–Munzenberg/Pohlgöns 12.0 km, Bad Nauheim Nord–Griedel 11.0 km. Friedberg–Friedrichsdorf (KBS 636 16.0 km); Friedberg–Nidda (KBS 632, 25.0 km); Friedberg–Hungen (KBS 632, 23 km).
Length: 23.7/31 km.   **Depot:** Butzbach Ost, Friedberg.
EVU Licence:

The BLE is part of the HLB empire (q.v.) and runs in three directions from Butzbach to Pohlgons (North West), Bad Neuheim (South East) and Munzenberg (North East). The line has not served Lich since 1961! The BLE has become a passenger train operator again in 1998 but not on its own line! As part of HLB it got the job of running the previously DB services from Friedberg–Friedrichsdorf. A year later BLE took over the passenger trains on two more lines: Friedberg–Nidda and Friedberg–Hungen. Initially some stock was hired in but now the Stadler type DMUs have taken charge. Those on the BLE services are second class only and no toilets. Toilets may be fitted later under a retro-fit scheme.

From January 2001 BLE took over passenger services over further stretches of DB Netz: Giessen -Nidda–Gelnhausen (KBS 631, 70.0km) and from June 2001 Friedberg–Hanau (KBS 633, 32.0 km).

No.	Builder, No. & Year	Type	kW	Details	Comments	
13	Jung 13408/1961	R42C	324	C DH	Stored	
17	Jung 13286/1961	R42C	324	C DH	Ex SK	
32	MaK 1000245/1965	G1300BB	992	B-B DH		
509 104	DWA Btz 509 001/1999	GTW2/6	550	2-Bo-2 DER	HLB VT 104	
509 105	DWA Btz 509 002/1999	GTW2/6	550	2-Bo-2 DER	HLB VT 105	
509 106	DWA Btz 509 003/1999	GTW2/6	550	2-Bo-2 DER	HLB VT 106	
509 107	DWA Btz 509 004/1999	GTW2/6	550	2-Bo-2 DER	HLB VT 107	
509 109	DWA Btz 509 006/1999	GTW2/6	550	2-Bo-2 DER	HLB VT 109	
509 110	DWA Btz 509 007/1999	GTW2/6	550	2-Bo-2 DER	HLB VT 110	
509 111	DWA Btz 509 008/1999	GTW2/6	550	2-Bo-2 DER	HLB VT 111	
509 112	DWA Btz 509 009/1999	GTW2/6	550	2-Bo-2 DER	HLB VT 112	
508 113	DWA Btz 508 004/1999	GTW2/6	550	2-Bo-2 DER	HLB VT 113	
508 114	DWA Btz 508 005/1999	GTW2/6	550	2-Bo-2 DER	HLB VT 114	
508 115	DWA Btz 508 006/1999	GTW2/6	550	2-Bo-2 DER	HLB VT 115	Wetterau
526 119	Bomb 526 119/2000	GTW2/6	550	2-Bo-2 DER	HLB VT 119	
526 120	Bomb 526 120/2000	GTW2/6	550	2-Bo-2 DER	HLB VT 120	
526 121	Bomb 526 121/2000	GTW2/6	550	2-Bo-2 DER	HLB VT 121	
~~526 122~~	~~Bomb 526 122/2000~~	~~GTW2/6~~	~~550~~	~~2-Bo-2 DER~~	~~HLB VT 122~~	
526 123	Bomb 526 123/2000	GTW2/6	550	2-Bo-2 DER	HLB VT 123	
526 124	Bomb 526 124/2000	GTW2/6	550	2-Bo-2 DER	HLB VT 124	
526 125	Bomb 526 125/2000	GTW2/6	550	2-Bo-2 DER	HLB VT 125	
526 126	Bomb 526 126/2001	GTW2/6	550	2-Bo-2 DER	HLB VT 126	
526 127	Bomb 526 009/2001	GTW2/6	550	2-Bo-2 DER	HLB VT 127	

526 128 Bomb 526 110/2001	GTW2/6	550	2-Bo-2 DER	HLB VT 128
526 129 Bomb 526 111/2001	GTW2/6	550	2-Bo-2 DER	HLB VT 139
526 130 Bomb 526 111/2001	GTW2/6	550	2-Bo-2 DER	HLB VT 130

NB: Nos. 13 and 17 are stored at Griedel. 526 127–130 used by DB Regio and in exchange BLE uses 628 448–450.

BODENSEE OBERSCHWABEN BAHN Gmbh   BOB

Friedrichshafen, Baden-Württemberg

Routes: Friedrichshafen Hafen–Friedrichshafen Hbf.–Ravensburg–Aulendorf (KBS 751)
Length: 42 km.   **Depot:** Friedrichshafen Stadt.
EVU Licence: Passenger 16/05/1995.

The BOB took over the local passenger services between Friedrichshafen Stadt and Ravensburg from DB in 1993 reopening several stations in the process. For a while Regio Sprinter sets were on loan from the DKB until its own stock was delivered. Starting with two NE 81 DMUs services went from strength to strength far exceeding expectations so soon a third unit was acquired. In September 1997 further growth took place when BOB extended operations to include the Friedrichshafen Hafen branch and services to Ravensburg were extended to Aulendorf. For these new services some Regio Shuttles were obtained. Now some more stations have been reopened and at least one new halt constructed. Passengers are flocking back to the railway and traffic is now reported to have doubled since BOB took over from DB. In 1995 the BOB was carrying 566,000 passengers; in 1999 766,000 passengers were moved and latest figures show 839,000 passengers–a real success story.

No.	Builder, No. & Year	Type	kW Details		Comments
VT 60	WagU 36107/1993	NE81	2 x 201	B-B DHR	
VT 61	WagU 36108/1993	NE81	2 x 201	B-B DHR	
VT 62	ABB 36289/1994	NE81	2 x 201	B-B DHR	
VT 63	Adtranz 36782/1998	RS1	2 x 257	B-B DMR	
VT 64	Adtranz 36783/1998	RS1	2 x 257	B-B DMR	
VT 65	Adtranz 36784/1998	RS1	2 x 257	B-B DMR	
VT 66	Adtranz 36785/1998	RS1	2 x 257	B-B DMR	

BAYERISCHE OBERLAND BAHN Gmbh   BOB (CONNEX)

Holzkirchen, Bayern

Routes: Holzkirchen–Bayrischzell (KBS 955), Holzkirchen–Lenggries (KBS 956), Schaftlach–Tegernsee (KBS 957). The first two are DB Netz tracks whilst the last is the former Tegernseebahn.
Length: 12.3 /13.7 km (being the former Tegernseebahn).
Depot: Lenggries.

This company was set up to run the local services from München to Lenggries, Tegernsee and Bayerischzell. It is a subsidiary of Connex and has a 15-year contract. The Tegernseebahn (TAG) was taken over as part of the reorganisation and its stock has been sold. To run the new services 17 5-car articulated sets were ordered off the drawing board from Jenbach in Austria. This untested design was called the Integral. Jenbach built the three main sections of the trains with PFA Weiden (Bayern) constructing two intermediate sections. MAN provided the engines. Thus it was a joint Austro-German venture. The units have had tremendous problems resulting in them all being taken out of traffic in 1999/2000 for various modifications to be done. Trains had to revert to being loco-hauled with DB Regio providing 218's as before but BOB hired in some Nohab diesels (former DSB locos) to help out. By late 2001/early 2002 things had settled down but what should have been a showpiece service with new units was a shambles. It will be interesting to see if anyone else buys any Integral units! In late 2003 BOB decided to order seven more sets!

No.	Builder, No. & Year	Type	kW	Details	Name
VT 101	JW J3155-01/1998	Integral	3 x 315	AA11AA DHR	*München*
VT 102	JW J3155-02/1998	Integral	3 x 315	AA11AA DHR	*Agatharied*
VT 103	JW J3155-03/1998	Integral	3 x 315	AA11AA DHR	
VT 104	JW J3155-04/1998	Integral	3 x 315	AA11AA DHR	*Bayerischzell*
VT 105	JW J3155-05/1998	Integral	3 x 315	AA11AA DHR	
VT 106	JW J3155-06/1998	Integral	3 x 315	AA11AA DHR	*Haushaun*
VT 107	JW J3155-07/1998	Integral	3 x 315	AA11AA DHR	*Bad Tölz*
VT 108	JW J3155-08/1998	Integral	3 x 315	AA11AA DHR	*Gaissach*

VT 109	JW J3155-09/1998	Integral 3 x 315	AA11AA DHR	
VT 110	JW J3155-10/1998	Integral 3 x 315	AA11AA DHR	*Holzkirchen*
VT 111	JW J3155-11/1998	Integral 3 x 315	AA11AA DHR	*Tegernsee*
VT 112	JW J3155-12/1998	Integral 3 x 315	AA11AA DHR	*Stadt Miesbach*
VT 113	JW J3155-13/1998	Integral 3 x 315	AA11AA DHR	*Lenggries*
VT 114	JW J3155-14/1998	Integral 3 x 315	AA11AA DHR	*Fischbachau*
VT 115	JW J3155-15/1998	Integral 3 x 315	AA11AA DHR	*Schaftlach*
VT 116	JW J3155-16/1998	Integral 3 x 315	AA11AA DHR	*Schliersee*
VT 117	JW J3155-17/1999	Integral 3 x 315	AA11AA DHR	

VERKEHRSBETRIEB BIBERACH–OBERHARMERS-BACH (SWEG)   BOH
Baden-Württemberg

Routes: Biberach–Zell–Oberharmersbach-Riersbach (KBS 722)
Length: 10.6 km.
Depot: Oberharmersbach-Riersbach.

This is another SWEG operation with the branch being only 10.5 km long. Local passenger trains only now as freight finished some years ago. School children and workers in the peaks with the odd tourist in between. The line is now served by OSB units (q.v.).

No.	Builder, No. & Year	Type	kW	Details	Comments
VT 102	Essl 23500/1952	Esslingen 2 x 107	1A-A1 DHR		Stored

boxXpress GmbH   boxXpress
Bad Honnef, Nordrhein-Westfalen

EVU Licence: Freight, 07/05/2003.

This company is involved in the movement of containers from the North Sea ports to the south of Germany.
It founded its own transport company on 29/05/02 made up as follows:
European Rail Shuttle B.V. (ERS) 47%(involving Maersk and P&O Nedlloyd)
Eurogate Intermodal 38%
Net Log Netzwerklogistik 15%(Subsidiary of TX Logistik AG)

Locomotives are hired from Dispolok; wagons from AAE; crews from MEV.

Workings in July 2002 were as follows

1. Bremerhaven–Kornwestheim and return
2. Gemunden–Hamburg Waltershof and return
3. Gemunden–Nürnberg Hafen and return
4. Bremerhaven–München Riem and return
5. Hamburg Waltershof–München Riem and return
6. München Riem–Augsburg Oberhausen and return

BAHNREINIGUNGS GESELLSCHAFT, LEIPZIG mbH BRG
Sachsen

This is a DB subsidiary which used to look after the two DB narrow gauge lines in Sachsen (Radebeul and Freital). It has a standard gauge shunting loco which it hires out to track contractors and others!

No.	Builder, No. & Year	Type	kW	Details	Comments
106 560	LEW 12315/1969	V60D	478	0-8-0 DH	Ex Bay Wa, Neumarkt, Sachs.

BREISGAU S–BAHN Gmbh   BSB
Freiburg, Baden-Württemberg

Route: Freiburg Hbf–Gottenheim–Breisach (KBS 729) 22.5 km. (DB Netz).
Length: 22.5 km.   **Depot:** Endingen (with SWEG).
EVU Licence: Freight and Passenger 24/01/1996.

This company is jointly owned by SWEG (50%) and Freiburger Verkehrs AG (50%). The new company has taken over passenger services from Freiburg to Breisgau and revolutionised the service with modern rolling stock leased from Rail Charter GmbH (q.v.). All sets are air-conditioned. Maintenance is carried out at the SWEG depot in Endingen. Late in 2000 BSB won a contract to run the services between Freiburg and Elzach which entailed ordering some more units which were delivered in 2002. These units differ from the earlier ones having air conditioning and a WC.

No.	Builder, No. & Year	Type	kW	Details	Comments
VT 001	Adtranz 36606/1998	RS1	2 x 257	B-B DMR	
VT 002	Adtranz 36607/1998	RS1	2 x 257	B-B DMR	
VT 003	Adtranz 36608/1998	RS1	2 x 257	B-B DMR	
VT 004	Adtranz 36609/1998	RS1	2 x 257	B-B DMR	WASENWEILER
VT 005	Adtranz 36610/1998	RS1	2 x 257	B-B DMR	IHRINGEN
VT 006	Adtranz 36611/1998	RS1	2 x 257	B-B DMR	GOTTENHEIM
VT 007	Adtranz 36612/1998	RS1	2 x 257	B-B DMR	STADT FREIBURG IM BREISGAU
VT 008	Adtranz 36613/1998	RS1	2 x 257	B-B DMR	BREISACH
VT 009	Adtranz 36614/1998	RS1	2 x 257	B-B DMR	MARCH
VT 010	Stadler 37153/2002	RS1	2 x 257	B-B DMR	WINDEN IN ELZTAL
VT 011	Stadler 37154/2002	RS1	2 x 257	B-B DMR	GUNDELFINGEN
VT 012	Stadler 37155/2002	RS1	2 x 257	B-B DMR	STADT ELZACH
VT 013	Stadler 37156/2002	RS1	2 x 257	B-B DMR	WALDKIRCH
VT 014	Stadler 37157/2002	RS1	2 x 257	B-B DMR	GUTACH IN BREISGAU
VT 015	Stadler 37158/2002	RS1	2 x 257	B-B DMR	ZWEITÄLELAND
VT 016	Stadler 37159/2002	RS1	2 x 257	B-B DMR	DENZLINGEN
VT 017	Stadler 37160/2002	RS1	2 x 257	B-B DMR	STADT FREIBURG
VT 018	Stadler 37161/2002	RS1	2 x 257	B-B DMR	
VT 019	Stadler 37162/2002	RS1	2 x 257	B-B DMR	

BROHLTAL-SCHMALSPUR EISENBAHN BETRIEBS GmbH — BSEG

Brohl-Lutzing, Rheinland Pfalz

Gauge: 1000 mm
Routes: Brohl–Brohl Hafen (dual gauge) 2.0 km; Brohl–Engeln (KBS 12426,17.6 km).
Length: 19.6/xxx km.   **Depot:** Brohl.
EVU Licence: Freight and Passenger 31/08/1996

This 19.6 km metre gauge line is located to the south of Bonn and its main depot is a short walk from the DB station. There is a branch down to a harbour on the Rhein which is dual-gauge. The line has had mixed times with freight traffic finishing some years ago. The railway kept operations going by running regular tourist trains as the top end of the line is quite scenic and to improve the attraction some steam locos were imported from Poland. Now with road congestion a problem there is the possibility of freight traffic again and for this a diesel has been acquired from Spain along with some container flat wagons.

No.	Builder, No. & Year	Type	kW	Details	Comments
V	Chrz 2135/1952	Px48		0-8-0	Ex PKP Px48-3906
VI	Chrz 2248/1952	Px48		0-8-0	Ex PKP Px48-3913
D 1	O&K 26528/1965	221		C D?	
D 2	O&K 26529/1965	221		C D?	
D 3	O&K 26623/1966	221		C D?	
D 5	Hens 31004/1966	DHG1200BB883		B-B DH	Ex FEVE 1405
005	U23A 24963/1984	L18H		0-6-0 DH	Ex Mansfeld
006	U23A 24964/1984	L18H		0-6-0 DH	Ex Mansfeld
7	LKM 250349/1967	V10C	75	C D?	Ex Mansfeld
VT 30	Fuchs 9053/1956		4 x 125	Bo-Bo DER	Ex WEG T30

BAHNEN DER STADT MONHEIM GmbH — BSM

Monheim am Rhein, Nordrhein Westfalen

Routes: Langenfeld–Monheim-Blee–Hitdorfer Kapelle 6.1 km; Wasserwerk–Monheim Nord 3.0 km.

Length: 9.5/11.3 km.   **Depot**: Daimlerstrasse, Monheim.
EVU Licence: 11/10/1995, Freight.

This local railway serves several industries around Monheim with some 9 km of track. The company can run over DB tracks and interchanges with DB at Düsseldorf- Reisholz. 33,000 tonnes were handled in 1998 and a similar amount in 2000.

No.	Builder, No. & Year	Type	kW	Details	Name
80	O&K 26880/1979	MC700C	500	C DH	MAX
81	O&K 26881/1979	MC700C	500	C DH	MORITZ

BREMEN–THEDINGHAUSER EISENBAHN GmbH   BTE
Weyhe Leeste, Niedersachsen/Bremen

Routes: Delmenhorst Süd–Bremen Huchting–Leeste–Thedinghausen 26.1 km
Length: 26.1/xxx km.   **Depot**: Leeste.
EVU Licence: Freight and Passenger 03/03/2000.

Basically a Bremen area industrial server having some 26 km of lines. BTE took over the former operator Eisenbahn Bremen Thedinghausen(BTh) from 29/2/2000. In 1998 BTh conveyed 30,000 tonnes of freight which increased to 35,000 tonnes in 2000. The line is also marketed by the "Weserbahn" (q.v.).

No.	Builder, No. & Year	Type	kW	Details	Comments
V 102	Mak 1000010/1958	1000D	736	D DM	For disposal
V 1001	LEW 16672/1981	V100.4	809	B-B DH	Ex V105; Ex BKW Welzow

BUG VERKEHRSBAU AG, BERLIN   BUG
Berlin

Livery: Green and black.

Founded in 1990 as Bug Bau und Unterhaltung von Gleisanlagen GmbH this firm is now getting into the privatised railway scene and hopes to get an EVU licence soon. In the meantime the locos are operated by OHE Spandau on behalf of BUG. Starting with one loco in 2002 the fleet is starting to build up nicely.

No.	Builder, No. & Year	Type	kW	Details	Comments
V60-BUG-01	LEW 15598/1977	V60D	478	0-8-0 DH	Ex DB 345 067
V60-BUG-02	LEW 17687/1982	V60D	478	0-8-0 DH	Ex DB 345 161
V60-BUG-03	LEW 15151/1976	V60D	478	0-8-0 DH	Ex DB 345 028
V60-BUG-04	LEW 13333/1972	V60D	478	0-8-0 DH	Ex DB 346 816
V60-BUG-05	LEW 14579/1975	V60D	478	0-8-0 DH	Ex DB 346 967
V100-BUG-01	LEW 12409/1969	V100	736	B-B DH	Ex Laubag 110-10, ex DR 110 108

BVO BAHN GmbH   BVO
Annaberg Buchholz,Sachsen

Gauge: 750 mm
Routes: Cranzahl–Kurort Oberwiesenthal (KBS 518) 17.4 km
Length: 17.4/22.8 km.   **Depot**: Oberwiesenthal.
EVU Licence: Freight and Passenger 23/02/1998.

When DB wanted to rid itself of the narrow gauge lines in Sachsen there were few takers. One company that did step in was the bus company in Annaberg-Buchholz which bought the line from Cranzahl to Oberwiesenthal (Fichtelbergbahn) taking over in 1998. There is talk of BVO doing something similar to the line on Rügen in as much as they are considering extending the narrow gauge line to Annaberg-Buchholz Obererbahnhof! In 1998 593,000 passengers used the line.

On 21 June 2004 this company took over the remaining DB operated narrow gauge lines in Sachsen at Radebeul and Freital Hainsburg, although the latter is still closed following the serious floods of August 2002.

Oberwiesenthal Line

No.	Builder, No. & Year	Type	kW	Details	Comments
99 772	LKM 32011/1952	DR	368	2-10-2T	
99 773	LKM 32012/1952	DR	368	2-10-2T	
99 776	LKM 32015/1953	DR	368	2-10-2T	Stored
99 785	LKM 32026/1954	DR	368	2-10-2T	
99 786	LKM 32027/1954	DR	368	2-10-2T	
99 794	LKM 32035/1955	DR	368	2-10-2T	
LH45-083	U23A/1985	L45H	331	B-B DH	Ex Romania IND.

Freital Hainsburg

No.	Builder, No. & Year	Type	kW	Details	Comments
99 1608-1	Hart 4521/1921	IV K		0-4-4-0T	At present used on Radebeul line
99 1734-5	Hart 4681/1928	DRB		2-10-2T	Stored
99 1741-0	Hart 4691/1928	DRB		2-10-2T	Stored
99 1746-9	BMAG 9535/1929	DRB		2-10-2T	
99 1747-7	BMAG 9536/1929	DRB		2-10-2T	Stored
99 1761-8	BMAG 10152/1933	DRB		2-10-2T	
99 1762-6	BMAG 10153/1933	DRB		2-10-2T	Stored
99 1771-2	LKM 32010/1952	DR		2-10-2T	
99 1777-4	LKM 32016/1953	DR		2-10-2T	
99 1780-8	LKM 32019/1953	DR		2-10-2T	Stored
99 1790-9	LKM 32031/1957	DR		2-10-2T	Stored

Radebeul

No.	Builder, No. & Year	Type	kW	Details	Comments
99 1713-9	Hart 4670/1927	DRB		0-10-0T	
99 1775-8	LKM 32014/1953	DR		2-10-2T	
99 1778-2	LKM 32017/1953	DR		2-10-2T	
99 1779-0	LKM 32018/1953	DR		2-10-2T	
99 1793-1	LKM 132034/1957	DR		2-10-2T	

BAYERISCHE ZUGSPITZBAHN AG   BZB
Garmisch Partenkirchen, Bayern

Gauge: 1000 mm.   **Electric System:** 1650 V DC.
Routes: Garmisch-Partenkirchen–Grainau (valley section)–Eibsee–Höllental–Schneefernerhaus/
Gletscherbhf Zugspitzplatt (KBS 11031) 18.7 km
Length: 18.7 km.   **Depot:** Grainau.
EVU Licence: Freight and Passenger 04/08/1995.

The BZB is a typical mountain railway of metre gauge having a valley section before the real
climb starts with Riggenbach rack assistance. The starting point at Garmisch Partenkirchen is
705 metres a.s.l. and the top station at Schneefernerhaus is 2649 metres a.s.l. There is talk of
closing the existing terminus at Garmisch and a new connection be laid in to allow trains to
terminate at or alongside the DB station. 459,000 passengers in 1996 but 500,000 in 1999.
Some new stock has been ordered from Stadler to arrive in 2004. (NB: no number 13!)

No.	Builder, No. & Year	kWDetails	Comments
1	AEG 4268/1929	2 x 112 Bo E	Valley loco
3	AEG 4270/1929	2 x 112 Bo E	Valley loco
4	AEG 4271/1929	2 x 112 Bo E	Valley loco
11	AEG 4260/1929	3 x 370 Bo E	Rack fitted
14	AEG 4263/1929	3 x 370 Bo E	Rack fitted
15	AEG 4264/1929	3 x 370 Bo E	Rack fitted
ET 1	MAN/SLM 140874/1954	4 x 114 Bo-Bo ER	Rack fitted
ET 2	MAN/SLM 141470/1956	4 x 114 Bo-Bo ER	Rack fitted
ET 3	MAN/SLM 143474/1958	4 x 114 Bo-Bo ER	Rack fitted
ET 4	MAN/SLM 143475/1958	4 x 114 Bo-Bo ER	Rack fitted
ET 5	SLM 5132/1978	4 x 117 Bo-Bo ER	Rack fitted
ET 6	SLM 5133/1978	4 x 117 Bo-Bo ER	Rack fitted
ET 7	SLM/BBC/1979	4 x 250 Bo-Bo ER	Ex Swiss BOB Abeh 4/4 309
ET 10	SLM 5316/1987	4 x 216 Bo-Bo ER	Rack fitted
ET 11	SLM 5317/1987	4 x 216 Bo-Bo ER	Rack fitted
ET 12	Stadler /2004		
ET 14	Stadler /2004		
ET 15	Stadler /2004		
ET 16	Stadler /2004		

CITY BAHN CHEMNITZ Gmbh   CBC
Chemnitz, Sachsen

Routes: Chemnitz Hbf.–Chemnitz Süd–Stollberg (KBS 522) 23.4 km.
Length: 23.4 km.   **Depot:** Stolberg.
EVU Licence: Passenger, 04/12/1997.

The passenger service on this former DB line from Chemnitz to Stolberg has been privatised as City Bahn Chemnitz. The long term intention is for Chemnitz to follow Karlsruhe and have a Stadtbahn (or Citybahn!) with the line to Stolberg being connected in to the city transport system via a new chord line in Altchemnitz. Six Variobahn Stadtbahn trams have been ordered for the first stage; late in 2001 a tender was issued for three units to work Stolberg–St. Egidien from autumn 2002–these are now confirmed as Regio Shuttles and were delivered early and hired out to other organisations–so they arrived well run in! Other routes likely to change to CBC are Chemnitz–Burgstädt and Niederwiesa–Hanichen.

No.	Builder, No. & Year	Type	kW	Details	Comments	Name
ET 411	Adtranz/2001	NGT-6LDZ	360	Bo-2-Bo	Regio Variobahn	
ET 412	Adtranz/2001	NGT-6LDZ	360	Bo-2-Bo	Regio Variobahn	
ET 413	Adtranz/2001	NGT-6LDZ	360	Bo-2-Bo	Regio Variobahn	*Stollberg*
ET 414	Adtranz/2001	NGT-6LDZ	360	Bo-2-Bo	Regio Variobahn	
ET 415	Adtranz/2001	NGT-6LDZ	360	Bo-2-Bo	Regio Variobahn	
ET 416	Adtranz/2001	NGT-6LDZ	360	Bo-2-Bo	Regio Variobahn	*Chemnitz*
VT 511	Stadler 37128/2002	RS1	2 x 257	B-B DMR		*Stadt Lichtenstein*
VT 512	Stadler 37129/2002	RS1	2 x 257	B-B DMR		*Stadt Oelsnitz*
VT 513	Stadler 37130/2002	RS1	2 x 257	B-B DMR		
VT 514	Stadler 37245/2003	RS1	2 x 257	B-B DMR		

CONNEX CARGO LOGISTICS Gmbh   CCL

This is the freight arm of the main Connex company and has been quite successful in obtaining traffic, some new to rail but no doubt some taken from DB. It operates via its other subsidiary companies e.g. Nord West Cargo (q.v.). Connex is also involved in the NeCoSs system (q.v.). It had a long distance service from Lübeck to Simbach but seems to have lost this flow. It is currently involved in using the reopened Groningen (NL)–Leer (D) line for freight, with trains from Veendam and Groningen, to Lübeck and Bremen. Connex in Germany is making full use of open access! The EVU licence is usually held by the subsidiary companies.

During 2003 Connex won contracts to move steel from Eisenhüttenstadt (Ziltendorf) to Dortmund Obereving, Ilsenburg and Rodange (LUX). The Rodange trains are worked by CCL to Ehrang where NEG takes over under the Euro Lux Cargo umbrella.

CHEMION LOGISTIK Gmbh BAHN-BETRIEBE CHEMION
Leverkusen, Nordrhein Westfalen

Routes: Köln-Mülheim–Köln-Stammheim–Köln-Flittard–Leverkusen Bayerwerk; and facorties at Leverkusen, Dormagen and Uerdingen
Length: 5.5/17.7 km.   **Depot:** Leverkusen Bayerwerk.
EVU Licence: Freight, 22/02/2002.

This railway title dates from 1/7/2001 prior to which it was known as the Eisenbahn Köln–Mülheim–Leverkusen (EKML). It is in effect another industrial server that now has main line access having obtained the status of an EVU 22.02.02. In this case the customer is the large chemical works of Bayer AG at Leverkusen. Instead of DB delivering some traffic to the works the Chemion goes and collects it itself. As EKML it has been running over DB since at least 1985. The depot and workshop remain in the factory complex. 530,000 tonnes handled in 1995; 631,000 tonnes in 2000.

No.	Builder, No. & Year	Type	kW	Details	Comments
01	VSFT 1001148/2001	G800BB	800	B-B DH	(Dormagen)
02	VSFT 1001149/2001	G800BB	800	B-B DH	(Leverkusen)
03	VSFT 1001318/2002	G800BB	800	B-B DH	(Dormagen)
04	VSFT 1001319/2002	G800BB	800	B-B DH	(Dormagen)
05	VSFT 1001320/2002	G800BB	800	B-B DH	
06	VSFT 1001321/2002	G800BB	800	B-B DH	

2	Mak 1000850/1990	G1203BB	745	B-B DH	(Dormagen)
3	Mak 1000893/1993	G1203	1180	B-B DH	(Dormagen)
11	Mak 700075/1985	G763C	559	C DH	(Uerdingen)
105	Mak 1000243/1963	G1300BB	956	B-B DH	
108	Mak 700088/1986	G763C	559	C DH	(Uerdingen)
109	Mak 700091/1987	G763C	559	C DH	(Leverkusen)
110	Mak 700094/1990	G763C	559	C DH	(Leverkusen)
?	VSFT1001022/2000	G1206	1570	B-B DH	On hire.

CHIEMSEE-SCHIFFAHRT LUDWIG FESSLER
CHIEMSEEBAHN

Prien, Bayern

Routes: Prien–Hafen Stock (KBS 10602) .8 km.
Length: 1.8/2.2 km. **Depot:** Hafen Stock.
EVU Licence: Freight and Passenger 04/08/1995.

This charming little railway continues to provide the link between the DB station of Prien and the landing stage on the Chiemsee. The steam loco and coaching stock were all original to the line. The loco had a new boiler some years back and until quite recently was the sole motive power on the line. It was decided a standby loco was needed so a suitable diesel loco was found and adapted to look like a replica of the steam loco. The line has had mixed fortunes recently and was facing possible closure but has been reprieved. It carried 120,000 passengers in 1998. If you have not been there please go and see this gem of a line.

No.	Builder, No. & Year	Type	kW	Details	Comments
–	KrMu 1813/1887	44		0-4-0T	Steam tram engine
–	Deutz 57499/1962	KG125BS	92	B DM	replica tram engine

CONNEX VERKEHRS Gmbh/DEG VERKEHRS Gmbh
CONNEX

Previously Deutsche Eisenbahn Gesellschaft it was taken over in 1997 by the French CFTA group (60%) and Energie Baden-Württemberg (40%). Now CFTA is part of the Vivendi group and Vivendi has bought out the EnBW share. In 2000 the Connex logo was brought into use. Connex is an umbrella organisation for the operation of several private railways in Germany. These are understood to be:

Bayerische Oberlandbahn (75%)	BOB/Connex
Farge-Vegesacker Eisenbahn Gmbh (98%)	FVE
Hörsetalbahn Gmbh (100%)	HTB/Connex
Industriebahn Geschellschaft Berlin mbH (25.1%)	IGB
Nord-Ostsee-Bahn (100%)	NOB
Nord Westbahn Gmbh (74%)	NWB
Ostmecklenburgische Eisenbahn Gmbh (74.8%)	OME
Regiobahn Bitterfeld Gmbh (100%)	RBB
Rheinisch Bergische Eisenbahn Gmbh (100%)	RBE
Teutoburger Wald Eisenbahn (53.9%)	TWE
Württembergische Eisenbahn Gesellschaft (96.9%)	WEG

Details of each line will be found under the respective individual entry. The EVU licences are held by these companies.

In 2003 Connex won the contract for the Nord Harz Netz covering lines from Magdeburg to Halberstadt/Thale/ Blankenburg and others. 19 Coradia LINT diesel units have been ordered (a mixture of LINT 27, LINT 41). The name of the new operating company has not yet been announced.

CONTRAIN Gmbh ConTrain
Bayern

This firm was due to start operating during 2001 but ran into problems and it was late in 2002 before operations started. Its intention was to run container trains from Hamburg to Coburg and Hof twice weekly but the terminal in Coburg has not materialised.

ConTrain is a subsidiary of the following companies:

Mannheim MVV;
Hanseatic Container and Train Operators Gmbh(responsible for marketing) whose HQ is in Hamburg and has many other co-operating companies;
Bremer Container Service (BCS), Bremen
Pöhland Spedition (Hof)
H. J. Sickert (Bremen)

ConTrain has opened its own container terminal at Hof–CTH–Container Terminal Hof.

Operations started 7/10/02. Southern terminals are now at Neuenmarkt Wirsberg, Hof and Zwickau. There are also two sources of traffic in the Kassel area at Baunatal and Beiseförth (auto traffic). The northern ports served are Bremerhaven (Eurogate) and Hamburg (Eurokombi).

ConTrain has no EVU licence so has contracted other operators to move the traffic. Two VSFT G2000 were obtained via Locomotion Capital and 80 wagons from AAE. RBG looks after the G2000 and has numbered them in its stock and has added a G1206 as a reserve locomotive.

RBG is responsible for the train working south of Leipzig. North of there two other partners are involved. OHE Spandau works from Beiseförth and Leipzig to the two ports. KNE trips traffic in the Kassel area. The two trains from the south met at first at Hannover Linden and exchange traffic before one departs for Bremerhaven and the other for Hamburg. This exchange now takes place at Elze.

The loco working to Hof/Neuenmarkt Wirsberg stables at the Deutsches Dampflok Museum Neuenmarkt Wirsberg, no doubt bringing in some extra income for the museum! ConTrain has succeeded in getting another flow of traffic this time a block train of empty wine and beer bottles from Bayern to France which one of the G2000s works to Ehrang. As traffic builds up other locos may have to be hired. Contrain has recently taken delivery of some 185s that have taken over the long haul under the wires. The diesels have much reduced work and their number may be reduced.

No.	Builder, No. & Year	Type	kW	Details	Comments
V1001.039	VSFT 1001039/2002	G2000	2240	B-B DH	(RBG D06)
V1001.041	VSFT 1001041/2002	G2000	2240	B-B DH	(OHE Sp)
V1001.043	VSFT 1001043/2002	G2000	2240	B-B DH	(RBG D07)

CARGO RAIL Gmbh   CRG
Dillingen, Saar.

Cargo rail is a subsidiary of the Dillinger Hüttenwerke AG having been founded in 1998 to service several factories: Dillinger Hüttenwerke; Roheisen Gesellschaft Saar mbh (ROGESA, also in Dillingen); Zentralkokerei Saar GmbH (ZKS) and other private sidings. In 1999 it appears to have become a fully-fledged EVU and started tripping from the various works to Dillingen sidings. In 2002 it took over workings between Dillingen and Limbach and by the year end had obtained locomotives D23/24 with a view to doing main line work.

No.	Builder, No. & Year	Type	kW	Details	Comments
D 7	Hens 30014/1959	DH440C	300	C DH	
D 9	Hens 30260/1960	DH440C	300	C DH	
D 10	Hens 31245/1967	DHG500C	400	C DH	
D 11	Hens 31238/1967	DHG500C	400	C DH	
D 14	Hens 29963/1959	DH500C	400	C DH	
D 16	Hens 31112/1965	DHG500C	400	C DH	
D 17	Hens 31687/1974	DHG700C	500	C DH	
D 18	KM 20342/1998	MH05	500	C DH	
D 23	VSFT 1001017/1999	G1206	1500	B-B DH	Via LSG/ATC ex NEG 06
D 24	VSFT 1001018/1999	G1206	1500	B-B DH	Via LSG/ATC ex NEG 07
R 1	Hens 31071/1965	DHG1000	750	B-B DH	
R 2	Hens 31203/1966	DHG1000	750	B-B DH	
R 3	KM 19917/1985	ME05	500	Co DE	
R 4	Hens 32566/1983	DE500	500	Co DE	
R 5	KM 20451/2001	MH05	500	C DH	
R 21	O&K 26711/1971	MC700N	700	C DH	
R 22	KM 20076/1993	MH05	500	C DH	
Z 1	KM 19915/1984	ME05	500	Co DE	

The prefix letters denote the usual place of employment, D: Dillinger Hüttenwerke; R: ROGESA; Z: ZKS. The smaller locos will normally be internal user but may be seen at exchange sidings from time to time.

DÖLLNITZBAHN GmbH   DBG
Mügeln, Sachsen

Gauge: 750 mm.
Routes: Oschatz–Mügeln–Kemmlitz
Length: 21 km.   **Depot:** Mügeln.
EVU Licence: Freight and Passenger 17/12/1993.

This short 750 mm gauge line is all that is left of a large network of narrow gauge lines radiating
from Mügeln. It was notable in DR days as being the last line using Sachsen Meyer type IV K 0-
4-4-0T three of which remained on the books when the line was privatised in 1993. There is a
kaolin factory at Kemmlitz which brings freight to the line and is the very reason why the line
lasted for so long. In 1995 regular passenger trains were reintroduced aimed at conveying school
children – one train doing the work of several buses. The line is intending to obtain some diesel
railcars to replace the old passenger coaches which will remain for use on tourist trains with the
steam locos. To cover the freight service some second hand diesel locos have been obtained.
The line also owns a standard gauge shunter for servicing the exchange sidings in Oschatz.

No.	Builder, No. & Year	Type	kW	Details	Comments
31	LKM 250271/1961	V10C	75	0-6-0 DH	Ex MaLoWa
35	LKM 250308/1962	V10C	75	0-6-0 DH	Ex MaLoWa
311 512	LKM 261314/1975	V15	162	0-4-0 DH	Ex DR (Standard gauge)
99 1561-2	Hart 3214/1909	IV K		0-4-4-0T	Ex DR
99 1574-5	Hart 3556/1912	IV K		0-4-4-0T	Ex DR
99 1584-4	Hart 3595/1912	IV K		0-4-4-0T	Ex DR. On loan to EBG Prora.
199 030	Simm 66765/1940	2091	150	1-Bo-1 DE	Ex ÖBB 2091 010
199 031	Simm 66767/1940	2091	150	1-Bo-1 DE	ex ÖBB 2091 012
199 032	LKM 250027/1957	V10C		C DH	Ex DR 199 008
199 033	U23A 24378/1981	L18DH	110	0-6-0 DH	Ex Poland Lyd2-71
199 034	U23A 24059/1981	L18DH	110	0-6-0 DH	Ex EBG, Ex Poland Lyd2-?
199 035	Gm 4234/1946	HF130C	97	C DH	Ex IRR Dornbirn
199 036	LKM 250482/1969	V10C	75	C DM	Ex Klinkerwerk Buchwaldchen

DEHN & DEHN EISENBAHN GESELLSCHAFT mbH
D&D

Hagenow Land, Mecklenburg-Vorpommern

Depot: Old DB depot at Hagenow Land.
Livery: Grey and blue.
EVU Licence: Freight and Passenger 10/02/2000.

This is another newly created firm dating from 1999/2000 and is based in the old depot at Hagenow
Land and takes advantage of any engineering contracts that are going and also spot hires its
locos. D&D is understood to provide the drivers for the WLB operation from Ybbs to Hamburg
over DB Netz.

No.	Builder, No. & Year	Type	kW	Details	Comments
121	Gm 5138/1959	Kof II	94	4w DH	Ex DB 323 686
651	LEW 270154/1963	V60D	478	0-8-0 DH	Ex Kaltwalzwerk Bad Salzungen 2
1401	LEW 12828/1970	V100.4	1050	B-B DH	Ex DB 202 319. CAT engine
1402	LEW 12887/1971	V100.4	1050	B-B DH	ex DB 202 378. CAT engine
1403	LEW 13896/1973	V100.4	1050	B-B DH	Ex ALS, ex DB 201 577, CAT engine
2401I	LKM 280125/1968	V180	2 x 736	C-C DH	Ex Jüterbog, DR 118 721
2401II	LKM 280105/1968	V180	2 x 736	C-C DH	Ex spare parts loco. DR 118 705
2402	LKM 280166/1969	V180	2 x 736	C-C DH	Ex Jüterbog, DR 118 757
2403	LKM 280167/1969	V180	2 x 736	C-C DH	Ex Jüterbog, DR 118 758

NB : 2401I sold to Uwe Adam.

DORTMUNDER EISENBAHN GmbH   DE
Dortmund, Nordrhein Westfalen

Routes: Dortmund Nord–Dortmund Stadthafen–Dortmund-Westerholz–Dortmund-Obereving
Süd–Dortmund-Stockheide–Dortmund-Körne–Dortmund-Remberg; branch to Dortmund-
Hardeberghafen; also works railways of Krupp Hoesch Stahl AG in Dortmund and in Bochum.

Length: 20.3/ 64 km (275 km including the steelworks lines and sidings!).
Depot: Westfalenhütte.
EVU Licence: Freight, 03/08/1995.

The DE serves numerous industries in the Dortmund area. Starting off as basic industrial railway it has grown over the years as industrial take-overs and contraction gave it more work. In 1980 it took over the railway needs of the Hoesch steelworks and as late as 1994 the railway network at the Krupp steelworks in Bochum was added to the DE empire. It has some 241 km of track and handled 30 million tonnes of traffic in 1999! This has risen to 39 million tonnes in 2000. Open access means that it can now move some traffic over DB lines in the area.

No.	Builder, No. & Year	Type	kW	Details	Comments
022	Mak 1000599/1975	G1600BB	1176	B-B DH	
023	Mak 1000600/1975	G1600BB	1176	B-B DH	
024	Mak 1000601/1975	G1600BB	1176	B-B DH	
026	Mak 1000602/1976	G1600BB	1176	B-B DH	
027	Mak 1000774/1976	G1600BB	1176	B-B DH	
028	Mak 1000775/1976	G1600BB	1176	B-B DH	
322	Mak 220100/1974	G320B	236	B DM	Ex Krupp
401	VSFT 1001008/1999	G1206BB	1500	B-B DH	Auto coupler
402	VSFT 1001009/1999	G1206BB	1500	B-B DH	Auto coupler
403	VSFT 1001010/1999	G1206BB	1500	B-B DH	Auto coupler
404	VSFT 1001011/1999	G1206BB	1500	B-B DH	Auto coupler
406	VSFT 1001017/2000	G1206BB	1500	B-B DH	On hire from LSG
730	Mak 700023/1978	G761C	500	C DH	Ex Krupp
734	Mak 700028/1979	G761C	500	C DH	Ex Krupp
735	Mak 700029/1979	G761C	500	C DH	Ex Krupp
736	KM 19929/1984	MH05	500	C DH	Ex Krupp
751	O&K 26817/1976	MC700N	515	C DH	Hoesch 751
752	O&K 26818/1976	MC700N	515	C DH	Hoesch 752
753	KM/20042/1992	MH05	500	C DH	Ex Krupp
754	KM 20043/1992	MH05	500	C DH	Ex Krupp
755	Mak 700032/1979	G761C	500	C DH	Ex Krupp
756	Mak 700033/1979	G761C	500	C DH	Ex Krupp
761	O&K 26954/1980	MEC502	510	Co DE	Stored
762	O&K 26955/1980	MEC502	510	Co DE	Stored
764	O&K 26957/1980	MEC502	510	Co DE	
765	KM 19888/1982	ME05	510	Co DE	Cab each end
766	KM 19889/1982	ME05	510	Co DE	Cab each end
768	KM 19891/1982	ME05	510	Co DE	Cab each end
769	KM 19892/1982	ME05	510	Co DE	Cab each end
801	Hens 31950/1975	DHG1200BB	882	B-B DH	Hoesch 801
802	Hens 31951/1975	DHG1200BB	882	B-B DH	Hoesch 802
803	Hens 31952/1975	DHG1200BB	882	B-B DH	Hoesch 803
804	O&K 26814/1975	MBB1200N	882	B-B DH	Hoesch 804
809	LEW 11212/1967	201	736	B-B DH	Hired from Adtranz
811	Mak 1000848/1990	G1203BB	745	B-B DH	
812	Mak 1000849/1990	G1203BB	745	B-B DH	
VT 13	Dessau	132		A-1 DxR	Ex RBG

NB: 401–4 fitted with Indusi and ZBF for working over DB e.g. coal trains Dortmund-Hardenberghafen–Elverlingsen power station.

DEUTSCHE GLEIS UND TIEFBAU Gmbh   DGT
Berlin
EVU Licence: 18/09/2003.

DGT was formed from the old DR track department being sold off by DB in 1997. It inherited most of the track equipment and the unusual V100.5 diesels that can be used to power track machines. Some have subsequently been sold to other firms. It is understood that there are several V22 type diesels for shunting at work sites. The 710 shown as rebuilt by Adtranz may in fact have been subcontracted to RBG Reichenbach!

NB: At a very late stage whilst researching the EVU licences it became clear that this firm is in fact a subsidiary of DB and should have been included in Part 1!

No.	Builder, No. & Year	Type	kW	Details	Comments
710 964	LEW 17313/1983	V100.5	1030	B-B DH	Rebuilt by Adtranz 1999
710 965	LEW 17314/1983	V100.5	1030	B-B DH	Rebuilt by Adtranz 1999
710 966"	Adtranz 72710/1999	V100.4	1030	B-B DH	Ex 201/202?
710 967	LEW 17316/1983	V100.5	1030	B-B DH	Rebuilt by Adtranz 1999
710 968"	Adtranz 72150/1999	V100.4	1030	B-B DH	Ex 202/202?
WL 2	LKM 262035/1968	V22	162	0-4-0 DH	Ex Gleisbau Magdeburg
WL 7	LKM 262197/1969	V22	162	0-4-0 DH	Ex Gleisbau Magdeburg
WL 10	LKM 261422/19xx	V18B		0-4-0 D	Rebuilt RFG 2/98. Ex Gleisbau Bitterfeld

DELMENHORST–HARPSTEDTER EISENBAHN GmbH DHE
Harpstedt, Niedersachsen

Routes: Delmenhorst Süd–Harpstedt (KBS 12398) 27.1 km
Length: 27.1/32.2 km. **Depot:** Harpstedt.
EVU Licence: Freight and Passenger 26/10/1995.

This short line lost its passenger service in the 1960's and since then has quietly served a few private sidings along the line. More recently passenger trains were reintroduced as tourist trains at weekends in the summer using at first the line's own diesel railcar and more recently a steam locomotive. 92,000 tonnes of freight handled in 1998 rising to 102,000 tonnes in 2000.

No.	Builder, No. & Year	Type	kW	Details	Comments
8	O&K 25624/1956	MV6b	107	B DM	
9	Schöma 5173/1991	CFL250DVR	286	B DH	
10	Gm 5266/1963	Köf III	176	4w DH	Ex MWB V245 ex DB 332 028
T 121	Wumag 71004/1940		2 x 107	A-A DHR	

DILLEN & LE JEUNE CARGO NV DLC
Boom, Belgium

This company is the first Belgian one to take advantage of open access not only in Belgium but also Germany! It is owned by Ronney Dillen (30%), Jersen Le Jeune (30%) and Hupac (40%). It started operating in April 2002 working container trains on behalf of Redderei Mediterranean Shipping Co. taking BMW car parts between Antwerpen and Wackersdorf (near Schwandorf, Bayern). A class 66 works from Antwerpen to Aachen West where at the moment a Hupac hire loco takes over for the run to Nurnberg Rbf. where the G2000 takes over for the final section. From January 2003 DLC started to work a container train from Antwerpen to Duisburg (via Tilburg and Venlo) and further new flows are expected thus the firm has acquired two further class 66's. During 2003 the Wackersdorf train operation changed to a class 66 working throughout. MVV provides the crews in Germany.

No.	Builder, No. & Year	Type	kW	Details	Comments
PB 03	GM 20008254-5/2001	66	2462	Co-Co DE	Hired from Porterbrook
PB 12	GM 20018360-2/2002	66	2462	Co-Co DE	Hired from Porterbrook
PB 14	GM 20018360-4/2002	66	2462	Co-Co DE	Hired from Porterbrook
PB 18	GM 20018360-8/2002	66	2462	Co-Co DE	Hired from Porterbrook
PB 19	GM 20018360-9/2002	66	2462	Co-Co DE	Hired from Porterbrook
ES64U2-100	SKM 20445/2000	ES64U2	6400	Bo-Bo E	Hired from Hupac.

DAMPFLOKWERK MEININGEN DLW
Thüringen

Surprisingly this steam locomotive works obtained a class 202 diesel during 2002. It is used for testing overhauled locos and stock (a standby in the case of steam locomotives). It is still fitted with a train heating boiler which is useful for pre-heating oil-fired steam locos.

No.	Builder, No. & Year	Type	kW	Details	Comments
50 3501-9	Borsig 14970/1940			2-10-0	
~~202 563~~	~~LEW 13881/1973~~	~~V100~~	~~883~~	~~B-B DH~~	~~Ex DB~~

DORTMUND MARKISCHE EISENBAHN (VOLMETALBAHN) DME

Dortmund, Nordrhein Westfalen

Routes: Dortmund Hbf.–Herdecke–Hagen–Brügge–Lüdenscheid (KBS 434) 57 km.
Length: 57 km (DB Netz).   **Depot:** Westfalenhütte (DE).
EVU Licence: Passenger, 01/08/1997.

This company was formed in 1997 by Dortmunder Stadtbahn (75%) and Markische Verkehrs Gesellschaft (25%). On 28/5/99 it started operating passenger trains as the Volmetalbahn Dortmund–Hagen–Lüdenscheid (KBS 434) obtaining four newly built 3-car Talent railcars from Bombardier (Talbot) Aachen. The stock is maintained by DE by local arrangement. Late in 2002 there was a shunting accident damaging several vehicles causing various other types of units to be hired in. Recently the franchise came up for renewal and it appears that DB will take over from DME in December 2004 with DME being expected to close down and the railcars sold.

No.	Builder, No. & Year	Type	kW Details	Comments
VT01 101	Bomb. 191014-016/1999	Talent	2 x 500 B-2-B DMR	
VT01 102	Bomb. 191017-019/1999	Talent	2 x 500 B-2-B DMR	
VT01 103	Bomb. 191020-022/1999	Talent	2 x 500 B-2-B DMR	
VT01 104	Bomb. 191023-025/1999	Talent	2 x 500 B-2-B DMR	

NB: The end power cars are 1xx, 2xx, the intermediate cars being 3xx

BERGBAHNEN IM SIEBENGEBIRGE AG, DRACHENFELSBAHN DRACHENFELS

Nordrhein Westfalen

Gauge: 1000 mm.
Routes: Königswinter–Plateau Drachenfels (KBS 11001) 1.5 km.
Electric System: 900 V DC.
Depot: Königswinter.

At Konigswinter just south of Bonn lies the Drachenfelsbahn. The metre gauge Riggenbach rack line runs for just 1.5 km. Originally steam it was electrified in the 1950's and still uses stock from this period. One of the line's steam locos is plinthed outside Königswinter station. In 1995 426,000 passengers were carried, 432,000 in 2001.

No.	Builder, No. & Year	Type	kW Details	Comments
II	Rastatt/1955	88	Bo ER	Rack fitted
III	Rastatt/1957	88	Bo ER	Rack fitted
IV	Rastatt/1959	88	Bo ER	Rack fitted
V	Rastatt/1960	88	Bo ER	Rack fitted
VI	Drachenfels/1979	88	Bo ER	Rack fitted

DEUTSCHE REGIONALEISENBAHN Gmbh   DRE

Schönefeld, bei Berlin

Depot: ?
EVU Licence: Freight and Passenger 22/1/.2003.

This company has been set up to run services Beeskow–Herzberg; At present responsible for freight trips DRE has recently been operating summer only passenger trains between Falkenberg /Elster and Lubben (KBS 13213) whilst Danneberg–Luchow is understood to have been taken over from DB on 31/10/2001. DRE has shown an interest in operating passenger trains Freiberg–Nossen. In 2003 it is understood that the summer passenger trains were stopped by the authorities concerned over the state of the rolling stock.

No.	Builder, No. & Year	Type	kW Details	Comments
V22 01	LKM 262038/1968	V22	162 0-4-0 DH	Ex DR/DB 312 004
V22 02	LKM 262626 /1976	V22	162 0-4-0 DH	Ex NVA Hangelsberg 04
?	Mak 600415/1962	650D	485 0-8-0 DH	Ex BLME, ex IIm V65.02
VT11	MAN 141757/1975	MAN	2 x 141 A-A DHR	Ex SWEG VT11

NB: The railcar is normally at Falkenberg with the locos at Lubben for freight trips.

DUISPORT RAIL GmbH
DUISPORT

Duisburg, Nordrhein Westfalen

Depot: Duisburg Hafen.
EVU Licence: Freight, 18/01/2001.
This company was set up in 2001 getting its EVU licence during the summer of that year. It is a 100% subsidiary of Duisburger Hafen AG. So what was an industrial railway for the Duisburg harbour lines is set to become a main line operator. Local trip workings followed the granting of the EVU licence. In late 2003 Duisport Rail co-operating with Rhenus rail started a Duisport – Stadtallendorf service running twice weekly using a hired in G1700. Later a container shuttle service was introduced between Duisport and Marl. Traffic is growing quickly with three locomotives needed in 2002 becoming ten towards the end of 2003. Duisport Rail together with others are reactivating the old DB freight yard at Rheinhausen as a private railways exchange yard.

No.	Builder, No. & Year	Type	kW	Details	Comments
7	MaK 700026/1978	G761C	550	6w DH	Ex Hafag 7
202 001	LEW14447/1974	V100DR	1086	B-B DH	CAT engine. Ex DB 202 746
202 002	LEW 14659/1975	V100	1086	B-B DH	CAT engine. Ex DB 202 778
~~203 003~~	~~LEW14853/1975~~	~~V100DR~~	~~1385~~	~~B-B DH~~	~~MTU engine. Ex DB 202 796~~
207 077	VL 5001477/2003	G1206	1500	B-B DH	
1001125	VSFT 1001125/2001	G1206	1500	B-B DH	Hired.
~~360 152~~	~~MaK 600037/1957~~	~~V60C~~	~~478~~	~~0-6-0DH~~	~~Ex DB~~
360 215	Hens 29295/1956	V60C	478	0-6-0DH	Ex DB
360 318	KHD 56721/1957	V60C	478	0-6-0DH	Ex DB
360 782	Hens 30071/1960	V60C	478	0-6-0DH	Ex DB
360 783	Hens 30072/1960	V60C	478	0-6-0DH	Ex DB
361 197	Krp 4517/1963	V60C	478	0-6-0DH	Ex DB

EISENBAHN BETRIEBS GESELLSCHAFT mbH
EBG

Prora, Mecklenburg Vorpommern

Depots: Altenbeken, Hameln.
EVU Licence: Feight and Passenger, 31/07/1998.

This organisation goes back some years under different guises. Trading once as "Historische Eisenbahn Paderborn" it was in effect just a loco dealer buying and selling locos–seeing opportunities and seizing them. Some of the more interesting acquisitions went to the new museum at Prora believed owned by the same person that owns EBG. Then came open access. First the loco dealing continued but instead of historic locos (steam) the accent was now on diesels. Many shunting and even main line locos were obtained from the DR fleet after unification often at knock down prices. Now a handsome profit is no doubt being made as these are sold on to Adtranz/Bombardier and other firms for overhaul and reuse. There is no doubting the entrepreneurial spirit which is shown by the importing of locos from the former Soviet Union in the shape of cl. TE109 diesels which of course are basically one and the same as DB Class 230 and thus have what is known in Britain as "grandfather rights". This firm even bought back from Kaliningrad two class 232 sold by DB! EBG has the former DB depots at Altenbeken (main workshop) and hameln (storage site). The loco fleet details are confusing as some locos have been on hire to several companies and returned to EBG whilst others have been purchased and sold on e.g. many 231 and 232. In 2002 EBG purchased four cl. 232 from Bosnia (these were donated to Bosnia by DB!) EBG is also understood to be part owner now of Nymburk workshops in the Czech Repblic.

EBG now operates the Klützer Ostsee Eisenbahn Gmbh (q.v.) and in 2000 EBG became the owner/operator of the Westfalische Almetalbahn GmbH (WAB) Paderborn–Büren which operated tourist trains to Borchen in 2001 and 2002. WAB has now been set up as a completely separate railway company (q.v.). EBG continues to hire out locos for ballast trains etc (spot hire). One to keep an eye on! In 2002 a contract was won to carry out the shunting duties at Sassnitz (Mukran) yard. Four V60D were converted for this work. The contract is understood to have commenced on 08/08/2002.

No.	Builder, No. & Year	Type	kW	Details	Comments
1	Deutz 57312/1960	Köf II	97	B DH	Ex VGH V124, DB 323 210
2	Jung 7000/1937	Köf II	97	B DH	Ex DR 100 711

3	LEW 12403/1969	V100	736	B-B DH	To TLG, See notes
3"	LKM 262369/1972	V22	162	0-4-0 DH	Ex EBG 5l,ex NVA Seltz, to KOE
4'	LEW 17851/1982	V100.4	736	B-B DH	To TLG, See notes
4"	LEW 11315/1965	V60D	478	0-8-0 DH	Ex WAB 18;ex Wismut V60-05. (Mukran)
5"	LEW 11314/1965	V60D	478	0-8-0 DH	Ex WAB 20 ex Wismut V60-04. (Mukran)
6	LEW 17416/1980	V60D	478	0-8-0 DH	Ex Buna 79 to TLG 4
6"	LEW 12380/1969	V60D	478	0-8-0 DH	Ex WAB 17.
7	LOB 262506/1974	V22	162	0-4-0 DH	Ex Stendal Milk *
8	LEW 13765/1973	V60D	478	0-8-0 DH	Ex EIB 3
9	LEW 16691/1979	V60D	478	0-8-0 DH	Ex Kieswerk Rüdersdorf
10	LEW 12596/1970	V60D	478	0-8-0 DH	Ex Kieswerk Rüdersdorf
V60-02	LEW 10925/1965	V60D	478	0-8-0 DH	Ex OGEG, Austria.
106-03	LEW	V60D	478	0-8-0 DH	Ex Laubag. *
220 013	MaK 2000013/1957	220		B-B DH	ex SBB 18461 ex DB. *
220 512	Lugansk	M62	1470	Co-Co DE	ex Wismut
VT 1	WMD 1300/1960	796	2 x 112	A-A DMR	Ex DB 796 760 now KOE
VT 2	MAN 145131/1960	796	2 x 112	A-A DMR	Ex DB 796 740 now KOE
VT 3	MAN 145607/1962	796	2 x 112	A-A DMR	Ex DB 796 825 now EfW
VT 4	MAN 145120/1960	798	2 x 112	A-A DMR	Ex DB 798 729

The following stock has been acquired and awaits overhaul or sale:

796 651	Uer 66532/1959	796	2 x 112	A-A DMR	Ex DB*
796 663	Uer 66547/1959	796	2 x 112	A-A DMR	Ex DB*
796 710	Uer 66606/1960	796	2 x 112	A-A DMR	Ex DB*
796 724	MAN 145115/1960	796	2 x 112	A-A DMR	Ex DB
796 734	MAN 145125/1960	796	2 x 112	A-A DMR	Ex DB
798 736	MAN 145127/1960	798	2 x 112	A-A DMR	Ex DB*
VT 22	Uer 62000/1956	798	2 x 112	A-A DMR	Ex StLB ex DB 798 645
VT 23	Uer 61998/1956	798	2 x 112	A-A DMR	Ex StLB ex DB 798 643*
VT 25	JW 1081.10/1965	798	2 x 112	A-A DMR	Ex StLB ex OBB 5081 020
701 009	WMD 1104/1955	701	2 x 110	A-A DMR	Ex DB *

EBG was involved in the purchase and resale of 230 012, 231 040/50/70.

Note: Loco 3: DR V100 072, then industrial at Kaliwerk Bernburg and returned to DR as V100 001" 1995 to Prora Museum then to EBG and hired to PEG as PEG 3, Returned to EBG and sold to TLG (2) in 1999.

Note Loco 4': Ex PCK Schwedt V100.4-17 to EBG then to PEG 2 back to EBG and sold in 1999 to TLG (5).

Note: Locos 4", 5", 6" are all 1520 mm gauge and used for shunting at Mukran.

* Some locos and railbuses are now stored at the old DB depot in Hameln.

EISENBAHN BETRIEBS GESELLSCHAFT OBERELBE mbH
EBGO

Pirna, Sachsen

This firm was based in the old DR depot at Pirna to take advantage of freight and ballast train opportunities in the Dresden area and elsewhere. Unfortunately the firm was declared bankrupt in early 2001 after a derailment involving one of its trains on the main line at Haspelmoor. As the locos were hired they all went back to Adtranz and are now in use with other operators. They are listed here in full to assist readers with what might have been seen in the last few years.

No.	Builder, No. & Year	Type	kW	Details	Comments
V115 001	Adtranz 72510/2000	V100.4	1030	B-B DH	Ex WAB 12
V115 002	Adtranz 72520/2000	V100.4	1030	B-B DH	Ex WAB 13. To EfW
V180 001	LKM 275155/1966	V180	1470	C-C DH	Ex WAB 26, ex 228 168. To EfW
V200.05	Lugansk 1239/1971	M62	1470	Co-Co DE	Ex CD 781 365
V200.06	Lugansk 1198/1971	M62	1470	Co-Co DE	Ex CD 781 412"(324!)
V200.07	Lugansk 1223/1971	M62	1470	Co-Co DE	Ex CD 781 430"(349!)
V200.08	Lugansk 1664/1972	M62	1470	Co-Co DE	Ex CD 781 448
V200.09	Lugansk 1769/1973	M62	1470	Co-Co DE	Ex CD 781 545
V200.10	Lugansk 1666/1972	M62	1470	Co-Co DE	Ex CD 781 540"(450)

Notes: All locos back to Adtranz/Bombardier and into hire fleet or sold.

EISENBAHN VERKEHRS GESELLSCHAFT mbH m BERGISCHE-MARKISCHE RAUM EBM
EBM CARGO GmbH & Co KG EBM

Gummersbach, Nordrhein Westfalen

Routes: Hagen Haspe–Ennepetal–Altenvoerde; (Köln)–Euskirchen–Gerolstein–Bitburg etc.
Length: **Depots:** Dieringhausen, Euskirchen.
EVU Licence: Freight, 27/01/2003.

In Dieringhausen there is a railway museum with some operational diesels. With the changing scene on German railways the museum set up a new company with a nation wide safety case for its locomotives. In 2000 it took over from DB the operation of freight trips on the Hagen Haspe–Ennepetal–Altenvoerde route. Later on in 2000 EBM took over the following lines from DB: Gerolstein–Daun–Kaisersesch; Gerolstein–Prüm–Pronsfeld; Jünkerath–Losheim (– Belgium). EBM Touristik will operate excursions over these lines in conjunction with local preservation groups. Freight traffic is to be sought after e.g. timber traffic. Euskirchen is also being looked at as a possible site for a depot. With traffic expanding EBM has formed two other companies: Vulkan Eifelbahn and Zugkraft with a reorganisation late in 2002 when a separate freight company was created – EBM Cargo. Whilst Zugraft and Vulcan Eifel have been retained as companies the loco fleet is now divided between EBM Cargo (for the regular freight traffic) and EBM which still looks after ballast train work. Late in 2002 EBM took over the movement of malt from Kulmbach to Bitburg using a hired in 212 from ALS.

EBM Cargo GmbH & Co KG

No.	Builder, No. & Year	Type	kW	Details	Comments
Ronneburg	LEW 11416/1967	V60D	478	0-8-0 DH	Ex Wismut WL 09, "105 972"
Beerwalde	LEW 11418/1967	V60D	478	0-8-0 DH	Ex Wismut WL 08 "105 973"
360 577	Krp 4000/1960	V60C	478	0-6-0 DH	Ex DB
202 269	LEW 12551/1970	V100.1	883	B-B DH	Ex DB.(New CAT engine)
203 004	LEW 13569/1973	V100	1240	B-B DH	Ex DB 202 530 MTU engine
203 005	LEW 13886/1973	V100	1240	B-B DH	Ex DB 202 568 MTU engine
203 006	LEW 14419/1974	V100.4	1240	B-B DH	Ex DB 202 718 MTU engine
203 007	LEW 13886/1973	V100.4	1240	B-B DH	Ex DB 202 568 MTU engine
203 203	LEW 12549/1970	V100	1086	B-B DH	Ex DB 202 267 CAT engine
203 204	LEW 12888/1971	V100	1086	B-B DH	Ex DB 202 379 CAT engine
212 044	MaK 1000180/1963	V100	992	B-B DH	Owned by Kallfelz & Stuch Gleisbau.
212 275	MaK 1000322/1965	V100	1050	B-B DH	Ex DB 212 275. CAT engine
212 325	MaK 1000372/1965	V100	1050	B-B DH	Ex DB 212 325. CAT engine
1116 912	SKM 20892/2003	Taurus	6400	Bo-Bo E	Intended to be ÖBB 1116 171. Used by RWB (q.v.)

EBM Hire loks

No.	Builder, No. & Year	Type	kW	Details	Comments
Merseburg	LEW 11975/1967	V60D	478	0-8-0 DH	Ex IND M'burg. "346 971"
Zwickau	LEW 16359/1980	V60D	478	0-8-0 DH	Ex IND, "346 970"
V200 503	Lugansk/1968	M62	1470	Co-Co DE	Ex Wismut ?
120 286	Lugansk 0689/1969	M62	1470	Co-Co DE	Ex DR
201 143	LEW 12444/1969	V100.1	736	B-B DH	Ex DR
202 487	LEW 13478/1972	V100.1	883	B-B DH	Ex DB. (New CAT engine)
202 487	LEW 13256/1972	V100.4	1030	B-B DH	Ex DB
228 742	LKM 280146/1968	V180	1470	C-C DH	Ex EFO Dieringhausen.

Current situation unclear.

No.	Builder, No. & Year	Type	kW	Details	Comments
Köf 4772	KHD 12673/1935	Köf II	97	4w DH	Ex DB 322 121 (Stored in Hagen)

EMSLÄNDISCHE EISENBAHN GmbH EEB

Meppen, Niedersachsen

Routes: Meppen–Haren–Lathen; Meppen–Essen (Oldb); Meppen–Meppen Emshafen; Lathen–Werlte.
Length: 76.7/87.7 km. **Depots:** Bhf Vormeppen, Werlte.
EVU Licence: Freight and Passenger 11/09/1998.

The EEB is the current owner and operator of two former private railways: Hümmlinger Kreisbahn (HKB: Lathen–Werlte 25 km); Meppen–Haselünner Eisenbahn (MHE: Meppen–Essen (Old)). Additionally it covers the Meppen–Meppen Emshafen branch. In 1995 59,000 tonnes were handled but 2000 saw a figure of 100,000 whilst in 2001 175,00 tonnes was reached. As can be seen from the routes it also works along the DB main line between Meppen and Lathen.

No.	*Builder, No. & Year*	*Type*	*kW*	*Details*	*Comments*
L 2II	Deutz 57504/1962	KG275B	202	B DH	
L 3	Deutz 56733/1960	V6M436	544	C Dx	
D 10	Krp 1373/1934	Köf II	97	B DH	Ex DB 322 642
Hummling	Deutz 56459/1956	MS650D	497	D DM	Ex Weserport B'haven 59
Emsland	KM 18904/1962	V100	845	B-B DH	Ex DB 211 308
Emsland II	Hens 30543/1964	V100	992	B-B DH	Ex DB 212 194
Emsland III	MaK 1000029/1961	V100	845	B-B DH	Ex DB 211 011
Emsland IV	MaK 1000030/1961	V100	845	B-B DH	Ex DB 211 012 Stored
T1II	Talbot 95135/1957			1A-1 DMR	Excursion use

EfW–Verkehrsgesellschaft mbH — EfW

Frechen, Nordrhein-Westfalen
Depot: **Worms (Hafen?)**
EVU Licence: Freight and Passenger 29/06/2001.

EfW stands for Eisenbahnfreunde Westerwald who formed a proper company for running railtours using locomotives that had been acquired in recent years. However the railtour business (EfW-Tours) went bankrupt in early 2002 and their other company remains as an EVU working ballast trains etc. Initially locomotives were all hired in from the Bombardier pool but late in 2002 EfW announced plans for the acquisition of many former DB locos which are listed below. Being formed by railway fans it is highly likely that all the former DB locos will be restored to original DB liveries and perhaps carry "old" numbers.

No.	*Builder, No. & Year*	*Type*	*kW*	*Details*	*Comments*
211 051	MaK 1000069/1962	V100	992	B-B DH	Ex ALS ex DB
212 047	MaK 1000183/1963	V100	992	B-B DH	Ex ALS ex DB
212 052	MaK 1000188/1963	V100	992	B-B DH	Ex ALS ex DB
212 057	MaK 1000193/1963	V100	992	B-B DH	Ex ALS ex DB
212 089	MaK 1000225/1964	V100	992	B-B DH	Ex ALS ex DB
212 240	MaK 1000287/1964	V100	992	B-B DH	Ex ALS ex DB
212 370	KHD 57770/1965	V100	992	B-B DH	Ex ALs ex DB
212 381	KHD 57781/1965	V100	992	B-B DH	Ex ALs ex DB
221 117	KM 19009/1963	V200.1	2x990	B-B DH	Ex OSE 415, ex DB
221 122	KM 19242/1964	V200.1	2x990	B-B DH	Ex OSE 420, ex DB
V180 168	LKM 275155/1966	V180	1470	B-B DH	Ex EBGO, ex WAB 26
232 714	Lugansk 0853/1978	232	2200	Co-Co DE	Ex W232.09 ex TE109 026. Returned to Lokpool?
332 129	O&K 26366/1964	Köf III	177	4w DH	Ex DB
332 137	O&K 26374/1964	Köf III	177	4w DH	Ex DB
332 153	O&K 26390/1964	Köf III	177	4w DH	Ex DB
332 287	O&K 26402/1965	Köf III	177	4w DH	Ex DB
333 002	Jung 14042/1968	Köf III	177	4w DH	Ex DB
333 008	Jung 14048/1968	Köf III	177	4w DH	Ex DB
335 108	Gm 5498/1973	Köf III	177	4w DH	Ex DB
335 127	Jung 14181/1973	Köf III	177	4w DH	Ex DB
360 109	MaK 600029/1956	V60C	478	0-6-0 DH	Ex DB
360 159	MaK 600080/1957	V60C	478	0-6-0 DH	Ex DB
360 239	Hens 29319/1956	V60C	478	0-6-0 DH	Ex DB
360 311	KHD 56714/1957	V60C	478	0-6-0 DH	Ex DB
360 312	KHD 56715/1957	V60C	478	0-6-0 DH	Ex DB
360 588	Krp 4011/1960	V60C	478	0-6-0 DH	Ex DB
360 770	Hens 30059/1960	V60C	478	0-6-0 DH	Ex DB
360 773	Hens 30062/1960	V60C	478	0-6-0 DH	Ex DB

ERFURTER GLEISBAU Gmbh   EGB

Erfurt, Thüringen

This company is an EIU with one loco for ballast trains and snow clearing duties. Normally operated by the Thüringer Eisenbahn Gmbh

No.	Builder, No. & Year	Type	kW	Details	Comments
211 074	MaK 1000092/1962	V100	992	B-B DH	Ex Pacton, ex BE D 20, ex DB 211 074

EISENBAHN UND HÄFEN Gmbh   EH
EISENBAHN UND HAFEN GÜTERVERKEHR Gmbh EHG

Duisburg, Nordrhein Westfalen

Routes: This company operates a vast system of branch lines and sidings around Dinslaken, Duisburg, Krefeld, Mülheim and Oberhausen.
Length: 572 km of which 234 km electrified.
Electric system: 600 V DC.
Depots: Duisburg-Hamborn, Duisburg-Ruhrort, Duisburg-Beeckerwerth, Oberhausen.
Workshop: Duisburg-Hamborn.
EVU Licence: Freight, 17/11/1998.

EH started off as an industrial railway in the Ruhr but over the years has taken over other operations and is now quite a big business perhaps the busiest of all the German private railways. It has 572 km of tracks of which 165 km are electrified and interchanges with DB at nine locations. Some 70 million tonnes of freight are handled each year. EH is owned by Thyssen Stahl (90%) and Ruhrkohle AG (10%) which in itself tells you the types of traffic handled! With the changes of the 1990's EH not only operates trains on its own system but also has running rights over various DB lines. If passing through Duisburg, Krefeld, Mülheim or Witten areas a visitor is likely to catch sight of mysterious green locos darting about with freight trips. Note the use of electro-diesel locomotives. The 1997/8 statistics show 68 million tonnes of freight of which 30 milion were handed over to DB. The 2000 figure was a total of 72 million tonnes. On its own system there were 398 million tonne kilometres. Short term hired in locos are numbered in the 9xx series. Locos numbered between 500 and 549 are all certified for use on DB Netz.

No.	Builder, No. & Year	Type	kW	Details	Comments
107	Jung 12800/1957	EDL	592/169	Bo-Bo ED	
118	Jung 13349/1961	EDL	592/169	Bo-Bo ED	
143	Jung 14072/1969	EDL	592/169	Bo-Bo ED	
144	Jung 14073/1969	EDL	592/169	Bo-Bo ED	
146	Jung 14075/1969	EDL	592/169	Bo-Bo ED	
147	Jung 14076/1969	EDL	592/169	Bo-Bo ED	
148	Jung 14077/1969	EDL	592/169	Bo-Bo ED	
150	Jung 14100/1970	EDL	592/169	Bo-Bo ED	
151	Jung 14101/1970	EDL	592/169	Bo-Bo ED	
163	Jung 14121/1971	EDL	592/169	Bo-Bo ED	
165	Jung 14123/1971	EDL	592/169	Bo-Bo ED	
171	Jung 14078/1969	EDL	592/169	Bo-Bo ED	Ex 149
172	Jung 14113/1971	EDL	592/190	Bo-Bo ED	Ex 155
173	Jung 13064/1959	EDL	592/190	Bo-Bo ED	Ex 115
174	Jung 14119/1971	EDL	592/190	Bo-Bo ED	Ex 116
175	Jung 13395/1961	EDL	592/190	Bo-Bo ED	Ex 126
258	KM 19814/1975	M700C	515	C DH	Ex Mannesman 11.
265	KM 19325/1966	M800BB	574	B-B DH	Ex HOAG 214. To be 574.
266	KM 19326/1966	M800BB	574	B-B DH	Ex HOAG 215
317	Wind 2291/1976		70		Ohle vehicle
320	Wind 2281/1976		70		Ohle vehicle
385	Jung 14120/1971	EDL	592/169	Bo-Bo ED	Ex 162
386	Jung 14122/1971	EDL	592/169	Bo-Bo ED	Ex 164
387	Jung 14116/1971	EDL	592/169	Bo-Bo ED	Ex 16x
388	Krp 3614/1957		162	B Dx	
389	KM 18163/1985	EDL	592/169	Bo-Bo ED	
501	KM 19573/1972	M1200BB	1119	B-B DH	Ex 281
502	KM 19574/1972	M1200BB	1119	B-B DH	Ex 282
503	KM 19575/1972	M1200BB	1119	B-B DH	Ex 283

504	KM 19576/1972	M1200BB	1119	B-B DH	Ex 284
505	KM 19578/1972	M1200BB	1119	B-B DH	Ex 285
506	KM 19579/1972	M1200BB	1119	B-B DH	Ex 286
507	KM 19580/1972	M1200BB	1119	B-B DH	Ex 287
508	KM 19580/1972	M1200BB	1119	B-B DH	Ex Neue Maxhütte Stahlwerk
511	Hens 31576/1973	DHG1200	1119	B-B DH	Ex 299
521	MaK 1000854/1991	G1205BB	1119	B-B DH	
522	MaK 1000855/1991	G1205BB	1119	B-B DH	
523	MaK 1000856/1991	G1205BB	1119	B-B DH	
524	MaK 1000857/1991	G1205BB	1119	B-B DH	
525	MaK 1000858/1991	G1205BB	1119	B-B DH	
526	MaK 1000859/1991	G1205BB	1119	B-B DH	
527	MaK 1000860/1992	G1205BB	1119	B-B DH	
528	MaK 1000861/1992	G1205BB	1119	B-B DH	
531	MaK 1000862/1992	G1205BB	1119	B-B DH	
532	MaK 1000863/1992	G1205BB	1119	B-B DH	
533	MaK 1000864/1992	G1205BB	1119	B-B DH	
534	MaK 1000865/1992	G1205BB	1119	B-B DH	
541	VSFT 1001134/2001	G1206BB	1500	B-B DH	
542	VSFT 1001135/2001	G1206BB	1500	B-B DH	
543	VSFT 1001145/2002	G1206BB	1500	B-B DH	
544	VSFT 1001151/2002	G1206BB	1500	B-B DH	
551	Deutz 57697/1964	DG1000BBM	760	B-B DH	Ex HKM Duisburg 01
552	Deutz 57878/1965	DG1000BBM	760	B-B DH	Ex HKM Duisburg 02
553	Deutz 57988/1966	DG1000BBM	760	B-B DH	Ex HKM Duisburg 03
554	Deutz 57989/1966	DG1000BBM	760	B-B DH	Ex HKM Duisburg 04
571	KM 19290/1966	M800BB	760	B-B DH	Ex 262 ex HOAG 211
572	KM 19291/1966	M800BB	760	B-B DH	Ex 263 ex HOAG 212
573	KM 19292/1966	M800BB	760	B-B DH	Ex 264 ex HOAG 213
576	KM 19327/1967	M800BB	735	B-B DH	Ex 267
651	O&K 26876/1976	MBB1200N	552	B-B DH	Ex HKM 05
652	O&K 26877/1976	MBB1200N	552	B-B DH	Ex HKM 06
701	Hens 32564/1983	DE500C	500	C DE	Ex TEW Witten 1
702	Hens 32563/1983	DE500C	500	C DE	Ex TEW Witten 3
703	Hens 32567/1983	DE500C	500	C DE	Ex TEW Witten 4
711	Hens 32750/1987	DHG700C	565	C DH	Ex TEW Witten 2
751	JW 3680059/1965	MG530C	397	C DH	Ex HKM 61
752	JW 3680060/1965	MG530C	397	C DH	Ex HKM 62
753	JW 3680061/1965	MG530C	397	C DH	Ex HKM 63
754	JW 3680062/1965	MG530C	397	C DH	Ex HKM 64
755	Deutz 58214/1967	MG530C	397	C DH	Ex HKM 65
756	O&K 26893/1978	MC700N	397	C DH	Ex HKM 66
757	O&K 26894/1978	MC700N	397	C DH	Ex HKM 67
758	Gm 5437/1983	DE500Co	496	Co DE	Ex HKM Duisburg 70
759	KM 19880/1981	ME05	500	Co DE	Ex On Rail
761	MaK 700043/1981	DE501	500	Co DE	Ex HKM Duisburg 71
762	MaK 700045/1981	DE501	500	Co DE	Ex HKM Duisburg 73
763	MaK 700048/1981	DE501	500	Co DE	Ex HKM Duisburg 76
764	MaK 700050/1981	DE501	500	Co DE	Ex HKM Duisburg 77
765	MaK 700052/1981	DE501	500	Co DE	Ex HKM Duisburg 79
766	MaK 700040/1980	DE501	500	Co DE	Ex Krupp 79
767	MaK 700046/1981	DE501	500	Co DE	Ex Krupp 84
771	MaK 700106/1993	G765	560	C DH	Ex HKM Duisburg 80
772	MaK 700107/1993	G765	560	C DH	Ex HKM Duisburg 81
780	Hens 31312/1968	DHG500C	368	C DH	Ex TEW Krefeld 12
801	Jung 13350/1961	EDL	592/375	Bo-Bo ED	Ex 119
802	Jung 13850/1964	EDL	592/375	Bo-Bo ED	Ex 140
803	Jung 13348/1961	EDL	592/375	Bo-Bo ED	Ex 117
804	Jung 13583/1962	EDL	592/375	Bo-Bo ED	Ex 129
805	Jung 13585/1963	EDL	592/375	Bo-Bo ED	Ex 131
806	Jung 13352/1961	EDL	592/375	Bo-Bo ED	Ex 121
807	Jung 13586/1963	EDL	592/375	Bo-Bo ED	Ex 132
808	Jung 13393/1961	EDL	592/375	Bo-Bo ED	Ex 124
809	Jung 13394/1961	EDL	592/375	Bo-Bo ED	Ex 125

810	Jung 13581/1962	EDL	592/375	Bo-Bo ED	Ex 127
811	Jung 13696/1963	EDL	592/375	Bo-Bo ED	Ex 135
812	Jung 13351/1961	EDL	592/375	Bo-Bo ED	Ex 120
813	Jung 13849/1964	EDL	592/375	Bo-Bo ED	Ex 139
851	KM 20329/1997	MH05	552	C DH	
852	KM 20330/1997	MH05	552	C DH	
853	KM 20331/1997	MH05	552	C DH	
854	KM 20332/1997	MH05	552	C DH	
855	KM 20333/1997	MH05	552	C DH	
856	KM 20334/1997	MH05	552	C DH	
857	KM 20335/1997	MH05	552	C DH	
858	KM 20336/1997	MH05	552	C DH	
859	KM 20337/1998	MH05	552	C DH	
860	KM 20338/1998	MH05	552	C DH	
861	KM 20339/1998	MH05	552	C DH	
862	KM 20340/1998	MH05	552	C DH	
863	KM 20341/1998	MH05	552	C DH	
864	KM 20343/1998	MH05	552	C DH	
865	KM 20344/1998	MH05	552	C DH	
866	KM 20345/1998	MH05	552	C DH	
867	KM 20346/1998	MH05	552	C DH	
868	KM 20440/1999	MH05	552	C DH	
869	KM 20441/1999	MH05	552	C DH	
870	KM 20442/1999	MH05	552	C DH	
871	KM 20444/1999	MH05	552	C DH	
872	KM 20451/2000	MH05	552	C DH	
873	KM 20454/2001	MH05	552	C DH	
874	KM 20452/2001	MH05	552	C DH	
875	KM 20453/2001	MH05	552	C DH	
876	KM 20347/1998	MH05	552	C DH	Ex Neuen Maxhütte 7
904	VSFT 1001017/2000	G1206BB	1570	B-B DH	On hire from VL.
905	VSFT 1001117/2000	G1206BB	1570	B-B DH	On hire from VL. Returned.

ERFURTER INDUSTRIE BAHN   EIB
Erfurt, Thüringen

Routes: Erfurt Nord–Erfurt Ost and sidings connections in the area.
Length: 15 km.   **Depot:** Erfurt Ost.
EVU Licence: Freight and Passenger 15/09/1997.

The Erfurter Industrie Bahn is a long established industrial railway and even existed under DDR days. In 1995 this railway changed its function from being the server of several sidings to being a fully-fledged private railway seizing the opportunities that were on offer after the fall of communism. Then came regionalisation and open access giving EIB even greater opportunities. EIB won the contract to provide local train services between Erfurt–Döllstädt–Leinefelde for which it acquired five new Regio Shuttles and later had to get three more. 30/5/99 saw the new service extended from Leinefelde via Eichenberg to Kassel Wilhelmshöhe. In 2000 EIB joined forces with Hessische Landesbahn GmbH to run services in the Meiningen area as the Südthuringenbahn GmbH (q.v.). In 2000 EIB handled 248,000 tonnes of freight.

2003 saw EIB being awarded the contract to run the Schweinfurt–Bad Kissingen–Gemünden and Schweinfurt – Meiningen passenger services. The contract is for 10 years and replaces DB local services. Whether EIB will run this service directly or sub-contract to STB is unclear. The new services are due to start in December 2004.

No.	Builder, No. & Year	Type	kW	Details	Comments
1	LEW 15583/1974	V60D	478	D DH	
2	LEW 11322/1966	V60D	478	D DH	
4	LEW 13765/1973	V60D	478	D DH	
5	LEW 16967/1980	V60D	478	D DH	
6	LEW 17589/1981	V60D	478	D DH	Sold
8	LEW 12247/1969	V60D	478	D DH	
20	LEW 16383/1978	V100.4	1060	B-B DH	Ex Adtranz, ex DB 201 889
21	LEW 16580/1981	V100.4	1060	B-B DH	Ex Adtranz, ex CSD 745 580

22	LEW 16385/1978	V100DR	1060	B-B DH	Ex199 891 Adtranz 72570/00	
ASF	LEW 20678/1990	EL16	17	Bo BE		
VT 001	Adtranz 36777/1998	RS1	2 x 228	B-B DMR	*Stadt Erfurt*	
VT 002	Adtranz 36778/1998	RS1	2 x 228	B-B DMR	*Stadt Kassel*	
VT 003	Adtranz 36779/1998	RS1	2 x 228	B-B DMR		
VT 004	Adtranz 36780/1998	RS1	2 x 228	B-B DMR		
VT 005	Adtranz 36781/1998	RS1	2 x 228	B-B DMR	*Stadt Mühlhausen*	
VT 006	Adtranz 36786/1998	RS1	2 x 228	B-B DMR	Ex Rail Charter VT301.	
					Nationalpark Hainich	
VT 007	Adtranz 36787/1998	RS1	2 x 228	B-B DMR	Ex Rail Charter VT302	
VT 008	Adtranz 36788/1998	RS1	2 x 228	B-B DMR	Ex Rail Charter VT303	
VT 009	Adtranz 36886/2000	RS1	2 x 228	B-B DMR	*Rosenstadt Bad Langensalza*	
VT 010	Stadler /2003	RS1	2 x 228	B-B DMR	*Landkreis Bad Kissingen*	
VT 011	Stadler /2003	RS1	2 x 228	B-B DMR	*Ilmenau*	
VT 012	Stadler 37280/2004	RS1	2 x 228	B-B DMR		
VT 013	Stadler 37281/2004	RS1	2 x 228	B-B DMR		
VT 014	Stadler 37282/2004	RS1	2 x 228	B-B DMR		
VT 015	Stadler 37283/2004	RS1	2 x 228	B-B DMR		
VT 016	Stadler 37284/2004	RS1	2 x 228	B-B DMR		
VT 017	Stadler 37285/2004	RS1	2 x 228	B-B DMR		
VT 018	Stadler 37286/2004	RS1	2 x 228	B-B DMR		
VT 019	Stadler 37287/2004	RS1	2 x 228	B-B DMR		
VT 020	Stadler 37288/2004	RS1	2 x 228	B-B DMR		
VT 021	Stadler 37289/2004	RS1	2 x 228	B-B DMR		

EICHHOLZ VERKEHR UND LOGISTIK Gmbh   EIVEL
Berlin

Depot: Haldensleben
EVU Licence: Freight, 27/03/2003.

Founded in 2002 this is yet another operator cashing in on the movement of infrastructure trains and hiring out locomotives. The base at Haldensleben is the old DR depot latterly used by Eurotrac, a subsidiary of Vossloh. Vossloh sold off part of Eurotrac that leased locos as this was now covered by arrangements with Angel Trains Cargo. Since then EIVEL has grown and acquired the fleet of Nohabs that had been with Eurotrac and Gamma Leasing.

No.	Builder, No. & Year	Type	kW	Details	Comments
01	Mak 220095/1962	240B	176	0-4-0 DH	Ex Eurotrac, ex NEG
02	LEW 13749/1973	V60D	478	0-8-0 DH	Ex Eurotrac, ex Laubag
03	LEW 14826/1975	V60D	478	0-8-0 DH	Ex Eurotrac, ex Laubag
V170 1125	Nohab 2366/1957	DSB MY	1433	A1A-A1A DE	Ex Eurotrac, ex DSB
V170 1127	Nohab 2368/1957	DSB MY	1433	A1A-A1A DE	Ex Gamma, ex Eurotrac, ex DSB
V170 1131	Nohab 2372/1957	DSB MY	1433	A1A-A1A DE	Ex Eurotrac, ex DSB
V170 1138	Nohab 2379/1958	DSB MY	1433	A1A-A1A DE	Ex Gamma, exEurotrac, ex DSB
V170 1142	Nohab 2383/1958	DSB MY	1433	A1A-A1A DE	Ex Eurotrac, ex DSB
V170 1143	Nohab 2384/1958	DSB MY	1433	A1A-A1A DE	Ex Eurotrac, ex DSB
V170 1147	Nohab 2598/1964	DSB MY	1433	A1A-A1A DE	Ex Eurotrac, ex DSB
V170.1149	Nohab 2600/1965	DSB MY	1433	A1A-A1A DE	Ex Gamma, ex Eurotrac, ex DSB
V170.1151	Nohab 2602/1965	DSB MY	1433	A1A-A1A DE	Ex Gamma, ex Eurotrac, ex DSB
V170.1155	Nohab 2606/1965	DSB MY	1433	A1A-A1A DE	Ex Gamma, ex Eurotrac, ex DSB

EKO TRANSPORTGESELLSCHAFT mbH   EKO
Eisenhüttenstadt, Brandenburg

Routes: Bhf. Ziltendorf into and around the works of EKO Stahl.
Length: 103/155 km.   **Depot**: EKO Works.
EVU Licence: Freight and Passenger 21/10/2003.

Yet another industrial operator that has grabbed the chance of working on the main line. In this instance EKO is the steelworks complex in the appropriately named former East German town of Eisenhüttenstadt. It started running its own trains from the steelworks to the refinery in Stendell

68

(PCK Schwedt). Two V100.4 work these trains. In 2000 another service to Castrop Rauxel in the Ruhr started up. The outward run is via Cottbus, Magdeburg and Minden but the return train is goes via Kassel, Halle and Eilenburg. EKO handled 6.7 million tonnes of freight traffic in 2000. Other locos are believed to be in stock but restricted to internal use.

No.	Builder, No. & Year	Type	kW	Details	Comments
2	LEW 17763/1986	ASF	17	Bo BE	
3	LEW 18844/1986	ASF	17	Bo BE	
27	LEW 12671/1970	V60D	478	D DH	
31	CKD 6573/1965	T334	365	C DH	Ex JLS 711 801, CD 710 657. CAT 3406 engine. FFS.
32	TSM 416 00092/1971	T334	365	C DH	Ex JLS 711 802, CD 710 445. CAT 3406 engine. FFS
34	LEW 12362/1969	V60D	478	D DH	
38	LEW 14196/1974	V60D	478	D DH	
42	Lugansk 0001/1972	242	2940	Co-Co DE	Ex DB 242 001
45	LEW 12637/1970	V60D	478	D DH	
47	LEW 10939/1965	V60D	478	D DH	Ex 346 248
48	LEW 11672/1967	V60D	478	D DH	Ex RBG D08 ex 346 391
52	LEW 13754/1973	V60D	478	D DH	
54	LEW 13793/1973	V60D	478	D DH	
55	LEW 13823/1973	V60D	478	D DH	
57	LEW 15146/1976	V60D	478	D DH	
58	LEW 16690/1979	V60D	478	D DH	
60	LEW 16384/1978	V100.4	1050	B-B DH	Ex 201 890
61II	LEW 17850/1982	V100.4	1050	B-B DH	Ex Leuna 135I
62	LEW 17852/1982	V100.4	800	B-B DH	CAT 3512 engine
63II	LEW 13936/1973	V100.4	1050	B-B DH	Ex DB 201 618
64	LEW 17730/1983	V100.4	1050	B-B DH	
65	LEW 17733/1983	V100.4	1050	B-B DH	
143 001	LEW 16323/1982	143	3720	Bo-Bo E	Ex Lokpool, ex AEG, ex DR.
DE 300.02	Lugansk 0248/1974	232	2200	Co-Co DE	Ex BGW, ex Kaliningrad, ex DB 232 057
711 703	CKD /1970	T334	365	C DH	Ex CD 710 402. EKO number not known. (33?)

Note: The V100.4 are locos rebuilt by Adtranz, Kassel (or RFG Reichenbach on behalf of Adtranz) with new CAT engines and fitted out for main line work having Mesa, Indusi I60R and passed for 100 km/h. Adtranz also modernised nine of the V60D which are now 485 kW but individual locos are not known as yet.

EURO LUX CARGO ELC
Rheinland Pfalz

In 2001 The CFL took over the Norddeutsche Eisenbahn Gesellschaft mbH (NEG) operating rights thus giving itself operating rights in Germany. Some trip workings around Trier have taken place but further developments are expected. ELC is hiring in locos as required. Some cross-border workings to Bettembourg and Thionville are to be expected. One to watch! It is not quite clear whether locomotives are being branded Euro Lux Cargo or NEG!

No.	Builder, No. & Year	Type	kW	Details	Comments
01	Mak 220061/1960	240B	176	0-4-0 DH	
02	MaK 800190/1978	G1100BB	809	B-B DH	
03	LEW 12524/1970	V100.4	1050	B-B DH	Ex ALS, ex DB 202 242. CAT engine
04	LEW 12939/1972	V100.4	1050	B-B DH	Ex ALS, ex DB 202 430, CAT engine
208	VSFT 1001208/2002	G1700	1700	B-B DH	On hire via ATC

EISENBAHN LOGISTIK, PIRNA ELP
Sachsen

This operator was derived from the EBGO operation and likewise was based in the old DB depot at Pirna. In 2002 it was hiring locos from VSFT for use on works trains. Operations ceased sometime in 2002/3.

EISENBAHNBETRIEB MITTLERER NECKAR GmbH EMN

Baden Württemberg

Depot: Kornwestheim Rbf.
Livery: Red.

This organisation was founded in 1999 and is believed to be the operating arm of the Stuttgart area preservation group Gesellschaft zur Erhaltung von Schienenfahrzeugen (GES). EMN has the shunting contract for Kornwestheim Pbf marshalling car sleeper trains.

No.	Builder, No. & Year	Type	kW	Details	Comments
V211 01	Jung 13305/1961	V100	992	B-B DH	Ex DB 211 031
V332 01	Jung 13802/1964	Köf III	176	B DH	Ex DB 332 189
V346 01	LEW 15584/1977	V60D	478	0-8-0 DH	Ex WL1 Kraftwerk Hagenwerder
V346 02	LEW 11346/1967	V60D	478	0-8-0 DH	Ex WL5 Kraftwerk Hagenwerder
V360-01	MaK 600171/1959	V60	478	0-6-0 DH	Ex DB 360 413
V360-02	Essl 5176/1957	V60	478	0-6-0 DH	Ex DB 360 335
Köf 6524	Gm 5158/1960	Köf	94	B DM	Ex DB 323 724
Köf 6624	O&K 26031/1960	Köf	94	B DM	Ex DB 323 250
701 052	WMD 1467/1962	701	2 x 110	A-A DMR	Ex DB 701 052
701 072	WMD 1495/1963	701	2 x 110	A-A DMR	Ex DB 701 072
V200 015	MaK 2000015/1957	V200	2 x 845	B-B DH	Ex SBB 18463, Ex DB 220 015
V200 016	MaK 2000016/1957	V200	2 x 845	B-B DH	Ex SBB 18464, Ex DB 220 016
??	Deutz 57788/1965		140	B DH	Ex Ulmer Weisskalkwerk, Blaustein
VT 11	Essl 25058/1958	Essl	2x162	B-B DHR	ex RAR, ex SWEG

It is understood that GES locos V100 1357, Köf 6169, 50 3636, 11 and 16 are also licensed for main line work under EMN. The two V200s were acquired by GES and are now in the Gmeinder works being overhauled.

NEBENBAHN EBINGEN–ONSTMETTINGEN EO (WEG)

Baden Württemberg

This WEG line ran for 8.2 km between the places mentioned in the title. It had one railcar to provide school train services but this contract was lost in 1998: the railcar (T09) has been transferred to Gaildorf-Untergroningen. Meanwhile EO is "sleeping".

EUROPEAN RAIL SHUTTLE RAILWAYS NV ERS

Netherlands

ERS Railways is a joint venture between Grossreedereien Maersk-Seeland AB (50%) and P&O Nedlloyd Ltd (50%). (Note ERS is also 47% into boxXpress!)

This company has existed for some years organising the movement of containers from Rotterdam, However during 2001/2 it decided to become an EVU and move its own traffic rather than contract this to NS and DB. These operations started in autumn 2002 when it commissioned the first of five Class 66 locos acquired through Porterbrook Leasing. The first train to get underway was the Rotterdam–Germersheim flow which cut over in October 2002. Early in 2003 workings to Mainz and Neuss cut over to ERS operation as more of its Class 66 locos came on line. There could be big growth here as ERS has container flows to Athus, Muizen, Praha, Lille, Budapest, Padova and Warszawa. Late in 2003 ERS announced that it would commence working trains to Italy through to Muttenz yard in Switzerland where trains would be handed over to SBB Cargo. Another batch of class 66s was added to stock and no doubt will be named in due course being numbered 6606-10 having been bought outright.

No.	Builder, No. & Year	Type	kW	Details	Comments
6601	GM 8254-9/2001	JT42CWR	2385	Co-Co DE	*BLUE ARROW* (Originally PB 07)
6602	GM 8254-10/2001	JT42CWR	2385	Co-Co DE	*BLUE BULLET* (Originally PB 08)
6603	GM 8254-11/2001	JT42CWR	2385	Co-Co DE	*BLUE CATAPULT* (Originally PB 09)
6604	GM 8254-12/2001	JT42CWR	2385	Co-Co DE	*BLUE DART* (Originally PB 10)
6605	GM 8360-1/2001	JT42CWR	2385	Co-Co DE	*BLUE EXCALIBUR* (Originally PB 11)
6606	GM 2002 8453-6/2003	JT42CWR	2385	Co-Co DE	
6607	GM 2002 8453-7/2003	JT42CWR	2385	Co-Co DE	
6608	GM 2002 8453-8/2003	JT42CWR	2385	Co-Co DE	
6609	GM 2002 8453-9/2003	JT42CWR	2385	Co-Co DE	
6610	GM 2002 8453-10/2003	JT42CWR	2385	Co-Co DE	

EISENBAHN SERVICE GESELLSCHAFT ESG

Baden Wurttemberg

Depot: Rudersberg.

Founded in 1998 and based in Rudersberg with a link to RAR for sales and marketing. Locomotives are hired out on demand.

No.	Builder, No. & Year	Type	kW	Details	Comments
1 CHRISSI	MaK 600154/1960	650D	478	0-8-0 DH	Ex TAG V65-12 CHRISSIE
2	LEW 16377/1978	201	736	B-B DH	Ex DWU 15, ex DB 201 883
3	Jung 13630/1963	Kof III	176	4w DH	Ex DB 332 046
4 RICHY		Kof III	176	4w DH	Ex DB 332 312
5 JOHNY	KM 15464/1934	Kof II	97	4w DH	Ex BGW ex DB 323 912
6	Essl 5169/1957	V60	478	0-6-0 DH	Ex DB 360 328
7 ERIKA	KHD 57383/1962	V100	992	B-B DH	Ex ÖBB 2048 024, ex DB 211 146
8	VL 5001478/2003	G1206	1500	B-B DH	Schwaben Sprinter
VT 09	WEG/Auwarter/1963		2x135	Bo DER	Ex WEG T 09
VT 36	Fuchs 9058/1956		2x154	B DMR	Ex WEG
VT 402	Essl 23343/1951	Essl	308	1A-A1 DHR	Ex WEG

ERNST SCHAUFFELE SCHIENENVERKEHRS GmbH & Co. KG ESS

Berlin

Depot: Berlin Nord Ost.
EVU Licence: Freight and Passenger 06/03/1997.

This Lübbenau based company is into the aggregates business and is acquiring locos to run its own trains. It has used some W232 locos hired from Adtranz but on expiry of the hire period Adtranz sold them to Eurorail! ESS is believed to be interested in acquiring some EMD class 66 locos and has used 259 003 for a while.

No.	Builder, No. & Year	Type	kW	Details	Comments
V60 001	LEW 16698/1979	V60D	478	0-8-0 DH	Ex Eisenhuttenstadt Binnenhafen
231 012	Lugansk 0114/1972	231	2200	Co-Co DE	Ex Falz, on hire to 2001, later purchased
W232.01	Lugansk 0003/1977	232	2200	Co-Co DE	Ex Lokpool, ex DB 242 003
W232.04	Adtranz 72100/2000	232	2200	Co-Co DE	Ex Lokpool, ex DB 242 004

EUROBAHN VERKEHRSGESELLSCHAFT mbH & Co K.G. EUROBAHN

Rheinland-Pfalz and Niedersachsen

Routes: Alzey–Kirchheimboladen (KBS 651 15 km); Bielefeld–Lemgo (30.3 km, KBS 404); Bielefeld–Rahden (61.6 km KBS 370/386).
Depots: Morscheim and Bielefeld-Sieker.
Length:
Livery: Bielefeld units white, black, yellow; Alzey units are white and yellow.
EVU Licence: Freight and passenger 26/10/1999.

Eurobahn is a Franco-German organisation being owned by VIA-GTI (60%) and BGW/Rhenus Logistik (40%). Whereas BGW itself is a freight operator this new off-shoot is for passenger services. In 1999 passenger services were reintroduced between Alzey and Kirchheimbolanden after a shut down of 48 years. To get the service off the ground two of the new generation of dmus were hired from the Bombardier/DWA pool. From May 2000 Eurobahn took over the operation of passenger services between Bielefeld and Rahden (KBS 386) and Bielefeld and Lemgo (KBS 405) for which six new Talent railcars were delivered from March 2000. Later in 2000 Eurobahn took over the passenger service on the Freiberg–Holzhau route (KBS 514) in Sachsen for which a new operating company was formed (FEG q.v.).

In 2002 Eurobahn and Verkehrsbetriebe Extertalbahn GmbH obtained an eight-year contract to run local trains on the "Weserbahn" (Hildesheim–Löhne) and "Lammetalbahn" (Hildesheim–

Bodenburg). 11 LINT 41 (Coradia) dmus are to be ordered and will be based at the existing Eurobahn depot in Bielefeld. Operations on these lines started on 14/12/2003 with a hourly service Monday–Friday and two-hourly at weekends. These units are in fact owned by the Land which acts as Leasing Company.

NB: From 3/9/2001 Eurobahn was reformed and changed its name to Rhenus Keolis GmbH & Co KG Mainz. The Rhenus group owns 51% whilst Keolis SA Paris owns 49%. (This latter firm itself is 48.7% Banque National de Paris and 43.5% SNCF!) Keolis is a merger of VIA-GTI and Carienne. The Eurobahn name is being kept for marketing.

No.	Builder, No. & Year	Type	kW	Details	Comments
VT1.01	Adtranz 36881/2000	RS1	2 x 268	B-B DMR	
VT1.02	Adtranz 36882/2000	RS1	2 x 268	B-B DMR	
VT2.01	Bom 191300-2/2000	Talent	2 x 315	B-2-2-B DMR	
VT2.02	Bom 191303-5/2000	Talent	2 x 315	B-2-2-B DMR	
VT2.03	Bom 191306-8/2000	Talent	2 x 315	B-2-2-B DMR	
VT2.04	Bom 191309-11/2000	Talent	2 x 315	B-2-2-B DMR	
VT2.05	Bom 191312-14/2000	Talent	2 x 315	B-2-2-B DMR	
VT2.06	Bom 191315-17/2000	Talent	2 x 315	B-2-2-B DMR	
VT2.07	Bom 191395-97/2000	Talent	2 x 315	B-2-2-B DMR	
VT4.01	Als /2003	LINT 41	2 x 315	B-2-B DMR	
VT4.02	Als /2003	LINT 41	2 x 315	B-2-B DMR	
VT4.03	Als /2003	LINT 41	2 x 315	B-2-B DMR	
VT4.04	Als /2003	LINT 41	2 x 315	B-2-B DMR	
VT4.05	Als /2003	LINT 41	2 x 315	B-2-B DMR	
VT4.06	Als /2003	LINT 41	2 x 315	B-2-B DMR	
VT4.07	Als /2003	LINT 41	2 x 315	B-2-B DMR	
VT4.08	Als /2003	LINT 41	2 x 315	B-2-B DMR	
VT4.09	Als /2003	LINT 41	2 x 315	B-2-B DMR	
VT4.10	Als /2003	LINT 41	2 x 315	B-2-B DMR	

NB: The numbering of the railcars indicates the lines to which they are allocated. VT1xx Rheinhessen units for Alzey–Kirchheimboladen whilst VT2xx are Ostwestfalen-Lippe units for the Bielefeld area services. VT3 sets are on the FEG (q.v) whilst the VT4 units are for the Lammentalbahn.

EUROPOOL–MAX KNAPE GLEISBAU GmbH

EUROPOOL

Bayern

This track engineering firm has acquired some of the V100.5 class that were DB 710 9xx. It is believed they have all been rebuilt by Adtranz probably under sub-contract to RFG at Reichenbach. The firm has many track machines and the four V100s.

Depots: Halle, Kreiensen.

No.	Builder, No. & Year	Type	kW	Details	Comments
V150.01	LEW 17310/1981	V100.5	1030	B-B DH	Ex DB 710 961
V150.02	LEW 17311/1983	V100.5	1030	B-B DH	Ex DB 710 962
V150.03	LEW 17312/1983	V100.5	1030	B-B DH	Ex DB 710 963
V150.04	LEW 17315/1983	V100.5	1030	B-B DH	Ex DB 710 966ᴵ

It has since been confirmed that locos were indeed rebuilt by Adtranz under order numbers 72440, 72450, 72460, 72470 of 2000. All are now to V100.4 standard.

EUROTRAC

EUROTRAC

Schleswig Holstein

A complicated story partly explained under Lokomotion Service GmbH. (LSG). Eurotrac was a leasing arm of Vossloh but when the new deals were struck with Angel Trains Eurotrac became a maintenance company and took over the old DB depot at Haldensleben from NEG; which it used it as a servicing centre for many private locos . The Danish Nohabs and the GM cl. 59 have been frequent visitors there. Eurotrac also has a depot at Kiel where it services the dmus of NOB and DB Regio. (Kiel is also the home of Vossloh!). The company was then reformed and now is a maintenance company only with most locos having gone to EIVEL (q.v.)

EISENBAHN & VERKEHRSBETRIEB ELBE–WESER Gmbh
EVB

Niedersachsen

Routes: Bremervörde Süd–Osterholz-Scharmbeck; Wilstedt–Zeven Süd–Tostedt; Rotenburg–Bremervörde–Hollenstedt; Hesedorf–Stade; Harsefeld–Buxtehude; Rotenburg–Brockel.
Length: 286/309 km.   **Depots:** Bremervörde Süd, Zeven Süd, Harsefeld Süd.

EVB was formed in 1981 by the fusion of Bremervörde–Osterholzer Eisenbahn Gmbh (BOE) and the Wilstedt–Zeven–Tostedter Eisenbahn Gmbh (WZTE). Passenger traffic on these lines had finished in the 1970s so on formation EVB was freight only. In 1991 it took over from DB the passenger services Bremerhaven–Stade–Bremervörde–Brockel and Hesedorf–Hollenstedt acquiring later several class 628.2 diverted from the DB order. In 1993 operations were extended further when the passenger traffic between Buxtehude and Harsefeld came to EVB. The most recent statistics are from 1998 when there were 880,000 passenger journeys and 171,000 tonnes of freight. With open access the freight has developed further and EVB works some container trains between the ports of Hamburg and Bremen/Bremerhaven. In late 2001 two more DB 211 were acquired from Stendal whilst in 2002 a new numbering scheme was introduced for its main line locos. Traffic continues to grow. Passenger traffic is up from 910,000 to 980,000 (1999-2001) whilst freight traffic has rocketed from 380,000 tonnes to 891,000 reflecting heavy container trains and aggregate traffic.

No.	Builder, No. & Year	Type	kW	Details	Comments
150	Duew 90323/4/1993	628	485	2-B + 2-2 DHR	(DB 628 405)
151	Duew 90321/2/1993	628	485	2-B + 2-2 DHR	(DB 628 406)
152	Duew 90325/6/1993	628	485	2-B + 2-2 DHR	(DB 628 407)
153	Duew 90327/8/1993	628	485	2-B + 2-2 DHR	(DB 628 409)
154	LHB 1351/2/1993	628	485	2-B + 2-2 DHR	
164	Talbot 97213/1955		2 x 107	1A-A1 DMR	Ex BOE
165	Uer 62001/1956	798	2 x 110	A-A DMR	Ex DB 798 648
166	WMD 1307/1960	798	2 x 110	A-A DMR	Ex DB 798 767
168	MAN 146608/1962	798	2 x 110	A-A DMR	Ex DB 798 826
170	LHW 1936/1959		2 x 107	B-2 DHR	Ex BOE,ex DB VT51 104
274	Hens 28641/1956	DH360	265	C DH	Ex WZTE, stored
276	BMAG 11449/1941	WR360C	65	C DH	Ex BHE stored
281	MaK 600414/1965	650D	478	D DH	Ex BHE
304.51	MaK 500041/1966	G500C	368	C DH	Ex 282II ex On Rail. FFS
306.51	MaK 500068/1975	G700C	559	C DH	Ex 283 ex BOE. FFS
410.51	Krp 4362/1962	V100	845	B-B DH	Ex 284 ex DB 211 252 FFS
410.01	KM 18919/1962	V100	845	B-B DH	Ex 285 ex DB 211 323
410.02	Jung 13457/1962	V100	845	B-B DH	Ex 286 ex DB 211 330
410.03	Jung 13451/1962	V100	845	B-B DH	Ex 287 ex DB 211 324
410.04	MaK 1000042/1961	V100		B-B DH	Ex DB 211 024. CAT engine
410.05	KM 1000079/1962	V100		B-B DH	Ex DB 211 061. CAT engine
417.01	KM 18297/1957	V200	2 x 845	B-B DH	Ex 288 ex SBB 18466, DB 220 053
420.01	KHD 57486/1965	V169	1580	B-B DH	Ex BGW DH280.01. DB 219 001I
622.01	Lugansk 0325/1974	232	2206	Co-Co DE	Ex BGW DE300.01, ex DB 232 103
Spares	Jung 13453/1962	V100	845	B-B DH	Ex DB 211 326

Notes: 150 named Buxtehude; 151 named Bremervörde; 153 Harsefeld; 154 Beverstadt. 285 received a new CAT engine in 1998. Some of the ex DB 211s have m.u. controls. 288 now fitted with 2 x CAT 3508 engines.
The new numbering system starts with a figure denoting the number of axles followed by the power rating in thousands. A running number over 50 denotes a radio controlled locomotive.

EIFELBAHN VERKEHRSGESELLSCHAFT mbH   EVG

Rheinland Pfalz

Routes: Linz–Kalenborn
Length: **Depot:** Linz.
EVU Licence: Freight and Passenger 18/12/1997.

This company appears to be a preservation group turned into a proper operating company as it operates tourist trains from Linz to Kalenborn whilst the sidings at Linz are used for the storage and marshalling of rolling stock for tourist trains. These trains are hired from Euro Express and Historische Eisenbahn Frankfurt/Main and see use on various excursion duties e.g. football specials. In 2002 EVG together with the Brohltalbahn formed Rheinische Eisenbahn GmbH (q.v.)

No.	Builder, No. & Year	Type	kW	Details	Comments
323 149	KHD 57294/1959	Köf II	97	4w DH	Ex Vennbahn, ex DB
323 351	KHD 57931/1965	Köf II	97	4w DH	Ex Industry, ex DB
323 972	KHD 10911/1934	Köf II	97	4w DH	Ex Industry, ex DB
798 598	WMD 1234/1956	798	2 x 110	A-A DMR	Ex EBG ex DB

EUREGIO VERKEHRSSCHIENENNETZ   EVS
Stolberg, Nordrhein Westfalen
EVU licence: Freight and Passenger 15/01/2001

Also known as the Regionalbahn Aachen. This company has been set up by DB Regio, Dürener Kreisbahn (now Rurtalbahn), NS Reizigers and Bahn Schotter Recycling (Stolberg) to operate services in the Aachen area. Various lines are to be reopened to passenger trains and linked into the existing service between Aachen and Heerlen. The lines involved are Stolberg to Walheim/Wurselen/Weisweiler and Herzogenrath–Alsdorf–Siersdorf. As a start existing DB Talent units were used between Aachen and Stolberg Hammer in 2001. Now DB is to operate the service using a new batch of Talent units in the 643.2 series. For details see Part 1.

BERND FALZ, HERMESKEIL MUSEUM   FALZ
Hermeskeil, Rheinlandfalz

Hr. Falz is the owner of Hermeskeil and Jüterbog museums. He has several former DR diesel locomotives that are in working order and makes additional money for the museum projects by hiring out these locomotives to anyone who needs one – spot hire mostly but some longer contracts do turn up.

No.	Builder, No. & Year	Type	kW	Details	Comments
220 355	Lugansk 2087/1974	M62	1470	Co-Co DE	
232 305	Lugansk 0518/1976	232	2200	Co-Co DE	
232 375	Lugansk 0610/1976	232	2200	Co-Co DE	
1	LEW 16969/1980	V60D	478	0-8-0 DH	Ex Umformtechnik Erfurt 1
7	LEW 16794/1980	V60D	478	0-8-0 DH	Ex EIB 7
346 594	LEW 12393/1970	V60D	478	0-8-0 DH	Ex Glaswerk Ilmenau

FREIBERGER EISENBAHNGESELLSCHAFT mbH   FEG
Freiberg, Sachsen
Route: Freiberg (Sachs)–Holzhau (KBS 514, 31 km)
Length: 31 km.   **Depot:** Mulda
EVU Licence: Freight and Passenger 10/01/2001.

This company has been set up by Eurobahn to operate the Freiburg–Holzhau branch taking over from DB late in 2000 and with a concession to run until 2019.

No.	Builder, No. & Year	Type	kW	Details	Comments
VT3.01	Adtranz 36883/2000	RS1	2 x 268	B-B DMR	*LOUISA*
VT3.02	Adtranz 36884/2000	RS1	2 x 268	B-B DMR	*HANNAH*
VT3.03	Adtranz 36885/2000	RS1	2 x 268	B-B DMR	*ESTHER*
V100 01	LEW 13520/1972	V100DR	883	B-B DH	Ex DB 202 481

The loco is actually owned by RRP-Eisenbahn, the EIU for the line.

FRANKFURT–KÖNIGSTEINER EISENBAHN AG   FKE
Frankfurt am Main, Hessen
Routes: Frankfurt/M-Höchst–Königstein (KBS 646, 16 km); Ffm-Hochst–Bad Soden (KBS 643, 7 km); Friedberg–Friedrichsdorf (KBS 636, 16 km); Friedrichsdorf–Brandoberndorf (KBS 637, 36.9 km).
Length: 75/85 km.   **Depots:** Königstein, Usingen.
EVU Licence: Freight and Passenger 25/10/2001.

This line comes under the HLB umbrella. Once a somewhat backwater the growth of commuting traffic has made these lines a virtual extension of the Frankfurt/M S-Bahn. Some rush hour trains run through to Frankfurt/M Hbf.

No.	Builder, No. & Year	Type	kW	Details	Comments
VT 1 A/B	LHB 01 A/B/1987	VT2E	463	Bo-2-Bo DER	
VT 2 A/B	LHB 02 A/B/1987	VT2E	463	Bo-2-Bo DER	
VT 3 A/B	LHB 03 A/B/1987	VT2E	463	Bo-2-Bo DER	
VT 4 A/B	LHB 04 A/B/1987	VT2E	463	Bo-2-Bo DER	
VT 5 A/B	LHB 05 A/B/1987	VT2E	463	Bo-2-Bo DER	
VT 6 A/B	LHB 06 A/B/1987	VT2E	463	Bo-2-Bo DER	
VT 7 A/B	LHB 07 A/B/1987	VT2E	463	Bo-2-Bo DER	
VT 8 A/B	LHB 08 A/B/1987	VT2E	463	Bo-2-Bo DER	
VT 9 A/B	LHB 09 A/B/1992	VT2E	463	Bo-2-Bo DER	
VT11	LHB 11A/B/1992	VT2E	463	Bo-2-Bo DER	
VT12	LHB 12A/B/1992	VT2E	463	Bo-2-Bo DER	
VT13	LHB 13A/B/1992	VT2E	463	Bo-2-Bo DER	
VT14	LHB 14A/B/1992	VT2E	463	Bo-2-Bo DER	
VT15	LHB 15A/B/1992	VT2E	463	Bo-2-Bo DER	
VT16	LHB 16A/B/1992	VT2E	463	Bo-2-Bo DER	
VT17	LHB 17A/B/1992	VT2E	463	Bo-2-Bo DER	
VT18	LHB 18A/B/1992	VT2E	463	Bo-2-Bo DER	
VT19	LHB 19A/B/1992	VT2E	463	Bo-2-Bo DER	
VT20	LHB 20A/B/1992	VT2E	463	Bo-2-Bo DER	
VT21	LHB 21A/B/1992	VT2E	463	Bo-2-Bo DER	
VT 51	Duew 91341/2/1994	628	485	B-2+2-2 DHR	
VT 71	Duew 91343/4/1995	629	2 x 485	B-2+2-B DHR	
VT 72	Duew 91345/6/1995	629	2 x 485	B-2+2-B DHR	
509 108	DWA 509 005/1998	GTW 2/6	550	Bo-2-Bo DER	

Note: VT11–21 carry Taunusbahn logos (TSB)

FLEX AG FLEX

Schleswig Holstein

When DB decided to take off the Inter Regio trains between Hamburg and Flensburg local organisations were up in arms. Consequently NNVG decided to do it themselves and together with its subsidiary NVAG, formed FLEX–Flensburg Express. They quoted for a two-hourly interval service from Hamburg to Flensburg and beyond–to Padborg just over the Danish border where connections would be made into DSB services. The quote was successful and so some Dispoloks were hired and some carriages found and refurbished and the new service started on 15/12/02–the day DB took off its own trains. FLEX started off quite well but in the latter part of 2003 signalled liquidity problems and was declared bankrupt. Although services were well used the cash flow from outlets was too slow. Connex in the shape of NOB has stepped into the breach and will run the trains until December 2005 during which time the contract will be relet. Some locos and stock still carry FLEX branding but Connex has moved in its own displaced stock from the Inter-Connex Köln – Rostock service.

Motive power is hired in with some locomotives provided by Dispolok or Connex may provide a loco in house. Early in 2004 Dispoloks 1116 063/64 were being used. Interestingly these are ÖBB locos hired by Dispolok. Quite complicated!

FRANKENBAHN GmbH FRANKENBAHN

Nürnberg, Bayern.

Depot: Würzburg
EVU Licence: Freight and Passenger 14/11/1996.

Registered in Nürnberg the Frankenbahn appears to be located in Würzburg and performs trip working in the harbour. The company is registered as a fully fledged EVU so may expand.

No.	Builder, No. & Year	Type	kW	Details	Comments
360 001	LEW 14555/1975	V60D	478	0-8-0 DH	Ex DB 346 953

FARGE–VEGESACKER EISENBAHN GmbH
FVE (CONNEX)

Bremen/Niedersachsen

Routes: Bremen-Farge–Bremen-Vegesack
Length: 10.4/15.6 km.
Depot: Bremen-Farge.

This is another of the DEG lines operating a short line in the Bremen area of just 10 km. Passenger traffic ceased in 1961 but the line is busy with freight as it has block coal trains going to a power station. 446,000 tonnes conveyed in 1995 but by 2000 this had reduced to 279,000 tonnes. 2003 has seen further changes. FVE has changed into an EIU with traffic now being worked by Nord West Cargo. The two line locos have been sold to Italy.

No.	Builder, No. & Year	Type	kW	Details	Comments
51	Mak 500071/1974	G500C	368	C DH	To NWC
161	MaK 1000513/1971	G1600BB	1176	B-B DH	Sold to Italy
162	MaK 1000514/1971	G1600BB	1176	B-B DH	Sold to Italy

GATX RAIL EUROPE
GATX

Zürich, Switzerland

American leasing company GATX has set up a European subsidiary. GATX is expected to take all the Bombardier Lokpool locos of class 232 besides having a couple of its own.

No.	Builder, No. & Year	Type	kW	Details	Comments
206 364	LEW 12873/1971	V100	883	B-B DH	Ex ALS, ex DB. On hire to TX Logistic
206 466	LEW 13505/1972	V100	883	B-B DH	Ex ALS, ex DB. On hire to TX Logistic
W232.09	Adtranz 72900/2000	232	2200	Co-Co DE	Ex Lokpool, Ex EfW 232 714 ex SZD TE109 026
W232.10	Adtranz 72910/2000	232	2200	Co-Co DE	Ex Lokpool, ex Russia, ex SZD TE109-015 On hire to KEG
W232.11	Adtranz 72920/2000	232	2200	Co-Co DE	Ex Lokpool, ex Russia, ex SZD TE109-033 On hire to KEG
W232.12	Lugansk 0847/1978	232	2200	Co-Co DE	Ex Lokpool, ex Russia, ex SZD TE109-020 On hire to KEG

GROSS BIEBERAU-REINHEIMER EISENBAHN GmbH
GBRE

Hessen

Routes: Gross-Biberau–Reinheim
Length: 3.0/3.7 km
Depot: Gross-Biberau
Once shown as a DEG line. Only 3 km long serving a few sidings and conveying stone and scrap with 32,000 tonnes forwarded in 2000.

No.	Builder, No. & Year	Type	kW	Details	Comments
V 36	O&K 26718/1971	MC360N	265	C DH	

GEORGSMARIENHÜTTEN EISENBAHN & TRANSPORT GmbH
GET

Osnabrück,Niedersachsen

Routes: Georgsmarienhütte - Hasbergen
Length: 7.3/8 km   **Depot:** Georgsmarienhütte.
EVU Licence: Freight and Passenger 14/01/1997.

This railway serves the industries in Georgsmarienhütte and once belonged to the steelworks there. Like other old steelworks towns, times have changed and the blast furnaces closed. Consequently the loco fleet has shrunk. From 1997 DB worked through from Osnabrück Rbf. just the opposite to what has happened elsewhere! Some locos have been sold off or scrapped since then. 1998 statistics reveal 750,000 tonnes carried with 2000 seeing 837,000 tonnes. There are plans to reopen the Osnabrück–Bielefeld line to passengers and at the same time provide a new connection into Georgsmarienhütte so that the existing line can be closed.

No.	Builder, No. & Year	Type	kW	Details	Comments
2	Deutz 57802/1965	MG530C	390	C DH	
5	Deutz 57805/1965	MG530C	390	C DH	
6	Deutz 57806/1965	MG530C	390	C DH	
7	Deutz 57807/1965	MG530C	390	C DH	
8	Deutz 57808/1965	MG530C	390	C DH	

NEBENBAHN GAILDORF–UNTERGRÖNINGEN   GU (WEG)
Baden Württemberg WEG

Routes: Gaildorf West–Untergröningen. (KBS 785)
Length: 18.8/20.7 km
Depot: Untergröningen

This 18km WEG line is quite busy with freight traffic for the local timber industry and consequently it is one of the few WEG lines to use a locomotive. The GU locos also work trips along the DB line from Backnang to Schwabish Hall Hessenthal. What passenger trains have run in recent years have been for school traffic but there are plans to increase passenger trains to an hourly service using new dmus possibly LVT/S single cars. In 1998 100,000 tonnes of freight.

No.	Builder, No. & Year	Type	kW	Details	Comments
T 36	Fuchs 9058/1956		2 x 154	B DMR	Stored
V 122	Mak 1000057/1961	1200D	883	D DH	Ex RStE
V 125	Krp 4383/1962	V100	845	B-B DH	Ex DB 211 273
VT 114	Essl 23497/1952		2 x 107	1A-A1 DHR	Hired from EMN

GVG VERKEHRSORGANISATION GmbH   GVG

This travel agency company took over the marketing and operation of the sleeping car trains from Berlin to Malmö via Sassnitz when DB lost interest in the service. GVG is now responsible for the Bratislava–Praha–Dresden–Sassnitz–Malmö train within Germany. This is useful as the Berlin–Malmö train is using hired sleeping cars from Slovakia! The actual haulage and running of the trains is done by WAB using its class 109 electric locos giving them some of the longest runs they have ever done!

No.	Builder, No. & Year	Type	kW	Details	Comments
608 801	WMD 1256/1956	608		B-2 DHR	Ex DB, US Army.
109-1	LEW 15116/1975	109	2920	Bo-Bo E	Ex Lokpool, ex DB 109 084
109-2	LEW 9904/1962	109	2920	Bo-Bo E	Ex Lokpool, ex DR 109 013
109-3	LEW 15105/1975	109	2920	Bo-Bo E	Ex Lokpool, ex DR 109 073

HESSISCHE GÜTERBAHN GmbH   HGB
Buseck, Hessen

This is a newcomer on the private scene first coming to light early in 2003. Just who owns it and what the aims are remain to be seen. Locomotives are hired in as required. One of the BUG V60 is known to be hired by HGB for shunting at Stadtallendorf. It is not clear whether HGB has purchased locos or simply hiring in. The following are understood to be being used by HGB: 212 285 (Ex ALS); V1200.02 (RAR) and V60 BUG 02 (BUG).

HAFEN & GÜTERVERKEHR KÖLN AG   HGK
Köln, Nordrhein Westfalen

Routes: Bonn–Brühl–Köln; Bonn–Wesseling–Köln; Wesseling–Brühl–Berrenrath; Benzelrath–Frechen–Köln–Niehl/Hafen.
Length: 102.2/310 km
Depots: Brühl-Vochem, Köln-Deutz Hafen, Köln-Bickendorf.
EVU Licence: Freight and Passenger 07/11/1988.

This company has its origins in Häfen Köln GmbH (HKG), originally just the railway serving the Köln docks. In 1992 the line merged with Köln Frechen Benzelrather Eisenbahn (KFBE) and at the same time took over the freight work from the Köln Bonner Eisenbahn (KBE). Freight traffic is quite heavy with the larger HGK locos working trips into nearby DB yards such as Köln Eifeltor. The main depots and workshops are at Brühl Vochem with sub depots at Köln Bickendorf and Köln Deutz Hafen. 102 km of track includes some electrification at 750 V DC used by KVG (ex KBE) services. 1998 traffic figures reveal 5.2 million tonnes handled with 2001 producing 5.8 million tonnes. In 1996/7 HGK obtained the three MaK demonstrator locos that had been DB 240 001– 003. These are intended to be used on container trains to Rotterdam in connection with the Dutch firm Short Lines. HGK has also obtained from GM several Class 66 diesel locos for similar work. HGK is owned by Stadtwerke Köln (54.5%), Stadt Köln (39.2%) and Erftkreise (6.3%).

2002 saw several developments. First several more GM diesels were acquired. HGK then formed Swiss Rail Cargo as a joint venture with the SBB. 2003 saw HGK class 66 locomotives roaming far and wide turning up at Grosskorbetha, Leipzig and Berlin. A new working late in 2003 was a coal train from Duisburg Hochfeld Süd to Bielefeld.

No.	Builder, No. & Year	Type	kW	Details	Comments
V3	Deutz 55547/1953	KS225B	166	D DH	Ex KBE V 5
V4	Deutz 55545/1953	KS225B	166	D DH	Ex KBE V 3
DE 11	MaK 300002/1989	DE1024	2650	Co-Co DE	DB/MaK 240 001
DE 12	MaK 300003/1989	DE1024	2650	Co-Co DE	DB/MaK 240 002
DE 13	MaK 300004/1989	DE1024	2650	Co-Co DE	DB/MaK 240 003
V 21	MaK 220105/1981	G321B	246	B DH	Ex HDK? 21
V 22	MaK 220106/1981	G321B	246	B DH	Ex HDK? 22
DH 31	Deutz 57187/1961	DG1200BBM	808	B-B DH	KBE V
DH 32	Deutz 57188/1961	DG1200BBM	808	B-B DH	KBE V 32
DH 33	Deutz 57189/1961	DG1200BBM	808	B-B DH	KBE V 33
DH 34	Deutz 57191/1961	DG1200BBM	808	B-B DH	KBE V 35
DH 35	Deutz 57541/1961	DG1200BBM	808	B-B DH	KBE V 37
DH 36	Deutz 57417/1961	DG1200BBM	808	B-B DH	KBE V 36
DH 37	Deutz 57982/1961	DG1200BBM	808	B-B DH	KFBE V 75
DH 38	Deutz 57983/1961	DG1200BBM	808	B-B DH	KFBE V 76
DE 61	GM 998101-1/1999	JT42CWR	2385	Co-Co DE	Ex 9902. ATBL
DE 62	GM 998101-2/1999	JT42CWR	2385	Co-Co DE	Ex 9901
DE 63	GM 20008254-6/2002	JT42CWR	2385	Co-Co DE	(PB 04) ATBL
DE 64	GM 20008254-8/2002	JT42CWR	2385	Co-Co DE	(PB 06) ATBL
DE 65	GM 20008360-3/2002	JT42CWR	2385	Co-Co DE	(PB 13) ATBL
DE 66	GM 20008360-5/2002	JT42CWR	2385	Co-Co DE	(PB 15) ATBL
DE 67	GM 20008360-6/2002	JT42CWR	2385	Co-Co DE	(PB 16) ATBL
DE 668	GM 20028453-1/2002	JT42CWR	2385	Co-Co DE	ATBL
DE 669	GM 20028453-2/2002	JT42CWR	2385	Co-Co DE	ATBL
DE 6610	GM 20028453-3/2002	JT42CWR	2385	Co-Co DE	ATBL
DE 6611	GM 20028453-4/2002	JT42CWR	2385	Co-Co DE	ATBL
DE 6612	GM 20028453-5/2002	JT42CWR	2385	Co-Co DE	ATBL
DE 71	MaK 1000833/1987	DE1002	1320	Bo-Bo DE	KBE DE 81
DE 72	MaK 1000834/1987	DE1002	1320	Bo-Bo DE	KBE DE 82. New Cummins engine.
DE 73	MaK 1000840/1987	DE1002	1320	Bo-Bo DE	KFBE DE 93
DE 74	MaK 1000836/1987	DE1002	1320	Bo-Bo DE	KBE DE 84
DE 75	MaK 1000837/1987	DE1002	1320	Bo-Bo DE	KBE DE 85
DE 76	MaK 1000839/1987	DE1002	1320	Bo-Bo DE	KFBE DE 92. New Cummins engine.
DE 81	MaK 1000882/1993	DE1002	1320	Bo-Bo DE	ATBL
DE 82	MaK 1000883/1993	DE1002	1320	Bo-Bo DE	ATBL
DE 83	MaK 1000884/1993	DE1002	1320	Bo-Bo DE	ATBL
DE 84	MaK 1000885/1993	DE1002	1320	Bo-Bo DE	
DE 85	MaK 1000886/1993	DE1002	1320	Bo-Bo DE	
DE 86	MaK 1000887/1993	DE1002	1320	Bo-Bo DE	
DE 91	MaK 1000838/1987	DE1002	1320	Bo-Bo DE	KFBE DE 91
DE 92	MaK 1000842/1987	DE1002	1320	Bo-Bo DE	KFBE DE 95
DE 93	MaK 1000835/1987	DE1002	1320	Bo-Bo DE	KBE DE 83
DE 94	MaK 1000841/1987	DE1002	1320	Bo-Bo DE	KFBE DE 94
2001	Adtranz 33386/2000	145	4200	Bo-Bo E	145 CL 011
2002	Adtranz 33821/2000	145	4200	Bo-Bo E	145 CL 012
2003	Adtranz 33826/2001	145	4200	Bo-Bo E	145 CL 013
2004	Adtranz 33828/2001	145	4200	Bo-Bo E	145 CL 014
2005	Adtranz 33842/2001	145	4200	Bo-Bo E	145 CL 015

VT 1	MAN 140896/1954	VT95	110	A-1 DMR	DB 795 398
VT 2	WMD 1221/1956	VT98	2 x 110	A-A DMR	DB 798 585

NB: Locos seen numbered in the DH 4x and DH 5x series are short term hire locos.

HEAVY HAUL POWER INTERNATIONAL GmbH   HHPI
Erfurt, Thüringen

Depot: ?
EVU Licence: Freight 09/05/2000.

Registered in Erfurt HHPI is the son of DB Foster Yeoman GmbH established as an independent EVU in 2000 using 59003 from the UK numbered as 259 003 in Germany. 29001/2 arrived in Europe late in 2001 and went to Tilburg (NL) for final fitting out. 29003 arrived later and was expected to emerge from Tilburg at the end of 2002 fitted up for operating into Poland. HHPI started hauling aggregates in the Rostock/Berlin area and now has contracts for the movement of imported coal from Hamburg Hafen to Lahde near Minden. This departs about 09.00 and runs via Verden and Nienburg.

No.	Builder, No. & Year	Type	kW	Details	Comments
259 003	GM 1985848002-3/1985	JT26CW-SS	2420	Co-Co DE	*YEOMAN HIGHLANDER*
29001	GM 20008254-3 2001	JT42CWR	2350	Co-Co DE	*ROBERT J.G. SAVAGE*
29002	GM 20008254-4 2001	JT42CWR	2350	Co-Co DE	*HANS CERMAK*
29003	GM 20008254-13 2001	JT42CWR	2350	Co-Co DE	

HESSISCHE LANDESBAHN GmbH   HLB
Frankfurt/Main, Hessen

The HLB was founded in 1955 taking over in 1966 the Butzbach–Licher Eisenbahn, Frankfurt–Königstein Eisenbahn, Hersfelder Kreisbahn and Kassel - –Naumburg Eisenbahn. More recently Verkehrsverband Hochtaunaus was also embraced. The HLB is an umbrella organisation for all these lines which are listed separately except for the Hersfelder Kreisbahn which no longer has rail traffic. New railcars have recently been delivered which are shown under the various lines where they work but note that the last three digits of the running number form one series within the HLB organisation and are also referred to as HLB VT 101–118. A further 12 are understood to have been ordered. A new contract has been started in 1999 running passenger trains from Dillenburg as the Hellertalbahn with the initials HTB. This duplicates an existing set so this particular HTB is shown as HTB/HLB.

Early in 2001 Giessen–Nidda–Gelnhausen and from June 2001 Friedberg–Hanau passenger services became operated by HLB via its BLE subsidiary.

HOYER RAILSERVE GmbH   HRS

What started off as a joint operation with RSE Cargo was taken over by Hoyer as it owned a 90% share and RSE 10%. Hoyer was running its own trains Brunnsbüttel–Neuss Hessentor–Dormagen–Köln. Locos are hired from Dispolok and other firms with ME26-01/6/7 and MWB 2001 being used in mid-2001. Local trips in the Hamburg area are diesel operated. In 2002 Hoyer merged with Rail4Chem (q.v.). Some hire locos may still carry HRS livery.

HARZER SCHMALSPURBAHNEN   HSB
Wernigerode, Sachsen Anhalt

Routes: Wernigerode–Nordhausen; Drei Annen Hohne–Brocken; Gernrode (Harz)–Hasselfelde; Alexisbad–Harzgerode; Stiege–Eisefelder Talmühle
Length: 131.2/150.0 km   **Depots:** Wernigerode, Nordhausen, Gernrode.
EVU Licence: Freight and Passenger 24/05/1995.

After the unification of Germany in 1990 the Harz area metre gauge system was sold off – privatised. These lines were originally private railways being nationalised after WW2 by the communist authorities. As private lines they were known as the Nordhausen–Wernigeroder Eisenbahn (NWE) and Gernrode–Harzgeroder Eisenbahn (GHE). Upon regaining their private status they are now one company. The railway's biggest earner is the line to the Brocken mountain peak (1125 metres a.s.l.) and makes the line very busy in the summer and winter tourist seasons. Elsewhere on the lines there is little traffic with school children being the regular passengers. In an attempt to reduce costs some DMUs have been acquired which are adequate for some areas. However the main business will see steam traction for years to come as HSB is gradually overhauling more and more locos. In 1997 over its 132 km network there were 1 million journeys and about 34,000 tonnes of freight. Passenger traffic is still holding up but freight traffic is now less than 10,000 tonnes per year.

An extension is being built from Gernrode to Quedlinburg, a town which is a world heritage site and sees lots of tourists. This is a conversion of a former standard gauge line.

No.	Builder, No. & Year	Type	kW	Details	Comments
99 7222-5	BMAG 9921/1931			2-10-2T	
99 7231-6	LKM 134008/1954			2-10-2T	
99 7232-4	LKM 134009/1954			2-10-2T	
99 7233-2	LKM 134010/1954			2-10-2T	
99 7234-0	LKM 134011/1954			2-10-2T	
99 7235-7	LKM 134012/1954			2-10-2T	
99 7236-5	LKM 134013/1955			2-10-2T	
99 7237-3	LKM 134014/1955			2-10-2T	
99 7238-1	LKM 134015/1955			2-10-2T	
99 7239-9	LKM 134016/1955			2-10-2T	
99 7240-7	LKM 134017/1955			2-10-2T	
99 7241-5	LKM 134018/1955			2-10-2T	
99 7242-3	LKM 134019/1955			2-10-2T	
99 7243-1	LKM 134020/1955			2-10-2T	
99 7244-9	LKM 134021/1955			2-10-2T	
99 7245-6	LKM 134022/1955			2-10-2T	
99 7246-4	LKM 134023/1955			2-10-2T	
99 7247-2	LKM 134024/1956			2-10-2T	
99 5901-6	Jung 258/1897	Mallet		0-4-4-0T	NWE 11
99 5902-4	Jung 261/1897	Mallet		0-4-4-0T	NWE 14 then 12
99 5903-2	Jung 345/1898	Mallet		0-4-4-0T	NWE 18 then 13. Stored.
99 5906-5	Karl 2052/1918	Mallet		0-4-4-0T	NWE 41
99 6001-4	Krp 1875/1939			2-6-2T	NWE 21
99 6101-2	Hens 12879/1914			0-6-0T	NWE 6
99 6102-0	Hens 12880/1914			0-6-0T	NWE 7
199 005	LKM 250352/1964	V10C	75	0-6-0 DM	
199 006	LKM 250353/1964	V10C	75	0-6-0 DM	
199 010	BMAG 10224/1934	Köf	92	B DH	Ex DR 100 325 Stored
199 011	Jung 5668/1935	Köf	92	B DH	Ex DR 100 639
199 012	BMAG 10164/1934	Köf	92	B DH	Ex DR 100 325 Stored
199 301	LKM 263001/1966	Java	250	C DH	Stored
199 861	LEW 15379/1976	V100	736	C-C DH	Ex DR 110 861
199 871	LEW 15389/1976	V100	736	C-C DH	Ex DR 110 871
199 872	LEW 15390/1976	V100	736	C-C DH	Ex DR 110 872
199 874	LEW 15392/1976	V100	736	C-C DH	Ex DR 110 874
199 877	LEW 16371/1978	V100	736	C-C DH	Ex DR 110 877 Stored
199 892	LEW 16386/1978	V100	736	C-C DH	Ex DR 110 892 Stored
187 001	Dess 3046/1933		40	A-1 DMR	GHE T1
187 011	Talbot 97519/1955	Eifel 2 x 107		1A-A1 DMR	Langeoog T1. BoStrab
187 012	Fuchs 9107/1955		2 x 154	B-B DHR	Langeoog T3
187 013	Talbot 97520/1955	Eifel 2 x 107		1A-A1 DMR	Langeoog T4. BoStrab
187 015	Wittenberge 1996		242	B-2 DHR	Prototype
187 016	Halberstadt 1999		242	B-2 DHR	New Build
187 017	Halberstadt 1999		242	B-2 DHR	New Build
187 018	Halberstadt 1999		242	B-2 DHR	New Build
187 019	Halberstadt 1999		242	B-2 DHR	New Build
187 025	Wismar 1940			Bo-Bo DER	NWE T3

HAMBURG SCHWERINER LOKFUHRERSERVICE GmbH
HSL LOGISTIC GmbH   HSL

A group of "retired" (redundant?) DB drivers started up this company. As the first title shows the first dealings were hiring out drivers but soon the firm got into the logistics business. It could well be hiring locos soon.

HÖRSELTALBAHN GmbH   HTB (CONNEX)
Eisenach,Thüringen

Routes: Eisenach area
Length: 9.2/11.2 km   **Depot:** Opel werksbahnhof
EVU Licence: Freight and Passenger 03/06/1999.

This firm grew up from an industrial shunting activity first under the old DDR at the Wartburg car factory and later at the same place but now for Opel. Privatised it now serves the Opel factory and other locations in the area around Eisenach. In 2003 HTB started tripping freight from Eisenach to Gerstungen on behalf of Railion Deutschland. (DB).

No.	Builder, No. & Year	Type	kW	Details	Comments
V 66	LEW 10758/1966	V60D	478	D DH	
V 67	LEW 11344/1967	V60D	478	D DH	To ?
V 71	MaK 700112/1994	G765C	560	C DH	
V 143	LEW 15395/1976	V100.4	1030	B-B DH	Ex DB 710 960

HELLERTALBAHN GmbH   HTB (HLB)
Steinebach, Rheinland Pfalz

Routes: Dillenburg–Haiger–Betzdorf(Sieg) (KBS 462, 35.8 km).
Length: 35.8 km   **Depot:** Bindweide (Westerwaldbahn)
EVU licence: Freight and Passenger 13/10/1999.

The Hellertalbahn is another new train company set up in 1998/9. It is a joint venture between the Hessische Landesbahn (who provide the rolling stock); the Siegener Kreisbahn (responsible for marketing and accounts); and the Westerwaldbahn (responsible for crews and operations). The HTB(HLB) has taken over from DB the local train service Dillenburg–Haiger–Betzdorf. The units are a follow on order after those for the BLE, KNE etc but are class 525 rather than 508/9. This is believed to due to these units having first class, second class and toilets. The last three digits are common numbers with the rest of the HLB fleet.

No.	Builder, No. & Year	Type	kW	Details	Comments
525 116	Bomb. 525 001/1999	GTW2/6	550	2-Bo-2 DER	HLB VT 116
525 117	Bomb. 525 002/1999	GTW2/6	550	2-Bo-2 DER	HLB VT 117
525 118	Bomb. 525 003/1999	GTW2/6	550	2-Bo-2 DER	HLB VT 118

HUPAC DEUTSCHLAND GmbH   HUPAC
Singen, Baden-Württemberg.

This container and intermodal operator is now running its own trains between Basel and Ludwigshafen/Köln jointly with HGK. Displolok 1116 901 was at first hired but has now been purchased.

No.	Builder, No. & Year	Type	kW	Details	Comments
ES64U2 100	SKM 20445/2000	ES64U2	6400	Bo-Bo E	Ex Dispolok ES64U2-901
ES64U2 101	SKM 20555/2001	ES64U2	6400	Bo-Bo E	Intended as 1116 904
ES64U2 102	SKM 20556/2001	ES64U2	6400	Bo-Bo E	Intended as 1116 905

Notes:
The locos are based on ÖBB class 1116/DB 182. They now have DB LZB numbers 182 600-602 and are passed for operation in Switzerland.

HOCHWALDBAHN EISENBAHNBETRIEBES UNDBAHN-SERVICE GESELLSCHAFT mbH   HWB
Hermeskeil, Rheinland-Pfalz.

Depot: Hermeskeil
EVU Licence: Freight and Passenger 22/07/2003

This company started out as an enthusiasts organisation running raibus trips over lines in the Trier area especially Trier–Hermeskeil but this line was later closed and lifted. Then came open access and so a company was formed and an EVU licence obtained. There are still trips to scenic places but now most time is spent overhauling railbuses and hiring them out! A workshop has been established at Hermeskeil. HWB is now involved in running the new service from Zittau under the SBE banner. Another possibility for HWB is tourist services from Hermeskeil to Turismühle which may well come about in 2004.

No.	Builder, No. & Year	Type	kW	Details	Comments
VL 1	Jung 12255/1956	R30C	200	B DH	Ex BE 1
VL 2^I	LKM 262412/1972	V22	162	0-4-0 DH	Ex Umformtechnik Erfurt 4. To NVAG?
VL 2^{II}	Jung 12981/1956	R30C	200	B DH	
VL 3	LKM 253010/1960	V15	110	0-4-0 DH	Ex DB 311 009. *MOLLI*
VL 5	KHD 57452/1962	MS530C	430	C DH	Ex GME V 11
VT 50	Uer 72448/1966	798	2 x 110	A-A DMR	Ex HEG VT 54
VT 51	WMD 1297/1962	798	2 x 110	A-A DMR	Ex Pfalzhahn VT 61 ex DB 796 757
VT 52	MAN 146567/1961	798	2 x 110	A-A DMR	Ex EBM ex DB 796 785. To SBE
VT 53^I	Uer 66555/1959	798	2 x 110	A-A DMR	Ex 798 668. Sold to ZSLM (NL)
VT 53^{II}	MAN 145115/1960	798	2 x 110	A-A DMR	796 724
VT 54	Uer 66692/1960	798	2 x 110	A-A DMR	Ex 798 711 ex EF Betzdorf, ex DB.
VT 55	MAN 145112/1960	798	2 x 110	A-A DMR	Ex KVG VT 55
VT 56	WMD 1212/1956	798	2 x 110	A-A DMR	Ex DKB 202, ex DB 798 576. To SBE
VT 57	MAN 146590/1962	798	2 x 110	A-A DMR	Ex DKB 208, ex DB 798 808. To SBE
VT	Uer 62000/1956	798	2 x 110	A-A DMR	Ex BNB, ex EBG, ex StLB VT 22, ex DB 798 645

HOHENZOLLERISCHE LANDESBAHN AG   HzL
Hechingen, Baden Württemberg

Routes: Eyach–Hechingen–Gammertingen–Sigmaringen; Gammertingen–Kleinengstingen; Hanfertal–Sigmaringendorf. Also over the following DB lines Tübingen–Hechingen–Sigmaringen–Aulendorf; Ulm–Sigmaringen–Tuttlingen. (KBS 755, 766, 768).
Length: 107.4/114.7 (286.4 if DB tracks included).
Depots: Gammertingen, Haigerloch
EVU Licence: Freight and Passenger 24/02/1995.

The HzL is no newcomer to the scene being over 100 years old. It has quietly been going about its business in a lovely part of Germany catering for local traffic both freight and passenger. Open access and Regionalisation opened up further opportunities resulting in HzL getting the contract to provide the local services on the Tübingen to Sigmaringen line. DB still provides the faster services with trains running through from Stuttgart etc. HzL was one of the first railways to acquire the Reggio Shuttles in any large number hiring them from Rail Charter. VT 44/5 are similar units but numbered differently because they are subsidised by the Tuttlingen area for services from Sigmaringen to Tuttlingen. Freight traffic has held up well for HzL thanks to salt traffic from Stetten which HzL now works through to Ulm Rbf. rather than handing over to DB at Sigmaringen. 1997 trafic figures were 1.1 million journeys and 305,000 tonnes of freight. The freight figure is very similar to 1970's levels. In 2001 it reached 414,000 tonnes. Within the next few years HzL is to take over all the local freight trips from DB in the Tübingen, Horb, Rottweil etc. areas. No doubt the locomotive fleet will have to be increased.

HzL is now operating the Ringzug services which started in December 2003 for which another bach of RS1 units were acquired.

No.	Builder, No. & Year	Type	kW	Details	Comments
VT 4	MAN 145274/1960		2 x 141	A-A DHR	Spare
VT 5	MAN 145275/1960		2 x 141	A-A DHR	Spare
VT 6	MAN 146631/1962		2 x 141	A-A DHR	Spare
VT 7	MAN 146632/1962		2 x 141	A-A DHR	Spare
VT 8	MAN 145163/1961		2 x 141	A-A DHR	Spare
VT 9	MAN 151129/1966		2 x 141	A-A DHR	Spare
V 23	MaK 220052/1958	240B	176	B DH	Stored at Haigerloch
V 25	MaK 220018/1958	240B	176	B DH	Stored at Haigerloch
V 34	Gm 5651/1985	D25B	261	B DH	Stetten pilot
VT 41	WagU 36100/1993	NE 81	2 x 201	B-B DHR	
VT 42	WagU 36101/1993	NE 81	2 x 201	B-B DHR	
VT 43	WagU 36102/1993	NE 81	2 x 201	B-B DHR	
VT 44	Adtranz 36585/1997	RS1	2 x 257	B-B DHR	

VT 45	Adtranz 36586/1997	RS1	2 x 257	B-B DHR		
V 81	Essl 5212/1957		699	D DH	Stored at Haigerloch	
V 118	KM 19855/1978	M1200BB	860	B-B DH		
V 119	KM 19856/1978	M1200BB	860	B-B DH		
V 122	MaK 1000247/1964	G1300BB	936	B-B DH	Spare	
V 124	MaK 1000258/1964	G1300BB	936	B-B DH	Spare	
V 150	Gm 5649/1985	D1000BB	1135	B-B DH	Salt trains	
V 151	Gm 5650/1985	D1000BB	1135	B-B DH	Salt trains	
V 152	Gm 5701/1992	D1000BB	1135	B-B DH	Salt trains	
VT 200	Adtranz 36563/1996	RS1	2 x 257	B-B DHR		
VT 201	Adtranz 36564/1997	RS1	2 x 257	B-B DHR		
VT 202	Adtranz 36565/1997	RS1	2 x 257	B-B DHR		
VT 203	Adtranz 36566/1997	RS1	2 x 257	B-B DHR		
VT 204	Adtranz 36567/1997	RS1	2 x 257	B-B DHR		
VT 205	Adtranz 36568/1997	RS1	2 x 257	B-B DHR		
VT 206	Adtranz 36569/1997	RS1	2 x 257	B-B DHR		
VT 207	Adtranz 36570/1997	RS1	2 x 257	B-B DHR		
VT 208	Adtranz 36571/1997	RS1	2 x 257	B-B DHR		
VT 209	Adtranz 36572/1997	RS1	2 x 257	B-B DHR		
VT 210	Adtranz 36573/1997	RS1	2 x 257	B-B DHR		
VT 211	Adtranz 36574/1997	RS1	2 x 257	B-B DHR		
VT 212	Adtranz 36575/1997	RS1	2 x 257	B-B DHR		
VT 213	Adtranz 36576/1997	RS1	2 x 257	B-B DHR		
VT 214	Adtranz 36577/1997	RS1	2 x 257	B-B DHR		
VT 215	Adtranz 36578/1997	RS1	2 x 257	B-B DHR		
VT 216	Adtranz 36579/1997	RS1	2 x 257	B-B DHR		
VT 217	Adtranz 36580/1997	RS1	2 x 257	B-B DHR		
VT 218	Adtranz 36581/1997	RS1	2 x 257	B-B DHR		
VT 219	Adtranz 36582/1997	RS1	2 x 257	B-B DHR		
VT 220	Adtranz 36583/1997	RS1	2 x 257	B-B DHR		
VT 221	Adtranz 36584/1997	RS1	2 x 257	B-B DHR		
VT 231	Stadler 37163/2003	RS1	2 x 257	B-B DHR	Ringbahn	
VT 232	Stadler 37164/2003	RS1	2 x 257	B-B DHR	Ringbahn	
VT 233	Stadler 37165/2003	RS1	2 x 257	B-B DHR	Ringbahn	
VT 234	Stadler 37166/2003	RS1	2 x 257	B-B DHR	Ringbahn	
VT 235	Stadler 37167/2003	RS1	2 x 257	B-B DHR	Ringbahn	
VT 236	Stadler 37168/2003	RS1	2 x 257	B-B DHR	Ringbahn	
VT 237	Stadler 37169/2003	RS1	2 x 257	B-B DHR	Ringbahn	
VT 238	Stadler 37170/2003	RS1	2 x 257	B-B DHR	Ringbahn	
VT 239	Stadler 37171/2003	RS1	2 x 257	B-B DHR	Ringbahn	
VT 240	Stadler 37172/2003	RS1	2 x 257	B-B DHR	Ringbahn	
VT 241	Stadler 37173/2003	RS1	2 x 257	B-B DHR	Ringbahn	
VT 242	Stadler 37174/2003	RS1	2 x 257	B-B DHR	Ringbahn	
VT 243	Stadler 37175/2003	RS1	2 x 257	B-B DHR	Ringbahn	
VT 244	Stadler 37176/2003	RS1	2 x 257	B-B DHR	Ringbahn	
VT 245	Stadler 37177/2003	RS1	2 x 257	B-B DHR	Ringbahn	
VT 246	Stadler 37178/2003	RS1	2 x 257	B-B DHR	Ringbahn	
VT 247	Stadler 37179/2003	RS1	2 x 257	B-B DHR	Ringbahn	
VT 248	Stadler 37180/2003	RS1	2 x 257	B-B DHR	Ringbahn	
VT 249	Stadler 37181/2003	RS1	2 x 257	B-B DHR	Ringbahn	
VT 250	Stadler 37182/2003	RS1	2 x 257	B-B DHR	Ringbahn	

IGENO SCHIENENFAHRZEUG GmbH   IGENO

Niedersachswerfen, Thüringen

EVU Licence: Freight, 03/11/2001.

This firm started up by purchasing the wagon repairs shops at Niedersachswerfen near Nordhausen. This works was an outpost of RAW Leipzig. It then expanded into locomotive work and bought or leased the old DB depot in Nordhausen. An early contract was helping out Adtranz with repairs to hire locos. Expansion has seen it develop into a major base for Rail4Chem who in late 2002 were on the verge of signing a contract for all their locomotive and wagons to be maintained by IGENO. Not only that but Rail4Chem was to make Nordhausen a central planning and control centre for the westward chemical flows from Grosskorbetha.

IKEA RAIL AB   IKEA

Helsingborg, Sweden

Yes IKEA! This furniture firm is now running it's own trains in Europe. In 2001 IKEA formed Rail Transport Team to haul its trains in Europe. RTT comprises TGOJ in Sweden; Traxxion in Denmark (since bankrupt) and RAG (BuH) in Germany. A Monday–Friday train started between Älmhult (Sweden)–København–Hamburg–Duisburg on 27/6/02. A TGOJ class 66 works to Padborg from where a RAG 145/185 CL takes over. Duisburg will become an IKEA logistics centre with connecting trains to and from Poland and the Benelux countries. The timings of these first trains are inbound to Germany: Padborg 23.29 arriving Duisburg Ruhrort Hafen 08.02; Outbound: Duisburg Ruhrort Hafen 18.46 Münster Kanal 20.09, Osnabrück 20.53-21.15. (These timings may change with each timetable revision). Late in 2003 IKEA intimated that it was going to withdraw the service but it now looks as if RAG will keep it going and allow all comers to put traffic on the train.

ILMEBAHN AG   ILM

Einbeck, Niedersachsen

Routes: Einbeck Salzderhelden - Dassel
Length: 13.1/16.4 km   **Depots:** Einbeck Mitte
EVU Licence: Freight and Passenger 26/10/1995.

Until recently the Ilmebahn only had one loco. Its passenger traffic was lost to buses in 1975 but the line continued to operate freight traffic but as elsewhere it was a decreasing traffic. Open access has meant a bigger opportunity as the railway now does trip working over nearby DB lines as an agent for DB Cargo and in 2000 acquired another loco. 20,000 tonnes of freight forwarded in 1998 but only 12,000 tonnes in 2001.

No.	Builder, No. & Year	Type	kW	Details	Comments
V100 01	MaK1000315/1965	V100	992	B-B DH	Ex DB 212 268
V100.02	LEW 12766/1970	V100	883	B-B DH	Ex DB 202 302
V60.03	MaK 500004/1954	600		0-8-0 DH	

IMOTRANs GmbH   IMOTRANS

Berlin

This company is a subsidiary of the Prignitzer Eisenbahn (PEG, q.v.) and appears to have been founded in 1999 but never came to light until 2001 when locos started appearing in IMOTRANS livery. It appears to be a PEG leasing firm with the locos below mostly having first served with PEG. Locos are numbered in a common fleet list for PEG/IMOTRANS/Rail Cargo Berlin.

No.	Builder, No. & Year	Type	kW	Details	Comments
V60.01	LEW 15147/1976	V60D	478	0-8-0 DH	Ex PCK Schwedt V60-41
V60.06	LEW 10875/1964	V60D	478	0-8-0 DH	ExKraftwerk Grossräschen 14
V200.04	Lugansk 1703/1973	M62	1470	Co-Co DE	Ex CD 781 335 (781 482!!)
V200.06	Lugansk 1891/1973	M62	1470	Co-Co DE	Ex PKP ST44 281 Stored
V200.07	Lugansk 3518/1979	M62	1470	Co-Co DE	Ex PKP ST44 934 Stored
V200.08	Lugansk 2558/1976	M62	1470	Co-Co DE	Ex EBM V200 506 ex Wismut V200 507
V200.09	Lugansk 0683/1969	M62	1470	Co-Co DE	Ex EBM ex DR 120 281

INFRA LEUNA-INFRASTRUKTUR & SERVICE GmbH
INFRA LEUNA

Leuna, Sachsen Anhalt

Routes: Chemical and refinery works in Leuna and Grosskorbetha
Length: -/65 km   **Depots:** Leuna, Werk 1.
EVU Licence: Freight and Passenger 04/05/2000.

This organisation has developed from the shunting organisation of the Leuna chemical complex. Under privatisation it has extended into being a provider of Infrastructure services to the industries around Leuna, Grosskorbetha and Merseburg running ballast trains etc as well as tripping to DB exchange sidings. Traffic handled in 2001 was 6 million tonnes.

No.	Builder, No. & Year	Type	kW	Details	Comments
131	LEW 16581/1981	V 100.4	1030	B-B DH	Ex Adtranz 1996

132	LEW 16582/1981	V 100.4	836	B-B DH	Ex Adtranz 1998
133	LEW 16676/1981	V 100.4	836	B-B DH	Ex Adtranz 2000
134	LEW 16677/1981	V 100.4	1060	B-B DH	Ex Adtranz 1996
135	LEW 17850/1982	V 100.4	836	B-B DH	Ex Adtranz 1998
174	LEW 13751/1973	V60D	478	D DH	Ex Leuna
181	MaK 700108/1993	G765C	560	C DH	New
182	MaK 700109/1994	G765C	560	C DH	New
183	MaK 700114/1994	G765C	560	C DH	New
184	MaK 700115/1994	G765C	560	C DH	New
191	SKM 20450/2000	MH05		6w DH	
204	LKM 280163/1968	V180BB	2 x 736	B-B DH	Ex Leuna. Stored 1998
205	LKM 280164/1968	V180BB	2 x 736	B-B DH	Ex Leuna. Stored 1998
ASF 04	LEW 18888/1987	ASF	17	Bo BE	Ex Leuna
1001-131	VSFT1001131/2001	G1206	1500	B-B DH	On hire from VL

INSELBAHN LANGEOOG

INSELBAHN LANGEOOG

Niedersachsen

Gauge: 1000 mm **Length:** 3.0/4.3 km
Routes: Bhf. Langeoog-Hafen Langeoog **Depots:** Langeoog

This island railway is metre gauge and connects the pier head with the town. With only three km of track, the railway was modernised in the 1990's. Most of its surplus railcars were sold to the HSB. 838,500 passengers and 13,000 tonnes of freight handled in 1998.

No.	Builder, No. & Year	Type	kW	Details	Comments
Kö 1	Schöma 1738/1956	CFL90	88	B DM	
Kö 4	Schöma 2860/1965	CFL80DB	65	B DM	Since sold.
Lok 1	Schöma 5344/1994	CFL250DCL	198	B DH	
Lok 2	Schöma 5345/1994	CFL250DCL	198	B DH	
Lok 3	Schöma 5346/1994	CFL250DCL	198	B DH	
Lok 4	Schöma 5347/1994	CFL250DCL	198	B DH	
Lok 5	Schöma 5348/1994	CFL250DCL	198	B DH	

INTERCONNEX

INTERCONNEX

A brief mention must be made of the long distance services being operated by Connex under the InterConnex banner (IC!). OME Talent units suitably modified are used on a Gera to Rostock service. This has proved extremely popular and when seen in August 2002 at Rostock was formed of two units and both were full. A second InterConnex service was due to start 15.12.2002 using Lausitzbahn units from Zittau to Berlin (daily) and on to Stralsund Friday–Monday. Desiro units will be used on this service. A Ruhr–Heidelberg service has not got off the starting block as the pathways were very poor (despite the loss of many DB IC trains along the route). Connex started a daily Rostock–Berlin–Halle–Kassel–Giessen–Köln loco hauled service in the spring of 2003 but loadings were poor and the service was soon withdrawn.

INDUSTRIE TRANSPORT GESELLSCHAFT BRANDEN-
BURG Gmbh ITB

Brandenburg

Routes: Brandenburg steelworks
Length:
Depot: Brandenburg steelworks?
This company started off as the internal shunting provider at the Brandenburg steelworks. It has since acquired the status of an EVU and thus can now be found on works trains etc anywhere on DB.

No.	Builder, No. & Year	Type	kW	Details	Comments
625	LEW 15367/1976	V60D	478	0-8-0 DH	
628	LEW 16464/1980	V60D	478	0-8-0 DH	
629	LEW 17594/1981	V60D	478	0-8-0 DH	
630	LEW 17595/1981	V60D	478	0-8-0 DH	
1101	LEW 17317/1983	V100.5	1100	B-B DH	Ex WAB 14, ex DB 710 968
V60-1036	LKM 270036/1962	V60D	478	0-8-0 DH	Ex Magdeburger Hafen 6
?	LEW 14443/1974	V100		B-B DH	Ex WAB 15, EWU 14, DB 201 742

ITL-EISENBAHNGESELLSCHAFT mbH   ITL

Dresden, Sachsen

Routes: Nationwide but particularly in Sachsen
Length: No lines owned.
Depots: Kamenz (old DB depot); Dresden (Nossener brücke)
EVU Licence: Freight & Passenger 08/12/1998

A firm that was unheard of just a few years ago is growing at a terrific rate. ITL stands for Import Transport Logistik. Based in the former East Germany this company quickly saw the developing opportunities and has gathered in locos from various sources. It is principally a works train contractor but having the locos it can take on any job. The numbering system was once the class number followed by a number in the 9xxx series; this has since changed to that shown below. At the end of 2002 ITL purchased many of the Lokpool M62 most of which were numbered as WAB locos. These will gradually be renumbered into the ITL scheme as they are inspected and put into traffic.

ITL has now moved into the freight business after years of engineering contracts. Glass for recycling is moving from Usti nad Labem (CZ) via Rumburk and Ebersbach to a destination north of the Berlin area. Summer 2003 saw new trains being worked from Bernburg to Konigs Wusterhausen (cement clinker) and Pardubice (CZ) – Hamburg the latter flow coming via Ebersbach border crossing. Another new flow that started about this time was cement from Duisburg to Regensburg Hafen. EH works the traffic to Oberhausen West where ITL takes over.

No.	Builder, No. & Year	Type	kW	Details	Comments
102 001	LKM 262367/1972	V22	162	0-4-0 DH	Ex Elbekies GmbH (102 9300)
102 002	LKM 262466/1973	V22	162	0-4-0 DH	Ex Papierfabrik Greiz(102 9301)
102 003	LKM 262364/1972	V22	162	0-4-0 DH	Ex VEB Gummiwerke Watterhausen (102 9303)
102 004	LKM 261128/1962	V22	162	0-4-0 DH	Ex Materialwerke Schwepnitz
102 005	LKM 262490/1974	V22	162	0-4-0 DH	Ex Materialwerke Schwepnitz
103 001	KM 18365/1958	ML500C		C DH	Ex WL53 Hattingen. Scrapped '02
106 001	LEW 11020/1965	V60D	478	0-8-0 DH	DR 106 302 (106 9301)
106 002	LEW 10944/1964	V60D	478	0-8-0 DH	Ex BKK Bitterfeld (106 9302)
106 003	LEW 11319/1965	V60D	478	0-8-0 DH	Ex MaLoWa 3 (106 9303)
106 004	LEW 10943/1965	V60D	478	0-8-0 DH	Ex Sprotta 4 (106 9304)
106 005	LEW 16680/1979	V60D	478	0-8-0 DH	Ex Binnenhafen Mittel Elbe
106 006	LEW 16576/1979	V60D	478	0-8-0 DH	Ex Edelstahlwerke Freital (106 9305)
106 007	LEW 16970/1979	V60D	478	0-8-0 DH	Ex DREWAG 2 (106 9307)
106 008	LEW 14546/1975	V60D	478	0-8-0 DH	Ex DREWAG 1 (106 9308)
106 009	LEW 14822/1975	V60D	478	0-8-0 DH	Ex Torgau Hafenbahn 4
106 010	LEW 13810/1973	V60D	478	0-8-0 DH	Wacker Chemie, Nünchritz 2.
111 001	Deutz 57397/1962	V100	?	B-B DH	Ex DB 211 160 See Note (111 9300)
111 002	Deutz 57371/1962	V100	809	B-B DH	Ex Bothe, exCTTG 22 ex DB 211 134
118 001	LKM 275106/1965	V180	2 x 736	B-B DH	Ex RBG D05,DB 228 119
118 002	LKM 651052/1983	V180	2 x 736	B-B DH	Ex RBG D06,DB 228 552
118 003	LKM 275111/1965	V180	2 x 662	B-B DH	Ex BEM ex DB 228 124
118 004	LKM 651085/1983	V180	2 x 736	B-B DH	Ex IGE WB, DB 228 585
120 001	Lugansk 1906/1973	M62	1476	Co-Co DE	Ex PKP ST44 296
120 002	Lugansk 1152/1971	M62	1476	Co-Co DE	Ex PKP ST44 204
120 003	Lugansk 1478/1972	M62	1476	Co-Co DE	Ex PKP ST44 240
120 004	Lugansk 1145/1971	M62	1476	Co-Co DE	Ex PKP ST44 197
120 005	Lugansk 0837/1970	M62	1476	Co-Co DE	Ex PKP ST44 110
120 006	Lugansk 1666/1972	M62	1470	Co-Co DE	Ex Lokpool V200.10, ex EBGO, ex CD 781 540[II]ex CD 781 450
120 007	Lugansk 1198/1971	M62	1470	Co-Co DE	Ex Lokpool V200.06, ex CD 781 412[II] Ex 781 324
120 008	Lugansk 1666/1972	M62	1470	Co-Co DE	Ex Lokpool, ex EBGO, ex CD 781 448
120 009	Lugansk 1690/1972	M62	1470	Co-Co DE	Ex WAB 37, ex CD 781 450[II] ex 781 469
120 010	Lugansk 1708/1973	M62	1470	Co-Co DE	Ex WAB 38 ex CD 781 487
WAB 39	Lugansk 3388/1979	M62	1470	Co-Co DE	Ex CD 781 530[II] ex 781 557
WAB 40	Lugansk 3424/1979	M62	1470	Co-Co DE	Ex CD 781 505[II] ex781 566[II] ex 781 598
WAB 41	Lugansk 1532/1972	M62	1470	Co-Co DE	Ex CD 781 324[II] ex 781 355[II] ex 781 412
WAB 42	Lugansk 3376/1978/9	M62	1470	Co-Co DE	Ex CD 781 469[II] ex 781 550
WAB 43	Lugansk 1209/1971	M62	1470	Co-Co DE	Ex CD 781 482[II] ex 781 335

WAB 44	Lugansk 1550/1972	M62	1470	Co-Co DE	Ex CD 781 349[II] ex 781 430
WAB 45	Lugansk 1553/1972	M62	1470	Co-Co DE	Ex CD 781 540[II] ex 781 433
WAB 46	Lugansk 1705/1973	M62	1470	Co-Co DE	Ex CD 781 484
WAB 47	Lugansk 1722/1973	M62	1470	Co-Co DE	Ex CD 781 555[II] ex 781 501
WAB 48	Lugansk 1742/1973	M62	1470	Co-Co DE	Ex CD 781 580[II] ex 781 518
V200 501	Lugansk 1305/1971	M62	1470	Co-Co DE	Ex Lokpool, Ex Wismut V200 501
V200 509	Lugansk 0431/1968	M62	1470	Co-Co DE	Ex Lokpool, Ex Wismut V200 509[I]

Notes:

111 001 ex On Rail Moers, Ex Heitkamp, ex CTTG 25, ex DB.
The V100, V180 and probably the V120 all have Indusi, MESA 2002.
118 003, 004 and 120 001,002 identities may have been transposed.

As this book went to press a big change was underway. Most of the 120s and WAB M62s were being sold to Poland for use by private operators there. ITL will use the money earned to purchase or hire some "Blue Tiger" diesel locomotives from the Bombardier Lokpool which just happens to have some spare! The full ITL list is shown with the hope that it may help some readers in identifying locomotives seen in Germany in the last few years.

VERKEHRSBETRIEB ENDINGEN –KAISERSTUHLBAHN KB (SWEG)

Baden Württemberg

Routes: Breisach–Endingen–Riegel Ort–Riegel (KBS 723) 26.4 km; Gottenheim–Bahlingen–Riegel Ort–Endingen (KBS 724) 17.5 km.
Length: 43.9/48.0   **Depots:** Endingen.

Another SWEG line that has changed at the end of the 1990s from being in something of a 1960s time-warp into a very modern operation. The line in fact dates back to the 1890's but has changed hands many times with the SWEG acquiring it from the Mittelbadische Eisenbahn Gesellschaft in 1971. The depot and workshops have recently been completely rebuilt and expanded to deal with expanding business under regionalisation. The KB depot looks after the BSB units as well as its own.

No.	Builder, No. & Year	Type	kW	Details	Comments
VT 9	MAN 151436/1969	MAN 2 x 155		A-A DHR	Reserve
VT 28	MAN 151210/1966	MAN 2 x 110		A-A DHR	Reserve
V 103	Gm 5648/1985	D75BB	754	B-B DH	
V70 01	Gm 5117/1959	D65BB	515	B-B DH	
VT 126	WagU 33637/1981	NE 812 x 199		B-B DHR	
VT 127	WagU 33638/1985	NE 812 x 199		B-B DHR	
VT 501	Adtranz 36555/1996	RS1 2 x 257		B-B DHR	*ENDINGEN*
VT 502	Adtranz 36556/1996	RS1 2 x 257		B-B DHR	*EICHSTETTEN*
VT 503	Adtranz 36557/1997	RS1 2 x 257		B-B DHR	*BAHLINGEN*
VT 504	Adtranz 36558/1997	RS1 2 x 257		B-B DHR	*MÜNSTAL*
VT 505	Adtranz 36559/1997	RS1 2 x 257		B-B DHR	*BÖTZINGEN*
VT 506	Adtranz 36560/1997	RS1 2 x 257		B-B DHR	
VT 507	Adtranz 36561/1997	RS1 2 x 257		B-B DHR	*RIEGEL*
VT 508	Adtranz 36562/1997	RS1 2 x 257		B-B DHR	*NIMBURG*

KARSDORFER EISENBAHN GESELLSCHAFT mbH   KEG

Karsdorf, Sachsen Anhalt

Routes: Karsdorf cement factory sidings and connections (30 km.); sidings around Zeitz (6.0 km); Burgenlandbahn (q.v.) Weissenfels–Teuchern (KBS 551 15.7 km); Laucha–Lossa (19.9 km);
Length: 71.6 km
Depots: Karsdorf, Zeitz, Weissenfels, Rheine, Troglitz.   **Workshops:** Karsdorf, Schwerte.
EVU Licence: Freight and Passenger 19/11/1997.

The KEG owes its beginnings to being the shunting organisation at the Karsdorf cement works in the former East Germany. When unification took place KEG was formed as a private business with help from a West German organisation - the Mainischen Feldbahnen. This latter organisation is a locomotive dealer/ repairer in Schwerte located near the old DB depot and workshops. After being founded in 1993 KEG continued with freight work but then came regionalisation and the company via its loco dealing friends got hold of a lot of second hand diesel railcars and got started in the passenger business in 1995. Open access gave bigger opportunities for freight traffic and the loco fleet has mushroomed since then and KEG locos can now be found anywhere in Germany on spot freight flows or ballast train work. With DB not selling locos foreign locos were obtained such as Romanian class 60. These had DB type approval as they used to work into Frankfurt/Oder being similar locos to PKP ST43!

KEG has revised its numbering scheme with locos now numbered according to their power range in horsepower.

One of the main freight flows captured by KEG was the transport of aviation fuel from Lingen (Ems) to München Flughafen for which an operating base was set up at Rheine. These trains usually have two of the Romanian diesels working throughout. KEG also has under its wing for operational matters the Rügensche Kleinbahn and the Burgenlandbahn. (q.v.).

In 2002 KEG bought the Waggonbau Brunghaus workshops in Schwerte and will use them for the heavy overhaul of locos amongst other purposes.

In 2003 KEG seems to have acquired lots of new contracts and is now moving Shell Oil trains from Flörsheim to Würzburg as well as other flows on behalf of Total, Fina and Elf. Consequently more locos have had to be hired in including Dispolok electric locos. KEG is getting into big time and late in 2002 announced that it would take eight "Blue Tigers" from Bombardier which are due to be delivered July 2003 – March 2004. Meanwhile from February 2003 KEG is likely to hire four W232 locos from Bombardier. New shunting contracts have also been obtained and KEG locos can now be found on shunting duties at Hof, Nürnberg Hafen and Würzburg.

As this book was closing for press KEG was in financial difficulties and most freight activities were suspended. The BLB and RKB operations are not affected. The hire or purchase of "Blue Tigers" was cancelled in late 2003 due to late delivery (locomotives not passed by EBA). Instead KEG was to obtain more 060DA from Romania.

The old (first numbering scheme) KEG numbers are shown in the comments column.

No.	Builder, No. & Year	Type	kW	Details	Comments
0001	Bor 14551/1934	Köll	94	B DM	(622) Zeitz pilot
0091	LEW 20238/1988	ASF	17	Bo BE	Ex Raab-Karche, Chemnitz.
0092	LEW 17233/1981	ASF	17	Bo BE	Ex Raab-Karche, Chemnitz
0093	LEW 13383/1973	ASF	17	Bo BE	Ex Raab-Karche, Chemnitz
0101	Deutz 56833/1958	A8L614	75	B DH	Rheine pilot
0201	Hens 29981/1960	DH240B	176	B DH	(01?) Ex Stadt Düsseldorf 4
0202	Hens 29709/1959	DH240B	176	B DH	(013) Ex RAG 303
0203	Hens 29704/1958	DH240B	176	B DH	(014) Ex RAG 321
0204	Hens 29703/1958	DH240B	176	B DH	(016) Ex Alusuisse Singen 349
0401	Jung 13288/1961	R42C	324	C DH	(018) Ex SK 18
0402	Jung 13423/1962	R42C	324	C DH	(020) Ex SK 20
0403	Jung 13267/1961	R42C	324	C DH	Ex Rheinbraun Bergheim D1
0501	Hens 30264/1960	DH500C	368	C DH	(015). Ex Mineralöl Wedel
0551	Deutz 57803/1964	MG530C	390	C DH	(011) (511)Ex GET V3
0552	Deutz 57896/1965	MG530C	390	C DH	(017) (512) Kruppstahl Hagen
0601	LEW 16574/1979	V60D	478	0-8-0 DH	(019) Zementwerk Karsdorf 8
0602	LEW 18112/1983	V60D	478	0-8-0 DH	(002) Zementwerk Karsdorf 2
0603	LEW 16687/1979	V60D	478	0-8-0 DH	(003) Zementwerk Karsdorf 3
0604	LEW 13757/1973	V60D	478	0-8-0 DH	(022)
0605	LEW 15672/1979	V60D	478	0-8-0 DH	(005) Zementwerk Karsdorf 5
0607	LEW 15628/1977	V60D	478	0-8-0 DH	(007) Zementwerk Karsdorf 7
0608	LEW 17697/1982	V60D	478	0-8-0 DH	Ex DWA Bautzeen.
0609	LEW 10870/1964	V60D	478	0-8-0 DH	(009)
0615	LEW 13870/1974	V60D	478	0-8-0 DH	(615) Ex Hydrierwerk Zeitz 15
0616	LEW 13811/1973	V60D	478	0-8-0 DH	(616) Ex Hydrierwerk Zeitz 16
0617	LEW 14818/1975	V60D	478	0-8-0 DH	(617) Ex Hydrierwerk Zeitz 17
0618	LEW 15356/1976	V60D	478	0-8-0 DH	(618) Ex Hydrierwerk Zeitz 18
0619	LEW 15579/1977	V60D	478	0-8-0 DH	(619) Ex Hydrierwerk Zeitz 1
0620	LEW 15684/1979	V60D	478	0-8-0 DH	(620) Ex Hydrierwerk Zeitz 20
0651	MaK 600138/1957	V60C	478	0-6-0 DH	(021) Ex WL 4 Maxhütte
0652	MaK 600026/1956	V60C	478	0-6-0 DH	Ex Swiss ex DB 260 106
0701	CKD 5075/1961	T435	551	Bo-Bo DE	(001) T435 0554, Karsdorf 1
0702	CKD 5698/1962	T435	551	Bo-Bo DE	(012) DR 107 018 Karsdorf 12
0703	CKD 5099/1961	T435	551	Bo-Bo DE	(010) T435 0556 Karsdorf 10

0704	CKD 5684/1962	T435		551	Bo-Bo DE	(004) DR 107 004 Karsdorf 4
0751	CKD 6808/1965	T435		551	Bo-Bo DE	Ex Czech 721 513
0752	CKD 6810/1965	T435		551	Bo-Bo DE	Ex Czech 721 515
1001	LEW 17729/1983	V100.4		808	B-B DH	Ex Kaliwerk Merkers
1002	LEW 12504/1970	V100.1		808	B-B DH	Ex DB 201 222
1003	LEW 16328/1981	V100.1		808	B-B DH	Ex Czech 745 528
1004	LEW 17709/1982	V100.4		808	B-B DH	Ex Czech 745 709
1005	LEW 13937/1973	V100.1		808	B-B DH	Ex DB 201 619
1111	Deutz 57801/1964	DG1000BBM		808	B-B DH	(211) Ex GET V1
2001	LOB 280160/1968	V180CC	2 x 736		C-C DH	(201) Ex Leuna 201
2002	LOB 280106/1968	V180CC	2 x 736		C-C DH	(202) Ex DB 228 706
2003	LOB 280162/1968	V180CC	2 x 736		C-C DH	(203) Ex Leuna 203
2004	LOB 280113/1968	V180CC	2 x 736		C-C DH	(204) Ex Buna 204
2101	Crai 1501/1975	060DA		1545	Co-Co DE	CFR 60 1030
2102	Crai 1712/1976	060DA		1545	Co-Co DE	CFR 60 1068
2103	Crai 1745/1978	060DA		1545	Co-Co DE	CFR 60 1105
2104	Crai 1762/1978	060DA		1545	Co-Co DE	CFR 60 1152
2105	Crai 1389/1973	060DA		1545	Co-Co DE	CFR 60 0905
2106	Crai 1392/1973	060DA		1545	Co-Co DE	CFR 60 0909
2107	Crai 1457/1974	060DA		1545	Co-Co DE	CFR 60 0933
2108	Crai 1549/1974	060DA		1545	Co-Co DE	CFR 60 0995
2109	Crai 0929/1970	060DA		1545	Co-Co DE	CFR 60 0620
2110	Crai 0930/1970	060DA		1545	Co-Co DE	CFR 60 0627
2111	Crai 0937/1970	060DA		1545	Co-Co DE	CFR 60 0675
2112	Crai 0993/1971	060DA		1545	Co-Co DE	CFR 60 0686
2113	Crai 1003/1971	060DA		1545	Co-Co DE	CFR 60 0692
2114	Crai 1009/1971	060DA		1545	Co-Co DE	CFR 60 0619
2115	Crai 1696/1976	060DA		1545	Co-Co DE	CFR 60 0918
2116	Crai 1497/1974	060DA		1545	Co-Co DE	CFR 60 0979
2117	Crai 1565/1975	060DA		1545	Co-Co DE	CFR 60 1297
2118	Crai 2413/1992	060DA		1545	Co-Co DE	CFR 60 1373
2119	Crai 2414/1992	060DA		1545	Co-Co DE	CFR 60 1020
2120	Crai 2086/1980	060DA		1545	Co-Co DE	CFR 60 1024
2121	Crai 1691/1976	060DA		1545	Co-Co DE	Expected 2003/4
2122	Crai 2056/1980	060DA		1545	Co-Co DE	Expected 2003/4
2123	Crai 2055/1980	060DA		1545	Co-Co DE	Expected 2003/4
2124	Crai 1547/1974	060DA		1545	Co-Co DE	Expected 2003/4
2125	Crai 2090/1980	060DA		1545	Co-Co DE	Expected 2003/4
2126	Crai 1701/1976	060DA		1545	Co-Co DE	Expected 2003/4
7001	Crai ../1979	060EA		5100	Co-Co E	CFR 40 0079
VT2.01	MAN 143403/1957	MAN	2 x 110		A-A DMR	Ex AKN ex WNB T21
VT2.02	MAN 143553/1957	MAN	2 x 110		A-A DMR	Ex AKN ex WNB T22
VT2.10	MAN 142777/1956	MAN	2 x 110		A-A DMR	Ex AKN (DB 771 909)
VT2.13	MAN 148085/1963	MAN	2 x 110		A-A DMR	Ex AKN (DB 771 901)
VT2.14	MAN 148086/1963	MAN	2 x 110		A-A DMR	Ex AKN (DB 771 907)
VT2.15	MAN 148087/1963	MAN	2 x 110		A-A DMR	Ex AKN (DB 771 902)
VT2.16	MAN 148088/1963	MAN	2 x 110		A-A DMR	Ex AKN (DB 771 904)
VT2.17	MAN 148090/1963	MAN	2 x 110		A-A DMR	Ex AKN (DB 771 906)
VT2.18	MAN 148089/1963	MAN	2 x 110		A-A DMR	Ex AKN (DB 771 908)
VT2.19	MAN 148091/1963	MAN	2 x 110		A-A DMR	Ex AKN (DB 771 903)
VT2.20	MAN 148092/1963	MAN	2 x 110		A-A DMR	Ex AKN (DB 771 905)
VT 12	MAN 142776/1956	MAN	2x147		A-A DMR	Ex WEG VT 12

Notes:
The fleet of ex Romanian class 60 are fitted with Indusi, MESA 2002. Works numbers and building dates of 2115–2120 uncertain. Another batch is due to arrive in 2003/4

The VT2 railcars are all ex AKN and retain their AKN numbers but also have been allotted DB numbers in the order of which the railcars were refurbished by Mainische Feldbahn.

KREISBAHN MANSFELDER LAND GmbH   KML
Helbra, Sachsen Anhalt

Routes: Helbra–Klostermansfeld–Wippra (KBS 337, 19.9 km), and industrial sidings totalling about 30 km.
Length: 49.9 km.   **Depots:** Klostermansfeld.
EVU Licence: Freight and Passenger 24/11/1995.

The KML is similar to KEG in that it owes its roots to an industrial beginning. The KML grew out of the works railway for the Mansfeld copper works. With unification and the following privatisation of former state businesses the railway company was formed first as Mansfeld Transport GmbH (MTG) later becoming KML 1995. Besides shunting and tripping in the Mansfeld area the company has also taken on passenger work covering the service on the 19.9 km Klostermansfeld–Wippra line. Locomotives are maintained at the old works locomotive depot and repair shop which trades as MaLoWa (Mansfelder Lokomotiv- und Wagenwerkstatt). The workshops take on a lot of private overhaul work specialising in overhauling former DR types for the emerging private operators.

No.	Builder, No. & Year	Type	kW	Details	Comments
1	LKM 270161/1964	V60D	478	D DH	Ex MTG
2	LEW 11040/1965	V60D	478	D DH	Ex MTG
6	LEW 15620/1977	V60D	478	D DH	Ex MTG
7	LEW 13826/1973	V60D	478	D DH	Ex EHW Thale
8	LEW 16572/1979	V60D	478	D DH	Ex Kali Steinsalz Stassfurt
9	LEW 16681/1979	V60D	478	D DH	Ex Kali Steinsalz Stassfurt
13	LKM 262292/1971	V22	162	B DH	Ex MTG
16	LKM 262011/1967	V22	162	B DH	Ex MTG
18	LKM 262006/1967	V22	162	B DH	Ex MTG
19I	LKM 262012/1967	V22	162	B DH	Ex MTG
19II	LKM 262346/1970	V22	162	B DH	Ex Leichtmetallwerk.
VT 104	Essl 25628/1961	Esslingen	2 x 210	B-B DHR	Ex FKE VT 104
VT 110	Essl 23385/1951	Esslingen	2 x 221	B-2 DMR	Ex DEW ex SWEG
VT 403	Essl 23493/1952	Esslingen	2 x 154	1A-A1 DHR	Ex Nürtingen (WEG)
VT 405	Essl 24999/1958	Esslingen	2 x 169	B-B DHR	Ex Nürtingen (WEG)
VT 406	Essl 25000/1959	Esslingen	2 x 210	B-B DHR	ex ENAG/WEG/FKE
VT 407	Essl 25001/1959	Esslingen	2 x 210	B-B DHR	Ex WEG ex FKE
VT 408	Essl 25628/1961	Esslingen	2 x 210	B-B DHR	Ex WEG ex FKE

KASSEL–NAUMBURGER EISENBAHN AG   KNE
Kassel, Hessen

Routes: Kassel-Wilhelmshöhe–Naumburg (32.6 km); Baunatal–Stahl Center (1.2 km.); Wabern–Bad Wildungen (KBS 621, 17.2 km - DB Netz)
Length: 32.6/39 km.   **Depots:** Baunatal-Grossenritte.
EVU Licence: Freight and Passenger 26/10/1993.

This line is part of the Hessische Landesbahn (HLB) group. The KNE lost its passenger trains in 1977 but has been very busy since with freight work tripping freights from Kassel Rbf. to the VW works located on its line. Although it lost its own passenger trains, part of the line is in fact electrified and used by the Kassel tramway network (KVG) consequently KNE owns two of the trams but recently more have been ordered and are believed to be under KNE stewardship for use between Kassel and Hessisch Lichtenau. More recently with HLB winning passenger train contracts the KNE now looks after the railcars for the Kassel - Wabern - Bad Wildungen service. On certain weekends in the year passenger trains traverse the whole of the former KNE route under the "Hessen Kurier" vintage train operation. One of the KNE original steam locomotives has been de-plinthed and overhauled for these trains.

No.	Builder, No. & Year	Type	kW	Details	Comments
DG 201	Deutz 57877/1965	DG2000CCM	1470	CC DH	
DG 202	Deutz 56955/1959	DG2000CCM	1470	CC DH	
475	Duew 1994	NGT6C	2 x 180	B-2-B ETm	
476	Duew 1994	NGT6C	2 x 180	B-2-B ETm	
508 101	DWA 508001/1999	GTW2/6	514	2-Bo-2 DER	
508 102	DWA 508002/1999	GTW2/6	514	2-Bo-2 DER	
508 103	DWA 508003/1999	GTW2/6	514	2-Bo-2 DER	

KLÜTZER OSTSEE EISENBAHN KOE

Mecklenburg-Vorpommern

Routes: Klütz–Grevemühlen
Length: 15.3/16.0 km   **Depots:** Klütz

This railway runs a passenger service over a line closed by DR and is part of the EBG organisation. Consequently locos and stock come and go according to needs of the main company. It is thought that passenger operations are in fact only run in the summer tourist season between Klütz and Grevesmühlen and as such it is really only a museum railway but is registered as a proper company. Operations in 2004 are thought unlikely.

No.	Builder, No. & Year	Type	kW	Details	Comments
VT 1	WMD 1300/1960	796	2 x 110	A-A DMR	EBG 1 ex DB 796 760
VT 2	MAN 145131/1960	796	2 x 100	A-A DMR	EBG 2 ex DB 796 740
V 5	LKM 262396/1972	V22	162	0-4-0 DH	EBG 5

KOMBIVERKEHR DEUTSCHE GESELLSCHAFT FU KOBINIERTEN GUTERVERKEHR mbH FRANKFURT/ MAIN KOMBIVERKEHR

Frankfurt am Main, Hessen

In 2001 this company started running its own trains between München and Verona (Italy) as a joint operation with Bayerische Trailerzuggesellschaft (BTZ). Trains are worked by Lokomotion locomotives that are hired for the München–Brenner section whilst in Italy RTC is handling the traffic with locos built new for PKP but rejected by the Poles.

KAHLGRUND VERKEHRSGESELLSCHAFT mbH KVG

Schöllkrippen, Bayern

Routes: Schöllkrippen - Kahl am Main (KBS 642)
Length: 30.5/33.3 km.   **Depots:** Schöllkrippen
EVU Licence: Freight and Passenger 04/08/1995.

Although in Bayern this line is located just about as far away from München as you can get within the Land – it is closer to Frankfurt/Main. The line is owned by DB, the Bavarian State and the town of Aschaffenburg. Trains run through from Kahl to Hanau. Three NE 81 sets have been the staple power for some time but a new Regio Shuttle was acquired to assist with the trains running through to Hanau. Four VT 642 have been ordered for delivery as shown after which VT80/1 are expected to be sold. As the units are part financed by DB some DB numbers have also been allocated.

No.	Builder, No. & Year	Type	kW	Details	Comments
VT 80	WagU 30903/1981	NE81	2 x 199	B-B DHR	*Spessart*
VT 81	WagU 30904/1981	NE81	2 x 199	B-B DHR	*Kahltal*
VT 82	WagU 36099/1993	NE81	2 x 250	B-B DHR	
VT 97	Adtranz 36603/1997	RS1	2 x 228	B-B DHR	
VT 2000	Duew 92403/4/2000	VT642	2 x 275	B-2-B DHR	DB 642 151/651
VT 2002	Sie 92854/5 /2002	VT642	2 x 275	B-2-B DHR	DB 642 152/652
VT 2003	Sie 93301/2 /2003	VT642	2 x 275	B-2-B DHR	DB 642 153/653
VT 2004	Sie /2004	VT642	2 x 275	B-2-B DHR	DB 642 154/654

NEBENBAHN KORNTAL WEISSACH "STROHGÄUBAHN" KW (WEG)

Baden Württemberg

Routes: Korntal - Weissach (KBS 790.7, 22.3 km)
Length: 22.3/24.5 km
Depots: Weissach

This 22 km long branch line is not far from Stuttgart and has a certain amount of commuter traffic with some trains running through to Stuttgart-Feuerbach station to connect into the S-

Bahn. Some freight is handled and hauled by the railcars. Weissach has a major depot for handling all WEG group rolling stock.

WEG now has a contract to work container trains Neu Ulm–Mannheim with locos hired from Vossloh and normally kept at Weissach at weekends.

No.	Builder, No. & Year	Type	kW	Details	Comments
VT 410	WagU 30901/1981	NE81	2 x 191	B-B DHR	
VT 411	WagU 30902/1981	NE81	2 x 191	B-B DHR	
VT 412	WagU 36104/1993	NE81	2 x 201	B-B DHR	
VT 413	WagU 36105/1993	NE81	2 x 201	B-B DHR	
VT 414	Adtranz 36456/1996	RS1	2 x 228	B-B DHR	
VT 416	Adtranz 36458/1996	RS1	2 x 228	B-B DHR	
VT 420	WagU 36234/1994	NE81	2 x 201	B-B DHR	
V1001 033	VSFT 1001033/2001	G2000BB	2240	B-B DH	On hire
V1001 034	VSFT 1001034/2001	G2000BB	2240	B-B DH	On hire

LAUSITZ BAHN GmbH   LBG (CONNEX)

Görlitz, Sachsen

Routes: Zittau–Görlitz (KBS 231, 34 km); Görlitz–Cottbus (KBS 2290, 93 km)
Length: All DB Netz.   **Depots:** Old DB depot in Görlitz?
EVU Licence: Freight and Passenger 31/07/2002.

In 2002 Connex won the right to operate the loco train service from Zittau to Görlitz and Cottbus. The contract is for three years 12/02–12/05. Desiro units have been hired from Angel Trains. Connex also plans to run one through from Zittau to Berlin/Stralsund. (See Interconnex).

No.	Builder, No. & Year	Type	kW	Details	Comments
VT 610	Sie 93147/8/2002	VT 642	2 x 275	B-2-B DHR	Görlitz/Zgorzelec
VT 611	Sie 93149/50/2002	VT 642	2 x 275	B-2-B DHR	Zittau
VT 612	Sie 93151/2/2002	VT 642	2 x 275	B-2-B DHR	Weisswasser
VT 613	Sie 93153/4/2002	VT 642	2 x 275	B-2-B DHR	Landkreis Bautzen
VT 614	Sie 93155/6/2002	VT 642	2 x 275	B-2-B DHR	Cottbus
VT 615	Sie 93157/8/2002	VT 642	2 x 275	B-2-B DHR	Berlin
VT 616	Sie 93159/60/2002	VT 642	2 x 275	B-2-B DHR	Spremberg
VT 617	Sie 93161/2/2002	VT 642	2 x 275	B-2-B DHR	Vorpommern
VT 618	Sie 93145/6/2002	VT 642	2 x 275	B-2-B DHR	

LOGISTIK DIENSTLEITUNG UND SERVICE GmbH   LDS

Eutin, Schleswig Holstein

Another company set up to exploit open access operations – mostly engineering works trains

No.	Builder, No. & Year	Type	kW	Details	Comments
1	Adtranz 72510/2000	V100.4	1030	B-B DH	Ex WAB 12!. Grüner Rose
2	Adtranz 73250/1999	V100.4	1030	B-B DH	Ex Lokpool. Weiser Beer

LEIPZIGER EISENBAHNVERKEHRSGESELLSCHAFT mbH
LEG

Leipzig, Sachsen

Depot: ?
EVU Licence: Freight and Passenger 17/12/2001.

This organisation started out as ASP Schienenfahrzeugdienst GmbH & Co KG but was restructured and became LEG in 2003. ASP was set up to take advantage of track work contracts in the former DR areas no doubt using redundant railway staff! Locos were hired in as work was found but the 120 is thought to be owned by one of the founders. Indeed the ASP name comes from the founders: André and Sylthe Pietz. The organisation dates from 07/06/1999. Now it is believed many of the locomotives are in fact owned by the firm.

No.	Builder, No. & Year	Type	kW	Details	Comments
120 295	Lugansk 1007/1970	M62	1470	Co-Co DE	Ex DB
V200 505	Lugansk 1239/1971	M62	1470	Co-Co DE	Ex Lokpool V200 005, ex CD 781 365
V200 506	Lugansk 1841/1973	M62	1470	Co-Co DE	Ex Wismut 120 506[II] ex BKK Geistal

No.	Builder, No. & Year	Type	kW	Details	Comments
V200 507	Lugansk 1223/1971	M62	1470	Co-Co DE	Ex Lokpool V200 007 ex CD 781 430[II] ex 781 349
V200 009	Lugansk 1769/1973	M62	1470	Co-Co DE	Ex Lokpool ex CD 781 545
W232.05	Lugansk 0117/1967	231	2200	Co-Co DE	Ex DB 231 015
W232.07	Lugansk 0113/1967	231	2200	Co-Co DE	Ex DB 231 011
W232.08	Lugansk 0120/1967	231	2200	Co-Co DE	Ex DB 231 018
232 158	Lugansk 0303/1974	232	2200	Co-Co DE	Ex ZBH, ex DB
V60-02	LEW 12687/1970	V60D	478	0-8-0 DH	Ex Wismut WL 02
V60-10	LEW 15572/1977	V60D	478	0-8-0 DH	Ex Wismut WL 10

LOCON LOGISTIK & CONSULTING AG — LOCON

Seehausen, Brandenburg.

Established in 2002 this firm first got into trackwork and later became a freight EVU on 02/07/03. The first locomotives were obtained in late 2003.

No.	Builder, No. & Year	Type	kW	Details	Comments
101	LEW 15151/1976	V60D	478	0-8-0 DH	Ex BUG V60 BUG 03 ex DB 345 028
102	LEW 12233/1969	V60D	478	0-8-0 DH	Ex NVAG 346 005 ex RAW Halle WL 5
103	LEW 15598/1977	V60D	478	0-8-0 DH	Ex BUG V60 BUG 01 ex DB 345 067
301	LKM 280056/1967	V180	1420	C-C DH	Ex Adam V180 256 ex DB 228 656

LOKOMOTION GESELLSCHAFT FUR SCHIENENVERKEHR mbH — LOKOMOTION

München, Bayern

EVU Licence: Freight, 17/06/2001.

Lokomotion is the German EVU involved in running intermodal trains from München to Verona in Italy. The traffic is organised by Kombiverkehr and Bayerische Trailerzeug GmbH. Lokomotion works the trains to and from the Italian border station of Brenner/Brenero handing over there to locos belonging to Rail Traction Company of Bolzano. But just look at who owns Lokomotion: DB Cargo 30%; RTC 30%; Kombiverkehr 20% and and Italian firm STR 20%. No doubt the train drivers are DB Cargo!

Starting with one pair of container trains a day on 16/10/01 2 car trains were added 1/4/02 and later the same year two more car trains were added but these ran through to Brescia in Italy. Since then more trains have been added to the timetable. Locomotives are hired from Dispolok as required.

LOKPOOL VERWALTUNGSGESELLSCHAFT mbH & Co VERMIETUNGS KG — LVG

Kassel, Hessen

This is the name given to the Bombardier hire pool which was set up when the firm was Adtranz. The customer support facility at its Kassel plant (former Henschel works) snatched the opportunity offered by open access to form a hire fleet. Basically customers having a locomotive overhauled can hire a replacement from Bombardier; a customer setting up a new traffic flow or taking over from DB Cargo the operation of its own trains (e.g. BASF) can hire locomotives for specific periods. The hiring out of locomotives is becoming a big business which is also being picked up by preservation groups as a good source of income! Many former DR V100 types have been rebuilt by Bombardier to V100.4 standards (as many as 50 plus) with several getting new CAT 3512 engines. Bombardier is expected to build some "Blue Tigers" and more class 185s for the hire pool. The story is really just starting!.

Arrangements are in place for hire fleet locos to be serviced at Köln (on HGK), Augsburg (AL), Viechtach (RBG), Mosbach (Gmeinder), Neumark (Sachs, VBG), and the Bombardier plants at Kassel and Hennigsdorf.

In 2002 Bombardier decided on a change of policy and henceforth would only hire out its own products – newly built locos of class 185 and "Blue Tigers". All the non Bombardier/Adtranz products are to be sold. ITL bought a big batch of M62 type locos at the end of 2002. These have been deleted from the list.

No.	Builder, No. & Year	Type	kW	Details	Comments
109-4	LEW 9937/1963	109	2920	Bo-Bo E	Ex Schwerte,ex BKK, ex DR 109 026
109-5	LEW 9943/1963	109	2920	Bo-Bo E	Ex Schwerte,ex BKK, ex DR 109 032
109-28	LEW 9939/1963	109	2920	Bo-Bo E	Ex BSW Leipzig, ex DR. To WAB ?
128 001	Adtranz 25200/1994	128	6400	Bo-Bo E	Test loco for cl. 185.
145 CL 001	Adtranz 33356/1999	145	4200	Bo-Bo E	On hire to BASF then Rail4Chem
145 CL 002	Adtranz 33366/2000	145	4200	Bo-Bo E	On hire to BASF then Rail4Chem
145 CL 003	Adtranz 33815/2000	145	4200	Bo-Bo E	On hire to BASF then Rail4Chem
145 CL 004	Adtranz 33841/2000	145	4200	Bo-Bo E	On hire to BASF then Rail4Chem
145 CL 011	Adtranz 33386/2000	145	4200	Bo-Bo E	On hire to HGK 2001
145 CL 012	Adtranz 33821/2000	145	4200	Bo-Bo E	On hire to HGK 2002
145 CL 013	Adtranz 33826/2000	145	4200	Bo-Bo E	On hire to HGK 2003
145 CL 014	Adtranz 33828/2000	145	4200	Bo-Bo E	On hire to HGK 2004
145 CL 015	Adtranz 33842/2000	145	4200	Bo-Bo E	On hire to HGK 2005
201 049	LEW 11887/1968	201	736	B-B DH	Ex B. Falz ex DR. Now ?
201 056	LEW 11894/1968	201	1030	B-B DH	On hire to DE 1807
201 075	LEW 11913/1968	201	1030	B-B DH	Blue Cat
201 833	LEW 14897/1975	201	1030	B-B DH	Grashopper
13	Adtranz 72520/2000	V100DR ?		B-B DH	Returned ex EfW
228 104	LEW 275091/1965	228	1470	B-B DH	Ex EBG, stored Eisenach.
228 548	LKM 651048/1964	228	1470	C-C DH	Waiting overhaul. New CAT 3606
228 550	LKM 651050/1964	228	1470	C-C DH	Ex B. Falz. Waiting overhaul. Now for scrap?
231 070	Lugansk 0184/1973	231	2200	Co-Co DE	Ex EBG, stored Eisenach.
2TE109 001B	Lugansk 1969	232	2200	Co-Co DE	Ex Russia.
2TE109 002B	Lugansk	232		Co-Co DE	Ex Russia
TE 125 001	Lugansk 0037/1971		2200	Co-Co DE	Ex Russia. Stored Eisenach
TE 129 001	Lugansk 0293/1971	142	2940	Co-Co DE	Ex Russia. Stored Eisenach
250 001	Adtranz 33293/1996	250	2430	Co-Co DE	"Blue Tiger" on hire to MKB
250 002	Bomb 33831/2002	250	2430	Co-Co DE	(KNE)
250 005	Bomb 33834/2003	250	2430	Co-Co DE	(ITL)
250 006	Bomb 33835/2003	250	2430	Co-Co DE	(ITL)
250 007	Bomb 33836/2003	250	2430	Co-Co DE	(ITL)
250 008	Bomb 33837/2003	250	2430	Co-Co DE	(S&S)
250 009	Bomb 33838/2003	250	2430	Co-Co DE	
250 010	Bomb 33839/2003	250	2430	Co-Co DE	
250 011	Bomb 33840/2003	250	2430	Co-Co DE	
1001	LEW 15084/1975	V100.4	1030	B-B DH	Ex 201 812 Hired by BASF
1002	Adtranz 72030/1998	V100.4	1030	B-B DH	Hired by BASF
1003	Adtranz 70110/1999	V100.4	1030	B-B DH	Hired by BASF

Former DWA Hire Pool:

VT3.00	DWA 1998	LVT/S	265	A-1 DMR	On hire to City Bahn
504 001	DWA		265	A-1 DMR	
504 002	DWA		265	A-1 DMR	
504 003	DWA		265	A-1 DMR	
504 004	DWA		265	A-1 DMR	
504 005	DWA		265	A-1 DMR	
670 905					

Notes:

The following locos were acquired by Adtranz and so far have not been traced although some of them no doubt are in use with new owners but their original identities are not known or confirmed: 199 863/870/879 (acquired 1999).

LAPPWALDBAHN Gmbh   LWB

Weferlingen, Sachsen Anhalt

Routes: Helmstedt–Weferlingen–Haldensleben.
Length: ?   **Depots:** Oebisfelde (old DB depot)
EVU licence: Freight and Passenger, 03/11/1997.

This EVU has taken over the Haldensleben–Weferlingen line from DB and probably also the previously freight only section on to Helmstedt. The intention was to run a tourist passenger

94

service but with open access the opportunity to run ballast trains etc. has meant all year round work. It is not intended to stray too far from the home base so most work will be in Sachsen Anhalt or close by Niedersachsen. It has found work on its own behalf or even as a sub-contractor to recognised engineering firms such as Wiebe. Initially starting off as a preservation outfit it was based in Weferlingen sugar factory but has now moved to the old DB depot in Oebisfelde.

No.	Builder, No. & Year	Type	kW	Details	Comments
V60 100	LEW 14828/1975	V60D	478	0-8-0 DH	Ex Filmwerke Wolfen 12
V60 101	LEW 18122/1983	V60D	478	0-8-0 DH	Ex Orbitalplast D4
V60 102	LEW 14142/1974	V60D	478	0-8-0 DH	Ex DB 344 892. FFS.
V60 103	LEW 15674/1979	V60D	478	0-8-0 DH	Ex Kiesgrube Sprotta
V60 104	LEW 14889/1976	V60D	478	0-8-0 DH	Ex DB 345 050
V60 105	LEW 17411/1980	V60D	478	0-8-0 DH	Ex DB 345 104
V60 106	LEW 16570/1979	V60D	478	0-8-0 DH	Ex DB 345 095
V60 107	LEW 17582/1981	V60D	478	0-8-0 DH	Ex DB 345 137
V100 120	LEW 15383/1976	V100.2	809	B-B DH	Ex DB 201 865
V100 121	LEW 12772/1970	V100	809	B-B DH	Ex DB 201 308
V100 122	LEW 14421/1974	V100	809	B-B DH	Ex DB 202 720
311 505	LKM 261294/1963	311	120	0-4-0 Dx	Ex DB 311 505
323 225	KHD 57328/1960	Köf II	98	4w DH	Ex DB 323 225
346 165	LKM 270182/1964	V60D	478	0-8-0 DH	Ex DR 346 165
701 045	WMD 1463/1962	701	2 x 110	A-A DM	Ex DB 701 045
TVT 1	WMD 1511/1964	701	2 x 110	A-A DM	Ex DB 701 098

VERKEHRSBETRIEB MECKESHEIM–AGLASTERHAUSEN–HÜFFENHARDT MAH (SWEG)

Baden Württemberg

Routes: Meckesheim–Neckarbischofsheim Nord–Aglasterhausen (KBS 707, 19.1 km); Neckarbischofsheim Nord–Hüffenhardt (KBS 707 17.0 km)
Length: 36.1/39.0 km
Depots: Neckarbischofsheim Nord, Hüffenhardt.

This line in fact splits after Meckesheim at Neckarbischofsheim Nord to reach the terminals mentioned in its name of Aglasterhausen and Hüffenhardt. There is little freight apart from military traffic to and from Siegelsbach. The SWEG railcars haul the wagons or a loco may have to be hired in. The military base has its own loco.

No.	Builder, No. & Year	Type	kW	Details	Comments
VT 26	MAN 146643/1962		2 x 110	A-A DHR	
VT 112	Essl 25058/1958	Esslingen	2 x 162	B-B DHR	Location uncertain. Sold?
VT 120	WagU 30895/1981	NE 81	2 x 199	B-B DHR	
VT 121	WagU 30896/1981	NE 81	2 x 199	B-B DHR	
VT 122	WagU 30897/1981	NE 81	2 x 199	B-B DHR	

VERKERHSBETRIEBE MÖCKMÜHL DÖRZBACH "JAGSTALBAHN" MD (SWEG)

Baden Württemberg

This line is currently "sleeping" following storm damage some years ago. During 2000 some money became available and it is highly likely that trains will start running again from the Dörzbach end sometime in 2004. However this is not clear whether it will be as a private railway or a museum line.

Gauge : 750 mm
Routes: Möckmühl–Dörzbach
Length: 39.1 km
Depots: Dörzbach

No.	Builder, No. & Year	Type	kW	Details	Comments
V22-01	Gm 5413/1955	V12-16	132	B DH	
V22-02	Gm 5414/1955	V12-16	132	B DH	
V22-03	Jung 11770/1953	L10B	77	B DH	

| VT 300 | Wismar 21147/1941 | 96 1A-A1 DMR |
| VT 303 | Dessau 3085/1935 | 107 1A-A1 DMR |

MECKLENBURGERBAHN GmbH   MEBA

Schwerin, Mecklenburg-Vorpommern

Routes: Industrial lines in and around Schwerin; Schwerin Hbf.–Parchim (KBS 152, 45.5 km); Schwerin–Rehna (KBS 153, 33.9 km)
Length: 79.4/104.9 km   **Depots:** Schwerin
EVU Licence: Freight and Passenger 30/11/2000.

This company has developed from an industrial railway in Schwerin having three lines and two locos. 150,000 tonnes originated in 1998. Now expansion into the passenger business is on the horizon as SWS has been awarded the contract to run the local passenger trains on the following DB lines: KBS 152 Schwerin–Parchim; KBS 153 Rhena–Gadebusch–Schwerin, total 79.4 km. The contract started in 2001 and will last for seven years. Six LINT 41 railcars were ordered 11/99 for delivery from 04/01 with the service starting 10/6/01. They are based at Schwerin tram depot and the trains are expected to run over part of the tramway system as in Zwickau

No.	Builder, No. & Year	Type	kW	Details	Comments
VT 701	Als 2001	LINT 41	2x315	B-2-B DHR	
VT 702	Als 2001	LINT 41	2x315	B-2-B DHR	
VT 703	Als 2001	LINT 41	2x315	B-2-B DHR	
VT 704	Als 2001	LINT 41	2x315	B-2-B DHR	
VT 705	Als 2001	LINT 41	2x315	B-2-B DHR	
VT 706	Als 2001	LINT 41	2x315	B-2-B DHR	
VT 707	Als 2001	LINT 41	2x315	B-2-B DHR	Extra unit owned by Alstom.
?	LKM 270050/1962	V60D	478	0-8-0 DH	Ex DR 106 050, stored

MITTELDEUTSCHE EISENBAHN GESELLSCHAFT MEG

Schkopau, Sachsen Anhalt

Routes: Works complexes at Schkopau and Böhlen; Köthen–Aken and has nationwide operating licence.
Length: 110 km.   **Depot:** Schkopau
EVU Licence: Freight and Passenger 18/10/1999.

Previously the railway operation of Buna AG /Chemische Werke Buna AG, the Buna works was part of a large complex of chemical and petro-chemical plants in the Merseburg area. The privatisation of state concerns in the former East Germany saw the internal rail system being set up as an independent operation as a subsidiary of DB Cargo! Now MEG is taking advantage of open access by running its own trains over DB and having sold off some of its locos has had to obtain some more, fortunately DB had some of the same type to sell. Over one millions tonnes of freight handled each year.

The company is now owned by DB Cargo (80%) and Transpetrol GmbH (20%). MEG diesel locos are often used to work some Rail4Chem trains over non-electrified lines. MEG itself in 2002 was working cement trains from Rüdersdorf to Regensburg, Schkopau and Rostock Seehafen often using two cl. 228 in multiple. Later some class 232 were purchased from DB. During 2003 ten new G1206 locomotives were acquired from Vossloh to work the Wählitz – Schkopau coal shuttles. Regrettably two of these trains collided head-on during Christmas Day 2003 – two brand new locomotives severely damaged! Another surprise in 2003 was DB selling to MEG electric locomotives 156 001–004 which had been put in store by DB.

No.	Builder, No. & Year	Type	kW	Details	Comments
02	LEW 17801/1980	V60D	478	0-8-0 DH	Ex Regis-Breitingen
03	LEW 13755/1973	V60D	478	0-8-0 DH	Ex Bohlen 3
04	LEW 11010/1965	V60D	478	0-8-0 DH	Ex Bohlen 4
05	LEW 10765/1966	V60D	478	0-8-0 DH	Ex Bohlen 5
06[II]	LEW 14284/1974	V60D	478	0-8-0 DH	Ex DB 346 931
62	LEW 11008/1965	V60D	478	0-8-0 DH	Ex Buna.
63	LEW 14320/1974	V60D	478	0-8-0 DH	Ex DB 346 933
68	LEW 13750/1973	V60D	478	0-8-0 DH	Modernised
71	LEW 15197/1976	V60D	478	0-8-0 DH	Modernised
72	LEW 15352/1976	V60D	478	0-8-0 DH	Modernised
73	LEW 15363/1976	V60D	478	0-8-0 DH	Modernised

74	LEW 15581/1977	V60D	478	0-8-0	DH	Modernised
75	LEW 15607/1977	V60D	478	0-8-0	DH	Modernised
76	LEW 16537/1979	V60D	478	0-8-0	DH	Modernised
77	LEW 16682/1979	V60D	478	0-8-0	DH	Modernised
78	LEW 15671/1979	V60D	478	0-8-0	DH	Modernised
80	LEW 12647/1970	V60D	478	0-8-0	DH	Ex DB 346 674
81	LEW 12667/1970	V60D	478	0-8-0	DH	Ex DB 346 692
82	LEW 12988/1971	V60D	478	0-8-0	DH	Ex DB 346 727
83	LEW 14544/1975	V60D	478	0-8-0	DH	Ex DB 346 942
84	LEW 15603/1977	V60D	478	0-8-0	DH	Ex DB 345 072
85	LEW 17578/1981	V60D	478	0-8-0	DH	Ex DB 345 133
86	LEW 17678/1982	V60D	478	0-8-0	DH	Ex DB 345 152
101	LEW 12867/1971	V100DR	889	B-B	DH	Ex DB 204 358
201	LKM 280110/1968	V180	2 x 736	C-C	DH	Ex Buna 201
202	LKM 280111/1968	V180	2 x 736	C-C	DH	Ex Buna 202
203	LKM 280112/1968	V180	2 x 736	C-C	DH	Ex Buna 203
205	LKM 280197/1969	V180	2 x 883	C-C	DH	Ex DB 228 788
206	LKM 280152/1968	V180	2 x 883	C-C	DH	Ex DB 228 748
207	LKM 280200/1969	V180	2 x 883	C-C	DH	Ex DB 228 791
208	LKM 280195/1969	V180	2 x 883	C-C	DH	Ex DB 228 786
228 700	LKM 280100/1968	V180	2 x 883	C-C	DH	Ex DB for spares
210	VL 5001465/2003	G 1206	1500	B-B	DH	
211	VL 5001466/2003	G 1206	1500	B-B	DH	Damaged 25/12/03.
212	VL 5001467/2003	G 1206	1500	B-B	DH	
213	VL 5001468/2003	G 1206	1500	B-B	DH	
214	VL 5001469/2003	G 1206	1500	B-B	DH	Damaged 25/12/03. Subsequently wdn.
215	VL 5001470/2003	G 1206	1500	B-B	DH	
216	VL 5001471/2003	G 1206	1500	B-B	DH	
217	VL 5001472/2003	G 1206	1500	B-B	DH	
218	VL 5001473/2003	G 1206	1500	B-B	DH	
219	VL 5001474/2003	G 1206	1500	B-B	DH	
220	VL 5001500/2004	G 1206	1500	B-B	DH	Ordered as replacement for 214
301	Krupp 5656/1992	229	2 x 1240	B-B	DH	Ex DB 229 120
302	Krupp 5663/1992	229	2 x 1240	B-B	DH	Ex DB 229 174
303	VSFT 1001035/2001	G2000	2240	B-B	DH	On hire from LSG.
Spares?	Krupp 5666/1992	229	2 x 1240	B-B	DH	Ex DB 229 184
Spares?	Krupp 5670/1992	229	2 x 1240	B-B	DH	Ex DB 229 199
310	Lugansk 0319/1974	232	2240	Co-Co	DE	Ex DB 232 104 mu fitted.
311	Lugansk 0627/1976	232	2240	Co-Co	DE	Ex DB 232 393 mu fitted
312	Lugansk 0689/1976	232	2240	Co-Co	DE	Ex DB 232 454 mu fitted
801	LEW 20004/1991	156	5580	Co-Co	E	Ex DB 156 001
802	LEW 20005/1991	156	5580	Co-Co	E	Ex DB 156 002
803	LEW 20006/1991	156	5580	Co-Co	E	Ex DB 156 003
804	LEW 20996/1991	156	5580	Co-Co	E	Ex DB 156 004

Notes: 71 last reported out-based at Rüdersdorf (Berlin) whilst 101 used on Bohlen-Trebsen trips.
204 sold to KEG. There are more V60D but these are thought to be internal shunters at the Schkopau and Böhlen plants of Buna. 68 – 79 were modernised by Adtranz and now have CAT 3412DITA engines, FFS and AK. 201 –203 have Indusi and ZBF.

VERKEHRSBETRIEB SCHWARZACH   MEN (SWEG)
Baden Württemberg

Routes: Bühl–Schwarzach–Stollhofen–Greffern/Söllingen
Length: 14.9 km
Depots: Schwarzach (Baden).

The initials are from a previous age when this line was part of a metre gauge network of the Mittelbadischen Eisenbahn and unlike most SWEG lines this one is freight only. Heavy freight traffic is handled as the line receives trainloads of chemicals mostly in tank wagons. Indeed it isthought that these trains originate in Ludwigshafen at the BASF plant and are now hauled by BASF locos to Bühl. Schwarzach is the principal centre and is a major SWEG maintenance centre for all its rolling stock.

No.	Builder, No. & Year	Type	kW	Details	Comments
V23 01	Gm 5491/1973	D25B	199	B DH	
V 102	Gm 5647/1985	D75BB	754	B-B DH	

METRONOM EISENBAHNGESELLSCHAFT mbH
METRONOM

Uelzen, Niedersachsen

Routes: Uelzen–Hamburg and Bremen–Hamburg
Length: (DB Netz) **Depot:** Uelzen.
EVU Licence: Passenger, 22/08/2002.

Metronom started off as Metrorail but was renamed before services started. It is a newly formed company set up to operate the Regio Express passenger services between Hamburg and Bremen/Uelzen. Metronom is a consortium comprising BSAG (5%); EVB (30%); HHA (25.1%) and OHE (39.9%). 10 class 146 were ordered and 66 double-deck carriages. A new depot has been built in Uelzen on a branch off the closed Uelzen–Danneburg line. The contract started in December 2003 for seven years.

No.	Builder, No. & Year	Type	kW	Details	Name
ME146-01	Bomb 33946/2003	146	4200	Bo-Bo E	Scheessel
ME146-02	Bomb 33953/2003	146	4200	Bo-Bo E	Lüneburg
ME146-03	Bomb 33954/2003	146	4200	Bo-Bo E	Bad Bevensen
ME146-04	Bomb 33955/2003	146	4200	Bo-Bo E	Buchholz in der Nordheide
ME146-05	Bomb 33956/2003	146	4200	Bo-Bo E	Rotenburg (Wumme)
ME146-06	Bomb 33957/2003	146	4200	Bo-Bo E	Winsen (Luhe)
ME146-07	Bomb 33958/2003	146	4200	Bo-Bo E	Lauenbrück
ME146-08	Bomb 33959/2003	146	4200	Bo-Bo E	Uelzen
ME146-09	Bomb 33960/2003	146	4200	Bo-Bo E	Tostedt
ME146-10	Bomb 33961/2003	146	4200	Bo-Bo E	Bienenbüttel

MAGDEBURGER HAFEN Gmbh MHG

Magdeburg, Sachsen Anhalt.

This is a new firm for 2003. No main line work as yet but obviously with a main line loco acquired they must have some intentions!

No.	Builder, No. & Year	Type	kW	Details	Comments
1	LEW 11212/1967	201	736	B-B DH	Rebuilt 1997. Ex Lokpool, Ex DR 201 004

MINDENER KREISBAHN Gmbh MKB

Nordrhein-Westfalen

Routes: Minden–Aminghausen(2.0 km); Minden–Hille–Hille Hafen Süd (15.2 km); Minden–Kleinenbremen (11.7 km); Minden–Todtenhausen (8.7 km) and sidings in Minden to Abstiegshafen (1.3 km); Osthafen (2.5 km); Westhafen (1.0 km).
Length: 45.5/59 km. **Depots:** Minden
EVU Licence: Freight and Passenger 18/06/1996

The MKB has been freight only since 1974 but passenger trains run on certain weekends by the Museums Eisenbahn Minden organisation often with steam traction. The MKB is also into the tourist market and uses a second hand railcar to take tourists to a mining museum in Kleinenbremen. The line has quite good freight traffic with coal being imported via the canal harbour at Hille or Minden which the MKB takes on to power stations in the area such as the one at Veltheim with MKB working over DB. At weekends from spring 2001 V6 has been working a rubbish train from Oldenzaal to Spreewitz and return.

In 2002 MKB obtained some contracts to move coal from Nordenham to the power station at Veltheim and had to hire in larger locos. It has also been successful with another contract to move chemicals from Hamburg and even more powerful locos are to be obtained. During the 2002 "INNOTRANS" exhibition in Berlin it was announced that MKB was to buy a "Blue Tiger" diesel loco from Bombardier and subsequently another announcement was made to the effect that a VSFT G1700 will be acquired.

No.	Builder, No. & Year	Type	kW	Details	Comments
V 4	Mak 1000805/1985	G1203BB	745	B-B DH	Sold 2003 to RCN
V 5	Mak 1000852/1991	G1203BB	745	B-B DH	
V 6	On Rail D1504/1/1999	D1504	1480	B-B DH	Rebuilt ex DB 216 014
V 19	VSFT 1001209/2003	G1700	1700	B-B DH	
V 20	Bomb 33833/2003	Blue Tiger	2430	Co-Co DE	
VT 01	Dessau 3184/1937	VT135	132	A-1 DMR	Ex Regentalbahn VT 12

MECKLENBURGISCHE BÄDERBAHN MOLLI Gmbh & Co MOLLI

Bad Doberan, Mecklenburg-Vorpommern

Gauge: 900 mm
Routes: Bad Doberan - Ostseebad Kühlungsborn West (KBS 157, 15.8 km)
Length: 15.8 km.   **Depot:** Ostseebad Kühlungsborn West
EVU Licence: Freight and Passenger 28/09/1995.

This former DR, later DB, narrow gauge line is unusual not only for running through the streets of Bad Doberan but also for its gauge - 900 mm. An early candidate of privatisation the line was not seen as part of DB and thus reverted to private ownership in 1995. As the name suggests it serves the beach resorts and is thus primarily a summer tourist line but does offer all year round services for the few commuters. Freight traffic ceased in 1969. Some diesel locomotives are now located on the line but these are understood to belong to an enthusiast supporters group.

No.	Builder, No. & Year	Type	kW	Details	Comments
99 2321-0	O&K 12400/1932			2-8-2T	
99 2322-8	O&K 12401/1932			2-8-2T	
~~99 2323-6~~	~~O&K 12402/1932~~			~~2-8-2T~~	
99 2331-9	LKM 30011/1951			0-8-0T	
99 2332-7	LKM 30013/1951			0-8-0T	Plinthed at Kühlungsborn

VERKEHRSBETRIEB STAUFEN (MÜNSTERTALBAHN) MT (SWEG)

Baden Württemberg

Routes: Bad Krozingen-Staufen-Münstertal (KBS 725, 11 km) (Staufen–Staufen Grunern out of use).
Length: 11 km
Depots: Staufen

Another little SWEG line with passenger trains feeding into the main line. What little freight traffic generated is handled by DB. Since the start of OSB services around Offenburg (q.v.), trains on this line now use OSB units.

MULDENTAL EISENBAHNVERKEHRSGESELLSCHAFT Mbh MTEG

Meerane, Sachsen

Depot: Glauchau (?)
EVU Licence: Freight and Passenger 19/01/2001.

This organisation appears to have started off as the operating arm of IG Traditionslok 58 3047 at Glauchau and is a fully-fledged EVU. Besides the preserved locomotives at Glauchau it has now acquired some diesel locomotives for track work and provides drivers for any other company that needs help.

No.	Builder, No. & Year	Type	kW	Details	Comments
345 061	LEW 15592/1977	V60D	478	0-8-0 DH	Ex Private, ex DB 345 061
346 756[II]	LEW 13787/1973	V60D	478	0-8-0 DH	Ex ESTEG 19
?	LEW 13349/1972	V60D	478	0-8-0 DH	Ex ESTEG 17
293 022	LEW 16584/1981	V100		B-B DH	Ex SWT 22
293 023	LEW 17849/1982	V100		B-B DH	Ex SWT 23

MITTELWESERBAHN GESELLSCHAFT für VERKEHR und TECHNIK mbH   MWB

Bruchhausen Vilsen, Niedersachsen

Routes: Nationwide.   **Depots:** Bruchhausen Vilsen.
EVU Licence: Freight and Passenger 18/10/1999.

This is quite a new operation. The German preservation society Deutsche Eisenbahn Verein DEV has a narrow gauge line at Bruchhausen Vilsen but also had a standard gauge operation from Hoya. To fall in line with current legislation it has formed itself into a proper operating company as an EVU. It is growing fast and has its main depot on the Hoya - Bruchhausen Vilsen line but also operates from Leeste on the BTE and Liebenau. It has transferred its "preserved" shunting engines into the new operating fleet and acquired locos from elsewhere including some newly overhauled V100's. V 246–249 were acquired late in 2000. 2001 was acquired from Hoyer. MWB locos can turn up anywhere on engineering trains or on hire to other users.

No.	Builder, No. & Year	Type	kW	Details	Comments
V 121	Gm 4887/1956	Köf II	97	4w DH	Ex DEV V127, DB 323 575
V 241	Gm 5121/1960	Köf III	176	4w DH	Ex DEV V241, DB 332 002
V 242[II]	Jung 13778/1964	Köf III	176	4w DH	Ex DB 332 165
V 243	O&K 26404/1965	Köf III	176	4w DH	Ex DB 332 289
V 244	O&K 26303/1962	Köf III	176	4w DH	Ex DB 332 008
V 246	Jung 13572/1963	Köf III	176	4w DH	Ex DB 332 030
V 247	O&K 26353/1964	Köf III	176	4w DH	Ex DB 332 115
V 248	Gm 5291/1963	Köf III	176	4w DH	Ex DB 332 050
V 249	O&K 26328/1963	Köf III	176	4w DH	Ex DB 332 090
V 250	Jung 13782/1964	Köf III	176	4w DH	Ex DB 332 169
V 251	Gm 5532/1977	Köf III	176	4w DH	Ex DB 333 245
V 601	SFT 220120/1996	G322	390	4w DH	Ex DSB 601. FFS
V 641	LEW 18002/1982	V60D	478	0-8-0 DH	Ex Werklok Skoda (CZ)
V 642	LEW 17421/1981	V60D	478	0-8-0 DH	Ex IND via ZOS Nymburk Sold to RAR
V 643	LEW 17639/1982	V60D	478	0-8-0 DH	Ex VNS Cekanice 716 530. Sold to RAR
V 661	Hens 30038/1959	V60C	478	0-6-0 DH	Ex Swiss, ex DB 260 749
V 662	Krp 3978/1960	V60C	478	0-6-0 DH	Ex DB 360 555
V 663	Krp 3995/1960	V60C	478	0-6-0 DH	Ex DB 360 572
V 664	Krp 4031/1960	V60C	478	0-6-0 DH	Ex DB 360 608
V 1101	KM 18893/1962	V100	940	B-B DH	Ex ÖBB 2048 001, DB 211 297 Sold 2002 to SLB V83 (A).
V 1201	LEW 14454/1974	V100DR	736	B-B DH	Ex DB 202 753
V 1202	LEW 14426/1974	V100DR	736	B-B DH	Ex DB 202 725
V 1203	LEW 13948/1973	V100DR	736	B-B DH	Ex DB 202 630
V 1204	LEW 15094/1975	V100.4	883	B-B DH	Ex DB 202 822. Sold to RAR 7/03.
V 1251	MaK 1000294/1965	V100	992?	B-B DH	Ex DB 212 247. FFS, CAT engine, GSM-R.
V 1351	MaK 1000386/1966	V100	940	B-B DH	Ex DB 213 339
V 1352	MaK 1000381/1966	V100	940	B-B DH	Ex DB 213 334. Sold 2003 to TRB.
V 1353	MaK 1000385/1966	V100	992?	B-B DH	Ex ALS, ex DB 213 338. CAT engine.
V 1354	MaK 1000388/1966	V100	992?	B-B DH	Ex ALS, ex DB 213 341
V 2001	Lugansk 3553/2979	M62	1470	Co-Co DE	Ex Hoyer 220.01. Ex-Poland PMP M62-08. Sold back to Poland!
V 2301	VSFT 1001210/2003	G1700	1700	B-B DH	CAT 3512 engine, FFS.
V 2302	VSFT 1001211/2003	G1700	1700	B-B DH	CAT 3512 engine. FFS.
V 2303	VSFT 5001488/2004	G1700	1700	B-B DH	Due 2004.
1020 034	AEG 5720/1943	E94	3000	Co-Co E	Ex ESG, ex ÖBB, ex DRG E94 095. Spare parts.
1020 041	AEG 5728/1953	E94	3000	Co-Co E	Ex ESG, ex ÖBB, ex DRG E94 103. To be Laufach banker.
1116 911	Sie 20852/2003	1116	6400	Co-Co E	ex ÖBB 1116 131[I].

NORDSEEBAHN   NB

Routes: Bremerhaven–Cuxhaven
Length: **Depot:** Bremervoerde.
EVU Licence:

This company started to work trains between Bremerhaven and Cuxhaven from December 2003. The company has been set up by DB Regio and EVB. An hourly train service will run on Monday–Friday with two-hourly intervals at weekends. Some trains will run through to Bremen. EVB staff will work the trains and a new maintenance hall will be built at the EVB depot at Bremervoerde to service the trains.

No.	Builder, No. & Year	Type	kW	Details	Comments
VT 101	Als /2003	LINT 41	2 x 315	B-2-B DH	LNVG Pool
VT 102	Als /2003	LINT 41	2 x 315	B-2-B DH	LNVG Pool
VT 103	Als /2003	LINT 41	2 x 315	B-2-B DH	LNVG Pool
VT 104	Als /2003	LINT 41	2 x 315	B-2-B DH	LNVG Pool
VT 105	Als /2003	LINT 41	2 x 315	B-2-B DH	LNVG Pool
VT 106	Als /2003	LINT 41	2 x 315	B-2-B DH	LNVG Pool
VT 107	Als /2003	LINT 41	2 x 315	B-2-B DH	LNVG Pool
VT 108	Als /2003	LINT 41	2 x 315	B-2-B DH	LNVG Pool
VT 109	Als /2003	LINT 41	2 x 315	B-2-B DH	LNVG Pool

NORDBAHN EISENBAHN GESELLSCHAFT mbH   NBE

Kaltenkirchen, Schleswig Holstein

Routes: KBS 142, Bad Segeberg–Bad Oldesloe–Neumünster.
Length: **Depot:** New depot to be built at Neumünster Süd.
EVU Licence: Passenger, 10/12/2002.

Founded in 2002 this firm is a joint venture between HHA 50% and AKN 50% having won the passenger contract for services on KBS 142 which were expected to start in December 2002. Units are numbered in the AKN scheme which company also has a spare set for NBE

No.	Builder, No. & Year	Type	kW	Details	Comments
VT 2.71	Alstom 2001	LINT 41	2 x 315	B-2-B DH	AKN Owned.
VT 2.72	Alstom 2001	LINT 41	2 x 315	B-2-B DH	AKN Owned. *DITHMARSCHEN*
VT 2.73	Alstom 2001	LINT 41	2 x 315	B-2-B DH	AKN Owned.
VT 2.74	Alstom 2001	LINT 41	2 x 315	B-2-B DH	AKN Owned. *SEGEBERG*
VT 2.75	Alstom 2001	LINT 41	2 x 315	B-2-B DH	HHA Owned.

STADTISCHEN HAFENBETRIEBE NEUSS–NEUSSER EISENBAHN   NE

Neuss, Nordrhein Westfalen

Routes: Various lines in and around Neuss including the harbour lines.
Length: Circa 20 km of tracks.   **Depots:** Neuss (Heerdterbuschstrasse)
EVU Licence: Freight, 03/08/1995.

The principal work of this railway is as its title suggests servicing the Neuss harbour lines. The branch is 19.6 km long but has over 52 km of tracks and many customers. The locos also work some trips on to DB lines in the area. Traffic handled in 1997 was 2.4 million tonnes.

No.	Builder, No. & Year	Type	kW	Details	Comments
I	KM 19815/1975	M700C	515	C DH	
II	MaK 700025/1978	G761C	470	C DH	
III	MaK 700061/1982	G761C	500	C DH	
IV	MaK 500057/1973	G700C	515	C DH	
V	MaK 1000244/1965	G1300BB	956	B-B DH	Ex OHJ Denmark
VI	MaK 1000890/1993	G1205BB	1120	B-B DH	
VII	MaK 1000906/1997	G1205BB	1120	B-B DH	
VIII	VSFT 1001113/2001	G1700BB	1500	B-B DH	
IX (9)	VSFT 1001040/2002	G2000BB	2240	B-B DH	(Loco carries"9")
11	Wind 260081/1991	RW110DH		B-B DH	Teletrac
12	Wind 260084/1991	RW90DH		B-B DH	Teletrac
14	Wind 260108/1994	RW60DH		B-B DH	Teletrac
15	Zephir 2001			4w DH	Lokotractor

NIEDERBARNIMER EISENBAHN AG NEB

Berlin/Brandenburg

Routes: Berlin-Wilhelmsruh–Basdorf–Gross Schönebech/Liebewalde and several industrial branches.
Length: 74.5 km.   **Depots:** Basdorf
EVU Licence: Freght and Passenger 24/11/2000

Anyone that went to Basdorf in DR days would have been surprised at the large shed there. The answer is simple as Basdorf was the operating centre of a once private railway that was nationalised in communist days. Now with reunification the line and its various branches have reverted to private ownership. The current situation is somewhat vague. The NEB will obviously take over the lines that have been running under DR/DB operation. But the line from Basdorf to Berlin Wilhelmsruh has been freight only for years; there is talk of it reopening to passengers. The NEB has taken back its old depot (which had become a museum as part of the Falz collection which has now moved on to Jüterbog) but the Berliner Eisenbahnfreunde are still here and will probably stay as it is a much smaller set up.

No.	Builder, No. & Year	Type	kWDetails	Comments
20	LEW 12834/1971	V100DR	736B-B DH	Ex DB 202 325
21	LEW 12897/1972	V100DR	736B-B DH	Ex DB 202 388

NB: Locos to Connex Cargo in 2002. 20 to be overhauled at the TWE depot on behalf of Bombardier; 21 to be overhauled by Bombardier at Kassel.

NEUTRAL CONTAINER SHUTTLE SERVICE NECOSS

Bremen

Necoss is a joint venture between Connex, EVB and Bremen freight forwarder ACOS (All Round Container service Helmut Frank GmbH). Trains started running from Bremerhaven, Bremen and Hamburg to southern Germany. EVB assembles the train at Bremen Grolland and a Connex 185 takes it south to Friedberg where it splits for Schweinfurt/Nürnberg and Kornwestheim with the parts being taken forward by BCB and WEG. Other connections are made into other private operations at Mannheim. The Connex operation is under its Nord West Cargo umbrella. On 6.6.2002 a Bremen–Bitterfeld service was started. A Connex 185 takes the train to Bitterfeld where traffic is handed over to RBB for local distribution in the Bitterfeld but also for onward forwarding to Riesa and Schawarzheide.

Traffic developed well during 2003 leading to a service revision. The Friedberg hub is no more as through trains now run from Bremen to Kornwestheim calling for traffic at Dortmund Obereving and Duisburg Rheinhausen. The Nürnberg train runs via Hannover and Bebra without traffic stops. Another train now runs Bremen to Erfurt. The Kornwestheim train now tends to use Connex 185s with EVB and WEG crews; the Nürnberg train uses a Dispolok with EVB and BCB crews.

In 2003 the shares were changed and are now understood to be distributed as follows: Connex 39%, EVB 20%, ACOS 10% and Rhenus Rail 31%

For locomotive details see the lists for the above mentioned firms.

NORDDEUTSCHE EISENBAHN GESELLSCHAFT mbH
NEG

Uetersen, Schleswig Holstein

Routes: UetersenHafen – Tornesch.
Length: 4.5 km   **Depots:** Uetersen Ost,
EVU Licence: Freight and Passenger 26/02/1998.

The NEG is a relative newcomer to the scene being formed in 1998 and absorbing at that time the Uetersener Eisenbahn AG (UeE). The new company soon got involved in open access arrangements and acquired a batch of former DSB MY Nohab GM locos then being made surplus in Denmark. No time was lost in finding work for these locos with some turning up in southern Germany helping out on the BOB/DEG when its Integral DMUs were all taken out of service.

Some have also been at Rottweil and have worked the Nostalgic Orient Express on tours in that area. Apart from hiring out locos NEG is a freight only operator still on the UeE but this line may well see passenger services reinstated within the next few years. In Spring 2000 NEG began using the old DR depot at Haldensleben as a base with a shunting loco and up to 7 V170's there. In 2001 the situation changed with NEG reverting to a local railway but later on in the same year it was taken over by CFL to be part of Euro Lux Cargo. This move gave CFL operating rights in Germany!

No.	Builder, No. & Year	Type	kW	Details	Comments
01	MaK 220061/1960	240B	176	0-4-0 DH	At Uetersen
02	MaK 220095/1962	240B	176	0-4-0 DH	To EIVEL
02II	MaK 800190/1978	G1100	809	B-B DH	Ex Seehaven Kiel 2
03	MaK 220020/1954	240B	176	0-4-0 DH	Ex UeE 1. Is at Kiel
03II	LEW 12574/1970	V100.4	1050	B-B DH	Ex ALS 203 209 ex DB 202 242
04	MaK 500045/1967	G500C	368	C DH	Ex Hydro Agri
04II	LEW 12939/1972	V100.4	1050	B-B DH	Ex ALS 203 210 ex DB 202 430
05	Gm 4905/1955	Köf II	94	B DH	Ex UeE 2. Stored

NECKAR–SCHWARZWALD–ALB–EISENBAHNVERKEHRS GESELLSCHAFT
NESA
Tübingen, Baden Württemberg

Routes: Nationwide
Length: -   **Depots:** Tübingen, Rottweil.
EVU Licence: Freight and Passenger 29/04/1999.

This new operating company is the operating arm of Eisenbahnfreunde Zollernbahn. The V170 was acquired for use with the MThB Orient Express train whilst the two V100 have been acquired as back up for EFZ steam locos. Whilst EFZ have first claim on their use it is likely that spot hire will take place from time to time.

No.	Builder, No. & Year	Type	kW	Details	Comments
V100 1041	Jung 13315/1962	V100DB	994	B-B DH	Ex DB 211 041
V100 2335	MaK 1000382/1966	V100DB	994	B-B DH	Ex DB 213 335

NIEDERRHEINISCHE VERKEHRSBETRIEBE AG   NIAG
Moers, Nordrhein Westfalen

Routes: Moers - Hoerstgen - Sevelen (20 km); Moers - Rheinberg - Millingen (15.8 km). There are through workings on to DB Netz to destinations in the Ruhr.
Length: 35.8/53.7 km.   **Depots:** Moers
EVU Licence: Freight and Passenger 17/11/1995.

NIAG is another predominately harbour railway with very heavy traffic handling some 3.7 million tonnes a year mostly ore and coal. The locos work on to DB and have been seen stabled at Oberhausen Osterfeld Süd depot over a weekend.

No.	Builder, No. & Year	Type	kW	Details	Comments
1	MaK 1000798/1981	G1204BB	1120	B-B DH	"Stadt Moers"
2	MaK 1000820/1985	G1204BB	1120	B-B DH	
3	MaK 1000894/1993	G1205BB	1120	B-B DH	
4	On Rail 1004/1/1997	DH1004	1030	B-B DH	Ex DB 211 162
5	MaK 1000781/1978	G1202BB	944	B-B DH	
6	MaK 1000782/1978	G1202BB	944	B-B DH	
7	O&K 26009/1959	Köf II	94	B-B DH	Ex DB 323 170
8	OnR DH1504/3/2000	216	1480 ?	B-B DH	Ex DB 216 111
9	OnR DH1504/4/2000	216	1480 ?	B-B DH	Ex DB 216 055
11	Hens 30872/1964	DHG160B	115	B DH	
12	Gm 5471/1972	D25B		B DH	
50	Wind 260149/1998	RW240DH			Teletrac at Hafen Orsoy
51	Wind 260184/1999	RW240DH			Teletrac at Hafen Orsoy

NB: No. 4 is a heavy rebuild of DB 211 162 and is like a MaK G12xx in appearance.

NEUKÖLLN–MITTENWALDER EISENBAHN
GESELLSCHAFT AG   NME

Berlin

Routes: Bermin Neukölln - Berlin Teltowkanal - Berlin-Britz - Berlin-Rudow Nord.
Length: 8.9/25.6 km   **Depots:** Teltowkanal
EVU Licence: Freight and Passenger 25/05/1990.

This private railway has quietly existed in West Berlin but lost part of its line in the east when the Berlin wall went up. It has continued to serve various industrial locations. Reunification has brought about an increase in traffic and more locomotives have had to be acquired. The line hands over to DB each day about three train loads of household rubbish and receives trainloads of coal for a power station so it keeps busy handling 1.8 million tonnes in 1998.

No.	Builder, No. & Year	Type	kW	Details	Comments
ML 00605	KM 19086/1965	M700C	515	C DH	
ML 00606	Hens 32559/1981	DHG700C	485	C DH	
ML 00607	Hens 32558/1981	DHG700C	485	C DH	
ML 00608	MaK 220117/1991	G321B	246	B DH	
ML 00612	Jung 14040/1970	R43C	323	C DH	
ML 00613	KM 19051/1965	M500C	441	C DH	

NEBENBAHN NÜRTINGEN–NEUFFEN "TALESBAHN"
NN (WEG)

Baden Württemberg

Routes: Nürtingen–Neuffen (KBS 762, 8.9 km)
Length: 8.9/-   **Depots:** Neuffen

Another short WEG line connecting with DB at Nürtingen on the Plochingen–Tübingen line. A small amount of freight traffic for a steelworks is handled by VT 401. In 2001 track improvements are being done in anticipation of getting some new railcars – Regio Shuttles. The line also runs steam trains organised by the GES organisation in Stuttgart. Two steam locos are usually found at the depot in Neuffen. VT 445-447 were built spare units to cover for the DEG/WEG fleet and hiring out to other operators in the DEG group. However during 2001 the Regio Shuttles were redistributed amongst the various lines to cope with traffic growth.

No.	Builder, No. & Year	Type	kW	Details	Comments
62	MaK 600129/1956	600D	441	D DH	Ex BTh V 62
VT 402	Essl 23343/1951	Esslingen	2 x 154	1A-A1 DHR	For Sale
VT 442	Adtranz 36848/1999	RS1	2 x 257	B-B DMR	
VT 445	Adtranz 36878/2000	RS1	2 x 257	B-B DMR	*AGNES*
VT 446	Adtranz 36879/2000	RS1	2 x 257	B-B DMR	*ALICE*
VT 447	Adtranz 36880/2000	RS1	2 x 257	B-B DMR	*MARA*

MARSCHBAHN   NOB

Kiel, Schleswig Holstein

Connex has won the concession to operate the Hamburg–Westerland local services. The NOB subsidiary will do the actual operating hence the name. On 20/11/2003 90 carriages and four 146.1 locomotives were ordered for the new service. Later an order for 13 new R 3000 diesel locmotives was placed with Vossloh. These are not expected to be ready until 2006 so to start the service off 13 ME26 locomotives will be used which Vossloh is to buy from Siemens. The electric locomotives are intended to be used on certain trains from Westerland which will be extended from Hamburg to places such as Köln and Berlin.

NORD OSTSEE BAHN GmbH   NOB (CONNEX)

Kiel, Schleswig Holstein

Routes: Kiel–Husum (KBS 134, 102 km); Husum–Bad St. Peter Ording (KBS 135, 44 km); Kiel–Neumünster (KBS 131, 31 km). All DB Netz.
Length: 177 km.   **Depots:** Kiel VKP
EVU Licence: Freight and Passenger 19/04/2002.

This is a very new organisation set up within the last few years being a joint operation between DEG and the Verkehrsbetrieben Kreis Plon (VKP). It ordered 12 air-conditioned LINT 41 railcars to operate train services on the above routes which will be 100% NOB except for KBS 131 which will be 50% DB and 50% NOB. A new depot has been built at Kiel Süd where Vossloh Schienenverkehrstechnik AG (under the Eurotrac banner) will maintain the units. There was a proposal to run car carrying trains from Niebüll to Westerland but DB declared that the car loading areas were not open access!

On 6/4/03 NOB took over the passenger train workings between Niebüll and Tonder (Denmark) – a recently re-introduced passenger service. A railcar has been drafted in from Baden Württemberg in the shape og WEG 411.

With NVAG declaring bankruptcy NOB has taken over the NVAG until such time as legal formalities have been completed.

No.	Builder, No. & Year	Type	kW	Details	Comments
VT 301	Als 2000	LINT 41	630	B-2-B DHR	
VT 302	Als 2000	LINT 41	630	B-2-B DHR	
VT 303	Als 2000	LINT 41	630	B-2-B DHR	
VT 304	Als 2000	LINT 41	630	B-2-B DHR	
VT 305	Als 2000	LINT 41	630	B-2-B DHR	
VT 306	Als 2000	LINT 41	630	B-2-B DHR	
VT 307	Als 2000	LINT 41	630	B-2-B DHR	
VT 308	Als 2000	LINT 41	630	B-2-B DHR	
VT 309	Als 2000	LINT 41	630	B-2-B DHR	

NORDFRIESISCHE VERKEHRSBETRIEBE AG NVAG
Niebüll, Schleswig Holstein

Routes: Niebüll - Dagebüll-Hafen.
Length: 26.6/29.8 km **Depots:** Niebüll
EVU Licence: Freight and Passenger 28/03/2001.

This little railway has quietly shuttled about on its 13.6 km line between Niebüll and Dagbüll Mole for many years. But things are changing here as elsewhere as on 15/09/99 NVAG took over the German section of the closed line into Denmark (Niebüll–Tønder). Temporary summer passenger services restarted on this line using DSB railcars. The NVAG railcar is one of the few Jenbach 5047s outside Austria/Hungary.

In 2002 even bigger changes took place on the freight front under open access as NVAG took over the local distribution network from DB Cargo. NVAG acquired some rebuilt diesels from Stendal and works trips from Maschen to Wilhelmsburg (connection into Hoyer/R4C trains) – Schleswig (connection into ABF trips) – Westerland.

2003 brought disaster as NVAG was declared bankrupt on 12/08/2003. It has now been taken over by a partnership of NEG, NOB, and Schmidt Reisen.

No.	Builder, No. & Year	Type	kW	Details	Comments
DL 2	Krupp 4343/1961	V100	845	B-B DH	Ex DB 211 233
203.003	LEW 14433/1974	V100DR	1240	B-B DH	Ex DB 202 732. FFS
203.004	LEW 12854/1971	V100DR	1240	B-B DH	Ex DB 202 345. FFS
203.005	LEW 13500/1972	V100DR	1240	B-B DH	Ex DB 202 461. FFS
346.006	LEW 12233/1969	V60D	478	0-8-0 DH	Ex RAW Halle 5
T 4	JW J3894-103/1995	5047	423	B-2 DH	
311 007	LKM 262412/1972	V22	162	0-4-0 DH	Ex HWB VL 2

NB: DL 2 heavily rebuilt by Henschel. Named "Nordfriesland"

NORDHARZ NETZ
Connex has won the contract to provide the local passenger service on the Nord Harz lines. These are KBS 315 Magdeburg–Halberstadt–Thale; KBS 328 Halberstadt–Blankenburg; KBS 330 Halle–Halberstadt–Wernigerode–Vienenburg; KBS 341 Könnern–Bernburg. 19 new DMUs of LINT 27 and LINT 41 types have been ordered. A depot will be established in Halberstadt (old DB depot?). More information is awaited.

NORDWESTBAHN GmbH   NWB (CONNEX)
Osnabrück, Niedersachsen

Routes: Osnabrück–Wilhelmshafen (KBS 392, 170.1 km); Sande–Esens (KBS 393, 33.7 km); Hespe–Delmenhorst (–Bremen), (KBS 394, 88.4 km). All DB Netz.
Length: 292.2 km. (DB Netz)   **Depots:** Osnabrück Hafen
Livery: Blue, yellow and white.
EVU Licence: Freight and Passenger 10/12/1999

Another new name in the list of German railways. The Nordwestbahn is 74% owned by the DEG and 26% by Stadtwerke Osnabrück. It has got the concession to run local passenger trains over three former DB routes as listed above. On the KBS 394 route the new train service will run through to Bremen Hbf. 23 LINT 41 railcars were ordered and the first arrived in Spring 2000. A new depot has been built on the Osnabrück harbour line as efforts to get use of the old DB depot in Oldenburg have been without success due to the site being reserved for redevelopment. The first route to be served was KBS 394 in November 2000 with the other lines changing over with the start of the 2001 timetable.

Traffic growth has been instantaneous so more units were requested from the supplier who could not meet the need. So Siemens stepped in and diverted some Desiro units intended for the DB! (deliveries to DB were running ahead of plan). Late in 2001 NWB reported patronage up by a staggering 70% in its first full year of operation. Six more LINT 41 railcars have been ordered for delivery in 2003. NWB has been in dispute with DB over train paths. It wants to increase the service between Osnabrück and Wilhelmshafen but DB would would not grant pathways as there is a once in a while freight train on the line. Also pathways have been declined for expresses between Osnabrück and Hannover. Some big arguments lie ahead which will end up in court.

In 2002 NWB together with TWE won the contract to operate local services from Münster to Bielefeld; Bielefeld to Paderborn; Bielefeld to Altenbeken and Paderborn to Holzminden. 28 3-car Talent DMUs were ordered for these services which may eventually be marketed under a separate operating name. Later the order appears to have changed to 19 3-car sets and 6 2-car sets.

No.	Builder, No. & Year	Type	kW	Details	Comments
VT 501	LHB 001/1999	LINT 41	2x315	B-2-B DHR	
VT 502	LHB 002/1999	LINT 41	2x315	B-2-B DHR	
VT 503	LHB 003/1999	LINT 41	2x315	B-2-B DHR	
VT 504	LHB 004/1999	LINT 41	2x315	B-2-B DHR	
VT 505	LHB 005/1999	LINT 41	2x315	B-2-B DHR	
VT 506	Als 006/2000	LINT 41	2x315	B-2-B DHR	
VT 507	Als 007/2000	LINT 41	2x315	B-2-B DHR	
VT 508	Als 008/2000	LINT 41	2x315	B-2-B DHR	
VT 509	Als 009/2000	LINT 41	2x315	B-2-B DHR	
VT 510	Als 010/2000	LINT 41	2x315	B-2-B DHR	
VT 511	Als 011/2000	LINT 41	2x315	B-2-B DHR	
VT 512	Als 012/2000	LINT 41	2x315	B-2-B DHR	
VT 513	Als 013/2000	LINT 41	2x315	B-2-B DHR	
VT 514	Als 014/2000	LINT 41	2x315	B-2-B DHR	
VT 515	Als 015/2000	LINT 41	2x315	B-2-B DHR	
VT 516	Als 016/2000	LINT 41	2x315	B-2-B DHR	
VT 517	Als 017/2000	LINT 41	2x315	B-2-B DHR	
VT 518	Als 018/2000	LINT 41	2x315	B-2-B DHR	
VT 519	Als 019/2000	LINT 41	2x315	B-2-B DHR	
VT 520	Als 020/2000	LINT 41	2x315	B-2-B DHR	
VT 521	Als 021/2000	LINT 41	2x315	B-2-B DHR	
VT 522	Als 022/2000	LINT 41	2x315	B-2-B DHR	
VT 523	Als 023/2000	LINT 41	2x315	B-2-B DHR	
VT 524	Als 2003	LINT 41	2x315	B-2-B DHR	LNVG Pool
VT 525	Als 2003	LINT 41	2x315	B-2-B DHR	LNVG Pool
VT 526	Als 2003	LINT 41	2x315	B-2-B DHR	LNVG Pool
VT 527	Als 2003	LINT 41	2x315	B-2-B DHR	LNVG Pool
VT 528	Als 2003	LINT 41	2x315	B-2-B DHR	LNVG Pool
VT 529	Als 2003	LINT 41	2x315	B-2-B DHR	LNVG Pool
VT 560	Sie 92843/4/2001	Desiro SR20D	2x275	B-2-B DHR	

VT 561	Sie 92845/6/2001	Desiro SR20D	2x275	B-2-B DHR
VT 562	Sie 92847/8/2001	Desiro SR20D	2x275	B-2-B DHR
VT 563	Sie 92849/50/2001	Desiro SR20D	2x275	B-2-B DHR
VT 564	Sie 92851/2/2001	Desiro SR20D	2x275	B-2-B DHR
VT 565	Sie 92853/4/2001	Desiro SR20D	2x275	B-2-B DHR
VT 701	Bomb /2003	Talent	2 x 315	B-2-2-B DHR
VT 702	Bomb /2003	Talent	2 x 315	B-2-2-B DHR
VT 703	Bomb /2003	Talent	2 x 315	B-2-2-B DHR
VT 704	Bomb /2003	Talent	2 x 315	B-2-2-B DHR
VT 705	Bomb /2003	Talent	2 x 315	B-2-2-B DHR
VT 706	Bomb /2003	Talent	2 x 315	B-2-2-B DHR
VT 707	Bomb /2003	Talent	2 x 315	B-2-2-B DHR
VT 708	Bomb /2003	Talent	2 x 315	B-2-2-B DHR
VT 709	Bomb /2003	Talent	2 x 315	B-2-2-B DHR
VT 710	Bomb /2003	Talent	2 x 315	B-2-2-B DHR
VT 711	Bomb /2003	Talent	2 x 315	B-2-2-B DHR
VT 712	Bomb /2003	Talent	2 x 315	B-2-2-B DHR
VT 713	Bomb /2003	Talent	2 x 315	B-2-2-B DHR
VT 714	Bomb /2003	Talent	2 x 315	B-2-2-B DHR
VT 715	Bomb /2003	Talent	2 x 315	B-2-2-B DHR
VT 716	Bomb /2003	Talent	2 x 315	B-2-2-B DHR
VT 717	Bomb /2003	Talent	2 x 315	B-2-2-B DHR
VT 718	Bomb /2003	Talent	2 x 315	B-2-2-B DHR
VT 719	Bomb /2003	Talent	2 x 315	B-2-2-B DHR
VT 771	Bomb /2003	Talent	2 x 315	B-2-B DHR
VT 772	Bomb /2003	Talent	2 x 315	B-2-B DHR
VT 773	Bomb /2003	Talent	2 x 315	B-2-B DHR
VT 774	Bomb /2003	Talent	2 x 315	B-2-B DHR
VT 775	Bomb /2003	Talent	2 x 315	B-2-B DHR
VT 776	Bomb /2003	Talent	2 x 315	B-2-B DHR

NORD WEST CARGO   NWC
Osnabrück, Niedersachsen (Connex)

Depot: Osnabrück Hafen
EVU Licence: Freight, 08/05/2002.

This is a development of Nord West Bahn with an eye on freight traffic. Formed by Connex (51%) and Stadtwerke Osnabruck (49%) operations started 2001/2. Stadtwerke Osnabrück already owns some shunting locomotives but main line locomotives are what is needed. The freights are now operated under the marketing of Connex Cargo Logistics with NWV/NWB as the EVU. In 2003 NWC took over the freight operations of the FVE including one of its locos.

In 2003, NWC in conjunction with the Dutch ATCS company started moving rubbish trains from Groningen to a power station near Bremen. These trains have brought back freight movements over the Nieuweschans – Leer route. Trains have been running Mondays and Wednesdays from Groningen and Tuesdays and Thursdays from Bremen. Locos on these trains are hired in from other Connex companies.

No.	Builder, No. & Year	Type	kW	Details	Comments
51	Mak 500071/1974	G500C	368	C DH	Ex FVE
V 132	MaK 1000256/1968	G1300BB	956	B-B DH	Ex TWE

OSTSEEBAHN GmbH   ??
Mecklenburg Vorpommern

This new company was established on 01/09/2002 by the Rostocker Strassenbahn AG (RSAG) and Connex Regiobahn GmbH. The purpose is to set up a local tram/train network around Rostock based on the "Karlsruhe Model" with operations expected to start in 2004. Services from Rostock would go to Bad Doberan, Warnemunde, Rostock Seehafen, Rövershagen and Gaal Müritz. Obviously one in its infancy but one to watch.

OSTDEUTSCHE EISENBAHN GmbH   ODEG
Parchim, Mecklenburg Vorpommern

Routes: Hagenow Land – Neustrelitz; Neustrelitz Süd – Mirow.
Length: 175 km (DB Netz).   **Depots:** Neustrelitz (main), Parchim (sub).
EVU Licence: Passenger, 02/12/2002.

ODEG is a joint venture by HHA and PEG to operate several lines in the period December 2003 to December 2009. The routes concerned are as above. At Hagenow Land there will be connections to and from Hamburg; Parchim for Schwerin; Neustrelitz for Berlin. At Parchim, Eurotrac staff will maintain the units. ODEG has won the contract to provide services east of Berlin for which another 25 Regio Shuttles have been ordered.

No.	Builder, No. & Year	Type	kW	Details	Comments
VT650.51	Stadler 37140/2002	RS	2x257	B-B DMR	Owned by PEG
VT650.52	Stadler 37141/2002	RS	2x257	B-B DMR	Owned by PEG
VT650.53	Stadler 37142/2002	RS	2x257	B-B DMR	Owned by PEG
VT650.54	Stadler 37143/2002	RS	2x257	B-B DMR	Owned by HHA
VT650.55	Stadler 37144/2002	RS	2x257	B-B DMR	Owned by HHA
VT650.56	Stadler 37145/2002	RS	2x257	B-B DMR	Owned by HHA
VT650.57	Stadler 37146/2002	RS	2x257	B-B DMR	Owned by HHA
VT650.58	Stadler 37304/2004	RS	2x257	B-B DMR	Owned by HHA
VT650.59	Stadler 37293/2004	RS	2x257	B-B DMR	Owned by HHA
VT650.60	Stadler 37. . . /2004	RS	2x257	B-B DMR	Owned by HHA
VT650.61	Stadler 37. . . /2004	RS	2x257	B-B DMR	Owned by HHA
VT650.62	Stadler 37. . . /2004	RS	2x257	B-B DMR	Owned by HHA
VT650.63	Stadler 37. . . /2004	RS	2x257	B-B DMR	Owned by HHA
VT650.64	Stadler 37. . . /2004	RS	2x257	B-B DMR	Owned by PEG
VT650.65	Stadler 37305/2004	RS	2x257	B-B DMR	Owned by PEG
VT650.66	Stadler 37306/2004	RS	2x257	B-B DMR	Owned by PEG
VT650.67	Stadler 37307/2004	RS	2x257	B-B DMR	Owned by PEG
VT650.68	Stadler 37308/2004	RS	2x257	B-B DMR	Owned by PEG
VT650.69	Stadler 37292/2004	RS	2x257	B-B DMR	Owned by PEG
VT650.70	Stadler 37309/2004	RS	2x257	B-B DMR	Owned by PEG
VT650.71	Stadler 373109/2004	RS	2x257	B-B DMR	Owned by PEG
VT650.72	Stadler 37311/2004	RS	2x257	B-B DMR	Owned by PEG
VT650.73	Stadler 37312/2004	RS	2x257	B-B DMR	Owned by PEG
VT650.74	Stadler 37313/2004	RS	2x257	B-B DMR	Owned by PEG
VT650.75	Stadler 37314/2004	RS	2x257	B-B DMR	Owned by HHA
VT650.76	Stadler 37. . . /2004	RS	2x257	B-B DMR	Owned by HHA
VT650.77	Stadler 37. . . /2004	RS	2x257	B-B DMR	Owned by HHA
VT650.78	Stadler 37. . . /2004	RS	2x257	B-B DMR	Owned by HHA
VT650.79	Stadler 37. . . /2004	RS	2x257	B-B DMR	Owned by HHA
VT650.50	Stadler 37. . . /2004	RS	2x257	B-B DMR	Owned by HHA
VT650.81	Stadler 37. . . /2004	RS	2x257	B-B DMR	Owned by HHA
VT650.82	Stadler 37. . . /2004	RS	2x257	B-B DMR	Owned by HHA

OBERRHEINISCHE EISENBAHN GESELLSCHAFT AG   OEG
Baden Württemberg

Gauge : 1000 mm
Electric System: 750 V dc
Routes: Mannheim–Heidelberg–Weinheim–Mannheim (53.1 km); Mannheim Käfertal–Heddesheim (6.5 km).
Length: 63.3/97.4 km.
Depots: Mannheim Käfertal; stabling points at Edingen, Viernheim.
EVU Licence: Freight and Passenger, 29/06/1964.

The metre gauge OEG could be considered a tramway but it has always been counted as a railway and until 1983 ran freight trains. Passenger traffic is heavy the railway connecting the three major centres of Mannheim, Heidelberg and Weinheim with a branch from Mannheim Käfertal to Heddesheim. In Mannheim and Heidelberg the OEG shares tracks with the local tramways – services are jointly operated.

No.	Builder, No. & Year	Type	kW	Details	Comments
16	Fuchs 1914		2 x 66	A1-1A ER	Departmental car
81	Rastatt 1961		2 x 115	B-2-2-B ER	
82	Duewag 33596/1966	GTW8	2 x 120	B-2-2-B ER	
83	Duewag 33597/1966	GTW8	2 x 120	B-2-2-B ER	
84	Duewag 33598/1966	GTW8	2 x 120	B-2-2-B ER	
85	Duewag 33599/1966	GTW8	2 x 120	B-2-2-B ER	
86	Duewag 33600/1966	GTW8	2 x 120	B-2-2-B ER	
87	Duewag 33601/1966	GTW8	2 x 120	B-2-2-B ER	
88	Duewag 33602/1966	GTW8	2 x 120	B-2-2-B ER	
89	Duewag 33603/1966	GTW8	2 x 120	B-2-2-B ER	
90	Duewag 34072/1969	GTW8	2 x 120	B-2-2-B ER	
91	Duewag 34073/1969	GTW8	2 x 120	B-2-2-B ER	
92	Duewag 34074/1969	GTW8	2 x 120	B-2-2-B ER	
93	Duewag 34075/1969	GTW8	2 x 120	B-2-2-B ER	
94	Duewag 34076/1969	GTW8	2 x 120	B-2-2-B ER	Accident in 1999
95	Duewag 34077/1969	GTW8	2 x 120	B-2-2-B ER	
96	Duewag 34078/1969	GTW8	2 x 120	B-2-2-B ER	
97	Duewag 34079/1969	GTW8	2 x 120	B-2-2-B ER	
98	Duewag 36147/1973	GTW8	2 x 150	B-2-2-B ER	
99	Duewag 36148/1973	GTW8	2 x 150	B-2-2-B ER	
100	Duewag 36149/1973	GTW8	2 x 150	B-2-2-B ER	
101	Duewag 36150/1973	GTW8	2 x 150	B-2-2-B ER	
102	Duewag 36151/1974	GTW8	2 x 150	B-2-2-B ER	
103	Duewag 36152/1974	GTW8	2 x 150	B-2-2-B ER	
104	Duewag 36153/1974	GTW8	2 x 150	B-2-2-B ER	
105	Duewag 36154/1974	GTW8	2 x 150	B-2-2-B ER	
106	Duewag 36155/1974	GTW8	2 x 150	B-2-2-B ER	
107	Duewag 36156/1974	GTW8	2 x 150	B-2-2-B ER	
108	Duewag 36157/1974	GTW8	2 x 150	B-2-2-B ER	
109	Duewag 36158/1974	GTW8	2 x 150	B-2-2-B ER	
110	Duewag 36159/1974	GTW8	2 x 150	B-2-2-B ER	
111	Duewag 37399/1987	GTW8	2 x 150	B-2-2-B ER	
112	Duewag 37400/1987	GTW8	2 x 150	B-2-2-B ER	
113	Duewag 37401/1987	GTW8	2 x 150	B-2-2-B ER	
114	Duewag 37402/1987	GTW8	2 x 150	B-2-2-B ER	
115	Duewag 37403/1987	GTW8	2 x 150	B-2-2-B ER	
116	Duewag 37404/1987	GTW8	2 x 150	B-2-2-B ER	
117	Adtranz 36472/1996	6MGT-LDZ	4 x 95	Bo-2-Bo ER	
118	Adtranz 36482/1996	6MGT-LDZ	4 x 95	Bo-2-Bo ER	
119	Adtranz 36492/1996	6MGT-LDZ	4 x 95	Bo-2-Bo ER	
120	Adtranz 36502/1996	6MGT-LDZ	4 x 95	Bo-2-Bo ER	
121	Adtranz 36512/1996	6MGT-LDZ	4 x 95	Bo-2-Bo ER	
122	Adtranz 36522/1996	6MGT-LDZ	4 x 95	Bo-2-Bo ER	
355	Rastatt 1958		4 x 60	Bo-Bo ER	Departmental
357	Rastatt 1960		4 x 60	Bo-Bo ER	Departmental
358	Rastatt 1963		4 x 60	Bo-Bo ER	Departmental
359	Rastatt 1963		4 x 60	Bo-Bo ER	Departmental

OSTHANNOVERSCHE EISENBAHNEN AG   OHE

Celle, Niedersachsen

Routes: Celle–Soltau (58.9 km); Celle–Wittingen–Ruhen (85.7 km); Beckedorf–Munster (Örtze) (23.9 km); Beedenbostel–Mariaglück (5.6 km); Soltau–Neunkirchen (12.0 km); Lüneburg–Soltau (57.1 km); Winsen–Hutzel (41.1 km); Winsen–Niedermarschact (18.1 km); Lüneburg–Bleckede (23.8 km).
Length: 333.1/396.9 km.   **Depots:** Bleckede (workshops), Celle, Lüneburg.
EVU Licence: Freight and Passenger 23/10/1995.

The OHE is a collection of eight former private railways grouped together now with headquarters in Celle. Total trackage is over 300 km with some really long branches e.g. Celle–Soltau and Celle–Wittingen. On 01/03/2000 OHE took over operation of the Steinhuder Meer Bahn (StMB).

In recent years the change to open access has seen OHE working more and more trains from its system over DB. Traffic for 1998 was 868,000 tonnes. The main depot is at Celle and its own workshops are at Blackede. Locos stable at the sub-sheds of Blackede (1), Lüneburg (3), Soltau (1), Wittingen (2), Winsen (1) and Wunstorf (1). Nostalgic passenger trains operate on certain routes during the summer.

No.	Builder, No. & Year	Type	kW	Details	Comments
Köf 0606	Deutz 56747/1957	KK130B	96	B DH	
Köf 0607	Gm 4196/1944	HF130C	88	0-6-0DH	
230 41	Deutz 57200/1961	KS230B	169	B DH	
230 42	Deutz 57201/1961	KS230B	169	B DH	
230 43	Deutz 57202/1961	KS230B	169	B DH	
600 22	MaK 600157/1959	650D	478	0-8-0 DH	For Sale
600 23	MaK 600158/1959	650D	478	0-8-0 DH	Stored
600 24	LHB 3136/1966	530C	504	6w DH	Ex VPS 545 in 2003
600 25	SFT 220121/1996	G322	390	4w DH	Ex VL, ex DSB MK 602
1000 32	MaK 1000015/1959	1000D	735	0-8-0 DH	Stored or sold
1200 51	MaK 1000016/1959	1200D	882	0-8-0 DH	For Sale
1200 52	MaK 1000045/1961	1200D	882	0-8-0 DH	Stored or sold
1200 54	MaK 1000156/1963	1200D	882	0-8-0 DH	For Sale
1200 68	Deutz 57465/1962	DG1000BBM	735	B-B DH	
1200 69	Deutz 57250/1961	DG1000BBM	735	B-B DH	
1200 70	Deutz 58241/1968	DG1000BBM	735	B-B DH	Stored 2000
1200 71	Deutz 57100/1960	DG1000BBM	882	B-B DH	
1200 72	Deutz 57101/1960	DG1000BBM	882	B-B DH	
1200 76	MaK 1000516/1971	G530C	504	6w DH	Ex BAG M19 2002
1400 01	MaK 1000786/1979	G1202BB	1000	B-B DH	
1400 02	MaK 1000788/1979	G1202BB	1000	B-B DH	
1500 03	MaK 1000814/1984	G1204BB	1120	B-B DH	
1500 04	MaK 1000822/1985	G1204BB	1120	B-B DH	
1500.05	Mak 1000891/1993	G1205	1120	B-B DH	Ex E-on M 21 12/02
1500.06	MaK 1000892/1993	G1205	1120	B-B DH	Ex E-on M 22 12/02
1500 73	Deutz 58250/1963	DG1500BBM	1104	B-B DH	*Soltau* (Sold to Italy)
1600 73	MaK 1000517/1971	G1600BB	1176	B-B DH	Ex OnRail 38,ex WHE 26
1600 74	MaK 1000518/1972	G1600BB	1176	B-B DH	*Winsen*
1600 75	MaK 1000597/1975	G1600BB	1176	B-B DH	*Wittingen*
?????	MaK 1000516/1971	G1600	1176	B-B DH	Ex E-on M 19 12/02
?????	MaK 1000492/1972	G1600	1176	B-B DH	Ex E-on M 20 12/02
2000 91	Deutz 57649/1963	DG2000CCM	2 x 735	C-C DH	*Celle*
2000 92	Deutz 57650/1964	DG2000CCM	2 x 735	C-C DH	*Lüneburg* (Stored)
2000 95	OnR 1504/6 2002	DH 1504	1480	B-B DH	Ex DB 216 121
2000 96	OnR 1504/5/2000	DH 1504	1480	B-B DH	Ex DB 216 158
2000 97	OnR 1504/2/2000	DH 1504	1480	B-B DH	Ex DB 216 123

2000 96/7 are heavily re-enginered DB locos having been fitted with FFS, ZBF and retaining Indusi.

OSTHAVELLÄNDISCHE EISENBAHN BERLIN–SPANDAU AG
OHE-Sp
Berlin

Routes: Berlin-Spandau (Gbf}–Johannesstift–Ober Havel and various industrial spurs.
Length: 15.8 km   **Depots:** Johannesstift
EVU Licence:

This OHE was once a much larger network around Berlin but the partition of the city after WW2 gave the OHE-Sp only 18 km of track in the Spandau area of the city. Most work was servicing private sidings from the main line interchange point. After many quiet years unification and open access have brought about some bigger opportunities and early in 2000 a V200 was acquired from Poland no doubt the figure of 512,000 tonnes handled in 1998 is likely to increase. V160.1 was acquired in 2002 for new trips from the former DB yard at Wustermark to Rathenow and Premnitz.

No.	Builder, No. & Year	Type	kW	Details	Comments
DL 5	Jung 13712/1963	R60D	478	0-8-0 DH	
DL 6	Jung 13931/1966	R60D	478	0-8-0 DH	
DL 7	Jung 14112/1972	RC70BB	773	B-B DH	For sale.
DL 8	MaK 1000779/1978	G1202BB	994	B-B DH	
V60.1	LEW 13362/1972	V60D	478	0-8-0 DH	Ex DB 346 823
V60.2	LEW 13819/1973	V60D	478	0-8-0 DH	Ex DB 346 833
V60.3	LEW 17793/1980	V60D	478	0-8-0 DH	Ex DB 345 112
V60.4	LEW 17794/1980	V60D	478	0-8-0 DH	Ex DB 345 113
V130.1	MaK 1000343/1965	V100DB	992	B-B DH	Ex ALS, ex DB 212 296
V130.2	Mak 1000173/1963	V100DB	992	B-B DH	Ex ALS, ex DB 212 037
V160.1	LEW 14081/1974	V100DR	1240	B-B DH	Ex ALS, ex DB 202 654. MTU engine.
V160.2	LEW 13905/1973	V100DR	1240	B-B DH	Ex ALS, ex DB 202 587, MTU engine.
V200.1	Lugansk 1109/1971	M62	1470	Co-Co DE	Ex PKP ST44 161
1001-037	VSFT 1001037/2002	G2000	2240	B-B DH	On hire 2002-2007

OSTMECKLENBURGISCHEN EISENBAHN mbH
OME (CONNEX)

Neubrandenburg, Mecklenburg Vorpommern

Routes: Pasewalk–Neubrandenburg–Parchim–Güstrow–Bützow (KBS 175, 154 km); Bützow–Schwerin (KBS 160, 57 km); Güstrow–Rostock (KBS 163, 45 km); Neubandenburg–Neustrelitz (KBS 185, 35.2 km); Pasewalk–Ueckermünde (KBS 192, 30 km), Stralsund–Neubrandenburg. All DB Netz.

Length: 321 km   **Depot:** Neubrandenburg.
EVU Licence: Freight and passenger 03/06/1997.

This new operator has its roots in the Industrieanschlusbahn Neubrandenburg which itself was set up after unification. Then came regionalisation and the opportunity to get into the passenger business. OME is 74.8% owned by DEG with local interests Stinnes Gruppe and Neubrandenburger Verkehrs AG having the remaining part. OME has the contract to run the passenger services over the above mentioned former DB routes. The stock includes the former industrial locos as well as the new Talbot Talent DMUs. When purely a freight operator it handled 144,000 tonnes. Connex shook DB when it started its InterConnex (IC trains!) between Gera and Rostock. These have proved very popular with passengers allowing through journeys not possible by DB. The trains have to be strengthened frequently and units from other Connex operations are drafted in to help out OME services. This also explains the acquisition of extra units in 2000. On 10/10/2002 a new depot was opened in Neubrandenburg and is operated by a subsidiary company Eisenbahn Werkstatt Neubrandenburg (EWN).

No.	Builder, No. & Year	Type	kW	Details	Comments
2	LOB 262471/1973	V22	162	0-4-0 DH	
3	LEW 18103/1983	V60D	478	0-8-0 DH	Stored
4	LEW 15623/1977	V60D	478	0-8-0 DH	
5	LEW 16693/1981	V60D	478	0-8-0 DH	Stored
6	LEW 18102/1983	V60D	478	0-8-0 DH	Stored
0001	Talb 190635-37/1998	Talent	2x315	B-2-2-B DMR	
0002	Talb 190638-40/1998	Talent	2x315	B-2-2-B DMR	
0003	Talb 190641-43/1998	Talent	2x315	B-2-2-B DMR	InterConnex
0004	Talb 190644-46/1998	Talent	2x315	B-2-2-B DMR	
0005	Talb 190647-49/1998	Talent	2x315	B-2-2-B DMR	
0006	Talb 190650-52/1998	Talent	2x315	B-2-2-B DMR	
0007	Talb 190653-55/1998	Talent	2x315	B-2-2-B DMR	InterConnex
0008	Talb 190656-58/1998	Talent	2x315	B-2-2-B DMR	
0009	Talb 190659-61/1998	Talent	2x315	B-2-2-B DMR	InterConnex
0010	Talb 191342-44/2000	Talent	2x315	B-2-2-B DMR	
VT 600	Sie 92834/5/2000	Desiro	2x275	B-2-B DHR	Leased from Angel Trains. Ex DSB MQ 4951/71
VT 601	Sie 92836/7/2000	Desiro	2x275	B-2-B DHR	Leased from Angel Trains. Ex DSB MQ 4952/72
VT 602	Sie 92838/9/2000	Desiro	2x275	B-2-B DHR	Leased from Angel Trains. Ex DSB MQ 4953/73

0003/7/9 have modified interiors for use on the InterConnex services from Gera to Rostock.

ORGANISATION NETZWERK BAHNLOGISTIK NRW
ONE.NRW
Nordrhein-Westfalen

This is a marketing organisation whereby the following companies co-operate with the movement of traffic: DKB, HGK, NIAG, RAG, StEK, NE, TWE, WAB, WLE and RSB Logistic GmbH.

ON RAIL GESELLSCHAFT FÜR EISENBAHNAUSRUSTUNG UND ZUBEHÖR mbH
ONRAIL
Nordrhein Westfalen

Routes: Moers–Rheinpreuseen
Length: 1.3/ 3.2 km   **Depots:** Moers

This is basically a loco dealing firm stemming from On Rail, Mettmann which has been involved in overhauling and rebuilding locos for private operators for some years. Now the glut of private operators has meant an increase in business in both the overhauling and leasing sides of the business. Two types are already specialities. Ex DB V100 are rebuilt to DH1004 series and DB 216 are rebuilt to DH1504 series. DB V200 009 has been obtained for someone and is being overhauled at Chemnitz works. Other DB locos reported on site are 211 276, 216 055/111 - these could be for spares or rebuilding.

No.	Builder, No. & Year	Type	kW	Details	Comments
07	Krp 4371/1962	V100		B-B DH	Ex DB 211 261 NIAG?
32	MaK 800161/1969	1100BB		B-B DH	Ex LB Denmark
36	LHB 3160/1973	LHB1300BB		B-B DH	Ex VPS To NIAG?
37	MaK 800186/1973	G1100BB	809	B-B DH	Ex WHE 20

ORTENAU S-BAHN
OSB (SWEG)
Lahr, Baden Württemberg

Routes: Offenburg–Hausach (KBS 720, 33.2 km); Offenburg–Kehl (KBS 719, 21.9 km); Offenburg–Oberkirch–Bad Griesbach (KBS 718, 37.2 km).
Length: 92.3 km all DB Netz.   **Depots:** Ottenhofen. Stabling at Offenburg (DB).
EVU Licence: Freight and Passenger: 19/11/1997.

Under regionalisation SWEG formed a new company Ortenau S-Bahn and got the contract for local services around Offenburg. New air-conditioned Regio-Shuttles were ordered and these are numbered after the ones obtained for the KB. The SWEG depot at Ottenhofen has been enlarged to maintain the units which thus have transfer trips from Offenburg to Achern. The units also turn up on other SWEG lines in the area having replaced older units. OSB also works to Strasbourg and SNCF is expected to participate using some of their X73900 single car DMUs. OSB has recently gained the contract to run from Hausach to Freudenstadt from December 2004. A further six units have been ordered.

No.	Builder, No. & Year	Type	kW	Details	Names
VT 509	Adtranz 36615/1998	RS1	2 x 257	B-B DMR	OBERHARMERSBACH
VT 510	Adtranz 36616/1998	RS1	2 x 257	B-B DMR	STADT OBERKIRCH
VT 511	Adtranz 36617/1998	RS1	2 x 257	B-B DMR	KAPPELRODECK
VT 512	Adtranz 36618/1998	RS1	2 x 257	B-B DMR	STADT OPPENAU
VT 513	Adtranz 36619/1998	RS1	2 x 257	B-B DMR	ACHERN
VT 514	Adtranz 36620/1998	RS1	2 x 257	B-B DMR	BAD PETERSTAL-GRIESBACH
VT 515	Adtranz 36621/1998	RS1	2 x 257	B-B DMR	STADT HASLACH
VT 516	Adtranz 36622/1998	RS1	2 x 257	B-B DMR	ZELL AM HARMERSBACH
VT 517	Adtranz 36623/1998	RS1	2 x 257	B-B DMR	STEINACH
VT 518	Adtranz 36624/1998	RS1	2 x 257	B-B DMR	STADT HAUSACH
VT 519	Adtranz 36625/1998	RS1	2 x 257	B-B DMR	OTTENHÖFEN
VT 520	Adtranz 36626/1998	RS1	2 x 257	B-B DMR	STADT OFFENBURG
VT 521	Adtranz 36627/1998	RS1	2 x 257	B-B DMR	KREISTADT KEHL
VT 522	Adtranz 36628/1998	RS1	2 x 257	B-B DMR	GEGENBACH
VT 523	Adtranz 36629/1998	RS1	2 x 257	B-B DMR	LAUTENBACH
VT 524	Adtranz 36630/1998	RS1	2 x 257	B-B DMR	BIBERACH
VT 525	Adtranz 36631/1998	RS1	2 x 257	B-B DMR	WILLSTADT
VT 526	Adtranz 36632/1998	RS1	2 x 257	B-B DMR	APPENWEIER

PLANUNG UND BAU VON SICHERUNGS UND VERKEHRS-
BAUSYSTEMEN GmbH   PBSV
Magdeburg, Sachsen Anhalt

Routes: Nation wide ballast and works trains.
Length: -   **Depots:** Magdeburg, Lübeck.
EVU Licence: Freight and Passenger 28/07/1997.

This company was formed in 1993 but was rather unknown until it acquired its loco No. 21 from the Czech Republic! The company had been quietly getting on with its shunting contract in the docks at Lübeck Travemünde for Railship then decided to expand. Usually three locos are at the Lübeck base whilst the others can be almost anywhere on trackwork contracts.

No.	Builder, No. & Year	Type	kW	Details	Comments
01	LEW 16533/1979	V60D	478	0-8-0 DH	At Lübeck. Ex Deusa GmbH.
02	LEW 15670/1974	V60D	478	0-8-0 DH	Ex Kieswerke Nordhausen
2	LEW 15355/1976	V60D	478	0-8-0 DH	On loan from IGE Werrabahn.
03	LEW 11680/1967	V60D	478	0-8-0 DH	At Lübeck. Ex DB 346 399
04	LEW 14291/1974	V60D	478	0-8-0 DH	Ex Walzwerk Hettstedt
05	LEW 15576/1977	V60D	478	0-8-0 DH	Ex Filmfabrik Wolfen
06	LEW 13786/1977	V60D	478	0-8-0 DH	Ex ITB 620
07	LEW 16972/1980	V60D	478	0-8-0 DH	Ex Magdeburg Hafen 1l
08	LEW 13827/1973	V60D	478	0-8-0 DH	Ex ITB 622
09	LEW 13866/1973	V60D	478	0-8-0 DH	Ex ITB?
10	LEW 13788/1973	V60D	478	0-8-0 DH	Ex SUSA GmbH
11	LEW 12751/1970	V100	883	B-B DH	Ex DB 202 287 (HU LSX 8.2000)
12	LEW 11904/1968	V100	883	B-B DH	Ex DR 202 066
13	LEW 11025/1966	V60D	478	0-8-0 DH	Ex ITB 611
14	LEW 11964/1968	V60D	478	0-8-0 DH	Ex ITB 615
345 037	LEW 15160/1976	V60D	478	0-8-0 DH	Ex DB
345 107	LEW 17419/1980	V60D	478	0-8-0 DH	Ex DB

PRIGNITZER EISENBAHN GmbH   PEG
Pulitz, Brandenburg

PEG CARGO   PEG CARGO
Berlin

Routes: Neustadt (Dosse)–Pritzwalk–Meyenburg (KBS 174, 209.73, 61 km); Pritzwalk–Putlitz (KBS 209.70, 17.0 km); Neustadt (Dosse)–Neuruppin (KBS 209.53, 28.4 km); Neustadt (Dosse)–Rathenow (KBS 209.50, 35.0 km). For freight PEG has a nationwide safety case.
Length: 160.7 (DB Netz).
Depots: Putlitz, Wittenberge, Meyenburg, Mülheim-Styrum.
EVU Licence: PEG Freight and Passenger 05/11/2003, PEG Cargo Freight only 30/01/2001.

The PEG was established in 1996 initially operating the local trains between Pritzwalk and Putlitz on KBS 209-70. Some redundant DB railbuses were obtained for this line and it was not long before operations expanded. Freight operations then started, the company acquiring locos, initially hiring through EBG at Altenbeken and then later getting its own from the Czech Republic. Late in 2000 PEG acquired use of the old DB depot in Wittenberge and took delivery of the old IC EMUs ("Donald Ducks") that were last used on the Lufthansa Express service. Just what are they going to do with them? PEG has set up two subsidiaries for hook and pull freight work and ballast trains. These are IMOTRANS and Rail Cargo Berlin. Locos are numbered in a common series.
Late in 2001 PEG pulled out of RCB and instead set up PE Cargo which would take over former DB feeder services under the MORA C concept serving the area around Bad Kleinen, Schwerin, Hagenow, Ludwiglust etc. The traffic handover point is Bad Kleinen where early in 2002 V60.07/09 were based.

PEG won the contract to provide passenger services from Oberhausen Hbf to Duisburg Ruhrort and Dorsten from December 2002.This is a long way from home and so a depot was set up at Mülheim-Styrum and some brand new Talent DMUs purchased. (A motly selection of DMUs was in fact brought in to start the service off). Whether a separate operating company will be formed for these lines is not clear. PEG together with Hochbahn Hamburg (HHA) won another passenger contract and subsequently formed ODEG (q.v.).

▲ Niederrheinische Verkehrsbetriebe (NIAG) has two ex-DB Class 216 locos. No.9 (ex 216 055) is seen stabled at Moers depot on 30/05/02. **Brian Garvin**

▼ EfW-Verkehrsgesellschaft is a company formed by railway enthusiasts which now works engineers' trains etc. They own 26 ex-DB locos, two of which are 221s repatriated from Greece. 221 122-5 is seen at Bullay on 21/03/04 with a permanent way train. **Keith Fender**

▲ HGK of Köln has a large number of modern mainline diesels including 12 GM type JT42CWR, better known as "Class 66". DE62 is seen at Brühl Vochem depot on 01/10/02.   **Brian Garvin**

▼ Mindener Kreisbahn's Bombardier "Blue Tiger" prototype 250 001-5 passes Ibbenbüren on 11/04/03 with a rubbish train from Coevorden (NL). This loco is now numbered V20.   **Keith Fender**

▲ Eichholz Verkehr und Logistik of Haldensleben runs infrastructure trains and hires out locomotives.It has a fleet of ten ex-DSB Class MY Nohab locos. V170 1131 is seen working a ballast train at Aschaffenburg on 14/04/02.

▼ Bayerische Zugspitzbahn (BZB) is a metre gauge rack and adhesion line which operates from Garmisch-Partenkirchen. Electric loco 11 (AEG 1929) was photographed at Grainau on 28/05/90.

Brian Garvin (2)

▲ The BZB has various EMUs. ET 11 is seen at Grainau on 28/05/90.   **Brian Garvin**

▼ The Frankfurt-Königsteiner Eisenbahn (FKE) operates articulated DMUs on commuter routes. VT5 is seen running empty into Königstein station on 23/03/04 to work the 14.31 to Frankfurt Höchst.
Keith Fender

▲ The Nordfriesische Verkehrsbetriebe (NVAG) runs the branch from Niebüll to Dagebüll Mole in Schleswig-Holstein. DMU T4 (ÖBB Class 5047) waits to leave Dagebüll on 10/05/03 with the 15.00 service to Niebüll which conveys two through Intercity coaches bound for Dresden.

▼ The Prignitzer Eisenbahn (PEG) owns a number of ex-DB Class 798 railbuses. VT2 and VT7 are seen at Neustadt (Dosse) on 01/06/02 with trains to Neuruppin and Rathenow respectively.

Keith Fender (2)

▲ The Burgenlandbahn operates services around Zeitz, Sachsen-Anhalt with these two-axle type LVT/S units. VT 3.02 is seen on a Nesa service at Zeitz-Welthau on 03/02/02.   **Steffen Scharf**

▼ The Bayerische Oberland Bahn (BOB) runs a fleet of five-section "Integral" DMUs built by Jenbach in Austria, which have been extremely unreliable. VT103 is seen at München Hbf with a Bayerischzell working on 19/05/02.   **W.J. Freebury**

DUAL-VOLTAGE TRAMS

▲ Albtalbahn Siemens dual voltage tram 846 (with "Bistro") at Karlsruhe Albtalbahnhof on 15/04/02 with a working to Baden-Baden which will take it along the DB main line. **Brian Garvin**

▼ The Saarbahn also operates dual-voltage vehicles known as "Tram-trains" built by Bombardier. They run through Saarbrücken streets, over DB main lines and even into France. 1010 is seen at the Saarbrücken terminus with a Kleinblittersdorf working on 26/04/00. **Peter Fox**

▲ Ex-DR V 100 003, preserved at Lutherstadt-Wittenberg, works a shuttle service to the Dresden "Dampflokfest" on 02/05/98.   **Colin Boocock**

▼ Gmeinder-built 0-6-0 diesel shunter Köf 0908 at Ochsenhausen on the Öchslebahn on 24/07/04.
                                                                                          Keith Fender

▲ 1935-built T3 (ex-DR VT 135 060) at Bohmte on the Museums-Eisenbahn Minden with trailer Wg8, both in Wittlager Kreisbahn livery on 13/04/03. **Keith Fender**

▼ Preserved 1B-B1 electric E7710 works the 11.45 special from Dresden Hbf to Bad Schandau on 02/05/98. **Colin Boocock**

▲ BLE 146 on a DGEG museum shuttle train at Bochum-Dahlhausen.   **Brian Garvin**

▼ 0-10-0T KNE 206 (Krauss Maffei, München 1942) at Hoof on a "Hessencourrier" service with the
12.30 Kassel Wilhelmshöhe Süd–Naumburg (Hessen) on 01/05/04.   **Keith Fender**

▲ Hohenzollerische Landesbahnen 0-8-0T No.11 calls at Linsenhofen station on 18/08/02.
Brian Garvin

▼ Kandertalbahn SWEG 0-6-0T No.30 (Borsig 1904) at Haltingen on 25/07/04 with the 14.15 service to Kandern.   **Keith Fender**

▲ 3-cylinder 4-6-2 01 1100 having worked a railtour, is seen coupled on the rear of a car shuttle to Niebüll on 01/06/02 to save a path on the single line over the Hindenburgdamm.   **Brian Garvin**

▼ DR Class 03 4-6-2 03 2295-8 at Kaiserslautern Hbf on 01/10/00 collecting stock during the weekend Plandampf.   **Colin Boocock**

▲ DR 4-6-2 18 201 is reputed to be the fastest serviceable steam loco in the world. It is seen approaching Pirna on a special to Decin on 19/05/02 having been painted in red livery sponsored by Model firm Märklin.

▼ DR 2-6-2 35 1019-5 leaves Dresden-Plauen on 18/05/02 with a return Dampflokfest special to Cottbus.   **Peter Fox (2)**

▲ DR 2-8-2 41 1150 near Berzhahn with the 15.03 Langenhahn–Limburg on 04/10/02 during the Westerwald Plandampf.   **Keith Satterly**

▼ Rebuilt DR Class 50.35 2-10-0 No.50 3648-8 runs through Dresden-Plauen on 18/05/02.
                                                                                          Peter Fox

▲ Rebuilt Class 52.8 "Kriegslok"
2-10-0 No. 52 8079 at Dresden
Hbf with a special for Altenberg
on 20/05/04.   **Mick Alderman**

► Ex-DR "Traditionslok" 2-8-2T
86 1001-6 at Dresden Hbf on
19/05/96 with a shuttle service to
the Dampflokfest.   **Keith Satterly**

    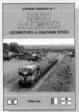

In 2002 PEG surprised everyone when it obtained en bloc all the former DB class 221 diesel hydraulic locos that had been sold to Greece. These are now being overhauled and it is clear that not all are for PEG as two locos are already reported sold to EfW – it is quite likely that the locos were purchased with cash provided by a consortium with PEG in the lead. For the moment all the locos are listed under PEG as V270 as it is understood that this is the intended PEG classification.

As 2002 was closing PEG learnt that it had acquired the contracts for various other lines. In Nordrhein-Westfalen it will operate Dortmund to Enschede from December 2003 for seven years. The company must surely look for a proper depot in this area. Also from December 2004 PEG jointly with HHA will operate the following services in Brandenburg:
KBS 207 Berlin Lichtenberg–Eberswalde–Wriezen–Frankfurt/O; KBS 2109.25 Berlin Lichtenberg–Tiefensee; KBS 209.36 Berlin Lichtenberg–Beeskow–Frankfurt/O; KBS 209.63 Eberswalde–Templin. These lines will be operated under the ODEG banner(q.v.)

Finally as this book went to presss PEG had ordered eight new Regio Shuttle units to replace the ageing DB 798 railbuses.

No.	Builder, No. & Year	Type	kW	Details	Comments
T 1	Uer 60278/1955	798	2 x 110	A-A DMR	Ex DB 798 538
T 2	Uer 61965/1956	798	2 x 110	A-A DMR	Ex DB 798 610
T 3	Uer 61999/1956	798	2 x 110	A-A DMR	Ex DB 798 644
T 4	Uer 66575/1960	798	2 x 110	A-A DMR	Ex DB 796 680
T 5	Uer 66570/1960	798	2 x 110	A-A DMR	Ex DB 798 698
T 6	Uer 66598/1960	798	2 x 110	A-A DMR	Ex DB 798 721
T 7	MAN 146598/1962	798	2 x 110	A-A DMR	Ex DB 798 816
T 8	MAN 146574/1960	798	2 x 110	A-A DMR	Ex DB 796 792
T 9	MAN 145144/1960	798	2 x 110	A-A DMR	Ex DB 798 723
T 10	Uer 61988/1956	798	2 x 110	A-A DMR	Ex DKB 201/ DB 798 633
T 11	Uer 66552/1959	798	2 x 110	A-A DMR	Ex DKB 208/ DB 798 667
T 12	Uer 66605/1960	798	2 x 100	A-A DMR	Ex DB 798 701
T xxx	Uer 60254/1955	798	2 x 110	A-A DMR	Ex DKB 203/ DB 798 514
T 20	MaK 513/1955	GDT	2 x 162	A1-A1 DHR	Ex ACT ALn 2460 ex OHE 0520. To Vossloh.
T 21	MaK 515/1959	GDT	2 x 162	A1-A1 DHR	Ex ACT ALn 2461 ex OHE 0522
T 22	MaK 509/1954	GDT	2 x 162	A1-A1 DHR	Ex ACT ALn 2457 ex OHE 0516
T 23	MaK 510/1955	GDT	2 x 162	A1-A1 DHR	Ex ACT ALn 2458 ex OHE 0517
T	WMD 1309/1960	796	2 x 110	A-A DMR	Ex EVB 166 ex DB 796 769
T	Uer 60272/1955	798	2 x 110	A-A DMR	Ex DB 798 532
T	WMD 1198/1956	798	2 x 110	A-A DMR	Ex DB 798 562
T	Uer 66544/1959	798	2 x 110	A-A DMR	Ex DB 798 658
T	Uer 66600/1960	798	2 x 110	A-A DMR	Ex DB 798 713
403 001	LHB/AEG 2/1974	403	960	Bo-Bo ER	Ex DB
403 002	LHB/AEG 1/1974	403	960	Bo-Bo ER	Ex DB
403 003	LHB/AEG 3/1974	403	960	Bo-Bo ER	Ex DB
403 004	LHB/AEG 4/1974	403	960	Bo-Bo ER	Ex DB
403 005	LHB/AEG 5/1974	403	960	Bo-Bo ER	Ex DB
403 006	LHB/AEG 6/1974	403	960	Bo-Bo ER	Ex DB
404 001	MBB/AEG 3001/1974	404	960	Bo-Bo ER	Ex DB
404 002	MBB/AEG 3002/1974	404	960	Bo-Bo ER	Ex DB
404 003	MBB/AEG 3003/1974	404	960	Bo-Bo ER	Ex DB
404 101	MBB/AEG 3004/1974	404	960	Bo-Bo ER	Ex DB
404 102	MBB/AEG 3005/1974	404	960	Bo-Bo ER	Ex DB
404 103	MBB/AEG 3006/1974	404	960	Bo-Bo ER	Ex DB
???	LKM 251142/1957	N4	96	0-4-0 DM	Wittenberge IND
V22.01	LKM 262593/1975	V22	162	0-4-0 DH	Wittenberge IND
V22.02	LKM 261386/1964	V22	162	0-4-0 DH	Ex IND.
?	LKM 262266/1970	V22	162	0-4-0 DH	Ex Industrieparke Calbe (Saale) 12
?	LKM 262267/1970	V22	162	0-4-0 DH	Ex Industrieparke Calbe (Saale) 13
?	LKM 262340/1971	V22	162	0-4-0 DH	Ex Industrieparke Calbe (Saale) 14
?	LKM 262341/1971	V22	162	0-4-0 DH	Ex Industrieparke Calbe (Saale) 15
V25.01	Essl 5283/1964		184	0-4-0 DH	Ex MEG 4. FFS
V60.02	LEW 11026/1965	V60D	478	0-8-0 DH	Ex Lauchhammer DI 242-60-B4
V60.03	LEW 16463/1980	V60D	478	0-8-0 DH	Ex Kraftwerk Guben 6
V60.04	LEW 16696/1979	V60D	478	0-8-0 DH	Ex Kraftwerk Guben 9

V60.05	LEW 16967/1980	V60D	478	0-8-0 DH	Ex Kraftwerk Guben 10
V60.07	LEW 11321/1964	V60D	478	0-8-0 DH	Ex Kraftwerk Grossräschen 15
V60.08	LEW 11028/1966	V60D	478	0-8-0 DH	Ex Kraftwerk Grossräschen 26
V60.09	LEW 13799/1973	V60D	478	0-8-0 DH	Ex Kraftwerk Grossräschen 29
V60	LEW 13858/1974	V60D	478	0-8-0 DH	Ex SWS Schwerin
V60	LEW 13776/1973	V60D	478	0-8-0 DH	Ex SWS Schwerin
V60	LEW 10925/1965	V60D	478	0-8-0 DH	Ex WTK Ampflwang(A) via EBG
201 026	LEW 12403/1969	V100	809	B-B DH	Stored. Sold 2003?
V200.01	Lugansk 1556/1972	M62	1470	Co-Co DE	Ex CD 781 436
V200.02	Lugansk 1547/1972	M62	1470	Co-Co DE	Ex CD 781 427
V200.03	Lugansk 1740/1973	M62	1470	Co-Co DE	Ex CD 781 516
V200.05	Lugansk 3428/1979	M62	1470	Co-Co DE	Ex PKP ST44 844
V200.	Lugansk 2944/1977	M62	1470	Co-Co DE	Ex PKP ST44 705 Stored
V200.10	Lugansk 3536/1979	M62	1470	Co-Co DE	Ex PKP ST44 952
V200	Lugansk 2518/1976	M62	1470	Co-Co DE	Ex PKP ST44 542
V200	Lugansk 3581/1980	M62	1470	Co-Co DE	Ex PKP ST44 1007
V200	Lugansk 0431/1968	M62	1470	Co-Co DE	Ex EBM V200 509, Ex Wismut, ex BKK Geisetal, ex DR 120 094
Kö 5731	BMAG 10315/1937	Köf III	96	B DH	Ex DR 100 931
E94.01	AEG 5331/1941	E94	3000	Co-Co E	Ex DR 254 052 ex Dieringhausen
E94.02	AEG 5330/1941	E94	3000	Co-Co E	Ex DB 194 051 ex Plinth at Singen
V270.	KM 18997/1962	V200.1	2x990	B-B DH	Ex OSE 411 ex DB 221 105
V270.	KM 18998/1962	V200.1	2x990	B-B DH	Ex OSE 412 ex DB 221 106
V270.	KM 18999/1962	V200.1	2x990	B-B DH	Ex OSE 424 ex DB 221 107
V270.	KM 19004/1963	V200.1	2x990	B-B DH	Ex OSE 421 ex DB 221 112
V270.	KM 19011/1963	V200.1	2x990	B-B DH	Ex OSE 422 ex DB 221 119
V270.	KM 19241/1964	V200.1	2x990	B-B DH	Ex OSE 427 ex DB 221 121
V270.	KM 19244/1964	V200.1	2x990	B-B DH	Ex OSE 419 ex DB 221 124
V270.	KM 19246/1964	V200.1	2x990	B-B DH	Ex OSE 425 ex DB 221 126
V270.	KM 19247/1965	V200.1	2x990	B-B DH	Ex OSE 426 ex DB 221 127
V270.	KM 19249/1965	V200.1	2x990	B-B DH	Ex OSE 414 ex DB 221 129
V270.	KM 19253/1965	V200.1	2x990	B-B DH	Ex OSE 413 ex DB 221 133
V270.	KM 19254/1965	V200.1	2x990	B-B DH	Ex OSE 418 ex DB 221 134
V270.	KM 19256/1965	V200.1	2x990	B-B DH	Ex OSE 417 ex DB 221 136
V270.	KM 19257/1965	V200.1	2x990	B-B DH	Ex OSE 430 ex DB 221 137
V270.	KM 19258/1965	V200.1	2x990	B-B DH	Ex OSE 428 ex DB 221 138
V270.	KM 19265/1965	V200.1	2x990	B-B DH	Ex OSE 423 ex DB 221 145
V270.	KM 19266/1965	V200.1	2x990	B-B DH	Ex OSE 429 ex DB 221 146
V270.	KM 19267/1965	V200.1	2x990	B-B DH	Ex OSE 416 ex DB 221 147

Oberhausen area services

VT 643.01	Bomb 191735/6/2002	Talent	2 x 315	B-2-B DMR	
VT 643.02	Bomb 191737/8/2002	Talent	2 x 315	B-2-B DMR	
VT 643.03	Bomb 191739-41/2002	Talent	2 x 315	B-2-2-B DMR	
VT 643.04	Bomb 191732-44/2002	Talent	2 x 315	B-2-2-B DMR	
VT 643.05	Bomb 191745-47/2002	Talent	2 x 315	B-2-2-B DMR	
VT 643.06	Bomb 191748-50/2002	Talent	2 x 315	B-2-2-B DMR	

Units ordered to replace old 798s. These are intended to work Neuruppin–Neustadt/Dosse–Pritwalk–Meyenburg and Pritwalk–Putlitz.

VT650.01	Stadler	RS1	2 x 257	B-B DMR	PEG Owned
VT650.02	Stadler	RS1	2 x 257	B-B DMR	PEG Owned
VT650.03	Stadler	RS1	2 x 257	B-B DMR	PEG Owned
VT650.04	Stadler	RS1	2 x 257	B-B DMR	HHA Owned
VT650.05	Stadler	RS1	2 x 257	B-B DMR	HHA Owned
VT650.06	Stadler	RS1	2 x 257	B-B DMR	HHA Owned
VT650.07	Stadler	RS1	2 x 257	B-B DMR	HHA Owned
VT650.08	Stadler	RS1	2 x 257	B-B DMR	HHA Owned

A further 11 Talent DMUs have been ordered for services from Dortmund to Enschede, service to be taken over in December 2004.
PEG has stored ex DB units 798 532/562/658/713/767. These may be overhauled eventually or just be used to provide spares.

Two steam locomotives have been acquired one of which is 50 3521. These may be future tourist services on some of its lines.

PFALZBAHN EISENBAHNBETRIEBESGESELLSCHAFT mbH
PFALZ

Frankenthal, Pfalz.

Depot: Worms?
EVU Licence: Freight and Passenger 24/09/1996.

This organisation appears to have been set up by various railfans in 1995 and obtained its EVU licence in 1996. It has been using the old DB depot at Worms but its current base is not known.

No.	Builder, No. & Year	Type	kW	Details	Comments
144 059	KM 15569/1936	E44	1860	Bo-Bo E	On loan from DB Museum
144 084	KM 15650/1938	E44	1860	Bo-Bo E	On loan from DB Museum
145 180	Hens 25585/1947	E44	1860	Bo-Bo E	On loan from DB Museum
310 275	O&K 20269/1934	Köf II	97	4w DH	Ex DR
310 278	O&K 20272/1933	Köf II	97	4w DH	Ex DR
798 622	Uer 61977/1956	798	2 x 110	A-A DMR	Ex DB
798 818	MAN 146600/1962	798	2 x 110	A-A DMR	Ex DB
VT 50	Essl 23608/1954	Esslingen	2 x 130	1A-A1 DHR	Ex KVG
V1001-041	VSFT 1001041/2002	G2000	2240	B-B DH	Hired via ATC for Contrain.

EISENBAHNBAU UND BETRIEBSGESELLSCHAFT
PRESSNITZTALBAHN mbH   PRESS
Jöhstadt, Sachsen

Depot: ?
EVU Licence: Freight and Passenger 07/06/2000.

The preservation society that runs the Jöhstadt–Steinbach line has formed its own EVU and is obtaining work on track construction works trains or simply hiring out its locos to other agencies. Locos are numbered with the DB style classification but the last three digits represent the numerical order.

No.	Builder, No. & Year	Type	kW	Details	Comments
346 001	LEW 11977/1968	V60D	478	0-8-0 DH	Ex Industry.
312 002	LKM 262607/1967	V22	162	0-4-0 DH	Ex WL 1 HKW Dresden
346 003	LEW 16956/1980	V60D	478	0-8-0 DH	Ex MEG 06I.
346 004	LEW 15693/1979	V60D	478	0-8-0 DH	Ex Czech 716 601
204 005	LEW 12859/1971	V100.4	1050	B-B DH	Ex 202 350. CAT 3512
346 006	LEW 17652/1982	V60D	478	0-8-0 DH	Ex Czech 716 602. Sold to ?
204 006	LEW 13564/1973	V100.4	1050	B-B DH	Ex 202 525, CAT 3512
199 007	LKM 250029/1957	Ns4	50	0-6-0 DH	Leased from Jöhstadt preservation group
199 008	LKM 250310/1962	V10C	70	0-6-0 DH	Leased from Jöhstadt preservation group
199 009	LKM 250 337/1964	V10C	70	0-6-0 DH	Leased from Jöhstadt preservation group
204 010	LEW 15388/1976	V100DR	1050	B-B DH	Ex ALS, ex HSB 199 870, DR 110 870. CAT engine
204 011	LEW 15229/1976	V100DR	1050	B-B DH	Ex ALS, ex DB 202 844
212 012?	MaK 1000323/1965	V100DB	?	B-B DH	Ex ALS, ex DB 212 276, (on order)

PRESS has also been hiring in locos to help out with contracts. These locos include 106 992 from the VSE preservation society. Similarly the two class 199 750mm gauge diesels belong to the Pressnitztalbahn preservation society but are available for use on lines elsewhere in Germany for ballast trains.

RAG AKTIENGESELLSCHAFT
RAG BAHN UND HAFENBETRIEB   RAG
Gladbeck, Nordrhein Westfalen

Electric System: 15kV ac 16.7 Hz.
Routes: Numerous lines around the Ruhr including servicing collieries and harbours.
Length: 452/582 km (192 km electrified).
Depots: Gladbeck, Dortmund-Mooskamp, Werne.
EVU Licence: Freight and Passenger 03/05/2001.

This company has its background in the coal industry. RAG originally stood for Ruhrkohle AG and was reponsible for servicing the Ruhr area collieries and connecting lines. The German coal industry has undergone great changes in a way similar to Britain forcing RAG to change with it. Thus the railway activities are now a division of Deutsche Steinkohle (DSK) with its sub title of Bahn und Hafenbetriebe. The railway continues to service the remaining collieries and has many workings over DB tracks taking coal to power stations etc. 58.4 million tonnes were handled in 1998 with 38 million of this being handed over to DB at some stage. The most recent diesel locomotives are Vossloh/Siemens/ MaK G1206BB "Ruhrpot Sprinter" specially tailored for RAG needs with heavy coal haulage. The arrival of these new locos will obviously see off some of the older locos. In 2001 RAG received some Adtranz 145CL electric locomotives to allow coal trains to work even further with RAG locos. They are used on coal trains from Oberhausen West/Marl Sinsen–Minden–Lahde and Beddingen. Under open access RAG is providing power for other services such as the Westerholt to Bremen Stahlwerke shuttle and the IKEA Duisburg–Sweden train. This latter working was taken over completely by RAG in January 2004 but is now operated by Railion.

No.	Builder, No. & Year	Type	kW	Details	Comments
001	Hens 32090/1976	E1200	1500	Bo-Bo E	
002	Hens 32091/1976	E1200	1500	Bo-Bo E	
003	Hens 32092/1976	E1200	1500	Bo-Bo E	
004	Hens 32093/1976	E1200	1500	Bo-Bo E	
005	Hens 32094/1976	E1200	1500	Bo-Bo E	
006	Hens 32095/1976	E1200	1500	Bo-Bo E	
011	Hens 32773/1984	E1200	1500	Bo-Bo E	
012	Hens 32774/1984	E1200	1500	Bo-Bo E	
013	Hens 32775/1984	E1200	1500	Bo-Bo E	
014	Hens 32776/1984	E1200	1500	Bo-Bo E	
015	Hens 32777/1984	E1200	1500	Bo-Bo E	
016	Hens 32828/1984	E1200	1500	Bo-Bo E	
017	Hens 32829/1984	E1200	1500	Bo-Bo E	
021	Hens 31336/1968	ED1600	1600/510	Bo-Bo ED	
022	Hens 31338/1968	ED1600	1600/510	Bo-Bo ED	
101	Hens 31330/1968	EA1000	720	Bo-Bo E	
103	Hens 31332/1968	EA1000	720	Bo-Bo E	
201	Adtranz 33844/2001	145	4200	Bo-Bo E	145 CL 201
202	Adtranz 33845/2001	145	4200	Bo-Bo E	145 CL 202
203	Adtranz 33846/2001	145	4200	Bo-Bo E	145 CL 203
204	Adtranz 33847/2001	145	4200	Bo-Bo E	145 CL 204
205	Bomb 33850/2002	145	4200	Bo-Bo E	145 CL 205
206	Bomb 33849/2002	145	4200	Bo-Bo E	145 CL 206
221	Bomb 33477/2002	185	5600	Bo-Bo E	185 CL 008
222	Bomb 33498/2002	185	5600	Bo-Bo E	185 CL 009
251	SKM 20573/2002	ES64U2	6400	Bo-Bo E	Dispolok ES64U2 017
252	SKM 20776/2003	ES64U2	6400	Bo-Bo E	Dispolok ES64U2 026 (Leased 2003–2006)
290	Hens 31132/1966	EA500	500	Bo E	
326	Hens 31088/1965	DH160	118	B DH	
362	KM 19398/1969	M350C	257	C DH	Stored 6/02
411	Gm 5277/1962	CDH5	441	C DH	Stored 1/02
413	Gm 5279/1963	CDH5	441	C DH	Stored 1/02
432	Hens 31187/1966	DHG500	368	C DH	Stored 1/02
433	Hens 31188/1966	DHG500	368	C DH	Stored 1/02
434	Hens 31189/1966	DHG500	368	C DH	
435	Hens 31232/1968	DHG500	368	C DH	
438	Hens 30583/1966	DHG500	368	C DH	Stored 1/02
440	Hens 30573/1963	DHG500	368	C DH	
441	Hens 30574/1963	DHG500	368	C DH	
442	Hens 30575/1963	DHG500	368	C DH	
443	Hens 30576/1963	DHG500	368	C DH	Sold to Italy
444	Hens 30577/1963	DHG500	368	C DH	
445	Hens 30854/1966	DHG500	368	C DH	
446	Hens 30855/1966	DHG500	368	C DH	
448	Hens 31072/1965	DHG500	368	C DH	Sold to Italy
449	Hens 31073/1965	DHG500	368	C DH	Stored 1/02
450	Hens 31075/1965	DHG500	368	C DH	

453	Hens 31183/1966	DHG500	368	C DH	
475	Hens 31074/1965	DHG500	368	C DH	
510	KM 19730/1974	M700C	515	C DH	
511	KM 19675/1973	M700C	515	C DH	Stored 1/02
512	KM 19679/1973	M700C	515	C DH	
513	KM 19680/1973	M700C	515	C DH	
514	KM 19687/1973	M700C	515	C DH	
515	KM 19689/1973	M700C	515	C DH	
516	KM 19678/1973	M700C	515	C DH	
517	KM 19688/1973	M700C	515	C DH	
518	KM 19695/1973	M700C	515	C DH	
519	KM 19729/1974	M700C	515	C DH	
522	Hens 31195/1966	DHG700C	515	C DH	
523	Hens 31468/1970	DHG700C	515	C DH	
551	MaK 700039/1980	DE501	510	Co DE	
552	MaK 700053/1981	DE501	510	Co DE	
554	MaK 700055/1981	DE501	510	Co DE	
555	MaK 700056/1981	DE501	510	Co DE	
556	MaK 700057/1982	DE501	510	Co DE	
557	MaK 700047/1981	DE501	510	Co DE	
558	MaK 700051/1981	DE501	510	Co DE	
559	MaK 700049/1981	DE501	510	Co DE	Ex 259 002
561	MaK 700095/1989	DE502	510	Co DE	
562	MaK 700096/1989	DE502	510	Co DE	
563	MaK 700097/1989	DE502	510	Co DE	
564	MaK 700098/1989	DE502	510	Co DE	
570	KM 19693/1973	M700C	515	C DH	
571	KM 19694/1974	M700C	515	C DH	
572	KM 19695/1973	M700C	515	C DH	
573	KM 19681/1973	M700C	515	C DH	
574	KM 19734/1975	M700C	515	C DH	
575	KM 19696/1973	M700C	515	C DH	
576	KM 19690/1974	M700C	515	C DH	
577	KM 19684/1973	M700C	515	C DH	
578	KM 19682/1973	M700C	515	C DH	
579	KM 19683/1973	M700C	515	C DH	
580	KM 19691/1974	M700C	515	C DH	
581	KM 19731/1975	M700C	515	C DH	
582	KM 19732/1975	M700C	515	C DH	
583	KM 19676/1973	M700C	515	C DH	Withdrawn
584	KM 19692/1974	M700C	515	C DH	
585	KM 19677/1973	M700C	515	C DH	
586	KM 19733/1975	M700C	515	C DH	
640	Hens 31178/1966	DHG1200	990	B-B DH	
641	Hens 31179/1966	DHG1200	990	B-B DH	
642	Hens 31180/1966	DHG1200	990	B-B DH	
643	Hens 31181/1966	DHG1200	990	B-B DH	
661	MaK 1000843/1988	DE1003	2 x 510	Bo-Bo DE	
662	MaK 1000844/1988	DE1003	2 x 510	Bo-Bo DE	
663	MaK 1000845/1988	DE1003	2 x 510	Bo-Bo DE	
664	MaK 1000846/1988	DE1003	2 x 510	Bo-Bo DE	
673	MaK 1000817/1984	G1204	1120	B-B DH	
674	MaK 1000797/1982	G1204	1120	B-B DH	
676	MaK 1000807/1983	G1204	1120	B-B DH	
677	MaK 1000812/1983	G1204	1120	B-B DH	
678	MaK 1000815/1984	G1204	1120	B-B DH	
679	MaK 1000821/1985	G1204	1120	B-B DH	
801	SFT 1000900/1997	G1206	1570	B-B DH	
802	SFT 1000901/1997	G1206	1570	B-B DH	
803	SFT 1000902/1997	G1206	1570	B-B DH	
804	SFT 1000903/1997	G1206	1570	B-B DH	
805	SFT 1000904/1997	G1206	1570	B-B DH	
806	SFT 1000905/1997	G1206	1570	B-B DH	
807	VSFT 1000913/1998	G1206	1570	B-B DH	

808	VSFT 1000914/1998	G1206	1570	B-B DH	
809	VSFT 1000915/1998	G1206	1570	B-B DH	
810	VSFT 1000916/1998	G1206	1570	B-B DH	
811	VSFT 1000917/1998	G1206	1570	B-B DH	
821	VSFT 1001012/1999	G1206	1570	B-B DH	Leased from ATC
822	VSFT 1001013/1999	G1206	1570	B-B DH	Leased from ATC
823	VSFT 1001014/1999	G1206	1570	B-B DH	Leased from ATC
824	VSFT 1001015/1999	G1206	1570	B-B DH	Leased from ATC
825	VSFT 1001016/1999	G1206	1570	B-B DH	Leased from ATC
826	VSFT 1001021/2000	G1206	1570	B-B DH	Leased from ATC
827	VSFT 1001023/2000	G1206	1570	B-B DH	Leased from ATC
828	VSFT 1001024/2000	G1206	1570	B-B DH	Leased from ATC
829	VSFT 1001026/2000	G1206	1570	B-B DH	Leased from ATC
830	VSFT 1001027/2000	G1206	1570	B-B DH	Leased from ATC
831	VL 5001479/2003	G1206	1570	B-B DH	
901	VSFT 1001030/2001	G2000BB	2240	B-B DH	Leased from ATC
902	VSFT 1001031/2001	G2000BB	2240	B-B DH	Leased from ATC
903	VSFT 1001032/2001	G2000BB	2240	B-B DH	Leased from ATC
904	VSFT 1001036/2001	G2000BB	2240	B-B DH	

NB: 821–830 leased for 15 years!

RAIL CHARTER FAHRZEUGBEREITSSTELLUNG
RAIL CHARTER

Baden Württemberg

This Mannheim based company is a financing arranger. Just look who owns it - 25% HzL, 25% SWEG and 50% Adtranz! It owns all the Regio Shuttles delivered to the railway companies - BSB 9, HzL 22, SWEG 8, OSB 18, RAB 20, and 3 spare. Note that RAB is listed under DB in part one. It appears that Adtranz is underwriting the purchase of its own units!

RAIL4CHEM EISENBAHNVERKEHRS-GELLSCHAFT mbH
Rail4Chem

Essen, Nordrhein-Westfalen

EVU Licence: Freight and Passenger 31/10/2001.

Rail4Chem was formed in 2001 and is a joint venture by BASF AG, Bertschi AG (Switzerland), Hoyer GmbH and VTG Lehnkering AG. It grew out of the early BASF chemical operations from Ludwigshafen but has expanded considerably. It still handles the former BASF main line runs from Ludwigshafen to Schwarzheide, Heimboldshausen and Antwerpen. The last mentioned is worked by a 145 to Aachen West. These are controlled from Ludwigshafen
Another flow is coal and pulverised coal (lignite) on the following routes:
Deuna–Spreewitz–Berlin–Spreewitz–Deuna
Deuna–Espenhain–Deutschenbora–Spreewitz–Deuna
Deuna–Berlin–Deutschenbora-Espenhain–Deuna
These flows are controlled from Nordhausen. On the non-electrified sections Rail4Chem has contracted out the haulage to local firms with MEG working Böhlen–Espenhain and vv whilst WAB works from Döbeln to Deutschenbora and vv.

The company has continued to grow and on 1.10.2002 absorbed all the Hoyer Railserv workings and locomotives. Another big step forward took place on 1/11/2002 when its presence at Nordhausen was enlarged as this has now become the major control centre not only for the trains but also for the locomotives and rolling stock. These are now maintained at Nordhausen by IGENO. Both IGENO and Rail4Chem share the same premises – the old DB locomotive depot! During 2002 further spot flows were acquired including chemicals from Leuna to Hamburg, Hannover, Berlin, and flows from Wittenberg to Linz (Austria) and Mazingarbe (France) which R4C takes to the respective border station. Another new flow is from Ludwigshafen to Duisburg Rheinhausen and Millingen. Besides taking traffic into Hamburg it is now engaged in working flows from there to Salzgitter and Seelze.

During 2003 Rail4Chem started a joint operation with Short Lines to move containers from Rotterdam to Worms whilst on the chemical side extra trips were being run from BASF Ludwigshafen and Schwarzenheide to Grosskorbetha.

Late in 2003 Rail4Chem combined forces with LTE in Austria to offer a Duisburg–Graz service three times a week. The train leaves Duisburg at 20.30 (TThSO) and is into Graz (Kalsdorf) at 16.30 the next day and gets away from Graz at 20.50 (MWFO) getting back to Duisburg at 20.50. The service was booked to start early in 2004 with 185 528 ordered for the service.

No.	Builder, No. & Year	Type	kW	Details	Comments
145 CL 001	Adtranz 33356/1999	145	4200	Bo-Bo E	
145 CL 002	Adtranz 33366/2000	145	4200	Bo-Bo E	
145 CL 003	Adtranz 33821/2000	145	4200	Bo-Bo E	
145 CL 004	Adtranz 33826/2000	145	4200	Bo-Bo E	
145 CL 005	Adtranz 33843/2001	145	4200	Bo-Bo E	
185 CL 004	Bomb 33453/2001	185	5600	Bo-Bo E	ex Hoyer
185 CL 005	Bomb 33451/2001	185	5600	Bo-Bo E	ex Hoyer
185 CL 006	Bomb 33458/2002	185	5600	Bo-Bo E	ex Hoyer
185 CL 007	Bomb 33456/2002	185	5600	Bo-Bo E	ex Hoyer
185 517	Bomb 33531/2002	185	5600	Bo-Bo E	
207 CL 116	VSFT 1001116/2000	G1206BB	1500	B-B DH	ex Hoyer
207 CL 138	VSFT 1001138/2001	G1206BB	1500	B-B DH	ex Hoyer
PB 05	EMD 20008254-7/2002	66	2462	Co-Co DE	
ES64U2 005	SKM 20561/2001	ES64U2	6400	Bo-Bo E	On hire from Dispolok

railogic GmbH   railogic
Kreuzau, Nordrhein-Westfalen

Depot:
EVU Licence: 15/07/2002.

Founded 21/02/2001 as an EIU/EVU it was not until 2002 that it acquired a locomotive and started working ballast trains etc. It is believed to have since taken over Eifelbahn Verkehrsgesellschaft mbH (EVG).

No.	Builder, No. & Year	Type	kW	Details	Comments
V60.01	LEW 12383/1969	V60D	478	0-8-0 DH	Ex Zement Rudersdorf 7

RAR EISENBAHN SERVICE AG   RAR
Depots: Neuoffingen

RAR is a joint venture leasing company formed by several small organisations in the greater Stuttgart area aimed at providing locomotives for hook and pull services that are cheaper to hire than from the bigger operators such as Bombardier, Angel Trains and Dispolok. Journeys tend to be over short distances. RAR = Rent a Rail! Locos numbered over 100 are generally hired in locos and subsequently move on to other railway operators.

No.	Builder, No. & Year	Type	kW	Details	Comments
VT11	Essl 25058/1958	Essl	2x162	B-B DHR	Ex SWEG Vt 112
V130.101	Gm 5153/1960	Köf II	97	4w DH	Ex DB 323 719
V130.102	KHD 57291/1959	Köf II	97	4w DH	Ex DB 323 146 (Neuoffingen 10/03)
V130.103	Gm 5205/1960	Köf II	97	4w DH	Ex DB 323 771
V130.104	Jung 13137/1959	Köf II	97	4w DH	Ex DB 323 697
V140.01	KHD 57788/1965	KK140B	90	4w DH	Ex WL3 Ulmer Weisskalkwerken
V140.02	KHD 56163/1956	KK130B	90	4w DH	
V240.01	Gm 5304/1964	Köf III	162	4W DH	Ex DB 332 901
V240.02	Gm 5357/1964	Köf III	162	4W DH	Ex DB 332 217
V240.03	Gm 5459/1964	Köf III	162	4W DH	Ex DB 335 063
V650.01	LEW 12363/1967	V60D	478	0-8-0 DH	Ex 11 ex EKO 35 "Bettina" (München area)
V650.02	LEW 12255/1969	V60D	478	0-8-0 DH	Ex IND, ex DR 346 545 "Andrea" (TXL Nürnberg)
V650.03	LEW 13760/1973	V60D	478	0-8-0 DH	Ex 10 ex EKO 32 "Barbel" (TXL München)
V650.04	LEW 12377/1971	V60D	478	0-8-0 DH	Ex DB 346 784 (DB Auto Zug, München Ost)
V650.05	LEW 17639/1982	V60D	478	0-8-0 DH	Ex MWB V643, on hire to TXL
V650.06	LEW 17421/1981	V60D	478	0-8-0 DH	Ex MWB V642, on hire to RCN
V650.107	LEW 17421/1981	V60D	478	0-8-0 DH	MWB V642 on hire
V650	LEW 17415/1980	V60D	478	0-8-0 DH	Ex MIBRAG Di482-65-B4 (Stored Neuoffingen)
V1200.01	LEW 15094/1975	V100DR	932	B-B DH	Ex MWB V1204, ex ALS, ex DB 202 822. "Steffi"
V1200.02	LEW 12774/1970	V100DR	932	B-B DH	Ex ALS, ex DB 202 310. "Brunhilde"

NB: Some of these locos that are in fact radio controlled are to be renumbered with a "5" at the start of the running number.

REGIOBAHN BITTERFELD GmbH   RBB (CONNEX)
Bitterfeld, Sachsen Anhal

Routes: Wolfen–Bitterfeld–Delitzsch
Length: 25.0/58.3 km   **Depots:** Wolfen Chemical works.
EVU Licence: Freight and Passenger 25/04/1996.

This company was formed after unification under the privatising arrangements for former state enterprises. Its background lies in the shunting and servicing of the chemical industry factories around Bitterfeld and coal mining concerns. Formed in 1995 RBB comes under the DEG umbrella. The network has some 105 km and as many as 35 different connections for serving over 80 customers. 593,000 tonnes originated in 1998 somewhat down on the 646,000 in 1997. As can be expected from a former East German operation most of the locos are V60D. The V100.4 locos have been modernised by Adtranz. Being a Connex company locos are often used in connection with other Connex traffic flows or on sub-contract to operators such as Rail4Chem where the diesel locos can take trains over non-electrified lines after a long journey by electric power. RBB has in recent times been hauling sand from Scharzfeld to Bitterfeld and Torgau for which some G2000 locos were hired. RBB also works trains to Riesa and Schwarzheide for which some G1206 locos were acquired on hire.

During 2003 under Connex Cargo Logistics, RBB started running a weekly block train of soda from Bernburg/Bitterfeld to Stolberg (Rheinland). A Connex 185 or G1206 is used.

No.	Builder, No. & Year	Type	kW	Details	Comments
1	Mein 03010/1984	CFL		0-6-0F	
9	Mein 03146/1986	CFL		0-6-0F	
20	LEW 15357/1976	V60D	478	0-8-0 DH	
21	LEW 11974/1968	V60D	478	0-8-0 DH	
22	LEW 16575/1979	V60D	478	0-8-0 DH	Ex HTB in 1999
24	LEW 14193/1973	V60D	478	0-8-0 DH	
26	LEW 15616/1977	V60D	478	0-8-0 DH	
27	LEW 16577/1979	V60D	478	0-8-0 DH	
28	LEW 15676/1979	V60D	478	0-8-0 DH	
29	LEW 17586/1981	V60D	478	0-8-0 DH	
33	LKM 262606/1975	V22	162	0-4-0 DH	
60	LEW 17769/1983	ASF	17	Bo BE	
75	LEW	ASF	17	Bo BE	
V 133	MaK 1000257/1968	G1300BB	956	B-B DH	To NWC 1203
V 141	LEW 17728/1983	V100.4	1050	B-B DH	Ex TWE V104/EKO 63. CAT engine
V 142	LEW 15382/1976	V100.4	1050	B-B DH	Ex DB 201 864. CAT engine. To BCB.
V 145	LEW 15381/1976	V100.4	1050	B-B DH	Ex Bombardier, ex HSB199 863 ex DR 199 863. CAT engine. To BCB.
V 146	LEW 12897/1971	V100	1050	B-B DH	Ex NEB 21, ex DB 202 388. CAT engine
V 147	LEW 12834/1971	V100	1050	B-B DH	Ex NEB 20, ex DB 202 325. CAT engine
V1001-021	VSFT 1001021/2000	G1206	1500	B-B DH	On hire from LSG
V1001-129	VSFT 1001129/2001	G1206	1500	B-B DH	On hire from LSG
V1001-042	VSFT 1001042/2002	G2000	2240	B-B DH	On hire from LC

RHEINGOLD ZUG BETRIEBESGESELLSCHAFT mbH
RBG

Nordrhein Westfalen

This organisation is the operating arm of the Kölner Eisenbahn Club that many former Rheingold vehicles. These are kept in the old loco depot at Köln Nippes and are often used on charter specials or as extra vehicles on service trains. The loco performs trip working in the Köln area but the EVU is not known.

No.	Builder, No. & Year	Type	kW	Details	Comments
332 RL 218	Gm 5358/1965	Köf III	162	4w DH	Ex DB

REGENTAL BAHNBETRIEBS GESELLSCHAFT RBG
REGENTAL CARGO GmbH RC
Vietach, Bayern

Routes: Kotzing–Lam (KBS 877); Viechtach–Gotteszell (own line). Cham–Waldmünchen (KBS 976, 22.1 km); Plattling–Bayerische Eisenstein (KBS 905, 71.7 km); Zwiesel–Grafenau (KBS 906 31.6 km); Zwiesel–Bodenmais (KBS 907, 14.5 km)
Length: 18.0/42.6 km plus DB Netz operations. **Depots:** Viechtach, Lam, Schwandorf
EVU Licence: Freight and Passenger 22/12/1994.

Formerly RAG (Regentalbahn AG) the RBG is a much changed organisation with its main operations now being over former DB lines. Its workshop division is now a separate entity - Regental Farhzeugwerkstätten GmbH using the old RAG workshops/depot in Vietach and new workshops at Neumarkt (Vogtl) which replaced those previously used at DR Bw Reichenbach. The RGB has been operating its "Waldbahn" services since 1996 and expanded since taking over former DR lines in the Reichenbach/Zwickau area under the "Vogtlandbahn" name (q.v.). 2000 saw further expansion on old DR lines followed by services on old DB routes in 2001 for which 11 more RS1 have been ordered. These routes around Schwandorf include Cham–Lam, Cham–Waldmünchen and Schwandorf–Cham–Furth in Wald to be marketed as "Oberpfalzbahn". DB RE services will continue to run so that DB and RBG will in effect share the services. In 1998 RBG handled 197,000 passengers and little freight.

In 2002 Regental Cargo was formed to act as the EVU for ConTrain (q.v.). RC locos work the container trains from Hof northwards and also cover other trips in the area. Locos D05-07 being acquired for the purpose. RBG also obtained the contract to run local services along the Hof–Regensburg line and is establishing a new depot in Schwandorf.

No.	Builder, No. & Year	Type	kW	Details	Comments
D 03	MaK 1000789/1980	G1202BB	1000	B-B DH	Viechtach area
D 04	MaK 1000791/1980	G1202BB	1000	B-B DH	Lam area
D 05	VSFT 1001142/2002	G1206	1500	B-B DH	
D 06	VSFT 1001039/2002	G2000	2240	B-B DH	
D 07	VSFT 1001043/2002	G2000	2240	B-B DH	
D 08	LKM 265108/1970	V22	162	0-4-0 DH	Ex DB 312 208
VT 02	WagU 30905/1981	NE81	2 x 201	B-B DHR	
VT 05	Essl 23437/1952	Esslingen	294	B-2 DHR	Ex BE VT 2. Museum car
VT 06	Essl 23438/1952	Esslingen	294	B-2 DHR	Ex HzL VT 10. Stored.
VT 07	Essl 23436/1952	Esslingen	294	B-2 DHR	Ex FKE VT 91
VT 08	WagU 33626/1985	NE81	2 x 201	B-B DHR	Spare
VT 09	O&K 320009/4/1959	515		Bo-2 DER	Ex DB 515 511 (rebuilt)
VT 10	O&K 320010/3/1960	515		Bo-2 DER	Ex DB 515 523 (rebuilt)
VT 15	Adtranz 36523/1996	RS1	2 x 228	B-B DMR	
VT 16	Adtranz 36524/1996	RS1	2 x 228	B-B DMR	*Naturpark Bayerische Wald*
VT 17	Adtranz 36525/1996	RS1	2 x 228	B-B DMR	
VT 18	Adtranz 36526/1996	RS1	2 x 228	B-B DMR	
VT 19	Adtranz 36527/1996	RS1	2 x 228	B-B DMR	*Frauenau*
VT 20	Adtranz 36528/1996	RS1	2 x 228	B-B DMR	*Deggendorf*
VT 21	Adtranz 36529/1996	RS1	2 x 228	B-B DMR	*Regen*
VT 22	Adtranz 36530/1996	RS1	2 x 228	B-B DMR	*Plattling*
VT 23	Adtranz 36531/1996	RS1	2 x 228	B-B DMR	*Gotteszell*
VT 24	Adtranz 36532/1996	RS1	2 x 228	B-B DMR	
VT 25	Adtranz 36533/1996	RS1	2 x 228	B-B DMR	*Bayerisch Eisenstein*
VT 26	Adtranz 36534/1997	RS1	2 x 228	B-B DMR	Ex Adtranz VT 300
VT 31	Adtranz 36888/2000	RS1	2 x 228	B-B DMR	Oberpfalzbahn
VT 32	Adtranz 36889/2000	RS1	2 x 228	B-B DMR	Oberpfalzbahn
VT 33	Adtranz 36890/2001	RS1	2 x 228	B-B DMR	Oberpfalzbahn
VT 34	Adtranz 36891/2001	RS1	2 x 228	B-B DMR	Oberpfalzbahn
VT 35	Adtranz 36892/2001	RS1	2 x 228	B-B DMR	Oberpfalzbahn
VT 36	Adtranz 36893/2001	RS1	2 x 228	B-B DMR	Oberpfalzbahn
VT 37	Adtranz 36894/2001	RS1	2 x 228	B-B DMR	Oberpfalzbahn
VT 38	Adtranz 36895/2001	RS1	2 x 228	B-B DMR	Oberpfalzbahn
VT 39	Adtranz 36896/2001	RS1	2 x 228	B-B DMR	Oberpfalzbahn
VT 40	Adtranz 36897/2001	RS1	2 x 228	B-B DMR	Oberpfalzbahn
VT 41	Adtranz 36898/2001	RS1	2 x 228	B-B DMR	Oberpfalzbahn
Werklok	Jung 5492/1934	Köf II	97	4w DH	Ex DB 323 486

RAIL CARGO BERLIN GmbH   RCB
Berlin

This is a new joint venture company formed by PEG and Industriebahn Berlin GmbH. M62s have been acquired from Poland for freight services from Berlin. In 2001 PEG pulled out of RCB and took back locos V200.06/7. PEG has since been replaced as part owner of RCB by Connex! The remaining two V200 have since been sold to a private operator in Poland (E. Burkhardt ?). An EVU licence for freight only was issued 24/11/2000.

To service the remaining traffic centres in Berlin RCB has hired in a G 2000.

No.	Builder, No. & Year	Type	kW	Details	Comments
V200.06	Lugansk 3184/1978	M62	1470	Co-Co DE	Ex PKP ST44 733 To PEG
V200.07	Lugansk 3200/1978	M62	1470	Co-Co DE	Ex PKP ST44 749 To PEG
V200.22	Lugansk 1819/1973	M62	1470	Co-Co DE	Ex PKP ST44 218
V200.23	Lugansk 3518/1979	M62	1470	Co-Co DE	Ex PKP ST44 934
V1001-042	VSFT 1001042/2002	G2000	2000	B-B DH	On hire

RAIL CENTRE NÜRNBERG GmbH & Co. KG   RCN
Nürnberg, Bayern

The DB rail centre in Nürnberg was bought in 2002 by Stahlberg Roensch of Hamburg forming RCN in the process. Two locomotives were also acquired for shunting at the works and delivering the long-welded rails etc. Since then further locomotives have been acquired for works trains. An EVU licence for freight trains was issued 20/11/2002.

No.	Builder, No. & Year	Type	kW	Details	Comments
RCN 0501	VSFT 1001136/2002	G1206	1500	B-B DH	Willi Wuhlbeck
RCN 0502	VSFT 1001139/2002	G1206	1500	B-B DH	Martin Lauer
RCN 0503	MaK 1000805/1985	G1203	745	B-B DH	Waldemar Cierpinski
RCN 0504	VSFT 1001141/2002	G1206	1500	B-B DH	
RCN 0505	LEW 14469/1975	V100DR1305		B-B DH	(Due to arrive in 2004). Ex DB 202 768 via ALS
RCN 0506	LEW 14891/1975	V100Dr 1305		B-B DH	(Due to arrive in 2004). Ex DB 202 827 via ALS

RHEINISCHE EISENBAHN   RE

Rheinland Pfalz

This company was founded in November 2002 by the Brohltal Schmalspureisenbahn Betriebes GmbH and Eifelbahn Verkehrsgesellsschaft mbH. Judging by the first acquisition it looks as if works trains are going to be sought after

No.	Builder, No. & Year	Type	kW	Details	Comments
212 309	MaK 1000356/1961	V100DB	992	B-B DH	Ex DB via ALS. Retains steam heat boiler
360 573	Krp 3996/1960	V60C	478	0-6-0 DH	Ex DB

REGIONAL BAHNGESELLSCHAFT GmbH   REGIOBAHN
Mettmann, Nordrhein Westfalen

Routes: Kaarst–Neuss–Düsseldorf–Erkrath–Mettmann (KBS 450.28).
Length: 34 km of which 16 km is DB Netz.   **Depots:** Mettmann.
EVU Licence: Passenger, 13/05/1997.

Founded in 1992 Regiobahn has since 25/09/1999 run the local service from Kaarst to Mettmann. Kaarst–Neuss and Düsseldorf-Gerresheim–Mettmann are over its own tracks but the bits in between are the DB lines between Neuss and Düsseldorf. Eight 2-car Talent DMUs work the service and are maintained at a new depot in Mettmann Stadtwald which also houses the "control" for the line. The service has been very successful leading to four more units being delivered in 2003.

No.	Builder, No. & Year	Type	kW	Details	Comments
VT 1001	Bom 190844–5/1999	Talent	2 x 315	B-2-B DMR	Stadt Mettmann
VT 1002	Bom 190846–7/1999	Talent	2 x 315	B-2-B DMR	Stadt Kaarst
VT 1003	Bom 190848–9/1999	Talent	2 x 315	B-2-B DMR	
VT 1004	Bom 190850–1/1999	Talent	2 x 315	B-2-B DMR	Stadt Neuss
VT 1005	Bom 190852–3/1999	Talent	2 x 315	B-2-B DMR	Kreis Neuss
VT 1006	Bom 190854–5/1999	Talent	2 x 315	B-2-B DMR	Düsseldorf
VT 1007	Bom 190856–7/1999	Talent	2 x 315	B-2-B DMR	Stadt Erkrath

VT 1008	Bom 190858-9/1999	Talent	2 x 315 B-2-B DMR
VT 1009	Bom 191841-2/2003	Talent	2 x 315 B-2-B DMR *Kreis Mettmann*
VT 1010	Bom 191843-4/2003	Talent	2 x 315 B-2-B DMR
VT 1011	Bom 191845-6/2003	Talent	2 x 315 B-2-B DMR
VT 1012	Bom 191847-8/2003	Talent	2 x 315 B-2-B DMR *Nordkanal*

EVU RENE RUCK   RENE

Hessen

Routes: Nationwide?   **Depot:** Darmstadt.
Length: -

This is a private operator of excursion trains from Darmstadt using old railbuses. However some of these have been sold and the company does not appear on the EBA list of EVUs! It is thought that the company is in fact gearing up for works contracts judging by the number of TVTs (701s) obtained!

No.	Builder, No. & Year	Type	kW	Details	Comments
701 074	WMD 1487/1963	701	2 x 110	A-A DMR	Spares or conversion?
701 082	WMD 1499/1963	701	2x110	A-A DMR	Ex DB
701 085	WMD 1502/1963	701	2x110	A-A DMR	Ex DB
798 731	MAN 145122/1960	798	2 x 110	A-A DMR	Ex DB
1	Adtranz 70120/2001	V100.4	1030	B-B DH	*Nobby*; now to S&S

RENNSTEIG BAHN GmbH & Co KG   RENNSTIEG

Stutzerbach, Thüringen

This new organisation became an EVU for Freight and Passenger and an EVI on 17/11/2003. It is the EVI for the Ilmenau–Schleusingen–Themar line but has a nationwide EVU licence. In effect it is the operating arm of the Verein Dampflokfreunde Mittlerer Rennsteig e.V.

No.	Builder, No. & Year	Type	kW	Details	Comments
V100	MaK 1000381/1966	V100	992	B-B DH	Ex MWB V1352 ex ALS ex DB 213 334

RENT A LOK GbR   RENT A LOK

Nordrhein-Westfalen

Founded 01/08/03 by two directors of EBM Cargo possibly as an umbrella organisation so that all their locos are not registered with one firm.

No.	Builder, No. & Year	Type	kW		Details	Comments
212 301	MaK 1000348/1965	V100	992	B-B DH	Ex ALS ex DB
212 375	KHD 57775/1965	V100	992	B-B DH	Ex ALS ex DB

The locos are used by EBM Cargo or leased out as required.

RHEIN–HAARDTBAHN GmbH   RHB

Bad Dürkheim, Rheinland Pfalz

Gauge: 750 mm
Electric System: 750 V dc
Routes: Bad Durkheim–Ludwigsafen–Oggersheim–Mannheim Paradeplatz–Mannheim Hbf.
Length: 16.3/30.4 km   **Depots:** Bad Durkheim Ost.
EVU Licence: Freight and Passenger 1909/1996.

This metre gauge line is like the OEG – more of a tramway but classed as a railway and like OEG gets into Mannheim and shares tracks with the local tramways using both VBL and MVG tracks. Freight traffic ceased in 1959 the diesel loco being for works trains. In connection with the shared running in Ludwigshafen and Mannheim some Ludwigshafen units work over RHB. At the time of introduction the 1022 type of vehicle was the longest tram in the world with a total length of 38 m. 1.7 million passengers were carried in 1998 but the total includes buses.

No.	Builder, No. & Year	Type	kW	Details	Comments
01	Gm 4826/1954		110	B DH	Ex OEG D 03
1015	Duewag 1963		2 x 225	B-2-B	
1018	Duewag 1963		2 x 225	B-2-B	
1022	Duewag 1967		2 x 150	B-2-2-2-2-B	

1041	Duewag 1995	4 x 95 Bo-2-2-Bo	*Deutsche Weistrasse*
1042	Duewag 1995	4 x 95 Bo-2-2-Bo	*Maxdorf*
1043	Duewag 1995	4 x 95 Bo-2-2-Bo	

RHENUS KEOLIS GmbH + Co. KG   RHENUS KEOLIS

Mainz, Baden Wurttemberg

This organisation was created in 2001 and owns amongst other things Eurobahn which name has been retained as a marketing name. Rhenus is Rhenus AG + Co. KG Dortmund which has 51% of the shares; Keolis is Keolis S.A. Paris which has 49%. Rhenus itself is owned by Rethmann AG + Co. KG, Selm. Keolis was formed by the merger of Cariane and VIA GTI and is part owned by SNCF (43.5%)! Private operators are complicated!

XAVER RIEBEL GLEISBAU GmBH & Co. KG   RIEBEL

Buchloe, Bayern

This company acquired a locomotive early in 2003 but has no EVU/EIU licence so the loco is used by BCB and numbered V200 001 . The name was given by Riebel

No.	Builder, No. & Year	Type	kW	Details	Comments
V200 001	VSFT 1001/2003	G1206	1500	B-B DH	"Kunigunde II"

RINGZUG   RINGZUG

Baden Württemberg

Baden Württemberg has contracted HzL to operate "Ringzug" – a new concept in local train services over four routes totalling 194 km. Operations commenced during 2003/4.

The routes are as follows:
1). Braunlingen–Donaueschingen–Villingen–Rottweil/Trossingen Stadt
2). Rottweil–Tuttlingen–Immendingen
3). Fridingen–Tuttlingen–Immendingen
4). Immendingen–Leipferdingen–Blumberg.
20 Regio Shuttle DMUs were ordered but differ from HzL units by having automatic couplers. A new depot has been constructed at Immendingen; possibly on the site of the old DB facilities! The wheel has gone full circle? Details of the stock can be found under the HzL entry.

REGIO INFRA SERVICE SACHSEN GmbH   RISS

Chemnitz, Sachsen

This company was established in 2002 to take over the infrastructure on routes around Chemnitz initially Chemnitz–Zwonitzbrücke–Chemnitz Süd and Hainchen–Niederwiesa. The closed line from Rosswein to Hainchen will also go to RIS. These are all routes that are currently DB Netz but will transfer to the local undertaking City Bahn Chemnitz.

No.	Builder, No. & Year	Type	kW	Details	Comments
112 708	LEW 14409/1974	V100DR	883	B-B DH	Ex 202 708

REGIONALVERKEHR RUHR–LIPPE GmbH   RLG

Soest, Nordrhein Westfalen

Routes: Hamm RLG–Vellingshausen (18.7 km?); Soest–Soest Süd (2.9 km); Arnsberg–Neheim–Hüsten–Sundern (25.4 km).
Length: 44.6/54.6 km   **Depots:** Hamm RLG, Neheim-Hüsten.
EVU Licence: Freight only 31/12/1987.

The RLG was only founded in 1979 but it goes back further being a name change for what was the Ruhr Lippe Eisenbahn (RLE) with some bits added not to mention the incorporation of local bus services into the company. Today the railway has been freight only for many years apart from excursion trains. The line serves numerous industrial locations moving chemicals and coal; 824,000 tonnes in 1998, 721,000 tonnes in 2000.

No.	Builder, No. & Year	Type	kW	Details	Comments
66	MaK 1000804/1983	G1203BB	745	B-B DH	"Arnsberg"
67	MaK 1000809/1983	G1203BB	745	B-B DH	"Neheim-Hüsten"
68	Deutz 57466/1962	DG1200BBM	1200	B-B DH	Ex KBE V36 or 38? CAT engine.

RÖBEL (MÜRITZ) EISENBAHN GmbH RME

Röbel (Müritz), Mecklenburg Vorpommern

This company was formed in 1997 by the "Hei Na Ganzlin" preservation group becoming the operating arm of that organisation allowing main line access with its steam loco and its diesel locos work freight along the closed branch Ganzlin to Röbel. Late in 2003 there were rumours of difficult times.

Routes: Röbel–Ganzlin–Karow
Length: 44.9 km   **Depot:** Röbel
EVU Licence: Freight and Passenger 23/05/2002.

No.	Builder, No. & Year	Type	kW	Details	Comments
100 927	BMAG 10521/1936	Köf II	92	B DH	Ex DB 310 927
V60 041	LEW 10874/1964	V60D	478	0-8-0 DH	
110 019	LEW 11228/1967	V100DR	736	B-B DH	Ex DB 201 019

NB: V60 041 and 110 019 understood to be under overhaul at WIG Industrieinstandhaltung GmbH, Brieske

RP EISENBAHN GmbH RPE

Wachenheim, Rheinland Pfalz

RP is understood to stand for Rheinland Pfalz. This company is the infrastructure owner for the following lines: Alzey–Kirchheimbolanden; Langenlonsheim–Stromberg–Simmern–Morbach; Freiberg (Sachs)–Holzhau.

The V100 it owns is listed under the FEG entry as it is allocated there for snowplough duties in winter but can be found on ballast trains etc. on the other lines at other times. An EVU licence for freight and passenger traffic was issued 25/02/99

RHEIN SIEG EISENBAHN BETRIEBSGESELLSCHAFT MBH RSE

Bonn, Nordrhein Westfalen

Routes: Bonn Beuel–Hangelar
Length: 4.6 km   **Depot:** Bonn Beuel
EVU Licence: 13/10/1995.

In 1994 some railway enthusiasts, local businesses (i.e. freight forwarders) and various other private people formed a new company Rhein Sieg Eisenbahn Betriebes GmbH. They started by taking over the Bonn Beuel–Hangelar line in 1995 after being upset that DEG had closed it. In 1999 the company started weekend tourist services on the Linz (Rh)–Kalenborn route. RSE holds the operating licenses for several museum line operations e.g. Dieringhausen–Waldbrol.

No.	Builder, No. & Year	Type	kW	Details	Comments
V1	O&K 26163/1962	MV9			Ex Sudzucker
V 07	LKM 251101/1956	N4	66	B DM	Ex Bundeswehr
V 14	LKM 261465/1967	V15B	110	0-4-0 DH	ExTrocknungswerk Erdeborn
V 22	LKM 262082/1968	V22	162	0-4-0 DH	Ex EM Rittersgrun
VT 6	MAN 141750/1955	MAN	2 x 110	A-A DHR	Ex SWEG
VT 23	MAN 142782/1956	MAN	2 x 110	A-A DHR	Ex SWEG
VT 25	MAN 145160/1960	MAN	2 x 110	A-A DHR	Ex SWEG
212 CL 326	MaK 1000378/1966	V100	1082	B-B DH	Ex ALS ex DB. CAT engine.
332 CL 109	O&K 26347/1964	Köf III		4w DH	Ex DB 332 109

RINTELN–STADTHAGENER VERKEHRS GmbH RStV

Celle, Niedersachsen

Routes: Rinteln Nord–Stadthagen West
Length: 20.4 km   **Depots:** Stadthagen West
EVU Licence: Freight and Passenger 4/10/1995.

The RStV was formed in 1995 taking over the bankrupt Rinteln-Stadthager Eisenbahn. Now it has no locos of its own with trains worked by the OHE (q.v.) although the loco listed below is usually allocated to the line. 102,000 tonnes of freight forwarded in 1998.

No.	Builder, No. & Year	Type	kW	Details	Comments
150005	SFT 1000897/1995	G1205BB	1120	B-B DH	

RHEIN–SIEG VERKEHRS GESELLSCHAFT mbH   RSVG
Troisdorf, Nordrhein Westfalen

Routes: Troisdorf West–Lülsdorf
Length: 15.3/17.8 km   **Depots:** Troisdorf-Sieglar
EVU Licence: Freight and Passenger 29/02/1996.

A freight only line with an interesting street running section in Sieglar which is the reason the locos are fitted with yellow flashing lights!

No.	Builder, No. & Year	Type	kW	Details	Comments
3	MaK 500053/1970	G700C	515	C DH	
4	MaK 500058/1972	G700C	515	C DH	

RURTALBAHN GmbH   RTB
Düren, Nordrhein Westfalen

Routes: Düren–Heimbach (KBS 484) 29.1 km; Düren–Jülich (KBS 483) 14.6 km; Jülich–Linnich 11.0 km; Julich Nord–Puffendorf 14.4 km; Düren–Düren Distelrath 2.0 km.
Length: 71.1/80.6 km.   **Depot:** Düren Distelrath.
EVU Licence: Freight and Passenger 23/10/2003.

Previously known as the Dürener Kreisbahn (DKB) and renamed in 2003. The DKB in the 1960s was a contracting railway with lines being closed as Germany regained its prosperity and the people obtained cars. Lorries started to polish off the freight traffic. Its fortunes began to change in 1984 when it took over the Julicher Kreisbahn. The 1990s then brought about big changes as regionalisation and open access came about. In 1993 DKB took over the passenger services on several DB lines in the area and to operate them at first got hold of some withdrawn class 798 railbuses from the DB. With passenger traffic improving an order was placed with Duewag for some of the new Regio Sprinters–the first of the new generation of railcars to appear. Since then the railway has gone from strength to strength and acquired more reconditioned locos from OnRail. Is freight traffic also set to increase as well? In 1998 1.3 million passengers and 103,000 tonnes of freight transported. Not bad for a railway that was somewhat moribund only a few years before! In 2002 DKB reintroduced passenger trains to Linnich. In October 2003 two locomotives were badly damaged in an accident and replacement locos have been hired in. These may vary from month to month.

No.	Builder, No. & Year	Type	kW	Details	Comments
6.301	MaK 220090/1968	G320B	250	B DH	Ex Julicher Krb V 35
6.302	Jung 14060/1968	Köf III	177	B DH	Ex DB 333 020
6.303	Deutz 56935/1959	MS650D	478	D DM	Ex HGK V 24. Scrapped 2003.
6.304	OnRail DH1004/4/2000	DH1004	1030	B-B DH	Ex DB 211 235
6.305	OnRail DH1004/5/2000	DH1004	1030	B-B DH	Ex DB 211 276. Damaged 2003.
6.306	OnRail DH1004/7/2002	DH1004	1030	B-B DH	ex DB 211 204. Damaged 2003.
T1	Talbot 94841/1952		107	1-A DMR	Ex JKB T1
6.001.1	Duewag 91345/1995	R.Sprinter	2 x 198	A-2-A DMR	
6.002.1	Duewag 91346/1995	R.Sprinter	2 x 198	A-2-A DMR	
6.003.1	Duewag 91347/1995	R.Sprinter	2 x 198	A-2-A DMR	
6.004.1	Duewag 91348/1995	R.Sprinter	2 x 198	A-2-A DMR	
6.005.1	Duewag 91349/1995	R.Sprinter	2 x 198	A-2-A DMR	
6.006.1	Duewag 91350/1995	R.Sprinter	2 x 198	A-2-A DMR	
6.007.1	Duewag 91351/1995	R.Sprinter	2 x 198	A-2-A DMR	
6.008.1	Duewag 91352/1995	R.Sprinter	2 x 198	A-2-A DMR	
6.009.1	Duewag 91353/1995	R.Sprinter	2 x 198	A-2-A DMR	
6.010.1	Duewag 91354/1995	R.Sprinter	2 x 198	A-2-A DMR	
6.011.1	Duewag 91355/1995	R.Sprinter	2 x 198	A-2-A DMR	
6.012.1	Duewag 91356/1995	R.Sprinter	2 x 198	A-2-A DMR	
6.013.1	Duewag 91357/1995	R.Sprinter	2 x 198	A-2-A DMR	
6.014.1	Duewag 91358/1995	R.Sprinter	2 x 198	A-2-A DMR	
6.015.1	Duewag 91359/1995	R.Sprinter	2 x 198	A-2-A DMR	
6.016.1	Duewag 91360/1995	R.Sprinter	2 x 198	A-2-A DMR	
6.017.1	Duewag 91361/1995	R.Sprinter	2 x 198	A-2-A DMR	

RÜGENSCHE KLEINBAHN GmbH & Co. RüKB
Putbus, Mecklenburg Vorpommern

Gauge: 750 mm
Routes: Lauterbach Mole–Putbus (KBS 198, 2.5 km, DB Netz); Putbus–Binz LB–Göhren (KBS 199, 26.7 km)
Length: 29.2/31.3 km   **Depots:** Putbus
EVU Licence: Freight and Passenger 21/12/1995.

This narrow gauge line was a private company before WWII but was nationalised under the post-war communist regime. With unification it is back in the private sector with KEG holding the operating licence. Amazingly some of the original steam locos survived the DR standardisation policy and have reverted to original style numbering. Since privatisation the line has been extended over the DB standard gauge branch from Putbus to Lauterbach Mole by adding a third running rail. The line is basically a summer tourist line but it does offer all year round service.

No.	Builder, No. & Year	Type	kW	Details	Comments
52 M^h	Vulcan 2951/1914		0-8-0WT	099 770/99 4632	
~~53 M^b~~	~~Vulcan 3851/1925~~		~~0-8-0WT~~	~~099 771/99 4633~~	
99 782	LKM 32023/1953		2-10-2T	099 746/99 1782	
99 783	LKM 32024/1953		2-10-2T	099 747/99 1783	
99 784	LKM 32025/1953		2-10-2T	099 748/99 1784	
99 4652	Hens 25983/1941		0-6-0T	On loan, ex *"Frank S"*	
99 4801	Hens 24367/1938		2-8-0T	099 780/99 4801	
99 4802	Hens 24368/1938		2-8-0T	099 781/99 4802	
"Nikki & Frank- S"	Hens 25982/1941		0-6-0T/T	Ex ÖBB 798 101	
Köf 6003	Gm 4205/1944	HF130C 97	0-6-0 DH	DR 100 902/199 002/310 901	
V51 901	Gm 5327/1964	V51 199	B-B DH	Ex StLB VL21 ex DB 251 901	
"Aquarius C"	Borsig 14806/1939		0-10-0T/T	Ex ZB 4, SKGLB 22	

REGIONAL VERKEHR MÜNSTERLAND GmbH RVM
Münster, Nordrhein Westfalen

Routes: Rheine–Altenrheine–Mettingen–Osnabrück-Eversburg (–Osnabrück Rbf).
Length: 46.6/53.3 km   **Depots:** Rheine Stadtberg
EVU Licence: Freight only, 16/12/1986.

Not many visitors to Germany in the last days of steam at Rheine were probably aware that the town also hosted a private railway – then known as the Tecklenburger Nordbahn which is today the RVM running between Rheine and Osnabrück more or less parallel to the DB line! The two locos are kept busy with usually one at each end of the line and in both cases running over DB tracks to local interchange facilities. 94,000 tonnes of freight originated in 1998 but 2001 figure understood to be only 50,936.

No.	Builder, No. & Year	Type	kW	Details	Comments
28	Deutz 57672/1964	DG1200BBM	883	B-B DH	Ex KFBE V73
45	Deutz 57673/1964	DG1200BBM	883	B-B DH	Ex KFBE V74 via Italy

RHEIN WESER BAHN GmbH RWB
Nordrhein Westfalen

This is a joint company formed by MWB (50%) and EBM Cargo (50%) to be the umbrella organisation for a new train service from the Köln area to Salzburg in Austria. RWB co-operates with STEG – Salzburger Eisenbahn Transport Logistik GmbH which is 45% owned by MWB! This new service is called "ECCO CARGO" and runs from Hürth Kalscheuren near Köln to Salzburg but with lots of connecting servicesThe train calls at Darmstadt where EBM has a loco positioned for trip working to places such as Ludwigshafen. At Donauwörth MWB has a loco positioned for trip workings to Wilburgstetten. At Salzburg Itzling the local Austrian railway SLB does the final distribution. The two locos listed here as RWB locos are finished off in the colours of their owners MWB and EBM Cargo!

No.	Builder, No. & Year	Type	kW	Details	Comments
1116 911	SKM 20852/2003	ES64U26400		Bo-Bo E	Owned by MWB. Intended to be ÖBB 1116 131
1116 912	SKM 20892/2003	ES64U26400		Bo-Bo E	Owned by EBM. Intended to be ÖBB 1116 171

RWE UMWELT
RWE
Essen, Nordrhein Westfalen

This company is a subsidiary of one of Germany's main power suppliers. It is not an EVU but has some locos that are hired out to other operators.

No.	Builder, No. & Year	Type	kW	Details	Comments
6	LEW 13784/1972	V60D	478	0-8-0 DH	Ex BKK Espenhain
7	LEW 15360/1976	V60D	478	0-8-0 DH	Ex BKK Bitterfeld Di 465 –22-B2
13	LEW 16327/1981	V100.5	1050	B-B DH	Ex Czech 745 527. New CAT engine.

STADTBAHN SAAR GmbH
SAARBAHN
Saarbrücken, Saarland

Electrical System: 750 V DC and 15 kV AC 16.7 Hz.
Routes: Saarbrücken–Ludwigstrasse–Brebach–Sarreguemines (France)
Length: 6 km newly built tramway and 13.5 km DB Netz (KBS 684).
Depots: Saarbrücken-Schleifmühle (planned)
EVU Licence: Passenger only 01/08/1997.

Saarbrücken has decided to follow Karlsruhe and integrate its city transport with the main line network. In the city it is a tramway, outside it is a railway running on former DB/SNCF tracks to Sarreguemines. The initial 15 units have been followed by many more as the system follows the lead of Karlsruhe and extends in all directions! Currently tramway conditions extend to Brebach and from there train conditions apply on to Sarreguemines. Like Karlsruhe the units are dual-voltage. 8 million passengers in 1998. Extensions to the system are being built and in 2001 the system reached Riegelsberg Süd. Further extensions are expected to Etzenhofen in 2003 and Lebach in 2004. It will be a newly built line to Etzenhofen but the last 11 km to Lebach will be over DB track. Meanwhile some spare vehicles have been leased to DB Kassel which is planning to do a "Karlsruhe".

No.	Builder, No. & Year	Type	kW	Details	Comments
1001	Bomb 1996		8 x 120	B-B-B-B	
1002	Bomb 1996		8 x 120	B-B-B-B	(Kassel)
1003	Bomb 1996		8 x 120	B-B-B-B	(Kassel)
1004	Bomb 1996		8 x 120	B-B-B-B	
1005	Bomb 1996		8 x 120	B-B-B-B	(Kassel)
1006	Bomb 1996		8 x 120	B-B-B-B	
1007	Bomb 1996		8 x 120	B-B-B-B	
1008	Bomb 1996		8 x 120	B-B-B-B	
1009	Bomb 1996		8 x 120	B-B-B-B	
1010	Bomb 1996		8 x 120	B-B-B-B	
1011	Bomb 1996		8 x 120	B-B-B-B	(Kassel)
1012	Bomb 1996		8 x 120	B-B-B-B	
1013	Bomb 1996		8 x 120	B-B-B-B	(Kassel)
1014	Bomb 1996		8 x 120	B-B-B-B	
1015	Bomb 1996		8 x 120	B-B-B-B	
1016	Bomb 2000		8 x 120	B-B-B-B	
1016	Bomb 2000		8 x 120	B-B-B-B	
1017	Bomb 2000		8 x 120	B-B-B-B	
1018	Bomb 2000		8 x 120	B-B-B-B	
1019	Bomb 2000		8 x 120	B-B-B-B	
1020	Bomb 2000		8 x 120	B-B-B-B	
1021	Bomb 2000		8 x 120	B-B-B-B	
1022	Bomb 2000		8 x 120	B-B-B-B	
1023	Bomb 2000		8 x 120	B-B-B-B	
1024	Bomb 2000		8 x 120	B-B-B-B	
1025	Bomb 2000		8 x 120	B-B-B-B	
1026	Bomb 2000		8 x 120	B-B-B-B	
1027	Bomb 2000		8 x 120	B-B-B-B	
1028	Bomb 2000		8 x 120	B-B-B-B	

SÄCHSISCHE BÖHMISCHE EISENBAHNGELLSCHAFT SBE

Sachsen

Routes: Zittau–Seifhennersdorf–Eibau.(KBS 236)
Length: **Depot:**
EVU Licence: Assumed to use EVU licence of HWB

This is a new consortium of Sächsisch-Oberlausitzer Eisenbahn Gesellschaft, Hochwaldbahn GmbH and Bohmische Nordbahn (Ceská Sevirni Dráha) set up to operate this former DB line from 19/06/2003. However from a date in the autumn of 2003 HWB has been solely involved. Units from the Hochwaldbahn are used.

No.	Builder, No. & Year	Type	kW	Details	Comments
VT 52	MAN 146567/1961	798	2 x 110	A-A DMR	Ex EBM ex DB 796 785
VT 56	WMD 1212/1956	798	2 x 110	A-A DMR	Ex DKB 202, ex DB 798 576
VT 57	MAN 146590/1962	798	2 x 110	A-A DMR	Ex DKB 208, ex DB 798 808

SCHRECK–MIEWES   SCHRECK

This construction firm has one locomotive that was last used on the Köln – Frankfurt NBS construction works. It was often stabled at Troisdorf and is in an orange livery. Current location unknown.

No.	Builder, No. & Year	Type	kW	Details	Comments
INGE	MaK 600139/1958	650D	500	0-8-0 DH	Ex Rheinarmee ex TWE V65

SIEMENS DISPOLOK GmbH   SDL

München, Bayern

With Adtranz/Bombardier getting in to hiring out locos it was not long before its great competitor Siemens got in on the act forming in 2000 a loco hire fleet company trading as Dispolok. Its main associate is Krauss Maffei where most of the locos associated with Siemens have been built in recent times (KM is in fact now owned by Siemens). A big surprise is the use of the former NSB class Di6 diesel locos which have been overhauled and modified to German standards in the DSB workshops in København. In 2003/4 the hire fleet has been expanded considerably with locos being hired from ÖBB to fill an urgent need! Now diesels are being built for hire known as the Euro Runner. These are the same as ÖBB class 2016. Locomotives have been given SDL numbers and also DB/ÖBB type numbers also as these are needed for the train radio and cab signalling etc. Late in 2002 a decision was taken to change radio numbers to the DB style and thus the locos now have DB 182 numbers. Siemens is also now building DB type 189s for the hire market as ES64F4 series. The numbering system is explained thus: ES64P001 where ES stands for Euro Sprinter (or as some would have it Electric Locomotive Siemens); 64 is the rating in this case 6400 kW; P is prototype whilst U2 is universal dual voltage, F is Freight and 4 is for four system locomotives. Siemens is understood to be using part of the old München Freimann works as a base and that is where *Parsifal* is to be found. With an ever increasing fleet Siemens is looking for more servicing centres.

The ES64U2 locos are quoted as being in up to nine versions: 0) standard ÖBB 1116; 1) DB 182; 2) SDL standard; 3) Hupac type; 4) MÁV 1047; 5) GySEV 1047; 6) SDL locos with Swiss fittings; 7) ?? 8) a new SDL version to have remote radio control for use in shunting operations.

In late 2003 Dispolok had so many orders for locomotives a deal was struck with ÖBB whereby ÖBB locomotives 1116 061-065 have been leased to Siemens for up to two years.

Surprisingly Siemens Displok has an EVU Licence for passenger and freight operations issued 05/07/2002.

No.	Builder, No. & Year	Type	kW	Details	Comments	Hirer
ES64P-001	KM 20075/1992	ES64P	6400	Bo-Bo E	Ex 127 001 (DB).	
ES64F-901	KM 20449/2000	ES64F	6400	Bo-Bo E	152 901	TXL
ES64F-902	KM 20448/2000	ES64F	6400	Bo-Bo E	152 902	TXL
ES64U2-001	KM 20557/2001	ES64U2	6400	Bo-Bo E	1116 701	Lokomotion
ES64U2-002	KM 20558/2001	ES64U2	6400	Bo-Bo E	1116 702	PEG
ES64U2-003	KM 20559/2001	ES64U2	6400	Bo-Bo E	1116 703	TXL
ES64U2-004	SKM 20560/2002	ES64U2	6400	Bo-Bo E	1116 704	TXL
ES64U2-005	SKM 20561/2002	ES64U2	6400	Bo-Bo E	1116 705	R4C
ES64U2-006	SKM 20562/2002	ES64U2	6400	Bo-Bo E	1116 706	TXL

ES64U2-007	SKM 20563/2002	ES64U2	6400	Bo-Bo E	1116 707	TXL
ES64U2-008	SKM 20564/2002	ES64U2	6400	Bo-Bo E	1116 708	TXL
ES64U2-009	SKM 20565/2002	ES64U2	6400	Bo-Bo E	1116 709	TXL
ES64U2-010	SKM 20566/2002	ES64U2	6400	Bo-Bo E	1116 710	TXL
ES64U2-011	SKM 20567/2002	ES64U2	6400	Bo-Bo E	1116 711	TXL
ES64U2-012	SKM 20568/2002	ES64U2	6400	Bo-Bo E	1116 712	TXL
ES64U2-013	SKM 20569/2002	ES64U2	6400	Bo-Bo E	1116 713	Lokomotion
ES64U2-014	SKM 20570/2002	ES64U2	6400	Bo-Bo E	1116 714	Lokomotion
ES64U2-015	SKM 20571/2002	ES64U2	6400	Bo-Bo E	1116 715	TXL
ES64U2-016	SKM 20572/2002	ES64U2	6400	Bo-Bo E	1116 716	TXL
ES64U2-017	SKM 20573/2002	ES64U2	6400	Bo-Bo E	1116 717	RAG
ES64U2-018	SKM 20574/2002	ES64U2	6400	Bo-Bo E	1116 718	TXL
ES64U2-019	SKM 20769/2002	ES64U2	6400	Bo-Bo E	1116 719	Lokomotion
ES64U2-020	SKM 20770/2002	ES64U2	6400	Bo-Bo E	182 520	WLB (A)
ES64U2-021	SKM 20771/2002	ES64U2	6400	Bo-Bo E	182 521	WLB (A)
ES64U2-022	SKM 20772/2002	ES64U2	6400	Bo-Bo E	182 522	WLB (A)
ES64U2-023	SKM 20773/2002	ES64U2	6400	Bo-Bo E	182 523	Lokomotion
ES64U2-024	SKM 20774/2003	ES64U2	6400	Bo-Bo E	182 524	(KEG)
ES64U2-025	SKM 20775/2003	ES64U2	6400	Bo-Bo E	182 525	TXL
ES64U2-026	SKM 20776/2003	ES64U2	6400	Bo-Bo E	182 526	RAG 252
ES64U2-027	SKM 20777/2003	ES64U2	6400	Bo-Bo E	182 527	WLB (A)
ES64U2-028	SKM 20778/2003	ES64U2	6400	Bo-Bo E	182 528	Lokomotion
ES64U2-029	SKM 20781/2003	ES64U2	6400	Bo-Bo E	182 529	Railogic
ES64U2-030	SKM 20782/2003	ES64U2	6400	Bo-Bo E	182 530	EVB
ES64U2-031	SKM 20446/2000	ES64U2	6400	Bo-Bo E	182 531	TXL (Ex 1116 902)
ES64U2-032	SKM 20447/2000	ES64U2	6400	Bo-Bo E	182 532	TXL (Ex 1116 903)
ES64U2-033	SKM 21037/2003	ES64U2	6400	Bo-Bo E	182 533	NOB
ES64U2-034	SKM 21038/2003	ES64U2	6400	Bo-Bo E	182 534	NOB
ES64U2-035	SKM 21039/2003	ES64U2	6400	Bo-Bo E	182 535	
ES64U2-036	SKM 21040/2003	ES64U2	6400	Bo-Bo E	182 536	
ES64U2-037	SKM 21041/2003	ES64U2	6400	Bo-Bo E	182 537	
ES64U2-038	SKM 21042/2003	ES64U2	6400	Bo-Bo E	182 538	
ES64U2-039	SKM 21043/2003	ES64U2	6400	Bo-Bo E	182 549	
ES64U2-040	SKM 21044/2004	ES64U2	6400	Bo-Bo E	182 540	
ES64U2-041	SKM 21045/2004	ES64U2	6400	Bo-Bo E	182 541	
ES64U2-042	SKM 21046/2004	ES64U2	6400	Bo-Bo E	182 542	
ES64U2-043	SKM 21047/2004	ES64U2	6400	Bo-Bo E	182 543	
ES64U2-044	SKM 21048/2004	ES64U2	6400	Bo-Bo E	182 544	
ES64U2-045	SKM 21049/2004	ES64U2	6400	Bo-Bo E	182 545	
ES64U2-046	SKM 21050/2004	ES64U2	6400	Bo-Bo E	182 546	
ES64U2-047	SKM 21051/2004	ES64U2	6400	Bo-Bo E	182 547	
ES64U2-048	SKM 21052/2004	ES64U2	6400	Bo-Bo E	182 548	
ES64U2-049	SKM 21053/2004	ES64U2	6400	Bo-Bo E	182 549	
ES64U2-050	SKM 21054/2004	ES64U2	6400	Bo-Bo E	182 550	
ES64U2-051	SKM 21055/2004	ES64U2	6400	Bo-Bo E	182 551	
ES64U2-052	SKM 21056/2004	ES64U2	6400	Bo-Bo E	182 552	
ES64U2-080	SKM 20779/2003	ES64U2	6400	Bo-Bo E	182 580	(Cargoserv). FFS
ES64U2-081	SKM 20780/2003	ES64U2	6400	Bo-Bo E	182 581	(Cargoserv). FFS
ES64U2-082	SKM 20783/2003	ES64U2	6400	Bo-Bo E	182 582	FFS
ES64U2-095	SKM 20784/2002	ES64U2	6400	Bo-Bo E	182 595	(KEG)
ES64U2-096	SKM 20785/2002	ES64U2	6400	Bo-Bo E	182 596	IGE
ES64U2-097	SKM 20786/2002	ES64U2	6400	Bo-Bo E	182 597	TXL
ES64U2-098	SKM 20787/2002	ES64U2	6400	Bo-Bo E	182 598	TXL
ES64U2-099	SKM 20788/2002	ES64U2	6400	Bo-Bo E	182 599	Spare
ES64U2-100	SKM 20445/2000	ES64U2	6400	Bo-Bo E	182 600	Sold to Hupac (Ex ES64U2-901)
ES64F4-001	SKM 20680/2003	ES64F4	6400	Bo-Bo E	182 901	RTC
ES64F4-002	SKM 20683/2003	ES64F4	6400	Bo-Bo E	182 902	RTC
ES64F4-003	SKM 20669/2002	ES64F4	6400	Bo-Bo E	182 903	RTC
ES64F4-004	SKM 20670/2002	ES64F4	6400	Bo-Bo E	182 904	RTC
ES64F4-005	SKM 20671/2002	ES64F4	6400	Bo-Bo E	182 905	RTC
ES64F4-006	SKM 20719/2004	ES64F4	6400	Bo-Bo E	182 906	
ES64F4-007	SKM 20724/2004	ES64F4	6400	Bo-Bo E	182 907	
ES64F4-008	SKM 20727/2004	ES64F4	6400	Bo-Bo E	182 908	

ES64F4-009	SKM 20727/2004	ES64F4	6400	Bo-Bo E	182 909	
ES64F4-010	SKM 20731/2004	ES64F4	6400	Bo-Bo E	182 910	
ES64F4-011	SKM 20735/2004	ES64F4	6400	Bo-Bo E	182 911	
ES64F4-012	SKM 20xxx/2004	ES64F4	6400	Bo-Bo E	182 912	
ES64F4-013	SKM 20xxx/2004	ES64F4	6400	Bo-Bo E	182 913	
ES64F4-014	SKM 20xxx/2004	ES64F4	6400	Bo-Bo E	182 914	
ES64F4-015	SKM 20xxx/2004	ES64F4	6400	Bo-Bo E	182 915	
ES64F4-016	SKM 20xxx/2004	ES64F4	6400	Bo-Bo E	182 916	
ES64F4-017	SKM 20xxx/2004	ES64F4	6400	Bo-Bo E	182 917	
ES64F4-018	SKM 20xxx/2004	ES64F4	6400	Bo-Bo E	182 918	
ES64F4-019	SKM 20xxx/2004	ES64F4	6400	Bo-Bo E	182 919	
ES64F4-020	SKM 20xxx/2004	ES64F4	6400	Bo-Bo E	182 920	
EF64F4-088	SKM 20732/2004	ES64F4	6400	Bo-Bo E	189 988	
EF64F4-089	SKM 20734/2004	ES64F4	6400	Bo-Bo E	189 989	
EF64F4-090	SKM 20736/2004	ES64F4	6400	Bo-Bo E	189 990	
EF64F4-091	SKM 20739/2004	ES64F4	6400	Bo-Bo E	189 991	
EF64F4-092	SKM 20721/2004	ES64F4	6400	Bo-Bo E	189 992	
EF64F4-093	SKM 20723/2004	ES64F4	6400	Bo-Bo E	189 993	
EF64F4-094	SKM 20695/2003	ES64F4	6400	Bo-Bo E	189 994	SBB
EF64F4-095	SKM 20698/2003	ES64F4	6400	Bo-Bo E	189 995	SBB
EF64F4-096	SKM 20701/2003	ES64F4	6400	Bo-Bo E	189 996	SBB
EF64F4-097	SKM 20704/2003	ES64F4	6400	Bo-Bo E	189 997	SBB
EF64F4-098	SKM 20707/2003	ES64F4	6400	Bo-Bo E	189 998	SBB
EF64F4-099	SKM 20730/2004	ES64F4	6400	Bo-Bo E	189 999	SBB
ME26-01	SFT 30005/1995	ME26	2650	Co-Co DE	Ex NSB Di6.661	Spare
ME26-02	SFT 30006/1995	ME26	2650	Co-Co DE	Ex NSB Di6.662	CFL
ME26-03	SFT 30007/1995	ME26	2650	Co-Co DE	Ex NSB Di6.663	CFL
ME26-04	SFT 30008/1995	ME26	2650	Co-Co DE	Ex NSB Di6.664	Spare
ME26-05	SFT 30009/1995	ME26	2650	Co-Co DE	Ex NSB Di6.665	CFL
ME26-06	SFT 30010/1995	ME26	2650	Co-Co DE	Ex NSB Di6.666	S&S
ME26-07	SFT 30011/1995	ME26	2650	Co-Co DE	Ex NSB Di6.667	S&S
ME26-08	SFT 30012/1995	ME26	2650	Co-Co DE	Ex NSB Di6.668	CFL
ME26-09	SFT 30013/1995	ME26	2650	Co-Co DE	Ex NSB Di6.669	CFL
ME26-10	SFT 30014/1995	ME26	2650	Co-Co DE	Ex NSB Di6.670	S&S
ME26-11	SFT 30015/1995	ME26	2650	Co-Co DE	Ex NSB Di6.671	S&S
ME26-12	SFT 30017/1995	ME26	2650	Co-Co DE	Ex NSB Di6.672	CFL
ER 20-001	SKM 21025/2003	ER	2000	Bo-Bo DE	Alex	
ER 20-002	SKM 21026/2003	ER	2000	Bo-Bo DE	Alex	
ER 20-003	SKM 21027/2003	ER	2000	Bo-Bo DE	Alex	
ER 20-004	SKM 21028/2003	ER	2000	Bo-Bo DE	Alex	
ER 20-005	SKM 21029/2003	ER	2000	Bo-Bo DE	Alex	
ER 20-006	SKM 21030/2004	ER	2000	Bo-Bo DE		
ER 20-007	SKM 21031/2004	ER	2000	Bo-Bo DE		
ER 20-008	SKM 21032/2004	ER	2000	Bo-Bo DE		
ER 20-009	SKM 21033/2004	ER	2000	Bo-Bo DE		
ER 20-010	SKM 21034/2004	ER	2000	Bo-Bo DE		
ER 20-011	SKM 21035/2004	ER	2000	Bo-Bo DE		
ER 20-012	SKM 21036/2004	ER	2000	Bo-Bo DE		
ER 20-013	SKM 21037/2004	ER	2000	Bo-Bo DE		
PARSIFAL	Jung 14126/1971	RK8B		4w DH	Ex IND Recklinghausen	

Notes: The ES64U2 numbered 080-084 are to be fitted with remote radio control for shunting duties; those numbered 095 onwards are suitable for working into Switzerland.
ME26.04 is numbered as DE2650-04.

SG LÜBECK mbH   SGL
Lubeck, Schleswig Holstein

This company is a subsidiary of Lübecker Hafen Gesellschaft mbH and is also known as LHG Service Gesellschaft mbH. It shunts the Lübeck harbour lines and terminals and also trips around the Lübeck area over DB Netz. About 80 km of tracks within the harbour area.

No.	Builder, No. & Year	Type	kW	Details	Comments
V60 01	LEW 17694/1983	V60D	478	0-8-0 DH	
V100 001	LEW 13498/1972	V100DR	1050	B-B DH	Ex ALS, ex DB 202 459 with CAT engine.

SEEHAFEN KIEL GmbH & Co. K.G.   SK

Kiel, Schleswig Holsten

Routes: Kiel Hgbhf–Kiel-Seefischmarkt; Neuwittenbek–Kiel–Schusterkrug; Suchsdorf–Kiel-Wik–Kiel-Nordhafen–Kiel Scheerhafen
Length: 18.7/30.1 km   **Depots:** Kiel-Wik, Kiel-Seefischmarkt.
EVU Licence: Freight only 28/11/1973.

Yet another railway formed from various industrial lines in Kiel. On one of its branches is the former MaK workshops (now Vossloh) which uses the line as a test bed for newly built locos. 67,000 tonnes of freight in 1998. One loco now shunts Kiel Hbf. station on behalf of DB R&T and DB Regio – the SK price being cheaper than DB Cargo!

No.	Builder, No. & Year	Type	kW	Details	Comments
1	MaK 400037/1961	450C	331	0-6-0 DH	
2	MaK 800190/1978	G1100BB	809	B-B DH	To NEG
3	MaK 220059/1960	240C	176	0-6-0 DH	
4	MaK 1000853/1991	G1203BB	745	B-B DH	
5	Deutz 57288/1959	Köf II	94	B DH	Ex DB 323 143
6	VSFT 1001137/2001	G1206	1500	B-B DH	

SIEGENER KREISBAHN GmbH   SK

Siegen, Nordrhein Westfalen

Routes: Siegen–Eintracht; Siegen Ost–Kaan–Marienborn; Kreuztal–Kreutztal-Buschhütten; Weidenau–Irmgarteichen; Herdorf–Salchendorf b.N.–Pfanneberg.
Length: 32/47 km **Depots:** Siegen-Eintracht, Weidenau Vorbahnhof (2 locos), Herdorf (1 loco).
EVU Licence: 10/10/1995.

This company operates various branches around the Siegen and Kreuztal areas including tripping on behalf of DB; loco 41 normally being used on these duties. 390,000 tonnes forwarded in 1998 with 440,000 tonnes reported for 2000. From 2/10/2000 SK took over freight work from DB on the Hellertalbahn; in late 2002 SK took over many more freight trips from Kreuztal including steel trains Kreuztal–Erndtebrück.

No.	Builder, No. & Year	Type	kW	Details	Comments
V 11	Jung 13119/1960	R42C	324	C DH	
V 12	Jung 13117/1959	R42C	324	C DH	
V 31	MaK 700093/1989	G763C	560	C DH	
V 32	MaK 700099/1990	G763C	560	C DH	
V 33	MaK 700110/1993	G763C	560	C DH	Spare
V 41	MaK 1000832/1988	DE1002	1120	Bo-Bo DE	Ex HLB 832
V 42	VSFT 1001108/2001	G1700BB	1500	B-B DH	
V 43	VSFT 1001327/2003	G2000	2240	B-B DH	
V44	VSFT 1001462/2003	G1000	1000	B-B DH	
V 651	MaK 1000793/1982	DE1002	1120	Bo-Bo DE	Ex RAG V 651

SPITZKE LOGISTIK GmbH. Hoch, Tief und Eisenbahnbau SLG

Berlin

Routes: Nation wide ballast train working.
Length: -   **Depots:** Berlin (Grossbeeren).
EVU Licence: Freight only,

Spitzke is a firm that has appeared on the scene since unification and is possibly part of the old DR system privatised. It has expanded considerably and continues to acquire locomotives.

No.	Builder, No. & Year	Type	kW	Details	Comments
V22 SP 030	LKM 262216/1969	V22	185	0-4-0 DH	Ex VEB Ziegelwerk
V22 SP 031	LKM 262136/1968	V22	185	0-4-0 DH	Ex Minol Lager Miltzow 1
V22 SP 032	LKM 262256/1969	V22	185	0-4-0 DH	Ex Minol Lager Miltzow 2
V60 SP 010	LEW 12628/1970	V60D	478	0-8-0 DH	Ex DB 346 657, Damaged in NBS crash.
V60 SP 011	LEW 13746/1973	V60D	478	0-8-0 DH	Ex Kraftwerk Elbe. CAT engine.
V60 SP 012	LEW 15202/1973	V60D	478	0-8-0 DH	Ex BKK Bitterfeld
V60 SP 013	LEW	V60D	478	0-8-0 DH	Ex ABC Coswig 319 ?

V60 SP 014	LEW 12686/1970	V60D	478	0-8-0 DH	Ex ABC Coswig 318
V60 SP 015	LEW 16966/1979	V60D	478	0-8-0 DH	Ex Filmfabrik Wolfen. CAT engine.
V100 SP 001	LEW 15231/1976	V100.4	883	B-B DH	Ex DB 202 846
V100 SP 002	LEW 13586/1973	V100.4	883	B-B DH	Ex DB 202 547
V100 SP 003	LEW 14378/1974	V100.4	1050	B-B DH	Ex DB 202 677 (Adtranz)
V180 SP 020	LKM 280003/1967	V180	2 x 736	C-C DH	Ex DB 228 203 (MaLoWa)
V232 SP 040	Lugansk 0002/1976	242	2200	Co-Co DE	Ex W232.02 ex DR 242 002
G1206 SP 021	VSFT 1001383/2003	G1206	1500	B-B DH	
G1206 SP 022	VL 5001475/2003	G1206	1500	B-B DH	

Note: V100Sp003 is in blue livery with a CAT 3512 engine having been installed by Adtranz

SÄCHSISCH–OBERLAUSITZER EISENBAHN
GESELLSCHAFT mbH   SOEG
Zittau, Sachsen

Gauge: 750 mm
Routes: Zittau–Bertsdorf–Oybin; Bertsdorf–Jonsdorf. (KBS 238).
Length: 16.1/21.3 km   **Depots:** Zittau, Bertsdorf
EVU Licence: Freight and Passenger 15/11/1996.

This is another former DR line that has been privatised. Sachsen always had a lot of narrow gauge lines but the Zittau system was one of the few that was not state built. Since unification the line was privatised but has been on hard times since the former "captive" passenger market now has cars! The line is located in a scenic tourist area and the future looks like being the running of DMUs in the off season and retaining steam locos and carriages for the heavy summer traffic. Long term the line ought to go in for overhauling its own stock in the off season. In the early 1990s some steam locos were rebuilt to oil firing but this was not successful as they have all now been converted back to coal firing.

No.	Builder, No. & Year	Type	kW	Details	Comments
99 731	Hart 4678/1928			2-10-2T	Stored
99 735	Hart 4682/1928			2-10-2T	
99 749	BMAG 9538/1929			2-10-2T	
99 750	BMAG 9539/1929			2-10-2T	Stored
99 757	BMAG 10148/1933			2-10-2T	Stored
99 758	BMAG 10149/1933			2-10-2T	
99 760	BMAG 10151/1933			2-10-2T	Stored
99 787	LKM 132028/1955			2-10-2T	
101 020	LKM 254020/1961	311		0-4-0 DH	Ex 311 020
199 013	U23A 24060/1980	L30H	240	0-6-0 DH	Ex Poland Lyd2- (IND?)

STAHLBERG ROENSCH GmbH & Co. KG   SR
Nordrhein Westfalen

This firm's Schienenschweisswerk in Duisburg obtained a diesel locomotive in 2002 with a view to using it to deliver products from the works.

No.	Builder, No. & Year	Type	kW	Details	Comments
SR 0501	VSFT 1001140/2002	G1206	1500	B-B DH	
SR 0502	MaK 1000803/1982	G1203	1120	B-B DH	Ex RAG 675

SWISS RAIL CARGO KÖLN GmbH   SRCK

This international company was formed 17/07/2002 by SBB (51%), HGK (44%) and Hupac (5%) and a freight EVU licence was issued the same day. The objective is to concentrate on freight traffic flows between Germany – Switzerland and Italy. It was expected that some 10 trains a day would be worked over the route by the end of 2002. HGK and SBB locos are to be used. As this book went to press it was expected that this company would be renamed SBB Cargo Deutschland.

SCHNEIDER & SCHNEIDER SCHIENENVERKEHRS GmbH S&S
Niedersachsen

This firm has been active in engineering work for some time but in 2002 went and obtained its first locomotive to power ballast trains.

No.	Builder, No. & Year	Type	kW	Details	Comments
NOBBY	Adtranz 70120/2001	V100.4	1050	B-B DH	Ex Adtranz Lokpool Ex DR?, "293 701"
V60.6	LEW 17589/1981	V60D	478	0-8-0 DH	Ex EIB 6

Other locomotives, mostly ME26s are on hire from Siemens Dispolok.

SAAR SERVICE GmbH — SSG

Saarbrücken, Saar.

Formed as long ago as 1992 this organisation has been rather unknown. It is a joint venture between DB (25.5%), Saarbrücken Stadt (24.5%) and five other organisations each with 10%. From 01/03/02 it acquired an EVU licence for passenger and freight train operations and looks likely to be more active from 2003 onwards and one to watch out for especially in the Trier, Saarbrücken and Kaiserslautern areas.

SÜD THÜRINGEN BAHN GmbH IG — STB

Erfurt, Thüringen

Routes: Sonneberg–Probstzella (KBS 564 48.8 km); Meiningen–Sonneberg(KBS 569, 80.5 km); Wernshausen–Zella Mehlis (KBS 573, 30.4 km); Eisenach–Meiningen (KBS 575, 60.7 km); Vacha–Bad Salzungen (KBS 576, 16.3 km). Parts of the above routes are currently closed due to the state of the infrastructure. Because of this STB has been given some work on the Meiningen–Erfurt route.
Length: Routes are all part of DB Netz. **Livery:** Green and white.
Depots: Former DB Meiningen depot being used with some maintenance done at a new depot in Erfurt on the EIB.
EVU Licence: Passenger only, 04/02/2000.

This is a new joint venture between Erfurter Industriebahn and Hessische Landesbahn each owning 50%. The STB was successful in obtaining the concession to run passenger trains in Thüringen for 15 years from June 2001 on the above lines: 21 Regio Shuttles were ordered which are air-conditioned and are fitted with toilets. Soon afterwards a further six units were ordered.

No.	Builder, No. & Year	Type	kW	Details	Comments
VT 101	Adtranz 36899/2000	RS1	2 x 257	B-B DMR	*STADT EISENACH*
VT 102	Adtranz 36900/2000	RS1	2 x 257	B-B DMR	*SPIELZUGSTADT SONNEBERG*
VT 103	Adtranz 36901/2000	RS1	2 x 257	B-B DMR	*STADT MEININGEN*
VT 104	Adtranz 36902/2000	RS1	2 x 257	B-B DMR	*WARTBURG, UNESCO WELTERBE*
VT 105	Adtranz 36903/2000	RS1	2 x 257	B-B DMR	
VT 106	Adtranz 36904/2000	RS1	2 x 257	B-B DMR	
VT 107	Adtranz 36905/2000	RS1	2 x 257	B-B DMR	
VT 108	Adtranz 36906/2000	RS1	2 x 257	B-B DMR	
VT 109	Adtranz 36907/2000	RS1	2 x 257	B-B DMR	
VT 110	Adtranz 36908/2001	RS1	2 x 257	B-B DMR	
VT 111	Adtranz 36909/2001	RS1	2 x 257	B-B DMR	
VT 112	Adtranz 36910/2001	RS1	2 x 257	B-B DMR	
VT 113	Adtranz 36911/2001	RS1	2 x 257	B-B DMR	
VT 114	Adtranz 36912/2001	RS1	2 x 257	B-B DMR	
VT 115	Adtranz 36913/2001	RS1	2 x 257	B-B DMR	
VT 116	Adtranz 36914/2001	RS1	2 x 257	B-B DMR	
VT 117	Adtranz 36915/2001	RS1	2 x 257	B-B DMR	
VT 118	Adtranz 36916/2001	RS1	2 x 257	B-B DMR	
VT 119	Adtranz 36917/2001	RS1	2 x 257	B-B DMR	
VT 120	Adtranz 36918/2001	RS1	2 x 257	B-B DMR	
VT 121	Adtranz 36919/2001	RS1	2 x 257	B-B DMR	
VT 122	Adtranz 36920/2001	RS1	2 x 257	B-B DMR	
VT 123	Adtranz 36921/2001	RS1	2 x 257	B-B DMR	
VT 124	Adtranz 36922/2001	RS1	2 x 257	B-B DMR	
VT 125	Adtranz 36923/2001	RS1	2 x 257	B-B DMR	
VT 126	Adtranz 36924/2001	RS1	2 x 257	B-B DMR	
VT 127	Bomb 37147/2002	RS1	2 x 257	B-B DMR	
VT 128	Bomb 37148/2002	RS1	2 x 257	B-B DMR	
VT 129	Bomb 37149/2002	RS1	2 x 257	B-B DMR	
VT 130	Bomb 37150/2002	RS1	2 x 257	B-B DMR	
VT 131	Bomb 37151/2002	RS1	2 x 257	B-B DMR	
VT 132	Bomb 37152/2002	RS1	2 x 257	B-B DMR	

STRAUSBERGER EISENBAHN GmbH STE

Brandenburg

Electrical System: 600 V d.c.
Routes: Strausberg Vorstadt–Strausberg Stadt
Length: 9.0/9.4 km
Depots: Strausberg

Not so much a railway as a tramway really. Todays company was founded in 1991 as a mixed passenger and freight operation but since unification the freight has all but gone. In 1995 three modern trams were acquired from Kosice (Slovakia) with the remaining older stock put into departmental use or in the case of No. 1 retained as a historic vehicle. The railway provides good connections into the Berlin S-Bahn.

No.	Builder, No. & Year	Type	kW	Details	Comments
1	Wismar 1921			Bo-Bo ER	Museum unit
14	LEW 9890/1960	EL4		Bo E	
15	LEW 10051/1963	EL4		Bo E	
21	CKD 1990			Bo-Bo+Bo-Bo ER	Kosice 527
22	CKD 1989			Bo-Bo+Bo-Bo ER	Kosice 503
23	CKD 1989			Bo-Bo+Bo-Bo ER	Kosice 505

STADTISCHE EISENBAHN KREFELD StEK

(Hafen und Bahnbetriebe der Stadt Krefeld)
Krefeld, Nordrhein Westfalen

Routes: Krefeld-Linn–into town and harbour areas.; also industrial spur from Krefeld Gbf.–Krefeld-Bäkerpfad
Length: 21.6/51.5 km
Depots: Krefeld-Linn, Krefeld-Oppum

This industrial railway serves the harbour lines around Krefeld and other industrial concerns including the rubbish disposal plant. 768,000 tonnes forwarded in 1998 but down to 390,000 tonnes in 2001.

No.	Builder, No. & Year	Type	kW	Details	Comments
D I	MaK 700069/1982	G763C	560	C DH	
D II	MaK 700070/1983	G763C	560	C DH	
D III	Jung 12347/1956	R40C	324	C DH	
D IV	VSFT 1001020/2000	G1206BB	1500	B-B DH	
D V	LKM 252537/1970	V10B	110	0-4-0 DM	
D VI	Jung 13430/1964	R42C	324	C DH	

STEINHUDER MEER BAHN GmbH StMB

Niedersachsen

This short line from Wunstorf was recently swallowed up by the OHE. Its own two locos were sold for preservation going to Graf MEC Bentheim. Now operated by OHE(q.v.).

SÜDWESTDEUTSCHE VERKEHRS AG SWEG

Baden Württemberg

Todays SWEG dates from 1971 when the old SWEG fused with another company and is now 100% owned by the state of Baden Württemberg. Most of its lines are heavily subsidised branch lines performing a public service to local communities with trains running instead of school buses. The railway services are linked into the SWEG bus network. The lines under SWEG control are:

- Verkehrsbetrieb Achern–Ottenhöfen (AO);
- Verkehrsbetrieb Biberach–Oberharmersbach (BOH);
- Verkehrsbetrieb Endingen "Kaiserstuhlbahn" (KB);
- Verkehrsbetrieb Meckesheim–Aglasterhausen–Hüffenhardt (MAH);
- Verkehrsbetrieb Möckmühl–Dörzbach (MD);
- Verkehrsbetrieb Schwarzach (MEN);
- Verkehrsbetrieb Staufen " Münstertalbahn" (MT).
- Ortenau S-Bahn (OSB)

Detailed descriptions are listed under each individual line. Note that the line from Möckmühl to Dörzbach has been closed for several years following storm damage. It was used for steam services by a preservation group and efforts are being made to reopen the line. Whether it will or not remains to be seen as does whether it reopens as a SWEG line or a museum line. During 2000 some money was made available to repair the storm damaged line but it looks as if the future will be purely a museum line operation. Time will tell. In 2004 the line was sold to the local community.

STÄDTISCHE WERKE KREFELD AG (KREFELDER EISENBAHN) SWK

Krefeld, Nordrhein Westfalen

Routes: Krefeld Süd–Krefeld Nord–Hüls–Hulserberg (13.8 km); Krefeld Nord–Tonisvorst (4.8 km).
Length: 18.6/21.0 km
Depots: Krefeld, Am Weserweg.

The 16.8 km SWK of today has shrunk from a former 62 km line that used to run out to Viersen and Moers. The line is a much smaller operation than SEK running into open countryside rather than the docks! The steam loco was acquired in the 1979 and regular tourist trains are operated in the summer. 20,000 tonnes of freight forwarded in 1998.

No.	Builder, No. & Year	Type	kW	Details	Comments
1	Hens 29893/1947	D600	480	0-8-0T	"98 8921"
V 6	MaK 500075/1975	G500C	515	C DH	
V 7	MaK 220051/1958	240B	176	0-4-0 DH	

STAHLWERKE THÜRINGEN GmBH SWT

Unterwellenborn, Thüringen

EVU Licence: Freight only 30/01/2001.

This steelworks has for some years operated local trips in the surrounding area but in 2001 became a fully fledged EVU. It has standard former DR types many having been modernised in recent years. Not all may be passed for mainline work.

No.	Builder, No. & Year	Type	kW	Details	Comments
22	LEW 16584/1981	V100.4	889	B-B DH	Sold to MTEG
23	LEW 17849/1982	V100.4	889	B-B DH	Sold to MTEG
24	LEW 12431/1969	V100.4	889	B-B DH	Ex DB 298 130
25	LEW 12436/1969	V100.4	889	B-B DH	Ex DB 298 135
26	LEW 11908/1968	V100.4	889	B-B DH	Ex DB 201 171
27	LEW 12472/1970	V100.4	889	B-B DH	Ex DB 201 870
28	LEW 15240/1976	V100.4	1240	B-B DH	Ex DB 202 885. MTU 12V4000R10 engine.
29	LEW 14841/1975	V100.4	1240	B-B DH	Ex DB 202 784. MTU 12V4000R10 engine.

TEGERNSEEBAHN A.G. TAG

Tegernsee, Bayern

In the late 1990s the TAG passenger train operations were bought out by BOB (q.v.) and the TAG loco stock disposed of. Now the TAG has risen from the ashes as an EVI as it still owns the infrastructure of the branch line. Consequently in 2002 a locomotive was obtained for the odd works trains. The EVU licence issued for freight and passenger trains on 22/12/1994 still applies.

No.	Builder, No. & Year	Type	kW	Details	Comments
332-15	Gm 5350/1965	Köf III	167	4w DH	Ex DB 332 210. OTTOKAR II

TROSSINGER EISENBAHN TE

Trossingen, Baden Württemberg

Electrification system: 600 V dc
Routes: Trossingen Bhf.–Trossingen Stadt (KBS 743)
Length: 4.5/5.8 km   **Depots:** Trossingen Stadt
EVU Licence: Freight and Passenger, 15/10/1909 (? 1999?)

Trossingen lies on the Rottweil–Villingen DB line but the railway when built by-passed Trossingen itself so that an electric railway was built to connect the town with its "main line" station. Whenever in the area do give the line a visit as plans exist to transform rail services in this area making the branch part of a Stadtbahn from Villingen. Latest figures available show 111,700 passengers a year. The "Ringzug" which started in 2003 will eventually swallow up the TE.

No.	Builder, No. & Year	Type	kW	Details	Comments
1	MAN 369/1898		2 x 50	Bo ER	
3	Essl 19254/1938		4 x 75	Bo-Bo ER	
5	Essl 24836/1956		2 x 60	Bo ER	
6	Rastatt 21-3/1968		2 x 60	Bo ER	
2	AEG 160/1902		2 x 40	Bo E	Number not carried. *Lina*

TRANSPORT UND LOGISTIK FÜR BAHNBAUSTELLEN Gmbh
TLG

Gründau, Sachsen Anhalt

Routes: Nationwide   **Livery:** Yellow with blue stripes.
Depots: Köthen, Berlin, Fürth, Hanau, Hannover, Leipzig, Neumünster.
EVU Licence: Freight only, 21/10/1998.

TLG is another operator that has jumped on the ballast train bandwagon eagerly providing locos for such trains or indeed spot hiring out of its own locos to other firms in need. Starting off with a base and registered office in Köthen it is now reported to have other bases at Koblenz Lützel and Hanau. TLG is growing fast. It is headquartered in Köthen but there are bases in Berlin, Fürth, Hanau, Hannover, Leipzig and Neumünster!

No.	Builder, No. & Year	Type	kW	Details	Comments
1	Adtranz 73240/1999	V100.4	1030	B-B DH	Ex Adtranz
2	LEW 16375/1996	V100.4	1030	B-B DH	Ex DB 201 999, 201 881. To Bombardier.
2[II]					ALS Hire loco 203 504 14/03/03.
3	LEW 13783/1973	V60D	478	0-8-0 DH	Ex Rudersdorf Zement
4	LEW 17416/1980	V60D	478	0-8-0 DH	Ex EBG 6, ex Buna 79
5	LEW 17851/1982	V100.4	883	B-B DH	Ex PEG 2, PCK Schwedt
6	LEW 12403/1969	V100.4	883	B-B DH	Ex PEG 3, Prora, DB 201 001[II]
7[I]	LEW 11212/1967	V100.4	1030	B-B DH	Ex DB 201 004 (Lokpool)
7[II]	LEW 12561/1970	V100.4	1050	B-B DH	Ex DB 202 279 in 2002.
8	Adtranz 73260/2000	V100.4	1030	B-B DH	Ex ?
9	Lugansk 0099/1972	230	2200	Co-Co DE	Ex Röbel, DB 230 077. *BÄRBEL*
10	Lugansk 0681/1976	232	2200	Co-Co DE	Ex BGW ex DB 232 446. *WALTRAUD*
11	LEW 13533/1972	V100.4	809	B-B DH	Ex DB 202 494
12[II]	LEW 15364/1976	V60D	478	0-8-0 DH	Ex IND
13[I]	Adtranz 72570/2000	V100.4	1050	B-B DH	Rebuilt at Lengerich To?
13[II]	LEW 13570/1973	V100	1050	B-B DH	Ex DB 202 531 2002
14	LEW 12489/1970	V100	883	B-B DH	Ex DB 202 207
15	LEW 16965/1980	V60D	478	0-8-0 DH	Ex Karsdorf Zement 006
16	LEW 13527/1972	V100	883	B-B DH	Ex DB 202 483
17	LKM 280135/1968	V180	1760	C-C DH	Ex DB 228 731
18	LEW	V100		B-B DH	

NB: Liveries vary: No. 1 is yellow; No. 5 is blue; No. 6 is Yellow with Blue stripe; No. 7 is green; No. 10 is yellow with two blue stripes; No. 16 is DB red. TLG 12[I] was Stendal 203 502 on hire.

TRANS REGIO DEUTSCHE REGIONALBAHN GmbH
TRANS REGIO

Trier, Rheinland Pfalz

Routes: Andernach–Mayen West–Kaisersech (KBS 478, 42.7 km); Kaiserslautern–Landstuhl–Kusel (KBS 671, 36.4); Bullay–Traben Trarbach (KBS 691, 10.6 km)
Length: 89.7 km   **Depots:** Mayen Ost, Altenglan.
Livery: Silver with yellow doors. Air conditioned. GPS for customer information.
EVU Licence: Freight and Passenger 01/12/1999.

This new company has been set up to operate passenger services on three different lines. The company is owned 51% by the Moselbahn (not a railway operator for many years) and 49% by Rheinischen Bahngesellschaft AG Düsseldorf. 19 RS1 were ordered for services between

Kaiserslautern–Landstuhl–Kusel; Andernach–Mayen West both services scheduled to commence in May 2000. In September 2000 the Mayen service was extended to Kaisersesch whilst in May 2001 Bullay–Traben Trarbach cut over to the new operator. During 2003 additional services were put on between Kusel and Neustadt (Weinstrasse) Sundays only and also between Kaiserslautern and Homburg (Monday–Friday) to fill gaps in the service.

No.	Builder, No. & Year	Type	kW	Details	Comments
001	Adtranz 36859/2000	RS1	2 x 257	B-B DMR	
002	Adtranz 36860/2000	RS1	2 x 257	B-B DMR	
003	Adtranz 36861/2000	RS1	2 x 257	B-B DMR	
004	Adtranz 36862/2000	RS1	2 x 257	B-B DMR	
005	Adtranz 36863/2000	RS1	2 x 257	B-B DMR	
006	Adtranz 36864/2000	RS1	2 x 257	B-B DMR	
007	Adtranz 36865/2000	RS1	2 x 257	B-B DMR	
008	Adtranz 36966/2000	RS1	2 x 257	B-B DMR	
009	Adtranz 36867/2000	RS1	2 x 257	B-B DMR	
010	Adtranz 36868/2000	RS1	2 x 257	B-B DMR	
011	Adtranz 36869/2000	RS1	2 x 257	B-B DMR	
012	Adtranz 36870/2000	RS1	2 x 257	B-B DMR	
013	Adtranz 36871/2000	RS1	2 x 257	B-B DMR	
014	Adtranz 36872/2000	RS1	2 x 257	B-B DMR	
015	Adtranz 36873/2000	RS1	2 x 257	B-B DMR	
016	Adtranz 36974/2000	RS1	2 x 257	B-B DMR	
017	Adtranz 36975/2000	RS1	2 x 257	B-B DMR	
018	Adtranz 36876/2000	RS1	2 x 257	B-B DMR	
019	Adtranz 36877/2000	RS1	2 x 257	B-B DMR	
020	Stadler 37127/2001	RS1	2 x 257	B-B DMR	

(8 for Mayen, 10 for Kaiserslautern area, 1 for Traben-Trarbach was the initial order but a supplementary unit has since been obtained).)

TRANSPORT SCHIENEN DIENST BURBACH   TSD

Nordrhein-Westfalen

This firm is a joint venture between EBM and Hering Bau of Burbach and came to light late in 2000. It works nationwide ballast trains but since being founded most of the work has been in the Köln area connected with the extension of the S-Bahn to Düren..

Depots: ?
Livery: Blue with yellow stripe.

No.	Builder, No. & Year	Type	kW	Details	Comments
1	LEW 12882/1971	V100DR	932	B-B DH	Ex DB 202 373. CAT Engine
2	LEW 12839/1971	V100DR	932	B-B DH	Ex DB 202 330. CAT engine
?	MaK 600252/1959	V60	478	0-6-0 DH	Ex DB 361 663

TX LOGISTIK AG   TXL

Bad Honnef, Nordrhein-Westfalen

EVU Licence: Freight, 06/12/2001.

This firm started off as KEP Logistik being the EVU for the Eurogate/boxXpress container services. It used MEV Eisenbahnverkehrs mbH Ludwigshafen crews and Siemens Dispolok locomotives. The name then changed to Netzwerk Logistik GmbH (Netlog). Services run from Hamburg and Bremerhaven to Stuttgart, München and Nürnberg. The old DB sidings at Gemünden are used as a hub with three trains from the south forming two trains to the north. Traffic has grown so much that now some trains run direct from the north to München. Late in 2001 a new flow started with Netlog taking over the movement of new Volkswagen cars from Glauchau to Emden with 145CL031 being obtained for this new flow. Interestingly this logo was adorned with TX Logistic markings which is the parent company. 206 364 was obtained for tripping at Emden and 206 466 for similar work at Bremerhaven. BMW cars started being moved from January 2002 from Regensburg/München/Dingolfing to Bremerhaven. NetLog and boxXpress workings are very much interlinked.

From 01/01/2003 the main company name has been used. 2003 saw many developments in particular the ABX block trains from Unna to Fürth on behalf of Karstadt Quelle, Woolworths and Metro AG. This train also has a portion worked in from Gütersloh and splits at Fürth for Nürnberg,

Augsburg and München Laim. RAR provides locos for shunting at Nürnberg and München. A 185 does the long haul – München. In April 2003 TXL started moving containers from MÜnchen Reim to Burgshausen. Early in 2004 this working became a job for a hired in Blue Tiger from Bombardier. The same month saw TXL take over the shunting duties at Unna Königsborn and Bönen. June 2003 saw yet another development with cars being moved from Regensburg to Lonato (Italy) involving TXL with LTE (Austria) and Trenitalia. Some of the hire locos are spare at weekends so TXL hires them out to others for use on special passenger trains etc! During 2003 TXL received a licence to move trains of rubbish and so once a week there is a Bremerhaven to Aken (Elbe) train. TXL uses an electric locomotive to Köthen and has sub-contracted MEG to provide a diesel for the trips to and from Aken. SBB 482 033/34 have been used in late 2003 for car trains from Regensburg to Bremerhaven.

2004 started with yet more progress with TXL taking over a Mannheim to Melzo (Italy) working using ES64U2-098 (passed for Switzerland) which works through to Chiasso.
Later the main company took over all the services and they are now marketed under the TX Logistik banner. Long term hire locos carry TX Logistik branding.
Electric locomotives are hired from Siemens Dispolok and Angel Trains Cargo. GATX Leasing provides two modernised 202s.

No.	Builder, No. & Year	Type	kW	Details	Comments
145 CL 031	Adtranz 33850/2001	145	4200	Bo-Bo E	
185 510	Bomb 33510/2002	185	5600	Bo-Bo E	
185 511	Bomb 33512/2002	185	5600	Bo-Bo E	
185 512	Bomb 33514/2002	185	5600	Bo-Bo E	
185 513	Bomb 33516/2002	185	5600	Bo-Bo E	
185 514	Bomb 33522/2002	185	5600	Bo-Bo E	
185 515	Bomb 33523/2002	185	5600	Bo-Bo E	
185 516	Bomb 33529/2002	185	5600	Bo-Bo E	
206 364	LEW 12873/1971	V100	883	B-B DH	Ex DB 202 364 via ALS.
206 466	LEW 13505/1972	V100	883	B-B DH	Ex DB 206 466 via ALS.
ES64F 901	KM 20449/2000	ES64F	6400	Bo-Bo E	
ES64F 902	KM 20448/2000	ES64F	6400	Bo-Bo E	
ES64U2 003	SKM 20559/2001	ES64U2	6400	Bo-Bo E	
ES64U2 004	SKM 20560/2002	ES64U2	6400	Bo-Bo E	
ES64U2 006	SKM 20562/2002	ES64U2	6400	Bo-Bo E	
ES64U2 007	SKM 20563/2002	ES64U2	6400	Bo-Bo E	
ES64U2 008	SKM 20564/2002	ES64U2	6400	Bo-Bo E	
ES64U2 009	SKM 20565/2002	ES64U2	6400	Bo-Bo E	
ES64U2 010	SKM 20566/2002	ES64U2	6400	Bo-Bo E	
ES64U2 011	SKM 20567/2002	ES64U2	6400	Bo-Bo E	
ES64U2 012	SKM 20568/2002	ES64U2	6400	Bo-Bo E	
ES64U2 014	SKM 20570/2002	ES64U2	6400	Bo-Bo E	
ES64U2 015	SKM 20571/2002	ES64U2	6400	Bo-Bo E	
ES64U2 018	SKM 20574/2002	ES64U2	6400	Bo-Bo E	
ES64U2 902	KM 20446/2000	ES64U2	6400	Bo-Bo E	
ES64U2 903	KM 20447/2000	ES64U2	6400	Bo-Bo E	

TEUTOBURGER WALD EISENBAHN GESELLSCHAFT
TWE (CONNEX)

Gütersloh, Nordrhein Westfalen

Routes: Ibbenbüren Ost–Lengerich–Gütersloh Nord–Hövelhof (92.6 km); Brochterbeck–Hafen Saerbeck (7.2 km); Harsewinkel–Harsewinkel West (3.0 km).
Length: 102.8/125.1 km.   **Depots:** Lengerich Hohne, Gütersloh Nord.
EVU Licence: 05/11/1996.

The TWE is quite a surprise having a main line of over 90 km and a couple of short branches on one of which is a plant manufacturing agricultural equipment and a source of freight traffic for TWE. Another good revenue earner is scrap from Paderborn to Lingen with a balancing turn to bring back steel billets. There are TWE depots at Lengerich Hohne and Gütersloh but Lengerich also has a well equipped workshop handling repairs and maintenance of locos for the whole DEG group. 429,000 tonnes forwarded in 1998; 500,000 tonnes in 2000. In December 2002 TWE received a new contract to move bananas from Hamburg to Dortmund but this seems to have lapsed in 2003.

No.	Builder, No. & Year	Type	kW	Details	Comments
Köf 11	Jung 13218/1960	Köf II	94	B DH	Ex DB 323 850
V 104	LEW 17728/1983	V100.4	1030	B-B DH	Ex EKO Stahl 63
V 131	MaK 1000255/1968	G1300BB	956	B-B DH	
V 144	OR DH1004/6/2001	DH 1004	1030	B-B DH	Ex DB 211 293
V 156	MaK 1000895/1968	G1205BB	1120	B-B DH	
V 157	MaK 1000896/1968	G1205BB	1120	B-B DH	
211 052	MaK 1000070/1962	V100	992	B-B DH	Ex DB 211 052 (spares)
VT 03	Wegm 35252/1926	VT70.9	2 x 154	Bo DMR	Ex WEG VT 03

Note: No. 11 is normally Lengerich pilot.

UWE ADAM TRANSPORTE GmbH   UAT
Sättelstädt, Thüringen

Depot: Old DB depot at Eisenach.
EVU Licence: Freight only, 02/04/2002.

This is a break away group from AMP Bahn Logistik. Mr & Mrs Adam formed their own company as Sylvia & Uwe Adam Transporte and had a deal with MaLoWa at Klostermansfeld for maintenance. Now the organisation has changed into two firms. Work remains the same – nationwide engineering trains.

No.	Builder, No. & Year	Type	kW	Details	Comments
3	LEW 13347/1972	V60D	478	0-8-0 DH	Ex Kali Bischhofferode (IND)
4	LEW 15613/1977	V60D	478	0-8-0 DH	Ex Kali Bischhofferode (IND).
7	LEW 12264/1969	V60D	478	0-8-0 DH	Ex DB 346 182 via Falz
8	LKM 280125/1968	V180	1470	C-C DH	Ex DB 228 721 via Falz. SYLVIA ADAM
9	LKM 13559/1973	V100	883	B-B DH	Ex DB 202 520 SEBASTIAN
10	LEW 14444/1974	V100	883	B-B DH	Ex DB 202 743 ANJA
11	LEW 13915/1973	V100	932	B-B DH	Ex DB 202 597 CHRISTINA
12	LEW 14439/1974	V100	932	B-B DH	Ex ALS, DB 202 738
13	LEW 11344/1967	V60D	478	0-8-0 DH	Ex HTB
14	Lugansk 0005/1977	242	2200	Co-Co DE	Ex Lokpool W232.03 ex 242 005
15	LKM 275155/1966	V180	1470	B-B DH	Ex EfW V180 168 ex DB
16	?				
17	LKM 280072/1967	V180	1470	C-C DH	Ex RAR 14, ex AMP 7, ex DB 228 672
18	MaK 1000160/1963	V100	992	B-B DH	Ex ALs, ex DB 212 024

USEDOMER BADER BAHN GmbH   UBB
Mecklenburg Vorpommern

This is a 100% DB Regio subsidiary set up to operate the services on the island of Usedom no doubt with a view to hiving off at a later date. Details of stock are shown in German Railways Part 1.

UEF EISENBAHNVERKEHRSGELLSCHAFT mbH   UEF
Baden

This is the operating arm of the Ulmer Eisenbahnfreunde set up principally to operate freight trains on the line it took over from the WEG – Amstetten to Gerstetten. Locomotives from the preserved fleet are used.

UNISPED SPEDITION und TRANSPORTGESELLSCHAFT mbH
USS

Saarbrücken, Saarland

Once a subsidiary of Deutsche Steinkohle AG USS is now under the control of P&O Trans European (Deutschland) GmbH. Besides shunting the former Saarbergwerk collieries etc. USS became an EVU 04.12.1996 and slowly started to expand with shunting and trackwork contracts. Locos 3 – 19 retain their old SBW numbers. During 2002 USS took over shunting duties at Worms Hafenbahn. It is not quite clear where the main depot is located.

No.	Builder, No. & Year	Type	kW	Details	Comments
3	KHD 56761/1958			0-4-0 DH	

9	KM 19293/1966	ML500C	368	0-6-0 DH	
10	KM 19097/1963	ML500C	368	0-6-0 DH	
11	Hens 31681/1973	DHG700C	515	C DH	
12	KM 19585/1972	M500C	368	C DH	
13	Hens 31866/1976	DHG700C	515	C DH	
14	Hens 31997/1978	DHG700C	515	C DH	
15	Hens 31993/1979	DHG700C	515	C DH	
16	Hens 32476/1981	DHG700C	515	C DH	
17	Hens 32561/1982	DHG700C	515	C DH	
18	Hens 32721/1982	DHG700C	515	C DH	
19	Gm 5281/1964	CDH5	478	C DH	
20	Gm 5376/1965	CDH5	478	C DH	Ex RAG 416
21	Gm 5278/1963	CDH5	478	C DH	Ex RAG 412
40	MaK 1000245/1965	G1300	956	B-B DH	Ex HEG V32, BLE 32
41	Krupp 4381/1962	V100DB	809	B-B DH	Ex DH 110 02 ex BGW 02 ex DB 211 271
45ᴵ	VSFT 1001017/2000	G1206	1500	B-B DH	Hired ex LSG
45ᴵᴵ	VSFT 1001133/2001	G1206	1500	B-B DH	Ex ATC 207CL133
411	Gm 5277/1962	CDH5	478	C DH	Hired ex RAG
413	Gm 5279/1963	CDH5	478	C DH	Hired ex RAG

VERKEHRS BETRIEBE EXTERTAL–EXTERTALBAHN Gmbh
VBE

Exertal, Nordrhein Westfalen

Electric System: 1500 V dc
Routes: Barntrup - Rinteln
Length: 23.8/28.6 km.   **Depots:** Bhf. Bösingfeld.
EVU Licence: Freight and Passenger, 30/04/1996.

As the name implies this line runs along the valley of the river Exter. The line was electrified upon opening and two original locos survive. Passenger services ceased in 1964 the line existing since then on freight traffic but this is now at a low ebb. Steam excursion trains run during the summer using bought in former OBB 93.1410 but do not miss the vintage wooden bodied electric locos or to be more correct baggage cars. Latest freight figures available show only 16,000 tonnes of freight originating. From January 2001 VBE took over the freight service from DB on the Barntrup–Lemgo line.

No.	Builder, No. & Year	Type	kW	Details	Comments
E 21	Killing 1927		4 x 110	BoBo E	
E 22	Killing 1927		4 x 110	BoBo E	

VOGTLANDBAHN Gmbh
VBG

Neumark, Sachsen

Routes: Zwickau Zentrum–Zwickau Hbf–Falkenstein–Klingenthal (KBS 539, 65 km); Reichenbach–Falkenstein–Adorf (KBS 539, 68 km); Plauen Oberer Bhf.–Schleiz West (KBS 543, 32.2 km); Zwickau Hbf.–Reichenbach–Plauen–Bad Brambach (KBS 544, 97 km). In 2001 took over local services Hof–Weiden from DB Regio and in 2002 took over some workings through to Regensburg! These later extensions caused more DMUs to be ordered with Desiro DMUs again in favour. From 1/7/02 started operating some through trains from Gera–Greiz–Plauen–Weischlitz. (62 km DB Netz).
Length: 260.2 km (All ex DB Netz except Zwickau town section).
Depots: Neumark.
EVU Licence: Freight and Pasenger, 18/03/1998.

Soon after unification local transport managers for Reichenbach and Land Sachsen wanted to improve the passenger service offered in the Reichenbach and Zwickau areas then along came regionalisation and the way to do it. A plan was agreed and track improvements put in hand on the Zwickau–Adorf and Reichenbach–Klingenthal routes. For the new service the RBG obtained the concession and ordered 8 Regio Sprinters from Duewag. RBG then took over the DB workshop part of Bw Reichenbach. The service has prospered and prompted Zwickau to do a Karlsruhe as a third running rail has been added to the metre-gauge street tramway allowing standard gauge DMUs to run through into the town. For this the Regio Sprinters had to be fitted with road warning lights etc. which were fitted to the new build VT 39–48 Now the VBG is expanding and more units have been ordered to allow it to take over services from DB on the following lines: KBS 545 Hof–Plauen Ob.Bhf; KBS 541 Gera–Greiz–Weischlitz; KBS 545/6 Hof–Schönburg–Zeulenroda Weida–Gera (84 km); KBS 866 Marktredwitz–Cheb (CZ)–Vojtnov (CZ)–Bad Brambach (27 km in Germany). In the Czech Republic the services will be jointly operated with the private operator Viamont. Nine more Regio Sprinters are believed ordered. A new depot has been built at Neumark (Sachs) and the old Bw Reichenbach facilities are no longer used. The VBG is a subsidiary of Regentalbahn.

No.	Builder, No. & Year	Type	kW	Details	Comments
VT 01	Duewag 92385/6/1999	Desiro	2 x 275	B-2-B DHR	
VT 02	Duewag 92387/8/1999	Desiro	2 x 275	B-2-B DHR	
VT 03	Duewag 92389/90/1999	Desiro	2 x 275	B-2-B DHR	
VT 04	Duewag 92391/2/1999	Desiro	2 x 275	B-2-B DHR	
VT 05	Duewag 92393/4/1999	Desiro	2 x 275	B-2-B DHR	
VT 06	Duewag 92395/6/1999	Desiro	2 x 275	B-2-B DHR	
VT 07	Duewag 92397/8/1999	Desiro	2 x 275	B-2-B DHR	
VT 08	Duewag 92399/00/1999	Desiro	2 x 275	B-2-B DHR	
VT 09	Duewag 92401/2/1999	Desiro	2 x 275	B-2-B DHR	
VT 10	Siemens 93046/7/2002	Desiro	2 x 275	B-2-B DHR	
VT 11	Siemens 93048/9/2002	Desiro	2 x 275	B-2-B DHR	
VT 12	Siemens 93050/1/2002	Desiro	2 x 275	B-2-B DHR	
VT 13	Siemens 93052/3/2002	Desiro	2 x 275	B-2-B DHR	
VT 14	Siemens 93054/5/2002	Desiro	2 x 275	B-2-B DHR	
VT 15	Siemens 93056/7/2002	Desiro	2 x 275	B-2-B DHR	
VT 16	Siemens 93127/8/2002	Desiro	2 x 275	B-2-B DHR	REGENSBURG
VT 17	Siemens 93129/30/2002	Desiro	2 x 275	B-2-B DHR	
VT 18	Siemens 93131/2/2002	Desiro	2 x 275	B-2-B DHR	
VT 19	Siemens 93133/4/2002	Desiro	2 x 275	B-2-B DHR	
VT 20	Siemens 93135/6/2002	Desiro	2 x 275	B-2-B DHR	
VT 21	Siemens 93137/8/2002	Desiro	2 x 275	B-2-B DHR	
VT 22	Siemens 93139/40/2002	Desiro	2 x 275	B-2-B DHR	
VT 23	Siemens 93141/2/2002	Desiro	2 x 275	B-2-B DHR	
VT 24	Siemens 93143/4/2002	Desiro	2 x 275	B-2-B DHR	VOGTLANDKREIS
VT 31	Duewag 91482/1996	Regio Sprinter	2 x 198	A-2-A DMR	
VT 32	Duewag 91483/1996	Regio Sprinter	2 x 198	A-2-A DMR	
VT 33	Duewag 91484/1996	Regio Sprinter	2 x 198	A-2-A DMR	
VT 34	Duewag 91485/1996	Regio Sprinter	2 x 198	A-2-A DMR	
VT 35	Duewag 91486/1996	Regio Sprinter	2 x 198	A-2-A DMR	
VT 36	Duewag 91487/1996	Regio Sprinter	2 x 198	A-2-A DMR	
VT 37	Duewag 91488/1996	Regio Sprinter	2 x 198	A-2-A DMR	
VT 38	Duewag 91693/1997	Regio Sprinter	2 x 198	A-2-A DMR	
VT 39	Duewag 91694/1997	Regio Sprinter	2 x 198	A-2-A DMR	Tramway fittings
VT 40	Duewag 91695/1997	Regio Sprinter	2 x 198	A-2-A DMR	Tramway fittings
VT 41	Duewag 91696/1997	Regio Sprinter	2 x 198	A-2-A DMR	Tramway fittings
VT 42	Duewag 91697/1997	Regio Sprinter	2 x 198	A-2-A DMR	Tramway fittings
VT 43	Duewag 91698/1997	Regio Sprinter	2 x 198	A-2-A DMR	Tramway fittings
VT 44	Duewag 91699/1997	Regio Sprinter	2 x 198	A-2-A DMR	Tramway fittings
VT 45	Duewag 91700/1997	Regio Sprinter	2 x 198	A-2-A DMR	Tramway fittings
VT 46	Duewag 91701/1997	Regio Sprinter	2 x 198	A-2-A DMR	Tramway fittings
VT 47	Duewag 91702/1997	Regio Sprinter	2 x 198	A-2-A DMR	Tramway fittings
VT 48	Duewag 91703/1997	Regio Sprinter	2 x 198	A-2-A DMR	Tramway fittings
WL 1	LKM 265050/1970	Class 312	162	0-4-0 DH	Ex RBG D07 ex DB 312 150

NEBENBAHN VAIHINGEN–ENZWEIHINGEN   VE (WEG)

Baden Württemberg

Routes: Vaihingen Nord–Enzweihingen (KBS 773, 7.3 km).
Length: 7.3 km
Depots: Enzweihingen

This is another of the WEG's classic short lines being just over 7 km long but of course with a DB link. The line was closed 13/12/2002.

No.	Builder, No. & Year	Type	kW	Details	Comments
T 04	Wegm 35254/1926	VT70.9	2 x 154	Bo DMR	Ex DB VT70 901

VULKAN EIFELBAHN BETRIEBSGESELLSCHAFT mbH VEB
Gerolstein, Rheinland Pfalz.

A subsidiary company of EBM to operate passenger and freight trains in the Gerostein area. During 2002 EBM reorganised the company's freight activity and formed EBM Cargo to which the locomotives were transferred. VEB is now understood to be the EVU for the tourist trains that run on the Gerolstein–Daun–Kaisersesch line. Railcars from the Dieringhausen collection are used.

In 2003 another reorganisation saw VEB combining with local forwarding companies in the Gerolstein area and together they constructed a container terminal and started running trains from Gerolstein to Wustermark (Berlin). A VEB diesel locomotive works from Gerolstein to Trier where a Dispolok ES64U2 takes over to Wustermark. Finally OHE Sp trips the train into the unloading terminal. The train connects south of Köln with the RWB train to and from Salzburg. Later VEB changed the work and the train now operates direct from Gerolstein to the Köln area where the ES64U2 takes over.

No.	Builder, No. & Year	Type	kW	Details	Comments
212 091	MaK 1000227/1964	V100	992	B-B DH	Ex ALs, ex DB
212 299	MaK 1000346/1965	V100	992	B-B DH	Ex ALs, ex DB
795 414	MAN 140972/1954	795	110	A-1 DMR	Ex EBM ex DB
796 784	MAN 146566/1961	796	2 x 110	A-A DMR	Ex EBM ex DB
798 670	Uer 61561/1961	798	2 x 110	A-A DMR	Ex EBM
798 751	WMD 1291/1960	798	2 x 110	A-A DMR	Ex EBM

NB: 798 670/751 also ex EAKJ, ex DKB VT207/5, ex DB.

VORWOHLE-EMMERTHALER VERKEHRSBETRIEBE GMbH   VEV
Bodenwerder, Niedersachsen

Routes: Vorwohle–Emmerthal.
Length: 31.8/35.1 km   **Depots:** Bodenwerder-Linse
EVU Licence: Freight and Passenger, 26/10/1995.

Although 31 km long this line does not have any main line locos with DB working what trains there are. The VEV loco is just used for shunting and the odd works train. A steam tourist service runs in the season using DBG locos from Bodenwerder. In 2000 it was reported that there were now more workings into Hameln.

No.	Builder, No. & Year	Type	kW	Details	Comments
V2-01	Gm 4885/1956	Köf II	88	B DH	Ex DB 323 574

VERKEHRSBETRIEBE GRAFTSCHAFT HOYA GmbH VGH
Hoya, Niedersachsen

Routes: Eystrup–Hoya–Syke
Length: 36.9/46.1 km   **Depots:** Hoya
EVU licence: 09/11/1995.

This old line has had a chequered existance but the new legislation might mean a new beginning. Regular passenger traffic ceased in 1972 after which the line relied on its freight traffic but this plummeted after the heavy sugar beet traffic ceased in the 1980s. Since then the odd wagon load has been handled plus some military traffic. As the line serves Bruchhausen Vilsen the DEV use a standard gauge railcar to run an occasional tourist service over the VGH. DEV are now involved with MWB and perhaps VGH may benefit from this connection.

No.	Builder, No. & Year	Type	kW	Details	Comments
60021	MaK 600155/1959	650D	478	0-8-0 DH	Ex OHE 60021
V 124	Deutz 57312/1959	Köf II	94	B DH	Ex DB 323 210
V 125	O&K 26032/1959	Köf II	94	B DH	Ex DB 323 251
V 126	Deutz 46541/1943	Köf II	94	B DH	Ex DB 324 011

VERKEHRSBETRIEBE KREIS PLÖN GmbH   VKP
Kiel, Schleswig Holstein

Routes: Kiel Süd–Schönberg; Oppendorf–Dietrichsdorf.
Length: 24.7 km   **Depots:** Schönberg.

EVU Licence: Freight only, 05/08/1913. (?)

A short branch northwards from Kiel that lost its passenger service in 1981. One loco suffices to move available freight. With a passenger renaissance elsewhere since regionalisation it is possible that the line may regain its passenger trains. However in the meantime it does see special passenger trains to the preservation centre at Schönberg. 788,000 tonnes of freight in 1998 which was mostly coal to a power station which is in danger of being transferred to coastal shipping. The NOB is to build its workshop on the VKP at Kiel.

No.	Builder, No. & Year	Type	kW Details	Comments
V 155	MaK 1000875/1992	G1205BB1120 B-B DH		

VERKEHRSBETRIEBE DES KREISES SCHLESWIG–FLENSBURG VKSF

Schleswig, Schleswig Holstein

This short line is all that is left of the former Schleswiger Kreisbahn which was over 100 km long. Today it has no motive power with DB tripping what freight traffic comes its way. Passenger traffic ceased in 1972. However a preservation group is based on the line thus it is possible to ride over it from time to time. Spot freight traffic is worked by AB or NVAG; 100,000 tonnes in 2000.

Routes: Süderbraraup–Kappeln. **Length:** 15 km
EVU Licence: Freight only, 14/06/1905.

No motive power.

VERKEHRSGESELLSCHAFT LANDKREIS OSNABRÜCK GmbH VLO

Bohmte, Niedersachsen

Routes: Holzhausen–Bohmte–Schwegermoor.
Length: 33.8/41.1 km **Depots:** Bohmte
EVU Licence: Freight only, 09/07/1996 (or 1896?).

This freight line is all that is left of the former Wittlager Kreisbahn. Regular passenger traffic ceased in 1971 passing to the local buses. Freight traffic still hangs on and it also possible to ride the line as Museums Eisenbahn Minden runs tourist trains from its base at Prussisch Oldendorf. In 1998 the freight traffic totalled 51,000 tonnes
In late 2000 it was announced that VLO is likely to take over the GET operations.

No.	Builder, No. & Year	Type	kW Details	Comments
DL 1	MaK 400005/1955	400C	294 0-6-0 DH	
T 3	Wumag 1935		81 A-1 DMR	Ex GME VT 1
VLO 1	O&K 26666/1970	MC360N 265 C DH		

VOSSLOH LOCOMOTIVES GmbH VL

Schleswig Holstein

This organisation started out as the leasing arm of Vossloh Schienfahrzeuge Technik - VSFT(MaK) and was once called Eurotrac. It became Locomotion Service GmbH (LSG) in 2000 owned by VSFT 90% and Angel Trains (UK) 10%. Another joint VSFT/Angel Trains company is Locomotion Capital. This company is also owned by Angel Trains and Vossloh but with the opposite share arrangement: Angel Trains 90%, VSFT 10%. In April 2003 this was renamed Angel Trains Cargo. (q.v.)

These Vossloh locomotives are short term hire locomotives as part of the overall Vossloh service to its customers. Vossloh can replace a locomotive should there be a failure (most unlikely) or accident, the latter being the usual scenario.

No.	Builder, No. & Year	Type	kW Details	Comments
06	VSFT 1001017/2000	G1206BB1500 B-B DH		Now to EH 904
07	VSFT 1001018/2000	G1206BB1500 B-B DH		
V1001-022	VSFT 1001022/2000	G1206	1500 B-B DH	
V1001-025	VSFT 1001025/2000	G1206	1500 B-B DH	
G2000.01	VSFT 1001028/2000	G2000	2240 B-B DH	Infra Leuna
G2000.02	VSFT 1001029/2000	G2000	2240 B-B DH	NE
V1001-033	VSFT 1001033/2001	G2000	2240 B-B DH	WEG

V1001-034	VSFT 1001034/2001	G2000	2240	B-B DH	EKO
V1001-035	VSFT 1001035/2001	G2000	2240	B-B DH	MEG for 2 years
V1001-037	VSFT 1001037/2001	G2000	2240	B-B DH	OHE
V1001-038	VSFT 1001038/2002	G2000	2240	B-B DH	BCB
V1001-114	VSFT 1001114/2000	G1206	1500	B-B DH	Ex HGK,to DLC
V1001-117	VSFT 1001117/2000	G1206	1500	B-B DH	Infra Leuna
V1001-125	VSFT 1001125/2001	G1206	1500	B-B DH	RAG
V1001-127	VSFT 1001127/2001	G1206	1500	B-B DH	NVAG
V1001-129	VSFT 1001129/2001	G1206	1500	B-B DH	RBB
V1001-130	VSFT 1001130/2001	G1206	1500	B-B DH	WEG
V1001-131	VSFT 1001131/2001	G1206	1500	B-B DH	Infra Leuna
V1001-133	VSFT 1001133/2001	G1206	1500	B-B DH	USS
V1001-138	VSFT 1001138/2001	G1206	1500	B-B DH	R4C
V1001-139	VSFT 1001139/2002	G1206	1500	B-B DH	
01	VSFT 1001148/2001	G800BB		B-B DH	Chemion
02	VSFT 1001149/2001	G800BB		B-B DH	Chemion
03	VSFT 1001318/2002	G800BB		B-B DH	Chemion
04	VSFT 1001319/2002	G800BB		B-B DH	Chemion
352 001	MaK 220139/1997	G322B		4w DH	DB

VERKEHRSBETRIEBE PEINE–SALZGITTER GmbH   VPS

Salzgitter, Niedersachsen

Routes: Salzgitter-Beddingen–Salzgitter–Vosspass and branches to Hütte Nord and Beddingen Hafen; Salzgitter–Immendorf West; other Salgitter area branches (38.2 km); Peine–Ilsede–Broistedt–Salzgitter Engelnstedt (31.3 km).
Length: 69.5/370.3 km   **Depots:** Hallendorf.
EVU Licence: Freight and Passenger 19/02/2003.

VPS shunts and trips around the steelworks complexes in Salzgitter and Peine. It also works freights from the works over DB tracks to and from destinations in the area using modern B-B locos which are thus fitted with Indusi and ZBF and some have been allocated DB numbers. 33 million tonnes handled in 1998 rising to 36 million in 2000. Besides the local trips VPS has now started moving steel from Lingen to Peine and freights from Salzgitter to Ilsenburg and Blankenburg.

No.	Builder, No. & Year	Type	kW	Details	Comments
501	LHB 3103/1964	530C	504	6w DH	
502	LHB 3114/1965	530C	504	6w DH	
503	LHB 3115/1965	530C	504	6w DH	
504	LHB 3116/1965	530C	504	6w DH	
506	LHB 3133/1966	530C	504	6w DH	
507	LHB 3134/1966	530C	504	6w DH	
508	LHB 3146/1966	530C	504	6w DH	
509	LHB 3153/1972	530C	504	6w DH	
510	LHB 3154/1972	530C	504	6w DH	
511	LHB 3155/1972	530C	504	6w DH	
512	LHB 3156/1972	530C	504	6w DH	
513	LHB 3157/1972	530C	504	6w DH	
514	LHB 3158/1972	530C	504	6w DH	
515	LHB 3095/1964	530C	504	6w DH	DB "351 001"
516	LHB 3096/1964	530C	504	6w DH	
517	LHB 3098/1964	530C	504	6w DH	
518	LHB 3101/1964	530C	504	6w DH	
519	LHB 3102/1964	530C	504	6w DH	
520	LHB 3104/1964	530C	504	6w DH	DB "351 002"
521	LHB 3108/1965	530C	504	6w DH	
522	LHB 3109/1965	530C	504	6w DH	
523	LHB 3110/1965	530C	504	6w DH	DB "351 003"
524	LHB 3111/1965	530C	504	6w DH	
525	LHB 3112/1965	530C	504	6w DH	
526	LHB 3113/1965	530C	504	6w DH	
527	LHB 3123/1966	530C	504	6w DH	
528	LHB 3124/1966	530C	504	6w DH	

529	LHB 3125/1966	530C	504	6w DH	
530	LHB 3126/1966	530C	504	6w DH	
531	LHB 3127/1966	530C	504	6w DH	
532	LHB 3128/1966	530C	504	6w DH	
533	LHB 3129/1966	530C	504	6w DH	
534	LHB 3130/1966	530C	504	6w DH	
535	LHB 3131/1966	530C	504	6w DH	
536	LHB 3145/1966	530C	504	6w DH	
537	LHB 3151/1972	530C	504	6w DH	
538	LHB 3152/1972	530C	504	6w DH	
539	LHB 3135/1966	530C	504	6w DH	
540	LHB 3099/1964	530C	504	6w DH	DB "351 004"
541	LHB 3100/1964	530C	504	6w DH	DB "351 005"
542	LHB 3105/1964	530C	504	6w DH	
543	LHB 3097/1964	530C	504	6w DH	
544	LHB 3106/1964	530C	504	6w DH	
545	LHB 3136/1966	530C	504	6w DH	Sold to OHE
701	KM 19885/1983	ME05	560	6w DH	
702	KM 19886/1983	ME05	560	Co DE	
703	KM 19887/1983	ME05	560	Co DE	
704	KM 19912/1984	ME05	560	Co DE	
705	KM 19913/1984	ME05	560	Co DE	
706	KM 19914/1984	ME05	560	Co DE	
1101	LHB 3139/1967	1100BB	1046	B-B DH	
1102	LHB 3140/1967	1100BB	1046	B-B DH	
1301	Gm 5708/1993	D1000BB	1320	B-B DH	Ex 1107
1302	Gm 5733/1996	D1000BB	1320	B-B DH	
1303	Gm 5734/1996	D1000BB	1320	B-B DH	
1501	Gm 5690/1990	D1000BB	1500	B-B DH	Ex 1104
1502	Gm 5691/1990	D1000BB	1500	B-B DH	Ex 1105
1503	Gm 5707/1993	D1000BB	1500	B-B DH	Ex 1106
1504	Gm 5739/2000	D1000BB	1500	B-B DH	
1505	Gm 5740/2000	D1000BB	1500	B-B DH	
1701	VSFT 1001213/2003	Mak1700BB	1700	B-B DH	Leased from ATC
1702	VSFT 1001214/2003	Mak1700BB	1700	B-B DH	Leased from ATC

Notes: Many of the 500 series have been rebuilt and there is some doubt as to actual identities of 539-545 which were possibly rebuilt out of order being previously numbered in the 600 series. 1501–5 work open access trains Salzgitter – Ilsenburg.

VERDEN–WALSRODER EISENBAHN GmbH   VWE
Niedersachsen

Routes: Verden (Aller) Süd - Stemmen (12.2 km); Walsrode–Böhme (12.6 km).
Length: 24.8/31.9 km   **Depots:** Verden (Aller) Süd.

This company operates three separate lines with the Verden line having heavy freight traffic at the Verden end. Its three locos are based on this section. The Walsrode section is serviced by the local Werkbahn Bomlitz - Walsrode (q.v.). 110,000 tonnes forwarded in 1998.

No.	Builder, No. & Year	Type	kW	Details	Comments
DL 1	Jung 13620/1964	R30C	246	C DH	
DL 2	Gm 4275/1947	V20	147	0-4-0 DH	
DL 3	LEW 12547/1971	V100	883	B-B DH	ex DB 202 265 in 2002.

WESTFALISCHE ALMETALBAHN GmbH   WAB
Nordrhein Westfalen

Routes: Paderborn–Büren
Length:
                         Depots: Altenbeken.
EVU Licence: (None appears to have been issued. Presumably operates under EBG banner).

This new railway company was set up to reintroduce passenger and freight services to the Paderborn–Büren line. It is an operating arm of the loco dealer at Altenbeken who is understood to live on the Büren branch! Be that as it may but WAB looks just now like another operator taking advantage of the big demand for locos as WAB locos are already being reported seen on works trains long distances from Altenbeken! The rebuilt DR V100 have been converted by Adtranz and given "new" Adtranz numbers which do not fall into a pattern with existing numbers. Consequently there is some doubt as yet as to the real identities. Under the Mora C concept WAB has picked up various freight flows serving customers on long circuitous routes from Altenbeken so that sidings get served once or twice a week. 30 staff are employed at Altenbeken including 21 drivers. The operations control is also here.

The owner of WAB is also involved with KOE and EBG and locos get moved from one company to another renumbered in the process.

Early in 2003 WAB purchased all the redundant cl. 142 from the bankrupt Mittelthurgaubahn/ Lokoop in Switzerland as SBB decided it did not want them! They are listed here with their Swiss numbers. Some may be sold on to other companies.

No.	Builder, No. & Year	Type	kW	Details	Comments
1	LKM 262634/1976	V22	162	0-4-0 DH	ExMaterialager Wittenhagen
2	LKM 261184/1962	V22	162	0-4-0 DH	Ex DB 311 665
3	MaK 2012/1948	V36	268	0-6-0 DH	Ex DB V36 255
4	MaK 400003/1955	400C	298	0-6-0 DH	Ex LEL V91
5	Deutz 57014/1959	Kof II	94	4w DH	Ex DB 323 104
9	BMAG 12359/1943	52	1200	2-10-0	Ex TE-5933, ex DRB 52 5933
10	Krupp 3113/1953	Knapsack		0-6-0T	Ex Lindener Hafenbahn 10
11	LEW 16675/1981	V100.4	908	B-B DH	Ex PCK Schwedt V100.4-16
12^I	Adtranz 72510/2000	V100	1050	B-B DH	To EBGO
12^{II}	Bomb 72540/2002	V100	1050	B-B DH	Ex DR 202?
13^I	Bomb 72520/2000	V100	1050	B-B DH	To EBGO
13^{II}	Bomb 72550/2002	V100	1050	B-B DH	Ex DR 202?
14	LEW 17317/1983	V100.5	1100	B-B DH	Ex DGT 710 968, Sold to ??
15	LEW 14443/1974	V100.1	883	B-B DH	Ex DWU 14 ex DR 201 742. To ITB ?
16	LEW 16756/1983	V100.5	1100	B-B DH	Ex DGT 710 970
17^I	LEW 12380/1969	V60D	478	0-8-0 DH	Ex Kaliwerk Bernburg 4, to EBG 6
18	LEW 11315/1966	V60D	478	0-8-0 DH	Ex EBM, ex Wismut 5 to EBG
19	LEW 14197/1974	V60D	478	0-8-0 DH	Ex Kaliwerk Merkurs 8
20^I	LEW 11314/1966	V60D	478	0-8-0 DH	Ex EBM, ex Wismut 4, to EBG
20^{II}	LEW 14816/1971	V60D	478	0-8-0 DH	Ex LAUBAG V106-03
21^I	LEW 12945/1971	V60D	478	0-8-0 DH	Ex Kaliwerk Merkurs 12, to EBG
22	LEW 15609/1977	V60D	478	0-8-0 DH	Ex EBG, ex Laubag 106-02
23	MaK 1000253/1963	1000D	800	0-8-0 DH	Ex Moerser Kreisbahn. Sold to Italy 9/2001
24	LKM 280033/1967	V180	2 x 736	C-C DH	Ex Glauchau, Ex 228 633
25	LKM 280123/1968	V180	2 x 736	C-C DH	Ex EBM, Ex 228 719.
26	Lugansk 2987/1977	M62	1470	Co-Co DE	Ex EBM, Ex Wismut V200 512
27^{II}	Lugansk 3383/1979	M62	1470	Co-Co DE	Ex PBSV 22 ex CD 781 418^{II} (781 557^I)
28	Lugansk 1536/1972	M62	1470	Co-Co DE	Ex PBSV 21 ex CD 781 416
30	Lugansk 0304/1974	232	2200	Co-Co DE	Ex JVA, ex 232 088
31	Lugansk 0227/1973	232	2200	Co-Co DE	Ex DB 232 037
50	LEW 11785/1967	142	2740	Bo-Bo E	Ex MThB 477 917, DB 142 154
51	LEW 11881/1968	142	2740	Bo-Bo E	Ex MThB 477 906, DB 142 157
52	LEW 11755/1968	142	2740	Bo-Bo E	Ex MThB 477 916, DB 142 134
53	LEW 11648/1967	142	2740	Bo-Bo E	Ex MThB 477 902, DB 142 132
54?					
55	LEW 13263/1972	142	2740	Bo-Bo E	Ex MThB 477 905, DB 142 191
56	LEW 15421/1968	142	2740	Bo-Bo E	Ex MThB 477 915, DB 142 287
57	LEW 11642/1967	142	2740	Bo-Bo E	Ex MThB 477 908, DB 142 126
101	Diema 2265/1959	DVL60		B DM	Ex Zuckerfabrik Uelzen
VT 1	Uer 66599/1960	796	2 x 110	A-A DMR	Ex DB 796 702
V36 204	BMAG 10991/1939	V36	270	0-6-0DH	Obtained for spares. 2003 to MaLoWa for repairs?
?	Lugansk 2990/1977	M62	1470	Co-Co DE	Ex Wismut V200 514 9/03
?	Lugansk 2991/1977	M62	1470	Co-Co DE	Ex Wismut V200 515 9/03
?	LEW 12736/1970	V60D	478	0-8-0 DH	Ex Wismut WL 13 9/03
(708)	KM 18990/1963	ML700C	505	0-6-0 D	Ex BT ex DE 708
(710)	KM 18992/1963	ML700C	505	0-6-0 D	Ex BT ex DE 710

Still to be overhauled and allocated WAB numbers are:

477 900	LEW 11646/1967	142	2740	Bo-Bo E	Ex DB 142 130
477 901	LEW 11781/1968	142	2740	Bo-Bo E	Ex DB 142 150

477 903	LEW 11649/1967	142	2740	Bo-Bo E	Ex DB 142 133
477 904	LEW 12150/1969	142	2740	Bo-Bo E	Ex DB 142 159
477 907	LEW 11634/1967	142	2740	Bo-Bo E	Ex DB 142 118
477 909	LEW 11644/1967	142	2740	Bo-Bo E	Ex DB 142 128
477 910	LEW 11619/1967	142	2740	Bo-Bo E	Ex DB 142 103
477 911	LEW 13630/1972	142	2740	Bo-Bo E	Ex DB 142 197
477 912	LEW 13632/1972	142	2740	Bo-Bo E	Ex DB 142 199
477 913	LEW 15004/1976	142	2740	Bo-Bo E	Ex DB 142 272
477 914	LEW 15845/1976	142	2740	Bo-Bo E	Ex DB 142 288

WAB 37–48 were M62s obtained from the CD. They had been in store for over a year with an acceptance problem. It then turned out the locos were in fact owned by the Adtranz Lokpool! The locos have all now been returned to Adtranz/Bombardier and subsequently to the Czech Republic for attention at Nymburk works which is now partly owned by the same person that owns EBG and WAB! As this book went to press it was learnt that ITL has bought the lot!

WESTERWALDBAHN GmbH   WEBA
Steinebach, Rheinland-Pfalz

Routes: Scheuerfeld–Oberdreisbach (18.4 km); Bindweide–Rosenheim (1.8 km); Betzdorf–Daaden (KBS 463, 9.9 km); Altenkirchen–Raubach (19.8 km).
Length: 49.9 km   **Depots:** Bindweide.
EVU Licence: No trace of licence to WEBA but could well operate under the Hellertalbahn licence.

The Westerwaldbahn is quite an old company having been founded in 1913. Its network has gradually shrunk and was down to two freight only routes when in 1994 under the regionalisation plans it took over from DB the passenger traffic between Betzdorf and Daaden buying, with help from the Lander, DB unit 628 677 and trailer. Passenger traffic grew again and extra carriages were purchased from WEG. WEBA will be expanding in the future and is already involved with the Hellertalbahn (q.v.) which it part owns.

On 14/11/02 WEBA learnt that its joint bid with HLB for local passenger services around Limburg had been accepted. The new company is 74.9% HLB and 25.1% WEBA. No details yet as to what title the new operation would operate under but it was soon confirmed that 28 LINT DMUs would be ordered from Alstom made up of 18 LINT 41 and 10 LINT 27. These will operate the following lines from 12/12/2004: Limburg–Koblenz/Siershahn/Altenkirchen-Au/Wiesbaden.

No.	Builder, No. & Year	Type	kW	Details	Comments
V26.1	Jung 12102/1956	R30B	191	0-4-0 DM	In use
V26.2	Jung 12103/1956	R30B	191	0-4-0 DM	Stored. Acc. 09/10/98
V26.3	Jung 12748/1957	R30B	191	0-4-0 DM	In Use
V26.4	Jung 12997/1959	R30B	191	0-4-0 DM	Stored – spares
05	OnR DH1004/2/1999	V100	1030	B-B DH	Ex DB 211 177
06	KM 19454/1962	M700C	515	C DH	Ex RAG 530 via On Rail
VT 24	Gm 5443/1968		2 x 154	Bo D?R	Ex WEG T 24
628 677	Duewag 91285/1994	628.4	485	B-B DHR	Ex DB 628 677

WÜRTTEMBERGISCHE EISENBAHN GESELLSCHAFT
WEG (CONNEX)

Baden Württemberg

The WEG is a subsidiary of DEG (now Connex) and as its name suggests it operates several lines in Baden Württemberg. These are:
• Nebenbahn Ebingen–Onstmettingen (EO);
• Nebenbahn Gaildorf–Untergröningen (GU);
• Nebenbahn Korntal–Weissach(KW);
• Nebenbahn Nürtingen–Neuffen (NN);
• Nebenbahn Vaihingen–Enzweihingen (VE);
• Zweckverbandes Schönbuchbahn (ZVS);
• Zweckverbandes Verkehrsverband Wieslaftalbahn (ZVVW).

Details of these various lines are listed under their respective names. Two other lines should be mentioned. Amstetten–Gerstetten (AG) has been closed by WEG but is now operated as a museum line by Ulmer Eisebahnfreunde who also trip any freight that comes for the line. The other line is

Jagstfeld–Ohnberg (JO) closed some years ago and believed to be still owned and in situ future unknown. WEG stock is all in one list but allocated to the different lines and only ever changes when major maintenance is to be done or units etc. damaged by accidents.

WENDELSTEINBAHN GmbH   WENDELSTEIN
Bayern

Gauge: 1000 mm
Electric System: 1500 V dc
Length: 7.7/8.4 km
EVU Licence: ?

Routes: Brannenburg–Wendelstein
Depots: Brannenburg

This is a typical mountain railway with a short valley section adhesion worked before the mountain climbing starts using the Strub rack system. The line starts at Brannenburg on the Rosenheim–Kufstein line with the station there at 508 m above sea level. The summit station on the Wendelstein is at 1723 m the 7.7 km taking 30 minutes. Note: The station is a long way from the DB one.

No.	Builder, No. & Year	Type	kW	Details	Comments
2	Essl 3628/1912		2 x 74	Bo E	Rack
3	Essl 3629/1912		2 x 74	Bo E	Rack
4	Essl 4239/1935		2 x 108	Bo E	Rack
11	SLM 5454/1990	Beh4/4	4 x 253	A1-A1+A1-A1	Rack. *Prinzregent Luitpold*
12	SLM 5455/1990	Beh4/4	4 x 253	A1-A1+A1-A1	Rack. *Otto v. Steinbeis*

WERNE BOCKUM HÖVELER EISENBAHN   WerBH
Nordrhein Westfalen

Routes: Werne–Stockum–Bockum–Hövel
Length: 12.0 km.   **Depots:** Werne.

This line still retains its identity but to all intents and purposes it is part of RAG. It is the only part of RAG to be counted as a proper railway and not as a sidings or industrial railway server. It ran passenger trains until the mid 1980s. The principal traffic today is coal to the power station at Stockum. For motive power see the RAG entry.

WESERBAHN   WESERBAHN
Bremen

Weserbahn is a subsidiary of the Bremer Strassenbahn A.G. (BSAG) and is the owner of the Bremer Vorortbahnen Gesellschaft. (BVG) which owns a series of lines linking sites around Bremen. Weserbahn also acts as an umbrella organisation for some other lines for which it holds the operating licence – VGH and BTE. Weserbahn is also active in promoting the extension of BSAG over DB lines in the area as done in Karlsruhe.

WANNE HERNER EISENBAHN UND HÄFEN GmbH WHE
Herne, Nordrhein Westfalen

Routes: Links in Wanne to the Osthafen and Westhafen and numerous other sidings and connections including to the power station in Herne.
Length: 13.7/40.0 km   **Depot:** Wanne Westhafen.
EVU Licence: Freight only 21/12/1995.

Another industrial operator on the edge of the Ruhr idustrial area. The main traffic handled is coal for Wanne Westhafen. To visit this line the first weekend in September is usually the best time as there is a regular open day about this time of year.

No.	Builder, No. & Year	Type	kW	Details	Comments
12	Deutz 55334/1952	KS5B	40	B DH	
20	MaK 800186/1973	G1100BB	809	B-B DH	
22	MaK 1000776/1978	G1600BB	1176	B-B DH	
23	MaK 1000777/1978	G1600BB	1176	B-B DH	
24	MaK 1000778/1978	G1600BB	1176	B-B DH	
25	MaK 1000783/1979	G1202BB	944	B-B DH	

27	MaK 1000813/1983	G1204BB	1119	B-B DH
28	MaK 1000816/1984	G1204BB	1119	B-B DH
29	MaK 700078/1984	DE502	560	Co DE
30	MaK 700079/1984	DE502	560	Co DE
-	Wind 130618/1980	RW150EM	32	B-B D??

N.F. WIEBE GmbH & Co. KG   WIEBE
Achim, Niedersachsen

Routes: Nationwide.   **Depots:** Nienburg.
EVU Licence: Freight only 27/10/1998.

The Wiebe company is a well known track maintenance firm which for many years only owned track machines. The change in circumstances on Germany's railways has allowed the firm to run its own locomotives. Based in Nienburg (the depot is actually built on the site of a former DB depot) the locos can be found anywhere in Germany where the firm gets a contract.

No.	Builder, No. & Year	Type	kW	Details	Comments
1	Gm 5026/1958	Köf II	97	B DH	Ex DB 323 639
2	Jung 13468/1962	V100 DB	994	B-B DH	Ex DB 211 341
3	Jung 13668/1964	V100 DB	994	B-B DH	Ex DB 212 192
4	Hens 30793/1963	V100 DB	994	B-B DH	Ex DB 212 107
5	O&K 26005/1959	Köf II	94	B DH	Ex IND, ex DB 323 166
6	Krp 4665/1965	V160	1397	B-B DH	Ex Italy, ex DB 216 032
7	Hens 30400/1963	V320 DB	2 x 1470	C-C DH	Ex Italy, ex DB 232 001
8	MaK 1000033/1961	V100 DB	992	B-B DH	Ex DB 211 015 in 2002
9	MaK 1000063/1962	V100 DB	992	B-B DH	Ex DB 211 045 in 2002
10	KHD 58144/1967	V160	1400	B-B DH	Ex DB 216 122
11	Krp 4831/1966	V160	1400	B-B DH	Ex DB 216 068

Note: No. 2 is now fitted with a CAT 3512 engine. All main line locos now fitted with Sifa, Indusi and ZBF. Numbers 8 and 9 understood to be marked BLP – this denotes Bauüberwachungs und Logistik GmbH – a Wiebe subsidiary.

WISMUT GmbH SANIERUNGSBETRIEBE RONNEBURG
WISMUT

BEREICH ANSCHLUSSBAHN. Thüringen

Routes: Seelingstädt (b. Werdau)–Paitzdorf, Kayna–Raitzhain W4.
Length: -/57 km   **Depot:** Lichtenberg
EVU Licence:

The Wismut concern serviced industrial concerns mining uranium. There are also sand deposits. Much reduced activity nowadays. The line once had a fleet of V200 (M62) but some have been sold off to other operators. Some may still be dumped on the line.

No.	Builder, No. & Year	Type	kW	Details	Comments
V200 506[II]	Lugansk 1843/1973	M62	1470	Co-Co DE	Stored
V200 514	Lugansk 2989/1977	M62	1470	Co-Co DE	Stored. Since sold to WAB
V200 515	Lugansk 2990/1977	M62	1470	Co-Co DE	Stored. Since sold to WAB
V300 001	Lugansk 0636/1976	232		Co-Co DE	Ex 232 404
V300 002	Lugansk 0640/1976	232		Co-Co DE	Ex 232 405
V300 003	Lugansk 0965/1981	232		Co-Co DE	Ex 232 684
V300 004	Lugansk 0664/1976	232		Co-Co DE	Ex 232 429
V300 005	Lugansk 0372/1974	232		Co-Co DE	Ex 232 155

NB: All the 232s understood to have been re-engined with CAT 3606 engines.

WESTFALISCHE LANDES EISENBAHN GmbH   WLE
Nordrhein Westfalen

Routes: Münster–Neubeckum–Lippstadt–Warstein (101.6 km with Neubeckum–Beckum actually DB Netz – 6 km); Neubeckum–Ennigerloh (7.2 km); Heidberg–Belecke (16.2 km); Wiedenbrück–Dellbrück.
Length: 111.3/130.9 km
Depots: Lippstadt, Beckum (3 locos), Warstein (3 locos).

The WLE is a long established private line dating back to 1883. It has been freight only since 1975 but may see passenger traffic return in the near future at the Münster end of the line. Ten locomotives are in use Monday–Friday with maybe just two on a Saturday. The railway is busy with traffic associated with cement works as there are two on the line generating freight traffic to the tune of 1.24 million tonnes in 1999 and a similar amount in 2001. In recent years many locomotives have been re-equipped with Caterpillar 3508 or 3512 engines. In 2003 WLE 51 was being used on weekend passenger services from Münster to Goslar or Wernigerode via DB routes in the Ruhr.

No.	Builder, No. & Year	Type	kW	Details	Comments
04	Wind 915/1944	Köf II	81	B DH	
05	Deutz 57876/1970	MG530C	465	C DH	
06	O&K 26744/1973	MG170N		B	
15	Gm 5373/1965		37	B DH	(Lippstadt pilot)
16	Breuer 3082/1964		55	B DM	(Lippstadt pilot)
30	Deutz 57651/1964	DG2000CCM	1616	C-C DH	*Helmut Ellinger* (Stored Warstein)
31	Deutz 56594/1957	DG1600BBM	808	B-B DH	(Stored)
34	Deutz 56288/1956	DG2000CCM	1940	C-C DH	*Erwitte*
35	Deutz 58107/1969	DG1200BBM	808	B-B DH	*Ennigerloh* (Sold to Italy)
36	Deutz 57419/1962	DG1000BBM	808	B-B DH	
37	Deutz 58251/1970	DG1500CCM	1400	C-C DH	*Münster* (from 17.03.2003).
38	Deutz 58252/1970	DG1500CCM	1400	C-C DH	
39	Deutz 57146/1961	DG1000BBM	1940	B-B DH	*Münster* (Sold to Italy)
40	Deutz 59254/1970	DG1100BBM	1940	B-B DH	*Warstein*
44	Deutz 57190/1961	DG1200BBM	808	B-B DH	
46	Deutz 57660/1963	DG1000BBM	808	B-B DH	
51	VSFT 1001150/2002	G1206BB	1500	B-B DH	*Kreis Warendorf*
61	MaK 1000596/1974	G1600BB	1176	B-B DH	*Kreis Soest*
62	MaK 1000599/1974	G1600BB	1176	B-B DH	
71	MaK 1000796/1981	G1204BB	1102	B-B DH	*Lippstadt*
72	MaK 1000806/1982	G1204BB	1102	B-B DH	*Beckum*

Notes: Locos 34, 39,40, 61 and 62 now have new CAT engines.

WOLFF WALSRODE AG WOLFF
Niedersachsen

Routes: Bomlitz–Cordingen–Walsrode
Length: 11.2 km   **Depots**: Bomlitz.

This line is included as it used to run a passenger service. The passenger traffic ceased in 1991. The full title of the line is Werkbahn Bomlitz - Walsrode der Wolff Walsrode AG. Locos carry Wolff Walsrode and the loco number. Both locos were sold in 2002 and OHE now works the line.

No.	Builder, No. & Year	Type	kW	Details	Comments
7	MaK 600345/1962	G650C	476	0-6-0 DH	To DBG Hildseheim
8	Mak 500054/1970	G700C	515	C DH	To On Rail

ZUGKRAFT GmbH ZUGKRAFT
Nordrhein-Westfalen

This company was set up in early 2002 by EBM and Kallfelz & Stuch Gleis und Tiefbau GmbH to hire out locos. Two locos were acquired but they were subsequently transferred to EBM Cargo. They may possibly still be owned by Zugkraft. This could merely be an accounting arrangement to spread risk.

ZURCHER GLEISBAU GmbH ZURCHER
Meissenheim, Baden Württemberg

This track contractor works all over Baden Württemberg. The loco was last reported at Heilbronn on works in connection with the Karlsruhe S-Bahn extension in that town.

No.	Builder, No. & Year	Type	kW	Details	Comments
11000050	Köf III	162	4w	DH	ex DB 332 152

ZWECKVERBAND SCHÖNBUCHBAHN ZVS (WEG)

Baden Württemberg (WEG)

Routes: Böblingen–Dettenhausen (KBS 790.9).
Length: 17.0 km
Depots: Dettenhausen

The Schönbuchbahn is a branch line from Böblingen to Dettenhausen once part of DB which had withdrawn the passenger service in 1965 and freight had just about died away when in 1988 the local government offices in Böblingen and Tübingen got together with WEG in an attempt to get passenger trains reinstated. They were eventually successful the leaning to regionalisation just about making their case. DB sold the branch for a nominal 1 DM! Since then the line has been modernised by the local authorities and a new passenger service introduced using Regio Shuttles. The project has been a great success with the number of people travelling far exceeding expectations. The units as delivered had 228 kW engines but these were not powerful enough and have since been replaced by a 257 kW version.

Traffic has grown rapidly and by 2001 trains were overcrowded. Platforms have since been extended and now 3-car trains can be operated. To assist this line and others with traffic growth WEG obtained some more Regio Shuttles and moved various units around the different lines that it operates.

No.	Builder, No. & Year	Type	kW	Details	Comments
VT 415	Adtranz 36457/1996	RS1	2 x 257	B-B	DMR	Schönbuch
VT 423	Adtranz 36554/1997	RS1	2 x 257	B-B	DMR	Schaichtal
VT 430	Adtranz 36459/1996	RS1	2 x 257	B-B	DMR	Dettenhausen
VT 431	Adtranz 36460/1996	RS1	2 x 257	B-B	DMR	Weilim Schönbuch
VT 432	Adtranz 36461/1996	RS1	2 x 257	B-B	DMR	Holzgerlingen
VT 433	Adtranz 36462/1996	RS1	2 x 257	B-B	DMR	Böblingen

ZWECKVERBAND VERKEHRSVERBAND WIESLAUFTAL-BAHN ZVVW (WEG)

Baden Württemberg (WEG)

Routes: Schorndorf - Rudersberg Nord (KBS 787, 10.6 km); Rudersberg Nord - Welzheim (currently closed).
Length: 23 km
Depots: Rudersberg.

This is a similar situation to ZVS. In this case officials from Schorndorf, Rudersberg and elsewhere got together with WEG to take over the DB line from Schorndorf to Rudersberg and Welzheim. Three NE 81 railcars and trailers being one of the last orders for this type of unit before the new generation of units came on the scene. Traffic growth here has also been strong and so an RS railcar had to be obtained to give some back up.

No.	Builder, No. & Year	Type	kW	Details	Comments
V 23	Gm 5124/1959	Köf III	162	4w DH	Ex DB 332 801
VT 421	WagU 36235/1994	NE81	2 x 201	B-B DHR	
VT 422	WagU 36236/1994	NE81	2 x 201	B-B DHR	
VT 440	Adtranz 36846/1999	RS1	2 x 257	B-B DMR	
VT 441	Adtranz 36847/1999	RS1	2 x 257	B-B DMR	Wiesel

4. RAILWAY MUSEUMS AND MUSEUM LINES

This section has been considerably extended covering extra sites in the old west German areas and of course many new sites in the east of the country. The lists are arranged in alphabetical order of the Länder and places within that area. A selection of tramway museums and garden/park railways is also included. Where there is a running line with regular services the DB Kursbuchstrecke number is shown (DB KBS) also the Kursbuch der Deutschen Museums Eisenbahnen number is shown (KME) as another cross reference. The latter publication appears each year and is indispensable when planning visits to German Museum lines (and a fraction of the weight of the DB Kursbuch!). The 2005 version will be published in April and will be available from Platform 5.

Perhaps the greatest differences between preservation in Germany and in the UK is that few groups in Germany own their own line and that few lines operate mid-week. A glance at the operating dates shows that a month of Sundays is required to ride many of the lines. A selection of tramway museums and garden railways is also included.

BADEN WÜRTTEMBERG

Achern–Ottenhöfen. 11 km. DB KBS 717. KME 205

The Achertäler Eisenbahnverein e.V. operate steam trains on two Sundays a month June to October using a former SWEG 0-6-0T

Amstetten–Gerstetten. 20 km. DB KBS 12758. KME 216.

Ulmer Eisenbahnfreunde. UEF Lokalbahn Amstetten–Gerstetten e.V. (LAG). This is former WEG line closed in 1996 and since then UEF has taken it over and operates whatever freight traffic is offered. This has allowed it to continue running museum trains which it does successfully on various Sundays between May and October but not usually the same Sundays as on its narrow gauge operation from Amstetten.

2 steam, 2 diesels, 2 railcars.

Amstetten–Oppingen. 5.7 km. 1000 mm gauge. DB KBS 12759. KME 217.

Museumsbahn Amstetten–Oppingen. This line former WEG line used to run through to Laichingen but closed in 1986. Local fans including Ulmer Eisenbahnfreunde saved a short section. Operations are on various Sundays May–October.

2 steam, 2 diesels, 1 railcar.

Blumberg–Weizen. 26 km. DB KBS 12737. KME 219.

Wutachtalbahn. This interesting line was a German strategic line avoiding Swiss territory and kept in good order for many years under NATO instructions. Now it is a museum line and has some spectacular viaducts and even a spiral. It operates Wednesdays, Saturdays, Sundays May–October and also Thursdays July–September. Afternoon trains run in these periods but in the peak season June–September there are some morning trains as well.

5 steam, 2 diesel, 1 railcar

Dörzbach. 750 mm gauge. KME 224.

Jagsttalbahnfreunde. Museum trains operated from Dörzbach from 1971 to 1988 but then the line suffered severe damage during storms and has been closed since. However there has been strong support to get the line open again or least part of it. Success is getting near as work started in 2000 clearing the station area at Dörzbach and hopefully getting the line reopened to Widden. 2004 could well see trains operating again.

1 steam, 3 diesels, 2 railcars.

Eschach-Seifertshofen.

Schwäbisches Bauern und Technik Museum. This private museum has collections of farming machinery, old cars, fire engines etc. and a railway section. Open daily 10.00–17.00

3 steam, 4 diesels, 1 battery electric.

Ettlingen–Bad Herrnalb. 19 km. DB KBS 715. KME 204.

Albtalbahn. Ulmer Eisenbahnfreunde (UEF) run steam trains over the Albtalbahn from Herrenalb using 50 3539 usually on the last Sunday of the month May–October.

1 steam.

Freiburg in Breisgau. 1000 mm gauge.

Freiburger Verkehrs AG. Freiburg is another city with a tram network and has a few nostalgic trams available for excursions and charters.

6 trams.

Gaildorf West–Untergröningen. 18.5 km. DB KBS 785. KME 211

Dampfbahn Kochertal (DBK). This society has operated over this private line for a number of years on selected Sundays and holidays. The locos also work trains from Schörndorf so some swapping of stock must take place occasionally.

4 steam, 3 diesels, 1 railcar

Heidelberg. 1000 mm gauge.

Heidelberger Strassen und Bergbahn AG. The local tramway has three historic trams one of which is available for excursions.

Heilbronn.

Süddeutsches Eisenbahn Museum, Heilbronn (SEH). Some time ago the old DB depot in Heilbronn was declared a historic monument. DB then had to decide what to do with it. An answer has now been found. Members of the Bayerische Eisenbahn Museum and Ulmer Eisenbahnfreunde together with local interests have founded a museum at the site. Locomotives soon starting arriving at the site including SNCF 231K22 and DB 01 1104 which used to be at Carnforth. UEF have several of its main line locos based there for excursions from Karlsruhe or Stuttgart both of which are easily reached.

15 steam, 11 diesels, 1 electric.

Kandern–Haltingen. 13 km. DB KBS 12733. KME 220.

Kandertalbahn. Eurovapor have operated museum trains over this private line for more than 30 years. Trains normally run on Sundays May–October with one round trip in the morning and two in the afternoon meaning that the line can be traversed from either end. Haltingen is on the DB main line from Freiburg to Basel.

3 steam, 1 diesel, 1 railcar.

Karlsruhe 2 .7 km. 600 mm gauge. KME 222.

Schlossgartenbahn. A somewhat unknown park railway with steam that has been operating since 1967. Trains run at weekends May to October and daily in the summer. Normally trains only run in the afternoon and steam comes out at weekends when the weather is fine.

1 steam, 1 diesel.

Karlsruhe.

Verkehrsbetriebe Karlsruhe. The tramway company has five nostalgic trams available for excursions and charters.

Karlsruhe–Baiersbronn. Km. DB KBS 716 . KME 204a

Ulmer Eisenbahnfreunde and AVG have a long standing degree of cooperation so now that AVG run the line to Bailersbronn UEF/AVG will now be operating steam trains on this line as well. Such is the determination to do this that watering facilities have been installed. Usual loco probably 50 3539 initially.

Korntal–Weissach. 22.5 km. DB KBS 790.7. KME 206

Gesellschaft zur Erhaltung von Schienfahrzeugen (GES). GES operate trains on this private line on various Sundays May to September.

Kornwestheim.

BSW Freizeitgruppe IG E93 07. This BSW group looks after not only E93 07 but also E94 279. Only the E94 is currently a runner.

Kornwestheim.

Gesellschaft zur Erhaltung von Schienfahrzeugen (GES). The main base for this society used to be the DB depot at Kornwestheim but now they have acquired use of an old wagon shop in the nearby rangierbahnhof. Active locos here are used on the line from Korntal.

9 steam, 9 diesels, 3 electrics.

Mannheim.

Landesmuseum fur Technik und Arbeit in Mannheim (LTA) This town museum has a railway section that includes an exhibition on the locomotive factory in Esslingen. 89 312 steams most days and is interesting in that it has been converted to fireless operation so as to not pollute the inside of the museum. One of the class 202 diesels that pioneered three-phase motors is also on show. Open Tuesday - Sunday 10.00 - 17.00 (20.00 Wednesday).

3 steam, 2 diesels.

Mannheim. 1000 mm gauge.

Oberrheinische Eisenbahn Gesellschaft (OEG). This railway has restored a 1928 twin set for excursions.

Marxzell.

Fahrzeugmuseum Reichert. This private museum opened in the late 1960s and is somewhat run down and very small compared to Sinsheim and Speyer. Four gauges are represented

6 steam, 3 diesels, 4 trams

Neresheim–Dischingen. 8 km. 1000 mm gauge. DB KBS ?. KME 215

Hartsfeld Museumsbahn (HMB). This society has preserved some locomotives and stock of the closed metre gauge line from Aalen to Dillingen. The section between Neresheim and Dichingen has been reopened. The line usually operates on the first Sunday of the month May to September.

2 steam, 2 railcars

Nürtingen–Neuffen. 8.9 km. DB KBS 762. KME 207.

Gesellschaft zur Erhaltung von Schienfahrzeugen (GES). This Stuttgart/Kornwestheim based society operates over this private line on the third Sunday of the month May to Octoberand keeps some locos here which are changed over with Kornwestheim when required. Former Hzl locos 11 and 16 are usually here.

Ochsenhausen–Warthausen. 19 km. 750 mm gauge. DB KBS 12752. KME 223.

This line is classed as a historic monument but in recent years there have been many troubled times. Once there were quite a few ex PKP Px48s here but these have all been removed (perhaps reflecting that it is a German historic monument) but some Austrian locomotives remain! The line operates Saturdays, Sundays and holidays May to October and also odd Thursdays in the main season.

2 steam, 3 diesels.

Reutlingen.

Freunde der Zahnradbahn Honau - Lichtenstein (ZHL). There used to be a rack railway here and this society hopes to reopen it! It has not only managed to get hold of some of the DB class 797 railcars but also has rack steam loco 97 501 under repair! An ambitious project. The base is in the old goods shed at Reutlingen West where some excellent facilities have been created and many fine tools and parts obtained.

1 steam, 3 diesels, 4 railcars

Riegel–Breisach. 26 km. DB KBS 723, 724. KME 218.

Kaiserstuhlbahn/Eisenbahnfreunde Breisgau (EFB). Using a former SWEG steam locomotive museum trains are run over the local private railway one weekend a month May – October.

1 steam, 1 diesel.

Schorndorf–Rudersberg. 9.9 km. DB KBS 787. KME 211

Dampfbahn Kochertal (DBK). This group based in Gaildorf West also operates steam trains on this line on selected weekends during the year.

Sinsheim.

Auto und Technik Museum (ATM). This museum is similar to the one at Speyer and is just as excellent. Allow a lot of time for a visit as there is plenty of interest here not only for the railfan but transport enthusiasts in general will find much of interest. A station (halt) has been opened to serve the museum and when last visited trains from here went through to Speyer so making both easily accessible in a day - if there is enough time. Do not miss the military section as there is a camouflaged class 52 in there!

9 steam, 1 diesel, 4 electrics.

Sinsheim.

Eisenbahnfreunde Kraichgau. A rather small society but with some interesting small diesels and a collection of carriages which are all to be found at the old sub-shed near the station.

4 diesels.

Stuttgart.

Freunde zur Erhaltung Historischer Schienenfahrzeuge (FzS). This society is interested in preserving EMUs that used to operate in the Stuttgart area and now has 425 120 in service. It has also obtained E18 19.

1 electric, 1 diesel, 4 EMUs.

Stuttgart.

BSW Freizeit Gruppe. Stuttgart railway staff have pledged to look after 612 506/7. The 612 unit has proved successful on railtours in the area and of course is not restricted to where the catenary goes.

1 railcar set.

Stuttgart, Parkeisenbahn Killesberg. 381 mm gauge. KME 203

Few people seem to be aware that Stuttgart also has a park railway that has two lovely Krauss Maffei pacifics from 1950. There is daily operation in the afternoons May to September but steam is not necessarily used every day. This particularly applies to early and late season and bad weather days.

2 steam 2 diesels.

Stuttgart-Zuffenhausen. KME 201, 202.

Strassenbahnmuseum. A good collection of Stuttgart area trams has a home here. Several are in working order and on Saturdays can be found working on two routes. On the last Saturday of the month they run between Stuttgart (Innenstadt) and the museum whilst the second Saturday of the month sees a circular route operated from the museum. Naturally the museum is also open on these days.

24 trams.

Tübingen. DB KBS 12763, 12767, 12774. KME 208, 208a, 209.

Eisenbahnfreunde Zollernbahn (EFZ). A very active society running excursion trains over the local DB and HzL networks. In the summer holiday period regular steam trains run along such scenic routes as Horb–Pforzheim.

5 steam, 5 diesels.

Tuttlingen.

Deutsche Dampflok Museum, Tuttlingen. This is located in the small roundhouse south of the station. The owner unfortunately died a few years ago and the project seems to have stalled. However it is believed to be open most Sundays. Most locomotives are from the DR fleet and in a "as received" condition.

26 steam, 6 diesels.

Ulm.

Ulmer Eisenbahnfreunde (UEF). Although still carrying the name of its founding city UEF has no operations based in Ulm with most of its large locos being kept on the AVG lines at Karlsruhe or at Heilbronn Museum. Besides operating main line excursion trains from Karlsruhe/Stuttgart the UEF has two operations at Amstetten.

Ulm.

Strassenbahn Nostalgie Ulm has a 1000 mm gauge tramway and there are a few old vehicles which usually operate on the last Sunday of the month May–October.

4 trams

BAYERN

Augsburg.

Freunde der Augsburger Strassenbahn. The supporting group has since 1985 helped to restore some of the 1000 mm gauge trams which are available for excursions and charters.

12 trams.

Bayerisch Eisenstein. KME 257.

Bayerische Localbahn Verein (BLV). The old roundhouse here is a listed building so what better place to have a railway museum. BLV have several locos here with local connections to either private lines or industry. Some steam trips do operate from Bayerische Eisenstein but these are normally into the Czech Republic using CD locos.

8 steam, 4 diesel, 1 electric, 2 railcars.

Ebermannstadt–Beringersmuhle. 16 km. DB KBS 12821. KME 251.

Dampfbahn Frankische Schweiz (DFS). Formed in the late 1970s this group started running trains over the line in 1983. Trains operate most Sundays but steam operation is variable.

3 steam, 4 diesels, 1 battery electric, 2 railcars

Fladungen-Ostheim-Mellrichstadt. DB KBS 12815. KME 264.

Frankische FreilanDMUseum Fladungen. A relative newcomer to the preservation scene having only started in the 1990s. Trains operate most Sundays but steam is only used once or twice a month.

2 steam, 4 diesels, 1 railcar

Garmisch Partenkirchen. KME 254.

BSW Gruppen in Garmisch Partenkirchen. At least three BSW Groups are now based in the old roundhouse having had to move out of München because of developments there. Open days are held several times a year at weekends between April and September.

8 electrics, 1 battery electric.

Heroldsbach–Parkeisenbahn. 2.1 km.

Freizeitpark Schloss Thurn has a 600 mm gauge railway which Is believed to operate daily May - August and other odd dates fringing the season.

2 steam

Kahl–Schöllkrippen. 23 km. KME 255.

Dampfbahnfreunde Kahlgrund e.V. (DK). Steam trains are run over the Kahlgrundbahn (KVG) about five times a year. Locos are actually based in the old DB depot in Hanau(Hessen) and the first train originates there and the last returns there. Excursions are also run over a wide area.

3 steam, 6 diesels.

Tegernsee.

Bayerische Localbahn Verein (BLV). For many years the BLV ran steam trains on the Tegernseebahn. However due to a more intensive regular service operations are now restricted to just a few days in the year but excursions organised by BLV operate around other parts of Bayern during the tourist season.

1 steam, 1 electric.

Lichtenfels.

BSW Freizeitgruppe Lichtenfels., Based in the old DB roundhouse this group looks after several DB Museum locos and in fact the depot can be counted as an annexe to the Nürnberg museum.

2 diesels, 6 electrics. 1 railcar.

München.

Deutsches Museum. A railway section can be found in this museum which is normally open daily 09.00–17.00 throughout the year. However rebuilding works are in progress. There is also the possibility of the old DB depot at Freilassing becoming an annexe.

6 steam, 1 steam railcar, 3 diesels, 6 electrics, 1 battery electric.

München.

Freunde des Münchner Trambahnmuseums e.V. (FMTM). München has a large tramway network and naturally there is a supporting group and some historic vehicles.

11 trams.

Neuenmarkt Wirsberg. KME 250.

Deutsches Dampflok Museum (DDM). It is amazing how private collections have outshone what is the national collection at Nürnberg. The DDM collection dates from the 1970's and is housed in a redundant loco shed and wagon shop and includes some rare items such as 10 001. Steam ups take place over various weekends and there are also special events. Open Tuesday–Sunday and holidays 10.00–17.00 and operates local steam trips in the summer up the famous "Schiefe Ebene".

27 steam, 6 diesels, 3 electrics (1435 mm) and 4 steam 16 diesel (600mm).

Neuoffingen. KME 261.

Schwaben Dampf. This society has changed in the last few years and no longer appears to be running main line excursions. The depot at Neuoffingen has been set up as a museum and is expected to be open on Sundays May to September..

3 steam, 2 diesels.

Nördlingen. KME 258.

Bayerische Eisenbahn Museum (BEM). Founded in 1969 as Eisenbahn Club München the club obtained more and more material and needed a bigger site than was available in München. Then DB closed the Nördlingen dept and BEM was formed when ECM transferred to its new home in Nördlingen. Now BEM has formed an operating company to run trains under open access on the main lines. Not only that, they have obtained from DB (in association with local government) the line from Nördlingen to Dombühl and possibly also to Gunzenhausen and operate services over these lines on a rotating basis. BEM also now has a depot in München Laim where normally two steam and one diesel are based for excursions from München. The museum is open on Sundays March to October and Tuesday–Saturday afternoons in July and August.

33 steam, 10 diesels, 8 electrics, 4 battery electrics, 5 railcars, 1 battery electric railcar.

Nürnberg. KME 252.

Verkehrsmuseum Nürnberg. The museum dates back to Bayerische Staatsbahn times and as the name implies is not only concerned with railways. The railway section became in recent times the DB Museum but with the railways in Germany heading towards privatisation the future arrangements seem unclear. When visiting the museum do not forget the annexe on the other side of the road and retain your ticket for this. Indeed retain your railway ticket to Nürnberg and get a reduced price admission ticket! Open Tuesday–Sundays 09.00–17.00 throughout the year.

12 steam, 5 electrics, 1 diesel, 2 railcars, 2 EMUs.

Nürnberg.

DB Bw Nürnberg West. Several active (and non-active) museum locos are kept in the old roundhouse and used on excursions from Nürnberg. The old roundhouse here is considered part of the museum and tickets for the museum are thought to be valid here. Ask.

5 steam, 3 diesels.

Nürnberg.

Freunde der Nürnberg - Fürther Strassenbahn. Based in the old depot at St. Peter this group has been preserving and restoring trams for over twenty years. The depot is open the first weekend of each month (except January) 10.00–18.00. Historic trams operate on Line 5 from the Hbf. 9 trams are active.

18 trams.

Nürnberg.

Frankische Museums Eisenbahn (FME). This group dates from 1985 the year of the DB 150 Celebrations. Today they are based in industrial sidings close to Nürnberg Nord Ost station. No main line excursions at the moment as running certificates have expired.

1 steam, 10 diesels.

Passau. KME 260.

Passauer Eisenbahnfreunde (PEF). Tucked away in the corner of the country bordering Austria this group has two specialities. Its principal excursions use a railbus to run tourist trains over freight only lines in the area. The majority of these trips are to Hauzenberg which run every Wednesday mid-July to the end of August and allows a combined rail/river excursion as it is possible to go one way by boat on the River Danube. The other trip goes to Freyung but these are on odd days between May and October. A UEF loco is also based here and is used for several trips a year with the PEF historic train. ÖGEG 86 501 (ex DR) is also used on excursions from here.

1 diesel, 1 electric, 1 railcar.

Selb.

Modell und Eisenbahnclub Selb/Rehau. Formed in the 1970's this group has found a home in the old sub-shed at Selb which unfortunately is now too small for the collection so some locomotives are kept outside in the open. The museum is normally open on a Saturday afternoon.

2 steam, 8 diesels, 2 electrics.

Würzburg.

BSW Gruppe Historische Fahrzeuge, Würzburg. From its base at Zell yard 52 7409 is used on excursions in the area.

1 steam.

BERLIN & BRANDENBURG

Berlin.

Deutsches Technik Museum. This excellent museum is located in the former locomotive depot for Berlin Anhalter Bahnhof. Everything has been restored – locomotives and buildings alike. Surplus stock is stored elsewhere on the site. The museum is open Tuesday–Sunday throughout the year.

24 steam, 15 diesels, 1 railcar, 11 electrics, 4 EMUs.

Berlin. 600 mm gauge. DB KBS 12299. KME 3.

Berliner Parkeisenbahn. Wuhlheide. 600 mm gauge. What was once a pioneer railway is now regarded as a park railway. It operates in the afternoon daily (except Mondays and Fridays) April–October.

4 steam, 12 diesels, 1 electric.

Berlin. KME 6

S-Bahn Berlin GmbH and Historische S-Bahn Berlin. The main company and a supporting group have restored some of the old Berlin S-Bahn cars. Some 18 sets have been saved and many are operational allowing tourist trains to run throughout the year. Watch out for trips on the fourth Saturday of each month.

Basdorf. DB KBS 12298. KME 5.

Berliner Eisenbahnfreunde has its museum collection is part of the old NEB depot at Basdorf from where it runs excursions from time to time over part of the old NEB between Berlin Wilhelmsruher Damm and Klosterfelde. Main line trips are also run from time to time. The museum at Basdorf is open each Saturday afternoon.

2 steam, 6 diesels, 1 railcar.

Belzig.

Eisenbahnfreunde Hoher Flaming. This small group started in 1994 by restoring a Köf and then went on to acquire more locos as DR types became spare.

6 diesels.

Cottbus.

Lausitzer Dampflok Club (LDC). This club started by restoring 03 204 then went on to acquire more locos. Slowly growing and operates main line excursions several times each year.

3 steam, 3 diesels.

Cottbus. Park Railway. 600 mm gauge. KME 384

This is another former pioneer railway now relegated to just a park railway. It operates at weekends April–September but is daily June–August. Steam operation is normally only at weekends and public/school holidays

2 steam, 3 diesels, 1 railcar.

Finsterwalde–Crinitz. 16.95 km. KME 385

Niederlausitzer Museumseisenbahn. Founded in 1995 and operates on the first Sunday of the month.

2 steam, 5 diesels, 1 railcar.

Gramzow.

Brandenburgisches Museum für Klein und Privatbahnen. A splendid museum has been established here since 1992 opening to the public in 1996. It is usually open 10.00–17.00 Wednesdays–Sundays May–October.

3 steam, 1 electric, 4 diesels, 2 railcars.

Falkenberg/Elster.

One of the old locomotive depots at Falkenberg is being set up as a museum. It is owned by the same person that owns Hermeskeil, Open days take place a few weekends each summer during the setting up period. Most locos are in "as received" condition.

30–40 locomotives, steam, diesel and electric.

HESSEN

Bad Nauheim–Munzenberg. 20.1 km. KME 153

Eisenbahnfreunde Wetterau e.V. run excursion trains on some Sundays and holidays during the holiday months.

1 steam, 1 diesel.

Borken.

Nordhessisches Braunkohle Bergbaumuseum. A project for a museum should come to fruition in 2001 when the old coal mining area is opened up as a museum. many of the items are in fact in the open depicting coal mining scenes. Stock is of 600, 900, and 1435 mm gauges.

1 steam, 2 electric, 4 electro-diesels, 3 diesels.

Darmstadt. KME 159 and 160.

Deutsche Museums Eisenbahn (DME). This group has its base in the old DB depot of Darmstadt Kranichstein and is easily accessible from the nearby station of that name opposite the depot. The museum is open every Sunday also Wednesdays April - September. Occasional specials are operated over lines in the area.

11 steam, 2 electric, 15 diesel, 4 railcars.

Darmstadt. Town tramway. 1000 mm gauge. KME 161.

A DME metre gauge steam locomotive runs over the town tramway at weekends during June and September. Operating dates do vary. The tramway also has 8 trams listed as historic vehicles.

Frankfurt am Main. Eiserner Steg–Mainkur/Griesheim. 11 km. DB KBS 12641. KME 155.

Historische Eisenbahn Frankfurt. This group runs trains along industrial lines alongside the river and into nearby DB interchanges. The only access is believed to be at Eisener Tor. Operating dates are rather spasmodic. 01 118 is often used on DB excursions in the area.

3 steam, 6 diesels, 1 railcar.

Frankfurt am Main. KME 154.

Frankfurter Feldbahnmuseum. The museum is not too far away from the old FF2 depot along Am Romerhof. A connection from the depot/museum into a nearby Rebstockpark allows an operating line of about 1.5 km. There is an excellent standard of restoration by a small but dedicated band of Feldbahn fans! The museum is open on the first Sunday of the month and also the first Friday. Limited operating dates.

14 steam, 14 diesels, 3 battery electric, 1 compressed air. (All 600 mm gauge).

Frankfurt am Main.

Verkehrsmuseum Schwanheim. This tramway museum at Rheinlandstrasse 132 is excellent and is open Saturdays, Sundays and holidays throughout the year. Nostaligic trams run throughout the year.

1 steam, 17 trams.

Giessen.

Oberhessisches Eisenbahnfreunde e.V. (OEF). This is a BSW group from the local DB depot at Giessen preserving railbuses for excursions in the area.

3 railcars.

Kassel–Naumberg. 33 km. KME 150.

Hessencourier e.V. This organisation runs trains over the private line from Kassel to Naumburg. There are depots at both ends of the line. Trains run alternate Sundays July–September and some other dates.

5 steam, 2 diesels

Kassel.

IG Nahverkehrsbetrieb Kassel. The city has trams and an active tramway society. A museum has been set up in the depot at Hollandische Strasse

9 trams

Solms Oberbiel. 600 mm gauge. KME 162.

Feld und Grubenbahnmuseum, Besucherbergwerk Fortuna. This iron ore mine closed about 1983 and is now a tourist attraction with the railway used to take people on sightseeing tours.

4 steam, 38 diesels, 7 battery electrics, 2 electrics, 1 compressed air.

Treysa. KME 151.

Eisenbahnfreunde Schwalm Knulll. Based in the old depot at Treysa this group runs trains several times a year over lines in the area including Marburg–Frankenberg.

3 steam, 9 diesels, 1 electric, 2 railcars.

Wiesbaden–Dolzheim–Bad Schwalbach–Hohenstein. 23.9 km. DB KBS 12628. KME 158.

Nassauische Touristik bahn e.V. (NTB). This line operates every Sunday and holiday from May to September.

2 steam, 3 diesels.

Walburg. KME 156.

Eisenbahnfreunde Walburg e.V. Once at Wanfried this group had to move and is now settled at Walburg from where they hope to run trains but just what they will do with three ex Berlin S-Bahn units is unclear.

3 steam, 9 diesels, 1 railcar, 3 EMUs

MECKLENBURG VORPOMMERN

Klutz–Gravesmuhlen. 15 km.

Klutzer Ostsee Eisenbahn GmbH was formed to operate museum trains over this line and is an offshoot of EBG Altenbeken from where most stock was obtained.

1 diesel, 2 railcars, 2 Berlin S-Bahns sets!

Prora. KME 400.

Eisenbahn und Technikmuseum, Prora. This relatively new museum is located in a former army base close to Prora station. In 2001 a new extension will be opening featuring Russian P36-0123 and DR "03 193" the latter being 03 002 streamlined as 03 193 once was.

10 steam, 20 diesels, 4 electrics, and 8 trams.

Röbel (Muritz).

Hei Na Ganzlin – Eisenbahnfreunde Röbel. This society is based at the terminus of Röbel where most of the rolling stock is kept. 52 8029 is active and used on railtours over a wide area including Berlin where it often does "Santa Specials".

7 steam, 13 diesels.

Schwerin.

Mecklenburgische Eisenbahnfreunde Schwerin and DB Museum. At the old DR depot the local staff have formed a BSW Group to look after what were previously DR Tradition Loks. DB Museum has since announced that this depot will open as an outpost of the museum but no date has yet been given.

4 steam, 6 diesels, 1 railcar.

NIEDERSACHSEN & BREMEN

Almstedt. KME 76.

Arge Historische Eisenbahn. This group has not operated for some years now but usually has a few open days each year. 800 metre demonstration line.

2 steam, 11 diesels.

Bohmte–Holzhausen–Heddinghausen. 20 km. DB KBS 12387. KME 100.

Museums Eisenbahn Minden (MEM) operate this line once a month April to October on dates different to the Rahden line. The depot is at Prussisch Oldendorf.

3 steam, 3 diesels, 2 railcars.

Borkum. 900 mm gauge. DB KBS 12100.

Borkumer Kleinbahn und Dampfschiffart GmbH operates the railway on this island and for the last few years has included a regular steam hauled train service. This usually runs in the afternoon. Besides the reconditioned steam loco there is also a vintage Wismar DMU.

1 steam, 1 railcar.

Braunschweigisches Eisenbahnmuseum des VBV e.V.

This museum is located in part of the old DB Ausbessungswerk and is expected to be open on the last Saturday of the month May to October.

5 steam, 19 diesel, 2 railcars.

Bremen–Kirchhucting–Leeste–Thedinghausen. 25 km. KME 61.

Kleinbahn Leeste operate diesel trains on about six Sundays between early May and late September.

3 diesels

Bremerhaven – Bederkesa. 21 km. KME 79

This line operates two Sundays a month May to September. The trip includes a run into the dock area fish quays.

4 diesels, 2 railcars.

Bremervörde – Stade/Osterholz Scharmbeck.   KME 80

The EVB runs excursions over these lines SSuO from May to September using vintage stock.

Bruchhausen Vilsen–Asendorf 8 km. 1000mm gauge. DB KBS. 12383. KME 59.

Deutsche Eisenbahn Verein (DEV) operate what is Germany's oldest preservation line with a wonderful selection of beautifully restored locomotives and rolling stock. It operates on Saturdays, Sundays and public holidays May to October running usually one morning and three afternoon round trips.

7 steam, 4 diesels, 6 railcars.

Buxtehude–Harsefeld. 14.8 km. DB KBS 12121. KME 55.

Buxtehuder–Harsefelder Eisenbahnfreunde operate a 1926 vintage railcar over the line one Sunday a month May–September doing four round trips.

1 railcar

Celle–Müden/Ortze 36 km and Celle–Wittingen–Brome 73 km. KME 62, 63.

Verein Braunschweiger Verkehrsfreunde (VBV). The depot and museum is in the old DB workshops at Braunschweig. Normally an OHE diesel loco operates over the above lines.

6 steam, 17 diesels, 2 railcars.

Eystrup–Bruchhausen Vilsen–Heiligenfelde. 31 km. DB KBS 12382. KME 60.

DEV also have a standard gauge operation over this VGH line. It operates only a few times each year.

1 diesel, 2 railcars.

Harpstedt–Delmenhorst Süd–Lemwerder. 36 km. KME 58.

The Delmenhorst Harpstedter Eisenbahnfreunde operate three return trips over the Harpstedt to Delmenhorst line on steam days but railcar trips over the complete line operate about three times during the season. Operating days usually on the first and third Sundays May–September.

2 steam, 3 diesels, 2 railcars

Hameln–Salzhemmendorf. 21 km. KME 69

Dampfzug Betriebs Gemeinschaft e.V. DBG operate about three times over this route in the season July–October.

Lüneburg Süd–Eyendorf. 31 km. KME 53.

Touristik Eisenbahn Lüneburger Heide GmbH. The full 31 km run only takes place a few times each year, otherwise there are numerous shorter workings over this OHE line.

5 diesels, 7 railcars.

Meppen–Essen–Quakenbrück. 57 km. DB KBS 12395. KME 51.

Eisenbahnfreunde Hasetal - Haselünne eV. Based in Haselünne the first trip to and from Meppen is normally a DMU connecting into the steam trains that covers the remainder of the service through to Quakenbrück, back to Meppen and then to base. A very busy line with many cyclists taking advantage of the baggage car and the buffet car!

1 steam, 1 diesel, 1 railbus.

Norden–Dorum. 17 km. DB KBS 12399. KME 74.

Museumseisenbahn Kustenbahn Ostfriesland e V. A fairly recent newcomer to the preservation scene. The group runs trains on most Sundays during June–September.

1 steam, 5 diesels.

Osnabrück. KME 75.

Osnabrück Dampflokfreunde. This group operates trains two or three times a year from Osnabrück Hbf to Zeche Piesberg. Trains also run to local events in the greater Osnabrück area.

1 steam, 7 diesels.

Rahden–Uchte. 25.3 km. KME 102.

Museums Eisenbahn Minden (MEM) operates over this line with railcars once a month May - October

2 diesels 2 railcars

Rinteln Nord–Stadthagen West. 20 km. DB KBS 12374.KME 68.

Dampfeisenbahn Weserbergland (DEW). This group not only runs over this line several times a year but also runs excursions over DB lines in the area. Usually a circular trip operates Rinteln–Löhne–Miden–Stadhagen–Rinteln.

Salzgitter.

Linke Hofmann Busch museum. This private museum can be visited by prior arrangement. It contains several locomotives and rolling stock built by the firm.

4 steam, 1 battery electric, 1 railcar, 1 EMU, 2 trams.

Salzgitter Bad–Borssum. 15 km. KME 71.

Dampflokgemeinschaft 41 096 e.V. This group is based at Klein Mahner and operates only three or four times a year.

4 steam, 12 diesels, 1 railcar.

Sehnde-Wehmingen. KME 66.

Hannoversches Strassenbahn Museum (HSM). This museum has a large collection of trams of which 12 are operational and many more under restoration. Trams are not only from Hannover but other places in Germany. The museum is open at weekends June–October and Tuesday–Sunday July–September 11.00–17.00

Soltau – Döhle. 30 km KME 64

Soltau Touristik run an old Wismar railcar over this line on Sundays July–September

Stemmen–Verden. 12 km. KME 65.

Verdener Eisenbahnfreunde operate on about eight occasions May–September

5 diesels, 1 railcar

Vienenburg.

Eisenbahnmuseum Vienenburg. This is located at Vieneburg station with most exhibits outside.

1 steam 2 diesels.

Werlte – Lathen. 25.2 km   KME 67

Museumseisenbahn Hummlinger Kreisbahn e.V. operate two return trips a few days each yaer usually in May and September.

2 railcars.

Westerstede–Ocholt–Sedelsberg. 34 km. KME 77.

Museumseisenbahn Ammerland–Saterland uses Ocholt as its base for operating railcars over this line on two Saturdays a month May–September.

1 diesel, 3 railcars.

Winsen Süd–Salzhausen–Amelinghausen–Sottorf. 55 km. KME 53a.
Winsen Süd–Niedermarsehacht. 17 km. KME 54.

These are more TELH operations over the OHE. Trains run once a month June to September.

NORDRHEIN WESTFALEN

Alsdorf.

Berbaumuseum Wurmrevier e.V. A new museum is being established at Alsdorf and will have a railway section associated with the local mining industry.

2 steam, 2 diesel.

Alstätte–Ahaus. 10 km. KME 122

Excursion trains run over this private freight railway on about six Sundays a year using a normal traffic locomotive.

Bochum Dalhausen. KME 109.

Deutsche Gesellschaft fur Eisenbahngeschichte (DGEG). This society used to have three sites around the country but now there are only two. Consequently a few extra items are now on show here. Located in a former DB depot the site has quite a few sidings and so extra storage buildings have been built on the site. A DMU shuttle operates from the station to the museum. Museum trains operate from Hattingen to Wengern Ost (22 km). A Feldbahn line has been constructed on the site. The museum is open Sundays and holidays 10.00–14.15 (12.15 in winter). Also Wednesdays and Fridays 10.00–16.15.

18 steam, 15 diesels, 4 railcars, 3 electrics, 1 battery electric, 2 EMUs, 1 battery electric railcar

Bösingfeld–Barntrup. 11.2 km. DB KBS 12376. KME 104.

Landeseisenbahn Lippe e. V. runs excursion trains over the Extertalbahn line using a mixture of traction.

2 steam, 2 diesels, 2 electrics.

Dahlhausen/Wupper.

A museum is being set up here and currently has 2 steam and 2 diesel locomotives.

Dieringhausen. KME 111

Eisenbahn Museum Dieringhausen/Eisenbahnfreunde Flugelrad Oberberg. This museum is located in the former DB roundhouse at Dieringhausen and expanded quite a lot in the 1990s obtaining locomotives from the eastern part of the country. The museum is open at weekends throughout the year. A few locomotives are active and are used on excursion trains. The museum has set up an operating company (q.v. EBM). Open each weekend 10.00–17.00.

14 steam, 20 diesels, 3 electrics, 1 battery electric, 5 railcars.

Dieringhausen–Oberwiehl. 16 km. KME 115

Stock from Dieringhausen museum is used on this line for a few weekends each year.

Dortmund. Westfalisches Industriemuseum.

This industrial museum is located in a former coal mine site which has retained many of the buildings and has a selection of locomotives etc. associated with the industrial past of the area. Open daily except Monday 10.00 - 18.00

8 steam, 10 diesels, 3 compressed air, 3 battery electrics, 1 electric.

Düren. KME 123.

Dampfbahn Rur–Wurm–Inde e.V runs regular steam excursions over lines of the RTB e.g. Julich–Heimbach.

1 steam

Eslohe.

Maschinen und Heimatmuseum. What started as a small private collection has grown and grown and includes lots of machinery and some locomotives. 600 mm, 1000 mm and 1435 mm gauges are represented.

4 steam, 2 diesels.

Essen Kupferdreh–Haus Scheppen. 3.3 km. DB KBS 12446. KME 108.

Verein zur Erhaltung des Hespertalbahn e.V. operates trains over this former colliery line on most Sundays May–September.

2 steam 4 diesel.

Geilenkirchen–Gillrath–Schierwaldenrath. 5.5 km. 1000 mm gauge. DB KBS 12422. KME 120.

Interessengengemeinschaft Historischer Schienenverkehr have over the last 30 years restored to a high standard locomotives and rolling stock from various narrow gauge lines. It operates every Sunday May to September and Saturdays in June.

5 steam, 3 diesels, 4 railcars

Gelsenkirchen.

Freunde des Bahnbetriebswerks Bismarck. The old DB depot is a listed building and consequently is attracting preservation groups. All locos currently present are former industrial ones.

3 steam, 5 diesels, 1 electric.

Gelsenkirchen. Emscher Park Eisenbahn.

This organisation runs tourist trains around the Ruhr industrial lines showing people the industrial past and present of the area.

1 steam, 2 diesels, 2 railcars

Gladbeck.

Museumsdampflok der Ruhrkohle AG. An RAG steam loco has been retained for special events

Gutersloh. KME 103.

Dampfkleinbahn Muhlenstroth e. V. 600 mm gauge. This short line (circa 1 km) runs around a park/gardens and is a purpose built line.

8 steam, 7 diesels.

Hamm–Lippborg. 18.7 km. KME 106.

Hammer Eisenbahnfreunde operate trains over this RLE route three or four times a year.

4 steam, 5 diesels, 1 railcar

Hattingen–Wengern. 18 km. KME 110.

This is a DGEG operation from their museum at Bochum Dahlhausen. Trains run on the first Sunday of the month April - November. Trains are usually steam but the last return trip is normally diesel operated.

Huinghausen–Plettenberg. 3.5 km. 1000 mm gauge. KME 117.

Markische Museums Eisenbahn e.V. is gradually building up its stock and operations here.

4 steam, 3 diesels, 1 railcar

Köln Nippes Rheinisches Industriebahn Museum. KME 114.

This museum is located in the old DB depot of Köln Nippes in the Lengerich area of the city at the north end of Köln Nippes freight yard. The museum is open every Sunday and holiday with trains operating once a month. Eight gauges are represented here – 600, 700, 750, 785, 800, 900, 1000 and 1435 mm!

8 steam, 57 diesels, 4 battery electric, 2 electrics, 1 EMU

Krefeld St Tonis–Hülser Berg. 13.6 km. DB KBS 12424. KME 112.

Stadtische Werk Krefeld AG. This industrial line operates tourist trains over its own network.

1 steam

Krefeld.

This former depot has recently changed hands and is now understood to belong to the Emscher Park Eisenbahn who are to use it as their base for tours around the industrial Ruhr lines.

Lengerich. DB KBS 12400. KME 105, 126.

Eisenbahn Tradition e.V. uses 24 009 or 50 3655 for excursions over the TWE lines radiating from Lengerich and on other lines in the area.

Minden Oberstadt–Hille. 13.4 km. DB KBS 12377. KME 101.
Minden Oberstadt–Kleinenbremen. 15 km. DB KBS 12377. KME 101.

Museums Eisenbahn Minden operates these lines from its Minden base with trains running on numerous Sundays May–October.

3 steam, 5 diesels, 1 railcar.

Oberhausen.

Dampflok Arge Oberhausen have their base at the old wagon shops at Oberhausen Osterfeld Süd. It is a BSW group looking after its own loco and some from the national collection. The "Lollo" that was here is now at Lübeck but no doubt the group will preserve one of their own 216s in due course.

3 steam, 3 diesels.

Oekoven. KME 113.

Feld und Werkbahnmuseum. A 600 mm gauge museum line close to the DB station with a short demonstration line. Operates first Sunday of the month May - October.

5 steam, 29 diesels, 4 electrics, 1 railcar, 1 battery electric.

Wanne Eickel. Emschertalmuseum.

An open air small collection of locos and trams associated with the area.

2 steam, 1 diesel, 1 electric, 4 trams.

Wesel Hafenbahn. 7 km. KME 107.

Historische Schienenverkehr Wesel operates occasional trains over the harbour lines at Wesel.

1 steam, 3 diesels.

Wesseling Köln-Bonner Eisenbahnfreunde e.V.

This group started off by preserving KBE ET 201 but now has various locomotives connected with local railways and industries.

1 steam, 1 diesel, 1 electric, 4 railcars, 1 EMU

Wuppertal-Kohlfurth. 1000 mm gauge. KME 116.

Strassenbahnmuseum der Bergischen Museumsbahnen (BMB). Another tramway museum open Saturdays all through the year also Sundays and holidays May–October. 5 trams are active.

19 trams.

RHEINLAND-PFALZ/SAARLAND

Brohl–Engeln. 1000mm gauge. 17.5 km. DB KBS 12426. KME 172.

IG Brohltal Schmalspureisenbahn, IBS. This is a supporting organisation for the Brohltalbahn. Steam and diesel excursions are organised Tuesdays, Thursdays and weekends plus holidays April–October. Many "Santa Specials" operate in December.

3 steam, 2 diesel, 1 railcar

Gerolstein.

Eifelbahn e V. A relatively new society in this part of Germany. Gerolstein depot has been declared a historical monument and this seemed to be the obvious base. Steam-hauled tours operate from here over various routes. Tours by railbus also operate over the scenic lines in the area including the freight only line to Kaiseresech

2 steam, 3 diesels, 2 railcars.

Hermeskeil. KME 171

Eisenbahn Museum Hermeskeil. A private museum set up in an old DB depot by Bernd Falz who started acquiring locos as long ago as the 1970s. The collection was moved to Hermeskeil in the 1980's and considerably enlarged when DR locos became available after the Berlin Wall came down. many of the steam locos are ex stationary boiler use and in as "received condition". Some of the diesels are in fact in working order and are hired out to earn money for the museum.

38 steam, 11 diesels, 4 electrics.

Hermiskeil–Türkismühle. 22.3 km. KME 170

Hochwaldbahn e.V. runs occasional excursions over this closed DB line using its own railbuses.

1 diesel, 2 railcars.

Koblenz Lützel.

This is an old DB locomotive depot latterly used as a wagon shop. It is now an official annexe of the DB Museum. The EMU is the old ET30 set that used to be at Hamm. Open every Saturday morning March–October.

1 steam, 4 diesels, 9 electric and 1 EMU.

Lambrecht–Elmstein. 13 km. "Kuckuksbähnel". DB KBS 12670. KME 173.

DGEG Neustadt/Weinstrasse locos ands stock are used for tourist trains over this pleasant line every other Sunday May–October with some extra days for local holidays. The first and last trains originate/terminate at Neustadt/W.

Losheim–Merzig/Delborner Mühle. 16.4 km. KME 190.

Museumseisenbahnclub Losheim (MECL). This group runs trains over part of the old Merzig - Buschfelder Eisenbahn between Losheim and Merzig Ost and Losheim and Delborner Mühle. Trains run once a month April - October (twice a month June, July, and August).

2 steam, 6 diesels.

Neustadt/Weinstrasse. KME 174.

Eisenbahn Museum. This museum is run by DGEG. Located close to Neustadt/Weinstrasse station it is an old loco depot. In 1999 the society obtained use of a more recent loco depot when DB gave up using a small roundhouse nearby. So DGEG has now got extended territory and the old mechanical signalbox that straddles the running lines. The museum is also the operating base for running trains on the line from Lambrecht. The museum is open Saturdays, Sundays and holidays 10.00 - 16.00

13 steam, 4 electric, 9 diesels, 1 railcar.

Schwarzerden–Ottweiler. 21 km. KME 192

A rather new set upwhich is operating on various weekends during the year using Köf!

4 diesel

Siegen.

Eisenbahnfreunde Betzdorf. Although founded in Betzdorf this group is now domiciled in the old DB roundhouse at Siegen which is understood to be a listed monument. Steam excursions are run in the area several times a year.

4 steam, 2 electric, 7 diesels, 1 railcar

Speyer.

Technik Museum, Speyer. This museum opened in the early 1990s and is excellent. Owned by the same people that run the museum at Sinsheim both can be visited quite easily using the local train services.. However such is the nature of the museums that a whole day could be spent at either. The railway collection is one part only of several themes in the museum which cover all forms of transport and also have military sections. Allow a lot of time! To get to the museum from Speyer station take the bus! Open daily 09.00–18.00

13 steam, 5 diesels, 3 electrics.

SACHSEN

Adorf.

Vogtlandische Eisenbahn Verein, Adorf (VEA). Another post-unification society now based in the old depot at Adorf but hoping to be able to run trains between Schönheide Ost and Muldenberg. Not open to the public yet but weekends will surely find someone at work at the depot.

5 steam, 6 diesel, 1 battery electric.

Bad Schandau–Lichtenhainer Wasserfall. "Kirnitzschtalbahn". 1000 mm gauge.

This delightful metre gauge tramway operates alongside the road and uses trams from various systems. It is open April–October. There are four historic vehicles available for charter, but the "normal" trams date from the 1960s!

3 trams + 1 trailer (not including the normal fleet).

Chemnitz. 600 mm gauge. DB KBS 12248. KME.

Parkeisenbahn, Kuchwaldring 24. Operates in the afternoons Tuesday - Sunday April - October. Steam usually operates on one weekend a month.

1 steam, 4 diesels, 1 battery electric

Chemnitz. KME 312a.

Sächsiches Eisenbahnmuseum, Chemnitz Hilbersdorf. Bw Hilbersdorf is a listed building as it retains much of its Sachsen beginnings. It was in use for steam traction until quite late and consequently has retained full steam facilities including a large coaling plant. With the closure of the nearby marshalling yard the depot was redundant and the fans moved in to make a museum out of it. Some interesting locomotives can be found there including a few Sachsen types and may industrial locos with local connection. Open Tuesday to Sunday throughout the year.

25 steam, 3 electrics, 3 battery electrics, 40 diesels, 4 railcars.

Chemnitz.

Strassenbahnfreunde Chemnitz. The Chemnitz tramway network was unusual in having two gauges 1435 mm and most unusually 925 mm! The museum collection is kept at the Kappel depot and can usually be seen by local arrangement. Only a short piece of 925 mm gauge remains for museum operation.

9 trams.

Dresden. KME 303.

Verkehrsmuseum Dresden (VMD). This museum is located within the city and naturally has railway and tramway sections. The VMD also owns may other locos which are spread around the former DDR as their is no space for them at the museum. many are at Bw Dresden Altstadt (q.v.). The museum is open Tuesdays - Sundays all year 10.00 - 17.00

4 steam, 3 electrics, 3 trams.

Dresden. KME 303a

Bw Dresden Altstadt. This depot was in DDR times planned to be an annexe of the VMD but now is an annex of the DB Museum. In early May each year the Dresden Dampflokfest brings large crowds to the depot but some of the land is to be given over to a new carriage washing plant and thus the future of the Dampffest is uncertain.

15 steam, 5 diesels, 1 electric, 2 trams, 2 railcars.

Dresden. Parkeisenbahn 381 mm gauge. DB KBS 12249. KME 304.

Alongside Wien Prater this must be one of the best known park railways in Europe. An intensive service can operate at times with the railway open daily May to October. Special events often take place.

2 steam, 2 battery electric

Glauchau.

BSW Freizeitgruppe IG 58 3047. This is another group set up after unification and stems from the fact that 58 3047 was a Traditions Lok. Now the local staff look after this and under locos under BSW auspices. The group has done a deal with the HE Frankfurt/Main and obtained 35 1097 (now working again) and ex DB 194 580 which is currently being overhauled. DR E42 001 is also in working order.

5 steam, 2 electrics, 9 diesels.

Jöhstadt–Steinbach. 750 mm gauge. 7.8 km DB KBS. KME 308.

IG Pressnitztalbahn. This society actually got going in DDR times but has really prospered since unification. Their objective is to preserve part of the Wolkenstein–Jöhstadt narrow gauge line which was closed in the mid 1980s – a line that used Sachsen Meyers to the end. The group forged ahead after unification restoring at first the depot at Jöhstadt and then laying track back towards Wolkenstein. Now 8 km has been laid to the former station of Steinbach which is the limit of the line. First class work has been done with the group setting themselves a high standard of restoration. The line operates most weekends May to September but steam locomotives only operate on selected dates.

4 steam, 3 diesels.

Klingenthal.

Eisenbahnfreunde Klingenthal. This little group has a small local museum at Klingenthal station.

1 tram, 1 diesel.

Leipzig.

BSW Kultur und Freizeit Gruppe "Historische Ellok". A group of DB staff at Bw Leipzig Hbf. West look after what were once the depot's "Tradition Loks". Some of these are usually exhibited at Leipzig Hbf station.

3 electrics.

Leipzig.

Eisenbahnmuseum Bayerische Bahnhof (EMBB). This society helps to look after the 1844 built Bayerische Bahnhof but has locos and stock at the old depot at Leipzig-Plagwitz. Excursions are run several times a year.

2 steam, 2 electrics, 1 diesel.

Leipzig. KME 301a

Historische Strassenbahnhof Leipzig-Möckern. The city of Leipzig has a large tramway network and naturally has some historic vehicles. There is no museum as yet but the Möchern depot usually has a few open days during the year. The historic trams normally operate on the third Sunday of the month from outside the Hauptbahnhof.

22 trams (10 in working order).

Leipzig. 600 mm gauge. KME 301.

Parkeisenbahn Auensee. Not as well known as the park railway in Dresden but it has one of the same steam locos. Operates most afternoons May–October.

1 steam, 1 battery electric

Löbau. KME 316.

Ostsächsiche Eisenbahnfreunde (OSE) was founded in the early 1990s and have their base at the old DR loco depot in Löbau. Some excursion trains operate each year and open days are held otherwise open each Wednesday 09.00–14.00

3 steam, 10 diesels.

Nossen.

BSW Freizeitgruppe IG Dampflok, Nossen. This society was formed after unification at the depot that used to look after 23 1113 once a Traditions Lok. When local branch lines lost their passenger services the depot became available as a base. It is hoped to run trains to Freiburg but for the present work is concentrated on restoration of locos and stock. A few open days are held each year.

4 steam, 6 diesels.

Oelsnitz.

Bergbaumuseum. A mining museum with a collection of industrial locomotives of various gauges. The only steam loco is a DR 52.8.

1 steam, 1 diesel, 3 electrics, 1 battery electric.

Oelsnitz.

Lugauer Eisenbahnfreunde (LEF). based at the old DR sub-shed this small society has some small ex DR shunting locos and a Ferkeltaxe!

6 diesels, 1 railbus.

Oschatz–Mügeln–Kemmlitz. 750mm gauge. 18.7 km. DB KBS 502, 12502. KME 309.

A preservation society helps to run steam excursions over this private railway usually on the last Sunday of the month April–September. But steam can occasionally be found in use on regular trains during the week when diesels are not available.

Plauen.

Strassenbahnnostalgie. The Plauen tramway is 1000 mm gauge and some vintage cars have been saved; the oldest in use dating from 1905.

4 trams

Radebeul Ost–Radeburg. 750 mm gauge. DB KBS 509. KME 307.

The Traditionsbahn Radebeul runs vintage trains on this line which is now owned by BVO Bahn. The historic stock is kept at Radeburg, although two locos are on static display at Radebeul Ost.

3 steam

Rittersgrün. KME 300.

Sächsisches Schmalspur Museum, Rittersgrün. This museum in fact dates from DDR days when the narrow gauge line here was closed in the early 1970s The collection has expanded since unification and is well worth a visit. The diesels are all ex industry.

3 steam, 6 diesels.

Schönheide Mitte–Stützengrün. 750 mm gauge. 3.9 km. KME 310.

Museumsbahn Schönheide/Carlsfeld. The Sachsen narrow gauge lines were always loved by fans in the DDR and as can be seen by these pages several groups are ensuring that Sachsen Meyers and the Heberleinbremse will not be forgotten. This group has saved part of the old Wilkau Hasslau–Carlsfeld narrow gauge line that had Meyers in use until it closed in the mid 1970s. The original depot in Schönheide Mitte has been restored.

3 steam, 1 diesel.

Schwarzenberg. KME 313

Eisenbahn Museum Schwarzenberg, Verein der Sächsische Eisenbahnfreunde (VSE). Another post unification success story helped along in the early days by a series of successful plandampfs. Located in a typical roundhouse the museum is open daily. Railtours and open days are held.

6 steam, 11 diesels.

Torgau.

Freunde der Eisenbahn, Torgau. (FET). This small society started by preserving small diesel shunters with local connections but have expanded to include a Class 52.80 and a fireless loco.

2 steam, 7 diesels.

Weisswasser–Bad Muskau/Kromlau. 600 mm gauge. 18.8 km. KME 380.

Waldeisenbahn Muskau (WEM) was a 600 mm gauge forest line that came into DR ownership. Two of the original steam locos and much original rolling stock survive but have been joined by a large number of second-hand industrial diesel locos made spare after unification. Trains run each weekend May–October but steam-hauled usually only on the first weekend of the month

4 steam, 37 diesels.

Zwickau.

Strassenbahn Nostalgie. This town has a metre gauge tramway and local fans have obtained and restored two historic trams to working order.

2 trams.

SACHSEN ANHALT

Aschersleben.

Eisenbahn Club Aschersleben. This group has taken over part of the old DR depot. Restricted opening but usually someone is there at weekends.

4 diesels, 1 railcar.

Gräfenhainchen.

Ferropolis Bergbau und Erlebisbahn. This museum is located at one of the old lignite centres and has many locomotives and rolling stock associated with the mining of brown coal.

1 steam, 10 diesels, 14 electrics, 3 battery electrics plus many narrow gauge items.

Halle.

One of the roundhouses at the old Halle P depot is now an outpost of the DB Museum. It is open on various Saturdays throughout the year.

5 steam, 3 diesels, 4 electrics, 1 railcar.

Halle.

Hallesche Strassenbahnfreunde. When in Halle remember the trams. There is a museum depot at Seebener Strasse 191 and historic trams run on tours of the town. The museum is open on Saturdays May to October.

18 trams.

Halle. 600 mm gauge. KME 354.

Park Railway. Another former Pioneerbahn. It is located on the Peissnitzinsel.

4 diesels, 3 battery electrics.

Hettstedt. KME 353a.

Mansfeld Museum. This museum deals with the history of mining in the area and has a railway section as the mines had narrow gauge networks.

1 steam, 3 diesels, 1 battery electric.

Klostermansfeld. 750 mm gauge. KME 353.

Mansfelder Bergwerksbahnverein (MBB). This society has managed to save part of the old 750 mm gauge mining railway network and restored some locomotives. It has also bought from Estonia a Gr type 0-8-0 a few of which used to work here many years ago. Steamings are held several times a year.

3 steam, 3 diesels.

Loburg. Loburg–Altengrabow 12 km. KME 354.

Arbeitskreis Loburger Bahn and Dampfzug Betriebsgemeinschaft (DBG) have come together to set up a museum depot and line at Loburg. DBG is a former West Germany society that has moved east. It is not clear whether all DBG stock is all Loburg but the totals include it. Operates on odd Saturdays in the summer.

2 steam, 10 diesels

Magdeburg.

Magdeburger Eisenbahnfreunde was formed about 1995 and has a base for the time being in the harbour lines area. They hope to be able to move into a former DR depot in the area eventually. (Buckau would be useful!).

1 steam, 6 diesels, 1 railcar.

Magdeburg.

This is another city with trams. There are six historic trams the oldest dating from 1898.

Naumburg. KME 356.

This town has a tramway and it would appear some active enthusiasts as some trams have been acquired from various other towns and cities. About three have been restored.

8 trams.

Rübeland.

Forderverein Rübelandbahn is based in the old depot at Rübeland where they are looking after 95 6676 "Mammut".

Salzwedel. KME 404.

Dampflokfreunde Salzwedel e.V. dates from 1994 and has set up home in the former DR depot which retains all its old infrastructure. The depot is open to visitors every Saturday. This part of East Germany was barred to visitors due to it being the border area. When here visit the splendid town which was held in a time warp whilst surrounded by the Iron Curtain.

6 steam, 6 diesels.

Stassfurt. KME 357.

Traditions Bahnbetriebswerk Stassfurt. The roundhouse and sidings have been taken over by this group and turned into a museum which is open on the first and third Saturdays of each month. There are some special weekends in June and October with locos in steam and perhaps some railtours around the area.

13 steam, 13 diesels, 1 electric, 1 railcar.

SCHLESWIG HOLSTEIN

Aumühle. KME 22.

There is a VVM depot and workshop here which is open to the public every Saturday and Sunday.

2 steam, 7 diesels, 1 DMU, 1 EMU

Bergedorf Süd–Geesthacht–Krummel. 15.7 km. KME 24.

Arbeitsgemeinschaft Geesthachter Eisenbahn runs trains over what is part of the AKN and an industrial branch on the first weekends of May, June, September and October plus other odd dates.

2 steam, 2 diesel, 1 railcar

Kappeln–Süderbrarup. 14.6 km. DB KBS 12146. KME 20.

Angeln Bahn and Freunde des Schienenverkehrs Flensburg e V. Former SJ and DSB locos are operated over the lines of Verkehrsbetriebe des Kreises Schleswig-Flensburg. Trains operate about twice a month June–September

4 steam, 5 diesel, 1 railcar

Lübeck.

BSW Gruppe Lübeck. This group of DB employees look after several locos and stock and have recently taken charge of the former TEE/IC set that was at Hamm. This has asbestos that must be removed and could be a big problem.

4 diesels, 1 DMU

Neumünster.

The old DB depot is now an outpost of the DB Museum and a base for the Rendsburger Eisenbahnfreunde. 01 1100 is the star locomotive here and works many excursions from Hamburg during the tourist season. The collection here has recently been enlarged by the arrival of a Class 64 2-6-2T from the closed works at Glückstadt and 82 008 formerly plinthed at Lingen.

6 steam, 2 diesels.

Schönberger Strand–Schönberg. 3.9 km. DB KBS 12131. KME 21.

Verein Verkehrsamateure und Museumsbahn, Hamburg (VVM). Operates Saturdays and Sundays June–September. Some trains may run through to and from Kiel.

2 steam, 5 diesels, 1 electric, 2 railcars, 1 EMU, 17 trams.

THÜRINGEN

Arnstadt.

Historisches Bw Arnstadt. Arnstadt depot was planned to be a steam centre by the DR where it would be the Traditions Bw for the area. However DBAG has no remit for this sort of operation so the local BSW group and others got together to form a society to save the depot and locos. It now looks secure and is used as a steam base for trains working into the area which is rich in tourist delights. The depot is open on Saturdays and Sundays throughout the year.

9 steam, 7 diesel, 2 battery electric.

Eisenach.

IG Werrabahn. This group started out at Gerstungen but lost the use of the depot there. They now seem to have a base in Eisenach but some of their stock is still stored on the Hersfelder Kreisbahn line.

3 steam, 3 diesels, one battery electric railcar.

Erfurt.

This is another city with a tramway. Three museum trams reported to be here.

Gera.

The local tramway has three museum trams.

Heiligenstadt.

Heiligenstadter Eisenbahnverein. This small society has collected some interesting exhibits which are displayed or stored at Heilgenstadt Ost station.

1 steam, 4 diesels, 1 battery electric.

Ilmenau. Ilmenau–Themar.

Dampfbahnfreunde Mittlerer Rennsteig e.V. A rather new venture aimed at keeping open this interesting route with its steep gradients. Spasmodic operations.

1 steam, 2 diesels.

Meuselwitz. Meuselwitz–Regis Breitingen. KME 340

Kohlebahn Haselbach. Excusrion trains are run over this 900 mm gauge coal railway. The old DR depot at Meuselwitz has been incorporated into the system and now has tracks of standard and narrow gauge. Some locomotives are on display at the outer end of the line.

6 steam, 4 electrics, 14 diesels.

Nordhausen.

When visiting the Harz narrow gauge lines remember that Nordhausen has a tramway with three historic vehicles.

Tammbach-Dietharz. KME 341

IG Hirzbergbahn Georgenthal-Tammbach is another new group set up since unification and still gathering stock. It is understood that there is a demonstration line at least within the confines of the station. It is still in the early stages of development.

1 steam, 4 diesels.

Weimar. KME 342

Thüringen Eisenbahnverein. This group is based in the old DR depot at Weimar and have concentrated on preserving electric locomotives.

3 steam, 5 diesels, 9 electrics, 3 battery electric and 2 railcars.

5. PRESERVED LOCOMOTIVES AND RAILCARS

A change has taken place in the status of the DB museum locomotives. After unification all operational museum locomotives were put in the care of DB InterCity later passing to DB Reise und Touristik. However the new business led railway getting ready for privatisation does not see operating and owning steam locomotives as part of its remit. So the locomotives have all been handed over to DB Museum which is now a separate "business". Part of the museum collection remains at the Verkehrsmuseum Nürnberg but the rest is spread far and wide. Indeed the new DB Museum staff found that they inherited a vast amount of locomotives and rolling stock that is too much to handle and house. Consequently there is no money to overhaul locomotives and in the last few years running certificates have expired on several locomotives.

However there is some good news to report. Joint arrangements are being formed with clubs and groups around the country who will look after locomotives on behalf of DB. This had led to the overhaul of 03 1010 (Halle P) and 01 1100 (Neumünster). 17 locations in particular have been nominated as places where DB Museum historic locomotives and rolling stock will be based and more importantly, housed. The places are: Arnstadt, Braunschweig, Dresden Altstadt, Düsseldorf Abstellbahnhof, Frankfurt/M, Garmisch Partenkirchen, Halle P, Koblenz-Lützel, Leipzig, Lichtenfels, Lübeck, Nürnberg West, Oberhausen Osterfeld Süd, Potsdam, Schwerin and Stuttgart.

Altogether some 220 items of rolling stock will be based at these locations leaving 260 items unplaced. Of these some will be loaned to other locations or sold to interested parties. DB Museum in fact owns several locos that have been plinthed in towns or at stations for many years. The situation with these "surplus" locomotives etc has not been clarified.

5.1. STANDARD GAUGE STEAM LOCOMOTIVES

The following are technical details of former DB and DR classes which are often seen on mainline use, either on excursions run by DB Nostalgie and by preservation societies etc. or on Plandampfs, which are events in which service trains are operated by steam locos. British enthusiasts are encouraged to support these events and details can be obtained from the website www.germansteam.info

CLASSES 01/01.5   4-6-2 (2'C1'h2)

After the first world war, the various German state railways were nationalised and the first of the new standard locomotives to appear was the Class 01 pacific. A few were built each year, there being altogether 232 locos plus 9 more rebuilt from Class 02. At the end of the second world war most of the class ended up on the DB. Both DB and DR modernised some of their locos in the 1950s and 1960s fitting new boilers, but only on the DR were the locos reclassified to 01.5.

Built: 1925–38. Rebuilt 1962–65.
Builder: Henschel
Driving Wheel Dia.: 2000 mm.   **Boiler Pressure:** 16 bar.
Length over Buffers: 23.94 m.   **Weight:** 170.6 tonnes.
Max. Speed: 130 km/h.   **Cylinders:** (2) 600 x 660 mm.

Some locos oil fired.

CLASS 01.10   4-6-2 (2'C1'h3)

Introduced in 1939, a three-cylinder heavy duty express locomotive built for a Germany that was
expanding its borders. After the second world war all of the class ended up on the DB. Originally streamlined this was removed soon after the second world war and in the 1950s most locos received new boilers and many became oil fired. 01 1102 has been restreamlined.

Built: 1940. Rebuilt 1953–58.
Builder: BMAG.
Driving Wheel Dia.: 2000 mm.   **Boiler Pressure:** 16 bar.
Length over Buffers: 24.13 m.   **Weight:** 180 tonnes.
Max. Speed: 140 km/h.   **Cylinders:** (3) 500 x 600 mm.

Oil fired.

CLASS 03
4-6-2 (2'C1'h2)

This class is a lightweight version of Class 01. After the second world war, the class was more or less evenly split between the DB and the DR. 03 001 has been retained in original condition, but other DR locos were rebuilt in the 1960s with modern boilers off withdrawn Class 22s.

Built: 1930–37.
Builder: Borsig.
Driving Wheel Dia.: 2000 mm.
Length over Buffers: 23.90 m.

Max. Speed: 130 km/h.
Boiler Pressure: 16 bar.
Weight: 160 tonnes.
Cylinders: (2) 570 x 660 mm.

CLASS 03.10
4-6-2 (2'C'1'h3)

As with Class 01.10 the 03.10 is a three cylinder version of the Class 03 and the class was also streamlined. All streamlining was removed after the second world war and both DB and DR rebuilt their locos with new boilers. On the DB the locos took on a completely different appearance having the same boiler as on Class 41, but all these locos lost out to diesels and electrics in the 1960s. The DR locos had new boilers, and the survivor owes its longivity to being fitted with counter pressure brakes and being kept by Halle Test Plant long after others had been scrapped.

Built: 1940. Rebuilt RAW Meiningen 1959.
Builder: Borsig.
Driving Wheel Dia.: 2000 mm.
Length over Buffers: 23.90 m.

Max. Speed: 140 km/h.
Boiler Pressure: 16 bar.
Weight: 163 tonnes.
Cylinders: (3) 470 x 660 mm.

CLASS 18.2
4-6-2 (2'C1'h3)

This one is a real cross breed. In the aftermath of the second world war, the DR found itself with a damaged 4–6–4T (61 002) for which there was no use. The driving wheels from this loco together with parts from a 2–10–2 (45 024) and a new boiler were put together by RAW Meiningen to make a new pacific tender locomotive. Fitted with counter pressure brakes the loco became part of the Halle Test Plant fleet and was the only steam loco passed for 160 km/h. It is now the fastest steam loco in the world as it is still passed for 160 km/h! It now has a supplementary tender.

Built: 1961.
Builder: RAW Meiningen.
Driving Wheel Dia.: 2300 mm.
Length over Buffers: 25.14 m.

Max. Speed: 160 km/h.
Boiler Pressure: 16 bar.
Weight:
Cylinders: (3) 520 x 660 mm.

Oil fired.

CLASS 23
2-6-2 (1'C1'h2)

After the second world war, the DB wanted to modernise its fleet of locomotives and to replace the ageing KPEV P8 4–6–0s, the Class 23 2–6–2 was introduced.

Built: 1959 for DB.
Builder: Jung.
Driving Wheel Dia.: 1750 mm.
Length over Buffers: 22.94 m.

Max. Speed: 110 km/h.
Boiler Pressure: 16 bar.
Weight: 136.6 tonnes.
Cylinders: (2) 550 x 650 mm.

Oil fired.

CLASS 23.10
2-6-2 (1'C1'h2)

This loco was the DR answer to the same problem that faced DB with the KPEV P8s. Between 1955 and 1959 the DR produced 113 of these and like the DB preserved the last example built. The class were renumbered as Class 35 in the DR computer numbering scheme.

Built: 1959 for DR.
Builder: LKM.
Driving Wheel Dia.: 1750 mm.
Length over Buffers: 22.66 m.

Max. Speed: 110 km/h.
Boiler Pressure: 16 bar.
Weight:
Cylinders: (2) 550 x 660 mm.

CLASS 38.10
4-6-0 (2'Ch2)

The famous Prussian P8. Some 3950 locomotives of this type were built between 1906 and 1925, and it is interesting to note that this "pre-nationalisation" design lasted right to the last days of steam operation, in some cases outliving locos built to replace it! The P8 was known as the "maid of all work" and was a good all round loco. Some examples have been repatriated from

Romania.
Built: 1910.
Builder: BMAG.
Driving Wheel Dia.: 1750 mm.
Length over Buffers: 18.59 m.

Max. Speed: 100 km/h.
Boiler Pressure: 12 bar.
Weight: 120.2 tonnes.
Cylinders: (2) 575 x 630 mm.

CLASS 41   2-8-2 (1'D1'h2)

366 locos were built between 1936 and 1941 and is basically a mixed traffic loco. The surviving locos differ in appearance. This is because both DB and DR rebuilt their locos in the 1950s. DB provided its locos with wide boilers, together with a large diameter chimney. 40 locos became oil burners and it is these that DB has preserved. On the DR the new boilers did not change the appearance dramatically.

Built: 1938–41. Rebuilt AW Braunschweig 1958.
Builder: MBA, Borsig, Jung
Driving Wheel Dia.: 1600 mm.
Length over Buffers: 23.90 m.
Max. Speed: 90 km/h.

Boiler Pressure: 26 bar.
Weight: 162.7 tonnes.
Cylinders: (2) 520 x 720 mm.

Some Oil fired.

CLASS 44   2-10-0 (1'Eh3)

The standard heavy freight loco built 1926–1944. These three cylinder locos were called "Jumbos" as all the real heavy loads were entrusted to them. DB had by far the largest part of the class after the second world war. Both DB and DR had oil fired locos and the DR Traditionslok was converted back to coal burning.

Built: 1926–44.
Builder: Floridsdorf.
Driving Wheel Dia.: 1400 mm.
Length over Buffers: 22.62 m.

Max. Speed: 80 km/h.
Boiler Pressure: 16 bar.
Weight: 170.8 tonnes.
Cylinders: (3) 550 x 660 mm.

CLASS 50   2-10-0 (1'Eh2)

Built 1939–1948, the class was intended as the standard loco to replace ageing KPEV G10 and G12 locomotives. However, with the outbreak of the second world war large numbers of this new class were built for the war effort until the class totalled over 3000. Its 15 tonnes axleload gave it a wide ranging route availability, making the class popular for main and branch line use.

Built: 1940-41.
Builder: Henschel, Krauss Maffei.
Driving Wheel Dia.: 1400 mm.
Length over Buffers: 22.94 m.

Max. Speed: 80 km/h
Boiler Pressure: 16 bar.
Weight: 135.1 tonnes.
Cylinders: (2) 600 x 660 mm.

CLASS 50.35   2-10-0 (1'Eh2)

Between 1958 and 1963, the DR reboilered many locos with new welded steel boilers and the Class 50 locos so treated were renumbered from 50 3501 upwards.

Rebuilt: 1958–63.
Builder: Henschel, Krauss Maffei.
Driving Wheel Dia.: 1400 mm.
Length over Buffers: 22.94 m.

Max. Speed: 80 km/h.
Boiler Pressure: 16 bar.
Weight:
Cylinders: (2) 600 x 660 mm.

CLASS 52.8   2-10-0 (1'Eh2)

Basically a Class 50 stripped of all non essential parts to become a wartime "Austerity" locomotive. Over 6000 were built, and the class ended up all over Europe with the Soviet Union having over 2000 of them. Again the light axleweight meant the loco had a good route availability, and the class is still in occasional use on the DR in the form of the reboilered examples, numbered in the 52.80 series. 200 locos were rebuilt by the DR with feed-water heaters, welded boilers etc.

Built: 1943. Rebuilt RAW Stendal 1965–67.
Builder: Skoda.
Driving Wheel Dia.: 1400 mm.
Length over Buffers: 23.05 m.

Max. Speed: 80 km/h.
Boiler Pressure: 16 bar.
Weight: 129.8 tonnes.
Cylinders: (2) 600 x 660 mm.

CLASS 58.3   2-10-0 (1'Eh3)

A class of 56 three cylinder 2–10–0s. These were DR rebuilds of KPEV G12s.

Built: 1917. Rebuilt 1963.
Builder: Henschel. RAW Zwickau
Driving Wheel Dia.: 1400 mm.
Length over Buffers: 21.65 m.

Max. Speed: 70 km/h.
Boiler Pressure: 16 bar.
Weight: 132.6 tonnes.
Cylinders: (3) 570 x 660 mm.

CLASS 62   4-6-4T (2'C2'h2t)

The DR saved a very interesting locomotive, as the Class 62 is in effect a tank version of the 01, albeit with smaller wheels. This strange 'Baltic' has its tank under the coal bunker. DB had a few examples and indeed one was put aside for preservation in the 1960s, but someone blundered and it was cut up. A fine fast locomotive.

Built: 1928.
Builder: Henschel.
Driving Wheel Dia.: 1750 mm.
Length over Buffers: 17.14 m.

Max. Speed: 100 km/h.
Boiler Pressure: 16 bar.
Weight: 117.5 tonnes.
Cylinders: (2) 600 x 660 mm.

CLASS 64   2-6-2T (1'C1'h2t)

A lightweight tank engine for branch line use, the class is a tank version of the Class 24 2–6–0 tender engine. 520 were built.

Built: 1928.
Builder: Borsig.
Driving Wheel Dia.: 1500 mm.
Length over Buffers: 12.40 m.
Max. Speed: 90 km/h.

Boiler Pressure: 14 bar.
Weight: 71 tonnes.
Cylinders: (2) 500 x 660 mm.

CLASS 65.10   2-8-4T (1'D2'h2t)

The DR built a very modern tank engine after the second world war, intended for use on suburban services and branch lines. Many worked in the Leipzig and Magdeburg areas. In the 1960s all were fitted with Giesl ejectors, but the preserved example has been restored to original condition.

Built: 1956 for DR.
Builder: LEW.
Driving Wheel Dia.: 1600 mm.
Length over Buffers: 17.50 m.
Max. Speed: 90 km/h.

Boiler Pressure: 16 bar.
Weight: 120 tonnes.
Cylinders: (2) 600 x 660 mm.

CLASS 86   2-8-2T (1'D1'h2t)

A standard locomotive which despite being classed as a freight locomotive, saw most use on mixed duties in mountainous areas. On the DR many were used in Saxony, and Aue was a well known centre for the class.

Built: 1928, 1942.
Builder: Karlsruhe, DWM.
Driving Wheel Dia.: 1400 mm.
Length over Buffers: 13.82 m.
Max. Speed: 80 km/h.

Boiler Pressure:
Weight: 83 tonnes.
Cylinders: (2) 570 x 660 mm.

CLASS 94   0-10-0T (Eh2t)

Originally KPEV Class T16.1, these locos were built for heavy shunting duties. Some were also used on mixed duties on steeply graded lines and this DR example was regularly used on the steep line from Schleusingen to Suhl. Over 1000 of these locomotives were built and several others have been plinthed.

Built: 1921.
Builder: BMAG.
Driving Wheel Dia.: 1350 mm.
Length over Buffers: 12.66 m.
Max. Speed: 60 km/h.

Boiler Pressure: 12 bar.
Weight: 81.2 tonnes.
Cylinders: (2) 610 x 660 mm.

5.2. LIST OF PRESERVED LOCOMOTIVES
5.2.1. STEAM LOCOMOTIVES

Old No.	Computer No.	Co.	Wheel	Type	Built	Status	Location
01 005	-	DR	4-6-2	2C1h2	1925	M	VMD, Stassfurt
01 008	001 008-2	DB	4-6-2	2C1h2	1925	M	DGEG. Bochum Dahlhausen
01 066	01 2066-7	DR	4-6-2	2C1h2	1928	MA	BEM. Nördlingen
01 111	001 111-4	DB	4-6-2	2C1h2	1934	M	DDM. Neuenmarkt Wirsberg
01 118	01 2118-6	DR	4-6-2	2C1h2	1934	MA	HE. Frankfurt/Main
~~01 137~~	~~01 2137-6~~	~~DR~~	~~4-6-2~~	~~2C1h2~~	~~1935~~	~~M~~	~~DBM. Dresden Altstadt~~
01 150	001 150-2	DB	4-6-2	2C1h2	1935	M	DBM. Nürnberg West
01 164	001 164-3	DB	4-6-2	2C1h2	1935	M	DBM. Nürnberg (On loan)
01 173	001 173-4	DB	4-6-2	2C1h2	1936	M	DTM. Berlin
01 180	001 180-9	DB	4-6-2	2C1h2	1936	P	Bowil, Switzerland.
01 202	001 202-1	DB	4-6-2	2C1h2	1936	MA	Lyss, Switzerland.
01 204	01 2204-4	DB	4-6-2	2C1h2	1936	M	Hermeskeil
01 220	001 220-3	DB	4-6-2	2C1h2	1937	P	Treuchtlingen
01 509	01 0509-8	DR	4-6-2	2C1h2	1963	MA	UEF. Heilbronn
01 514	01 1514-7	DR	4-6-2	2C1h2	1964	M	TM. Speyer
01 519	01 1519-6	DR	4-6-2	2C1h2	1964	MA	EFZ. Tübingen
~~01 531~~	~~01 1531-1~~	~~DR~~	~~4-6-2~~	~~2C1h2~~	~~1964~~	~~M~~	~~DBM. Arnstadt~~
01 533	01 1533-7	DR	4-6-2	2C1h2	1964	MA	ÖGEG. Ampflwang, Austria
~~01 1056~~	~~011 056-9~~	~~DB~~	~~4-6-2~~	~~2C1h3~~	~~1940~~	~~M~~	~~DME. Darmstadt Kranichstein~~
01 1061	012 061-8	DB	4-6-2	2C1h3	1940	M	DDM. Neuenmarkt Wirsberg
01 1063	012 063-4	DB	4-6-2	2C1h3	1940	P	Braunschweig Hbf.
01 1066	012 066-7	DB	4-6-2	2C1h3	1940	MA	UEF. Heilbronn
01 1075	012 075-8	DB	4-6-2	2C1h3	1940	MR	SSN. Rotterdam Noord, Netherlands
01 1081	012 081-6	DB	4-6-2	2C1h3	1940	M	UEF. Heilbronn
01 1082	012 082-4	DB	4-6-2	2C1h3	1940	M	DTM. Berlin
01 1100	012 100-4	DB	4-6-2	2C1h3	1940	MA	DBM Neumünster
01 1102	012 102-0	DB	4-6-2	2C1h3	1940	MR	Trans Europe, Giessen
01 1104	012 104-6	DB	4-6-2	2C1h3	1940	M	SEH. Heilbronn
03 001	03 2001-0	DR	4-6-2	2C1h2	1930	M	DBM. Dresden Altstadt
03 002	03 2002-8	DR	4-6-2	2C1h2	1930	M	TM. Prora
03 098	03 2098-6	DR	4-6-2	2C1h2	1933	M	TM. Speyer
03 131	003 131-0	DB	4-6-2	2C1h2	1933	M	DDM. Neuenmarkt Wirsberg
03 155	03 2155-4	DR	4-6-2	2C1h2	1934	M	Dieringhausen
03 188	003 188-0	DB	4-6-2	2C1h2	1935	P	DBM. Kirchheim (Teck).
03 204	03 2204-0	DR	4-6-2	2C1h2	1936	MA	LDC. Cottbus
~~03 295~~	~~03 2295-5~~	~~DR~~	~~4-6-2~~	~~2C1h2~~	~~1937~~	~~MA~~	~~BEM. Nördlingen~~
~~03 1010~~	~~03 1010-2~~	~~DR~~	~~4-6-2~~	~~2C1h3~~	~~1940~~	~~MA~~	~~DBM Halle P.~~
03 1090	03 0090-5	DR	4-6-2	2C1h3	1940	MS	DBM. Schwerin
05 001	-	DB	4-6-4	2C2h3	1935	M	DBM. Nürnberg
10 001	010 001-6	DB	4-6-2	2C1h3	1957	M	DDM. Neuenmarkt Wirsberg
15 001	-	DRG	4-4-4	2B2h4v	1906	M	DBM. Nürnberg
17 008	-	DRG	4-6-0	2Ch4	1911	M	DTM. Berlin
17 1055	-	DR	4-6-0	2Ch4v	1913	M	VMD. Dresden Altstadt
18 201	02 0201-0	DR	4-6-2	2C1h3	1961	MA	Dampf Plus. Nossen.
18 314	02 0314-1	DR	4-6-2	2C1h4v	1919	M	TM. Sinsheim
18 316	018 316-0	DB	4-6-2	2C1h4v	1919	M	LTA/HEM. Mannheim
18 323	018 323-6	DB	4-6-2	2C1h4v	1920	P	DBM. Offenburg
18 451	-	DB	4-6-2	2C1h4v	1912	M	Deutsches Museum, München
18 478	-	DB	4-6-2	2C1h4v	1918	M	BEM. Nördlingen
18 505	018 505-8	DB	4-6-2	2C1h4v	1924	M	DGEG. Neustadt (Weinstrasse)
18 508	-	DB	4-6-2	2C1h4v	1924	S	Wettingen, Switzerland
18 528	-	DB	4-6-2	2C1h4v	1928	M	Siemens Krauss Maffei, München Allach
18 612	-	DB	4-6-2	2C1h4v	1926	M	DDM. Neuenmarkt Wirsberg
19 017	-	DR	2-8-2	1D1h4v	1922	M	VMD. Dresden Altstadt
22 029	39 1029-6	DR	2-8-2	1D1h3	1959	MS	BEM. Nördlingen
22 047	39 1047-8	DR	2-8-2	1D1h3	1960	M	Falkenberg/Elster
22 064	39 1064-3	DR	2-8-2	1D1h3	1960	MS	BEM Nördlingen

22 066	39 1066-8	DR	2-8-2	1D1h3	1960	M	Hermeskeil
22 073	39 1073-4	DR	2-8-2	1D1h3	1961	M	Falkenberg/Elster
23 019	023 019-3	DB	2-6-2	1C1h2	1952	M	DDM. Neuenmarkt Wirsberg
23 023	023 023-5	DB	2-6-2	1C1h2	1952	MA	SSN. Rotterdam Noord, Netherlands.
23 029	023 029-2	DB	2-6-2	1C1h2	1954	P	Aalen
23 042	023 042-5	DB	2-6-2	1C1h2	1954	MR	DME. Darmstadt Kranichstein
23 058	023 058-1	DB	2-6-2	1C1h2	1955	MR	Eurovapor. Sulgen. Switzerland
23 071	023 071-4	DB	2-6-2	1C1h2	1956	MA	VSM. Beekbergen, Netherlands
23 076	023 076-3	DB	2-6-2	1C1h2	1956	MA	VSM. Beekbergen, Netherlands
23 105	023 105-0	DB	2-6-2	1C1h2	1959	MS	DBM. Nürnberg West
23 1019	35 1019-5	DR	2-6-2	1C1h2	1958	MA	LDC. Cottbus
23 1021	35 1021-1	DR	2-6-2	1C1h2	1958	M	TM. Prora
23 1074	35 1074-0	DR	2-6-2	1C1h2	1959	MS	Görlitz (for Röbel)
23 1097	35 1097-1	DR	2-6-2	1C1h2	1959	MA	IG. Glauchau
23 1113	35 1113-6	DR	2-6-2	1C1h2	1959	MS	DBM. Leipzig
24 004	37-1004-3	DR	2-6-0	1Ch2	1928	M	VMD. SEM. Chemnitz Hilbersdorf
24 009	37 1009-2	DR	2-6-0	1Ch2	1928	MA	ET Lengerich
24 083	(Oi2-22)	PKP	2-6-0	1Ch2	1938	MA	Loburg
38 205	38 5205-0	DR	4-6-0	2Ch2	1910	M	DBM, SEM Chemnitz Hilbersdorf
38 1182	38 1182-5	DR	4-6-0	2Ch2	1910	M	DBM. Arnstadt
38 1444	-	DB	4-6-0	2Ch2	1913	M	LHB. Salzgitter
38 1772	038 772-0	DB	4-6-0	2Ch2	1915	M	Siegen
38 2267	38 2267-3	DR	4-6-0	2Ch2	1918	MA	DGEG. Bochum Dahlhausen
38 2383	038 382-6	DB	4-6-0	2Ch2	1918	M	DDM. Neuenmarkt Wirsberg
38 2425	(Ok1-296)	PKP	4-6-0	2Ch2	1919	M	DTM. Berlin
38 2460	(230 094)	CFR	4-6-0	2Ch2	1919	MA	Treysa. Restored as Posen 2455.
38 2884	038 884-3	DB	4-6-0	2Ch2	1921	M	DBM. Nürnberg
38 3650	038 650-8	DB	4-6-0	2Ch2	1922	P	Böblingen
38 3711	038 711-8	DB	4-6-0	2Ch2	1922	P	Berebostel
38 3180	-	CFR	4-6-0	2Ch2	1921	MA	BEM Nördlingen.(CFR 230 105)
38 3199	-	CFR	4-6-0	2Ch2	1921	MA	SEH Heilbronn (CFR 230 106)
38 3999	-	CFR	4-6-0	2Ch2	1923	MA	DME Darmstadt. (CFR 230 111)
39 184	-	DB	2-8-2	1D1h3	1924	M	LHB. Salzgitter
39 230	-	DB	2-8-2	1D1h3	1925	M	DBM. DDM Neuenmarkt Wirsberg
41 018	042 018-2	DB	2-8-2	1D1h2	1938	MA	IG. Augsburg
41 024	042 024-0	DB	2-8-2	1D1h2	1938	M	DME. Darmstadt Kranichstein
41 025	41 1025-0	DR	2-8-2	1D1h2	1938	M	Hermeskeil
41 052	042 052-1	DB	2-8-2	1D1h2	1938	M	Osnabrück
41 073	042 073-7	DB	2-8-2	1D1h2	1939	MR	Eurovapor. Haltingen
41 096	042 096-8	DB	2-8-2	1D1h2	1938	MA	IG. Salzgitter
41 105	042 105-7	DB	2-8-2	1D1h2	1938	MR	SSN. Rotterdam Noord, Netherlands.
41 113	042 113-1	DB	2-8-2	1D1h2	1938	M	TM. Sinsheim
41 122	41 1122-5	DR	2-8-2	1D1h2	1938	MS	Meiningen Works
41 125	41 1125-8	DR	2-8-2	1D1h2	1938	MS	Falkenberg/Elster
41 137	41 1137-3	DR	2-8-2	1D1h2	1938	M	Hermeskeil
41 144	41 1144-9	DR	2-8-2	1D1h2	1938	MA	IG Werrabahn, Eisenach.
41 150	41 1150-6	DR	2-8-2	1D1h2	1938	MA	BEM. Nördlingen
41 185	41 1185-2	DR	2-8-2	1D1h2	1938	M	DBM Halle P.
41 186	042 186-7	DB	2-8-2	1D1h2	1938	M	Dieringhausen
41 225	41 1225-6	DR	2-8-2	1D1h2	1938	M	SEM. Chemnitz Hilbersdorf
41 226	042 226-1	DB	2-8-2	1D1h2	1938	M	Tuttlingen
41 231	41 1231-4	DR	2-8-2	1D1h2	1939	MA	Stassfurt
41 241	042 241-4	DB	2-8-2	1D1h2	1939	MA	DBM Oberhausen Osterfeld Süd
41 271	042 271-7	DB	2-8-2	1D1h2	1939	M	EF Rendsburg. Neumünster.
41 289	41 1289-2	DR	2-8-2	1D1h2	1939	M	Falkenberg/Elster
41 303	41 1303-1	DR	2-8-2	1D1h2	1939	MS	Röbel
41 360	042 360-8	DB	2-8-2	1D1h2	1939	MA	DBM Oberhausen Osterfeld Süd
41 364	042 364-0	DB	2-8-2	1D1h2	1941	M	DDM. Neuenmarkt Wirsberg
42 1504	(Ty43-127)	PKP	2-10-0	1Eh2	1944	M	TM. Speyer
42 2754	-	BDZ	2-10-0	1Eh2	1949	P	Opladen (BDZ 16.15)
42 2768	-	BDZ	2-10-0	1Eh2	1949	M	BEM Nördlingen. (BDZ 16.18)
43 001	-	DR	2-10-0	1Eh2	1926	M	VMD. Dresden Altstadt
44 100	043 100-7	DB	2-10-0	1Eh3	1937	M	TM. Sinsheim
44 105	44 2105-3	DR	2-10-0	1Eh3	1938	M	Falkenberg/Elster

44 140	44 2140-0	DR	2-10-0	1Eh3	1938	M	Falkenberg/Elster
44 154	44 2154-1	DR	2-10-0	1Eh3	1938	M	Falkenberg/Elster
44 167	44 2167-3	DR	2-10-0	1Eh3	1939	M	Hermeskeil
44 177	44 2177-2	DR	2-10-0	1Eh3	1939	M	Hermeskeil
44 196	44 2196-2	DR	2-10-0	1Eh3	1939	M	Hermeskeil
44 225	44 2225-9	DR	2-10-0	1Eh3	1939	MS	LDC Cottbus
44 264	44 2264-8	DR	2-10-0	1Eh3	1939	M	Hermeskeil
44 276	044 276-4	DB	2-10-0	1Eh3	1940	M	DDM. Neuenmarkt Wirsberg
44 351	44 0351-5	DR	2-10-0	1Eh3	1941	S	VSE. Wülknitz
44 381	043 381-3	DB	2-10-0	1Eh3	1941	M	BEM. Nördlingen
44 389	044 389-5	DB	2-10-0	1Eh3	1941	P	Altenbeken
44 394	44 2394-3	DR	2-10-0	1Eh3	1941	M	Falkenberg/Elster
44 397	44 2397-6	DR	2-10-0	1Eh3	1941	M	TM. Prora
44 404	044 404-2	DB	2-10-0	1Eh3	1941	M	DME. Darmstadt Kranichstein
44 434	044 434-9	DB	2-10-0	1Eh3	1941	M	Hermeskeil
44 481	044 481-0	DB	2-10-0	1Eh3	1941	P	Kassel. Thyssen Works.
44 500	44 2500-5	DR	2-10-0	1Eh3	1941	M	Hermeskeil
44 508	044 508-0	DB	2-10-0	1Eh3	1941	MS	Montabaur or Westerburg.
44 546	44 2546-8	DR	2-10-0	1Eh3	1941	M	BEM. Nördlingen
44 594	044 594-0	DB	2-10-0	1Eh3	1941	M	Salzwedel
44 606	043 606-3	DB	2-10-0	1Eh3	1941	M	Bahnpark, Augsburg
44 635	44 2635-9	DR	2-10-0	1Eh3	1941	M	Hermeskeil
44 661	44 2661-5	DR	2-10-0	1Eh3	1941	MA	ÖGEG. Ampflwang. Austria
44 663	44 2663-1	DR	2-10-0	1Eh3	1941	M	Stassfurt
44 687	44 2687-0	DR	2-10-0	1Eh3	1941	M	Altenbeken.
44 903	043 903-4	DB	2-10-0	1Eh3	1943	P	Emden Hbf.
44 1040	44 1040-3	DR	2-10-0	1Eh3	1942	M	Hermeskeil
44 1056	44 1056-9	DR	2-10-0	1Eh3	1942	M	Hermeskeil
44 1085	043 085-0	DB	2-10-0	1Eh3	1942	P	Porz Westhofen
44 1093	44 1093-2	DR	2-10-0	1Eh3	1942	M	DBM Arnstadt
44 1106	44 1106-2	DR	2-10-0	1Eh3	1942	M	Hermeskeil
44 1121	043 121-3	DB	2-10-0	1Eh3	1942	M	Tuttlingen
44 1182	44 1182-3	DR	2-10-0	1Eh3	1942	MA	Stassfurt
44 1203	043 196-5	DB	2-10-0	1Eh3	1942	P	Salzbergen Bhf.
44 1251	44 1251-6	DR	2-10-0	1Eh3	1942	M	Hermeskeil
44 1338	043 315-1	DB	2-10-0	1Eh3	1943	MS	Kornwestheim
44 1377	44 1338-1	DR	2-10-0	1Eh3	1943	M	SEM Chemnitz Hilbersdorf
44 1378	044 377 0	DB	2-10-0	1Eh3	1943	M	DGEG. Bochum Dahlhausen.
44 1412	44 1378-7	DR	2-10-0	1Eh3	1943	M	SEH Heilbronn
44 1424	44 1412-4	DR	2-10-0	1Eh3	1943	M	Hermeskeil
44 1486	044 424-0	DB	2-10-0	1Eh3	1943	M	Gemünden
44 1489	44 1486-8	DR	2-10-0	1Eh3	1943	M	Stassfurt
44 1537	44 1489-2	DR	2-10-0	1Eh3	1943	MR	SEH Heilbronn
44 1558	44 1537-8	DR	2-10-0	1Eh3	1943	M	Hermeskeil
44 1569	044-556-9	DB	2-10-0	1Eh3	1943	M	Hamm (or now at Gelsenkirchen Bismarck?)
44 1593	44 1569-1	DR	2-10-0	1Eh3	1943	S	Frankfurt/Oder
44 1595	44 1593-1	DR	2-10-0	1Eh3	1943	MA	VSM. Beekbergen, Netherlands.
44 1614	44 1595-6	DR	2-10-0	1Eh3	1943	S	ÖGEG. Ampflwang. Austria.
44 1616	44 1614-5	DR	2-10-0	1Eh3	1943	S	ÖGEG. Ampflwang. Austria.
44 1681	44 1616-0	DR	2-10-0	1Eh3	1943	S	Menzingen
45 010	043 681-6	DB	2-10-0	1Eh3	1942	M	Dieringhausen
50 001	045 010 6	DB	2-10-2	1E1h3	1941	M	DBM. Nürnberg
50 413	050 001-7	DB	2-10-0	1Eh2	1939	M	DTM. Berlin
50 607	050 413-4	DB	2-10-0	1Eh2	1940	M	TM. Sinsheim
50 622	050 607-1	DB	2-10-0	1Eh2	1940	M	Hermeskeil
50 682	050 622-0	DB	2-10-0	1Eh2	1940	M	DBM Nürnberg West
50 685	050 682-4	DB	2-10-0	1Eh2	1950	P	Grafenwöhr
50 778	(50.685)	GKB	2-10-0	1Eh2	1940	M	TM. Speyer
50 794	050 778-0	DB	2-10-0	1Eh2	1941	M	BEM. Nördlingen
50 849	050 794-7	DB	2-10-0	1Eh2	1941	P	Tolk, Kreis Schleswig
50 904	50 1849-4	DR	2-10-0	1Eh2	1941	MA	DBM Glauchau
50 955	050 904-2	DB	2-10-0	1Eh2	1940	M	DDM. Neuenmarkt Wirsberg
50 975	50 1955-9	DR	2-10-0	1Eh2	1941	S	BEM. Nördlingen
	050 975-2	DB	2-10-0	1Eh2	1941	M	DDM. Neuenmarkt Wirsberg

50 1002	50 1002-0	DR	2-10-0	1Eh2	1941	MS	ÖGEG. Ampflwang. Austria
50 1255	051 255-8	DB	2-10-0	1Eh2	1941	MR	SSN. Rotterdam Noord, Netherlands.
50 1446	051 446-3	DB	2-10-0	1Eh2	1941	M	Hermeskeil
50 1650	051 650-0	DB	2-10-0	1Eh2	1942	P	Aulendorf (Bhf.)
50 1724	051 724-3	DB	2-10-0	1Eh2	1941	MS	Linz/Rhein
50 1832	051 832-4	DB	2-10-0	1Eh2	1941	M	Hermeskeil
50 2146	50 2146-4	DR	2-10-0	1Eh2	1943	P	Weiden
50 2404	052 404-1	DB	2-10-0	1Eh2	1942	MS	DBM/BSW Oberhausen
50 2429	052 429-8	DB	2-10-0	1Eh2	1942	MS	Oberhausen
50 2613	052 613-7	DB	2-10-0	1Eh2	1942	P	Seifertshofen
50 2652	50 2652-1	DR	2-10-0	1Eh2	1943	P	Kaiserslautern
50 2740	50 2740-4	DR	2-10-0	1Eh2	1942	MS	UEF. Busenbach
50 2838	052 838-0	DB	2-10-0	1Eh2	1943	M	Tuttlingen
50 2908	052 908-1	DB	2-10-0	1Eh2	1942	P	Lauda (Bhf.)
50 2988	052 988-3	DB	2-10-0	1Eh2	1942	MA	WTB. Fützen
50 3014	50 3014-3	DR	2-10-0	1Eh2	1942	M	Hermeskeil
50 3031	053 031-1	DB	2-10-0	1Eh2	1942	M	SHE. Heilbronn
50 3075	053 075-8	DB	2-10-0	1Eh2	1943	M	DGEG. Bochum Dahlhausen.
50 3502	50 0072-4	DR	2-10-0	1Eh2	1957	MA	BEM. Nördlingen
50 3506	50 3506-8	DR	2-10-0	1Eh2	1957	MS	ÖGEG. Ampflwang. Austria
50 3517	50 3517-5	DR	2-10-0	1Eh2	1958	M	Salzwedel
50 3518	50 3518-3	DR	2-10-0	1Eh2	1958	M	Falkenberg/Elster
50 3519	50 3519-1	DR	2-10-0	1Eh2	1958	MS	ÖGEG. Ampflwang. Austria
50 3520	50 3520-9	DR	2-10-0	1Eh2	1958	M	VSM. Beekbergen, Netherlands.
50 3521	50 3521-7	DR	2-10-0	1Eh2	1958	MS	Rostock
50 3522	50 3522-5	DR	2-10-0	1Eh2	1958	M	Röbel
50 3523	50 3523-3	DR	2-10-0	1Eh2	1958	M	Selb
50 3527	50 3527-4	DR	2-10-0	1Eh2	1958	M	Pasewalk
50 3535	50 3535-7	DR	2-10-0	1Eh2	1958	M	Stassfurt
50 3538	50 3538-1	DR	2-10-0	1Eh2	1958	M	Röbel
50 3539	50 3539-9	DR	2-10-0	1Eh2	1958	MA	SEH. Heilbronn
50 3540	50 3540-7	DR	2-10-0	1Eh2	1958	M	Tuttlingen
50 3545	50 3545-6	DR	2-10-0	1Eh2	1958	MA	Crailsheim
50 3552	50 3552-2	DR	2-10-0	1Eh2	1958	MA	Salzwedel
50 3553	50 3553-0	DR	2-10-0	1Eh2	1958	M	Hermeskeil
50 3554	50 3554-8	DR	2-10-0	1Eh2	1959	MS	Tuttlingen
50 3555	50 3555-5	DR	2-10-0	1Eh2	1959	M	Hermeskeil
50 3556	50 3556-3	DR	2-10-0	1Eh2	1958	M	Stassfurt
50 3557	50 3557-1	DR	2-10-0	1Eh2	1959	M	Falkenberg/Elster
50 3559	50 3559-7	DR	2-10-0	1Eh2	1959	P	Liblar/Erfstadt
50 3562	50 3562-1	DR	2-10-0	1Eh2	1959	P	Kirchweyhe
50 3564	50 3564-7	DR	2-10-0	1Eh2	1959	MA	VSM. Beekbergen, Netherlands.
50 3568	50 3568-8	DR	2-10-0	1Eh2	1959	M	Falkenberg/Elster
50 3570	50 3570-4	DR	2-10-0	1Eh2	1959	M	Salzwedel
50 3576	50 3576-1	DR	2-10-0	1Eh2	1959	MA	NTB. Wiesbaden
50 3580	50 3580-3	DR	2-10-0	1Eh2	1960	MR	EFZ. Tübingen (Restored as 50 245)
50 3600	50 3600-9	DR	2-10-0	1Eh2	1960	MA	BEM. Nördlingen
50 3603	50 3603-3	DR	2-10-0	1Eh2	1960	M	Tuttlingen
50 3604	50 3604-1	DR	2-10-0	1Eh2	1960	M	Tuttlingen
50 3606	50 3606-6	DR	2-10-0	1Eh2	1960	MA	Magdeburg
50 3610	50 3610-8	DR	2-10-0	1Eh2	1960	MA	Dieringhausen
50 3616	50 3616-5	DR	2-10-0	1Eh2	1960	MA	VSE. Schwarzenberg
50 3618	50 3618-1	DR	2-10-0	1Eh2	1960	M	Stassfurt
50 3624	50 3624-9	DR	2-10-0	1Eh2	1960	M	Salzwedel
50 3626	50 3626-4	DR	2-10-0	1Eh2	1960	M	Weimar
50 3628	50 3628-0	DR	2-10-0	1Eh2	1960	M	SEM Chemnitz Hilbersdorf
50 3631	50 3631-4	DR	2-10-0	1Eh2	1960	M	Falkenberg/Elster
50 3635	50 3635-5	DR	2-10-0	1Eh2	1960	M	Falkenberg/Elster
50 3636	50 3636-3	DR	2-10-0	1Eh2	1960	MA	GES. Kornwestheim
50 3637	50 3637-1	DR	2-10-0	1Eh2	1960	M	Röbel (Existence now doubted).
50 3638	50 3638-9	DR	2-10-0	1Eh2	1960	MS	Röbel
50 3642	50 3642-1	DR	2-10-0	1Eh2	1960	M	Falkenberg/Elster
50 3645	50 3645-4	DR	2-10-0	1Eh2	1961	MS	Rommerode/EF Walburg
50 3648	50 3648-8	DR	2-10-0	1Eh2	1961	MA	SEM Chemnitz Hilbersdorf

50 3649	50 3649-6	DR	2-10-0	1Eh2	1961	M	Hermeskeil
50 3652	50 3652-0	DR	2-10-0	1Eh2	1961	M	Falkenberg/Elster
50 3654	50 3654-6	DR	2-10-0	1Eh2	1961	MA	VSM. Beekbergen, Netherlands
50 3655	50 3655-3	DR	2-10-0	1Eh2	1961	MA	ET. Lengerich
50 3657	50 3657-9	DR	2-10-0	1Eh2	1961	M	Tuttlingen
50 3658	50 3659-7	DR	2-10-0	1Eh2	1961	M	Adorf
50 3661	50 3661-1	DR	2-10-0	1Eh2	1961	MS	CFT Pontarlier – Vallorbe, France
50 3662	50 3662-9	DR	2-10-0	1Eh2	1961	M	Hermeskeil
50 3666	50 3666-0	DR	2-10-0	1Eh2	1961	MA	Trans Europe, Giessen.
50 3670	50 3670-2	DR	2-10-0	1Eh2	1961	MA	Berlin.
50 3673	50 3673-6	DR	2-10-0	1Eh2	1961	MA	Treysa
50 3680	50 3680-1	DR	2-10-0	1Eh2	1961	P	Linde bei Lindlar
50 3681	50 3681-9	DR	2-10-0	1Eh2	1961	MA	VSM. Beekbergen, Netherlands.
50 3682	50 3682-7	DR	2-10-0	1Eh2	1961	M	Salzwedel
50 3684	50 3684-3	DR	2-10-0	1Eh2	1961	MA	Treysa
50 3685	50 3685-0	DR	2-10-0	1Eh2	1961	M	Salzwedel
50 3688	50 3688-4	DR	2-10-0	1Eh2	1961	M	DBM. Arnstadt
50 3689	50 3689-2	DR	2-10-0	1Eh2	1961	M	ÖGEG Ampflwang, Austria.
50 3690	50 3690-0	DR	2-10-0	1Eh2	1961	MR	Nossen
50 3691	50 3691-9	DR	2-10-0	1Eh2	1961	S	EBG. Altenbeken
50 3693	50 3693-4	DR	2-10-0	1Eh2	1961	M	Falkenberg/Elster
50 3694	50 3694-2	DR	2-10-0	1Eh2	1961	M	EF Rendsburg. Neumünster
50 3695	50 3695-9	DR	2-10-0	1Eh2	1961	MA	Stassfurt
50 3696	50 3696-7	DR	2-10-0	1Eh2	1961	MA	CFV3V. Mariemburg, Belgium
50 3700	50 3700-7	DR	2-10-0	1Eh2	1961	M	Stassfurt
50 3703	50 3703-1	DR	2-10-0	1Eh2	1961	M	Prora
50 3705	50 3705-6	DR	2-10-0	1Eh2	1962	M	Treysa
50 3707	50 3707-2	DR	2-10-0	1Eh2	1962	P	Berlin Naturpark Süd
50 3708	50 3708-0	DR	2-10-0	1Eh2	1962	MA	Goslar
50 4073	50 4073-8	DR	2-10-0	1Eh2	1959	MR	BEM. Nördlingen
52 360	52 1360-8	DR	2-10-0	1Eh2	1942	MA	Vienenburg
52 662	52 1662-7	DR	2-10-0	1Eh2	1944	M	Hermeskeil
52 1423	52 1423-4	DR	2-10-0	1Eh2	1943	M	Hermeskeil
52 2093	52 2093-4	DR	2-10-0	1Eh2	1943	M	Hermeskeil
52 2195	52 2195-7	DR	2-10-0	1Eh2	1943	M	BEM. Nördlingen
52 2202	52 2202-1	DR	2-10-0	1Eh2	1943	MS	Altenbeken. To be scrapped.
52 2751	52 2751-7	DR	2-10-0	1Eh2	1943	M	Marl
52 3109	(152.3109)	GKB	2-10-0	1Eh2	1943	M	TM. Sinsheim
52 3548	52 3548-6	DR	2-10-0	1Eh2	1943	M	BEM. Nördlingen
52 3915	(TE-3915)	SZD	2-10-0	1Eh2	1944	M	Speyer (ex TE-3915)
52 4544	(Ty2-4544)	PMP	2-10-0	1Eh2	1943	MR	Naumburg
52 4867	(152.4867)	GKB	2-10-0	1Eh2	1943	MA	HEF.Frankfurt/M
52 4900	52 9900-3	DR	2-10-0	1Eh2	1943	MS	Halle P.
52 4924	52 4924-8	DR	2-10-0	1Eh2	1943	M	SEM Chemnitz Hilbersdorf
52 4966	52 4966-9	DR	2-10-0	1Eh2	1943	M	DTM. Berlin
52 5448	52 5448-7	DR	2-10-0	1Eh2	1943	MS	Leipzig
52 5679	52 5679-7	DR	2-10-0	1Eh2	1943	P	Falkenberg/Elster
52 5804	(52.5804)	ÖBB	2-10-0	1Eh2	1943	M	DDM. Neuenmarkt Wirsberg
52 5933	(TE-5933)	SZD	2-10-0	1Eh2	1943	MR	Altenbeken (ex TE-5933)
52 6358	52 6358-7	DR	2-10-0	1Eh2	1944	MS	Berlin Buchholz
52 6666	52 6666-3	DR	2-10-0	1Eh2	1943	MS	DBM Berlin Schöneweide
52 6721	52 6721-6	DR	2-10-0	1Eh2	1943	M	Hermeskeil
52 7409	(52.7409)	ÖBB	2-10-0	1Eh2	1943	MA	Würzburg
52 7596	(52.7596)	ÖBB	2-10-0	1Eh2	1944	MR	EFZ. Tübingen
52 8001	52 8001-1	DR	2-10-0	1Eh2	1960	MS	Oebisfelde
52 8003	52 8003-7	DR	2-10-0	1Eh2	1960	MS	ÖGEG Ampflwang, Austria
52 8004	52 8004-5	DR	2-10-0	1Eh2	1960	MS	Sassnitz
52 8006	52 8006-0	DR	2-10-0	1Eh2	1960	M	Hermeskeil
52 8007	52 8007-8	DR	2-10-0	1Eh2	1960	S	München
52 8008	52 8008-6	DR	2-10-0	1Eh2	1960	M	Falkenberg/Elster
52 8009	52 8009-4	DR	2-10-0	1Eh2	1961	M	Falkenberg/Elster
52 8010	52 8010-2	DR	2-10-0	1Eh2	1961	MR	VSM. Beekbergen, Netherlands
52 8012	52 8012-8	DR	2-10-0	1Eh2	1961	P	Zollhaus Blumberg
52 8013	52 8013-6	DR	2-10-0	1Eh2	1961	M	Falkenberg/Elster

52 8014	52 8014-4	DR	2-10-0	1Eh2	1961	S	Lutherstadt Eilsleben
52 8015	52 8015-1	DR	2-10-0	1Eh2	1961	P	Lehrte
52 8017	52 8017-7	DR	2-10-0	1Eh2	1961	M	Basdorf
52 8019	52 8019-3	DR	2-10-0	1Eh2	1961	M	Tuttlingen
52 8020	52 8020-1	DR	2-10-0	1Eh2	1961	M	Tuttlingen
52 8021	52 8021-9	DR	2-10-0	1Eh2	1961	M	Falkenberg/Elster
52 8023	52 8023-5	DR	2-10-0	1Eh2	1961	M	Falkenberg/Elster
52 8028	52 8028-4	DR	2-10-0	1Eh2	1961	MS	Oebisfelde
52 8029	52 8029-2	DR	2-10-0	1Eh2	1961	MA	Röbel
52 8034	52 8034-2	DR	2-10-0	1Eh2	1961	P	Simbach (Inn)
52 8035	52 8035-9	DR	2-10-0	1Eh2	1961	M	Falkenberg/Elster
52 8036	52 8036-7	DR	2-10-0	1Eh2	1961	M	Falkenberg/Elster
52 8037	52 8037-5	DR	2-10-0	1Eh2	1961	M	DEW Rinteln
52 8038	52 8038-3	DR	2-10-0	1Eh2	1961	MA	DEW Rinteln
52 8039	52 8039-1	DR	2-10-0	1Eh2	1962	M	SEM Chemnitz Hilbersdorf
52 8041	52 8041-7	DR	2-10-0	1Eh2	1962	MS	Lutherstadt Wittenberg
52 8042	52 8042-5	DR	2-10-0	1Eh2	1962	M	Falkenberg/Elster
52 8043	52 8043-3	DR	2-10-0	1Eh2	1962	M	Tuttlingen
52 8044	52 8044-1	DR	2-10-0	1Eh2	1962	M	Falkenberg/Elster
52 8047	52 8047-4	DR	2-10-0	1Eh2	1962	MS	Nossen
52 8051	52 8051-6	DR	2-10-0	1Eh2	1962	M	Tuttlingen
52 8053	52 8053-2	DR	2-10-0	1Eh2	1962	MA	VSM. Beekbergen, Netherlands
52 8055	52 8055-7	DR	2-10-0	1Eh2	1962	MA	DLM. Winterthur, Switzerland. (Or Wil).
52 8056	52 8056-5	DR	2-10-0	1Eh2	1962	P	Bautzen Bhf.
52 8057	52 8057-3	DR	2-10-0	1Eh2	1962	M	Tuttlingen
52 8058	52 8058-1	DR	2-10-0	1Eh2	1962	S	Eisenach. (For France)
52 8060	52 8060-7	DR	2-10-0	1Eh2	1962	MS	Rommerode
52 8062	52 8062-3	DR	2-10-0	1Eh2	1962	P	Treuenbritzen
52 8063	52 8063-1	DR	2-10-0	1Eh2	1962	MS	Falkenberg/Elster (Existance now doubted)
52 8064	52 8064-9	DR	2-10-0	1Eh2	1962	MS	Klein Mahner
52 8068	52 8068-0	DR	2-10-0	1Eh2	1962	M	SEM. Chemnitz Hilbersdorf
52 8069	52 8069-8	DR	2-10-0	1Eh2	1962	M	Meuselwitz
52 8070	52 8070-6	DR	2-10-0	1Eh2	1962	MS	Herrnhut
52 8072	52 8072-2	DR	2-10-0	1Eh2	1963	M	Falkenberg/Elster
52 8075	52 8075-5	DR	2-10-0	1Eh2	1963	MA	IG Werrabahn. Eisenach
52 8076	52 8076-3	DR	2-10-0	1Eh2	1963	MS	Oebisfelde
52 8077	52 8077-1	DR	2-10-0	1Eh2	1963	MS	DBK. Crailsheim
52 8079	52 8079-7	DR	2-10-0	1Eh2	1963	MA	Dampf Plus, Glauchau
52 8080	52 8080-5	DR	2-10-0	1Eh2	1963	MA	Löbau
52 8082	52 8082-1	DR	2-10-0	1Eh2	1963	MR	Stadskanal, Netherlands
52 8083	52 8083-9	DR	2-10-0	1Eh2	1963	MS	Altenbeken
52 8085	52 8085-4	DR	2-10-0	1Eh2	1963	M	Falkenberg/Elster
52 8086	52 8086-2	DR	2-10-0	1Eh2	1963	M	Dalhausen (Wupper)
52 8087	52 8087-0	DR	2-10-0	1Eh2	1963	MS	Worms
52 8089	52 8089-6	DR	2-10-0	1Eh2	1963	M	Falkenberg/Elster
52 8090	52 8090-4	DR	2-10-0	1Eh2	1963	M	Hermeskeil
52 8091	52 8091-2	DR	2-10-0	1Eh2	1963	P	Amsterdam, Netherlands
52 8092	52 8092-0	DR	2-10-0	1Eh2	1963	M	Falkenberg/Elster
52 8095	52 8095-3	DR	2-10-0	1Eh2	1963	MA	Dieringhausen
52 8096	52 8096-1	DR	2-10-0	1Eh2	1963	M	ÖGEG Ampflwang, Austria
52 8097	52 8097-9	DR	2-10-0	1Eh2	1963	S	Frankfurt/O
52 8098	52 8098-7	DR	2-10-0	1Eh2	1963	M	BEM. Nördlingen
52 8100	52 8100-1	DR	2-10-0	1Eh2	1963	M	Falkenberg/Elster
52 8102	52 8102-7	DR	2-10-0	1Eh2	1964	M	Falkenberg/Elster
52 8104	52 8104-3	DR	2-10-0	1Eh2	1964	M	Falkenberg/Elster
52 8106	52 8106-8	DR	2-10-0	1Eh2	1964	MA	Treysa
52 8109	52 8109-2	DR	2-10-0	1Eh2	1964	M	Weimar
52 8111	52 8111-8	DR	2-10-0	1Eh2	1964	M	Tuttlingen
52 8113	52 8113-4	DR	2-10-0	1Eh2	1964	M	Hermeskeil
52 8114	52 8114-2	DR	2-10-0	1Eh2	1964	S	Halle G (Believed scrapped)
52 8115	52 8115-9	DR	2-10-0	1Eh2	1964	M	Knappenrode
52 8116	52 8116-7	DR	2-10-0	1Eh2	1964	M	Dieringhausen
52 8117	52 8117-5	DR	2-10-0	1Eh2	1964	S	Eisenach. (For France)
52 8120	52 8120-9	DR	2-10-0	1Eh2	1964	M	Hermeskeil

52 8121	52 8121-7	DR	2-10-0	1Eh2	1964	M	Siegen
52 8122	52 8122-5	DR	2-10-0	1Eh2	1964	M	Falkenberg/Elster
52 8123	52 8123-3	DR	2-10-0	1Eh2	1965	M	Hermeskeil
52 8124	52 8124-1	DR	2-10-0	1Eh2	1965	M	ÖGEG Ampflwang, Austria
52 8125	52 8125-8	DR	2-10-0	1Eh2	1965	M	Tuttlingen
52 8126	52 8126-6	DR	2-10-0	1Eh2	1965	M	Falkenberg/Elster
52 8130	52 8130-8	DR	2-10-0	1Eh2	1965	M	Tuttlingen
52 8131	52 8131-6	DR	2-10-0	1Eh2	1965	M	Salzwedel
52 8132	52 8132-4	DR	2-10-0	1Eh2	1965	M	Falkenberg/Elster
52 8133	52 8133-2	DR	2-10-0	1Eh2	1965	M	Falkenberg/Elster
52 8134	52 8134-0	DR	2-10-0	1Eh2	1965	MA	Siegen
52 8135	52 8135-7	DR	2-10-0	1Eh2	1965	P	Wildau
52 8137	52 8137-3	DR	2-10-0	1Eh2	1965	M	Stassfurt
52 8138	52 8138-1	DR	2-10-0	1Eh2	1965	M	Tuttlingen
52 8139	52 8139-9	DR	2-10-0	1Eh2	1965	MA	VSM Beekbergen, Netherlands
52 8141	52 8141-5	DR	2-10-0	1Eh2	1965	MS	Löbau
52 8143	52 8143-1	DR	2-10-0	1Eh2	1965	?	Schwarzenberg (? Scrapped)
52 8145	52 8145-6	DR	2-10-0	1Eh2	1965	S	Frankfurt/O
52 8147	52 8147-2	DR	2-10-0	1Eh2	1965	P	Quedlinburg
52 8148	52 8148-0	DR	2-10-0	1Eh2	1965	MA	Düren
52 8149	52 8149-8	DR	2-10-0	1Eh2	1965	M	SEM Chemnitz Hilbersdorf
52 8150	52 8150-6	DR	2-10-0	1Eh2	1965	M	Stassfurt
52 8154	52 8154-8	DR	2-10-0	1Eh2	1965	MA	Leipzig
52 8156	52 8156-3	DR	2-10-0	1Eh2	1966	M	Oebisfelde
52 8157	52 8157-1	DR	2-10-0	1Eh2	1966	S	Falkenberg/Elster
52 8160	52 8160-5	DR	2-10-0	1Eh2	1966	MA	VSM Beekbergen, Netherlands
52 8161	52 8161-3	DR	2-10-0	1Eh2	1966	M	Stassfurt
52 8163	52 8163-9	DR	2-10-0	1Eh2	1966	S	Last reported at Neuenberg, Baden, en route to France.
52 8165	52 8165-4	DR	2-10-0	1Eh2	1966	S	Worms
52 8168	52 8168-8	DR	2-10-0	1Eh2	1966	M	BEM. Nördlingen
52 8169	52 8169-6	DR	2-10-0	1Eh2	1966	M	Tuttlingen
52 8170	52 8170-4	DR	2-10-0	1Eh2	1966	M	Falkenberg/Elster
52 8171	52 8171-2	DR	2-10-0	1Eh2	1966	M	Tammbach Dietharz
52 8173	52 8173-8	DR	2-10-0	1Eh2	1966	S	Helbra
52 8174	52 8174-6	DR	2-10-0	1Eh2	1966	M	Torgau
52 8175	52 8175-3	DR	2-10-0	1Eh2	1966	M	Falkenberg/Elster
52 8176	52 8176-1	DR	2-10-0	1Eh2	1966	M	Tuttlingen
52 8177	52 8177-9	DR	2-10-0	1Eh2	1966	MA	Berlin Schöneweide
52 8183	52 8183-7	DR	2-10-0	1Eh2	1967	M	VSE Schwarzenberg
52 8184	52 8184-5	DR	2-10-0	1Eh2	1967	MA	Stassfurt
52 8186	52 8186-0	DR	2-10-0	1Eh2	1967	M	ÖGEG Ampflwang, Austria
52 8187	52 8187-8	DR	2-10-0	1Eh2	1967	M	Falkenberg/Elster
52 8189	52 8189-4	DR	2-10-0	1Eh2	1967	M	Stassfurt
52 8190	52 8190-2	DR	2-10-0	1Eh2	1967	M	Prora
52 8191	52 8191-1	DR	2-10-0	1Eh2	1967	M	Tuttlingen
52 8194	52 8194-4	DR	2-10-0	1Eh2	1967	M	Falkenberg/Elster
52 8195	52 8195-1	DR	2-10-0	1Eh2	1967	MA	FME. Nürnberg
52 8196	52 8196-9	DR	2-10-0	1Eh2	1967	M	ÖGEG Ampflwang, Austria
52 8197	52 8197-7	DR	2-10-0	1Eh2	1967	M	Hermeskeil
52 8198	52 8198-5	DR	2-10-0	1Eh2	1967	M	Tuttlingen
52 8199	52 8199-3	DR	2-10-0	1Eh2	1967	M	Oelsnitz
52 8200	52 8200-9	DR	2-10-0	1Eh2	1967	MA	CFV3V. Mariembourg, Belgium
53 7002	-	DRG	0-6-0	Cn2	1884	M	DBM. Nürnberg
55 669	-	DR	0-8-0	Dn2	1905	M	VMD. Dresden Altstadt
55 3345	055 345-3	DB	0-10-0	DH2	1915	M	DGEG. Bochum Dahlhausen
55 3528	055 528-4	DB	0-10-0	DH2	1915	M	TM. Speyer
56 3007	-	DB	0-10-0	1DH2	1928	M	DME. Darmstadt Kranichstein
57 3088	057 088-7	DB	0-10-0	Eh2	1922	M	DBM/EFB Siegen
57 3297		DR	0-10-0	Eh2	1923	M	VMD. Dresden Altstadt
"57 3525"		CFR	0-10-0	Eh2	1926	M	BEM Nördlingen. (CFR 50.227)
"57 xxxx"		CFR	0-10-0	Eh2	1930	M	SEH. Heilbronn. (CFR 50.397)
58 261	58 1261-5	DR	2-10-0	1Eh3	1921	M	VMD. Chemnitz Hilbersdorf
58 311	58 1111-3	DR	2-10-0	1Eh3	1921	MR	UEF. Menzingen

58 1616	58 1616-0	DR	2-10-0	1Eh3	1920	M	Hermeskeil
58 3047	58 3047-6	DR	2-10-0	1Eh3	1963	MA	DBM Glauchau
58 3049	52 3049-2	DR	2-10-0	1Eh3	1963	MR	VSE Schwarzenberg
62 015	62 1015-8	DR	4-6-4T	2C2h2t	1928	M	DBM Dresden Altstadt
64 006	064 006-0	DB	2-6-2T	1C1h2t	1926	M	DGEG. Neustadt/Weinstr.
64 007	64 1007-0	DR	2-6-2T	1C1h2t	1928	M	DBM Schwerin
64 019	064 019-5	DB	2-6-2T	1C1h2t	1927	M	Selb
64 094	064 094-6	DB	2-6-2T	1C1h2t	1928	MS	GES. Kornwestheim
64 250	064 250-4	DB	2-6-2T	1C1h2t	1932	MA	CFV3V. Mariembourg, Belgium
64 289	064 289-2	DB	2-6-2T	1C1h2t	1933	MA	EFZ. Tübingen
64 295	064 295-9	DB	2-6-2T	1C1h2t	1933	M	DDM. Neuenmarkt Wirsberg
64 305	064 305-6	DB	2-6-2T	1C1h2t	1934	M	NVR Peterborough, UK.
64 317	64 1317-3	DR	2-6-2T	1C1h2t	1934	P	Frankfurt/Oder Hbf.
64 344	064 344-5	DB	2-6-2T	1C1h2t	1934	P	DBM. Plattling
64 355	064 355-1	DB	2-6-2T	1C1h2t	1934	P	Hillstedt
64 393	064 393-2	DB	2-6-2T	1C1h2t	1935	P	Konz
64 415	064 415-3	DB	2-6-2T	1C1h2t	1935	MA	VSM Beekbergen, Netherlands
64 419	064 419-5	DB	2-6-2T	1C1h2t	1935	MA	DBK. Crailsheim
64 446	064 446-8	DB	2-6-2T	1C1h2t	1938	M	DBM. Neumünster
64 491	064 491-4	DB	2-6-2T	1C1h2t	1940	MA	DFS Ebermannstadt
64 518	064 518-4	DB	2-6-2T	1C1h2t	1940	MA	Eurovapor, Huttwil, Switzerland
64 520	064 520-0	DB	2-6-2T	1C1h2t	1940	P	Engen
65 018	065 018-4	DB	2-8-4T	1D2h2t	1955	MA	SSN. Rotterdam Noord, Netherlands
65 1008	65 1008-5	DR	2-8-4T	1D2h2t	1955	M	Pasewalk
65 1049	65 1049-9	DR	2-8-4T	1D2h2t	1956	MA	DBM Arnstadt
65 1057	65 1057-2	DR	2-8-4T	1D2h2t	1956	MA	Basdorf
66 002	066 002-7	DB	2-6-4T	1C2h2t	1955	M	DGEG Bochum Dahlhausen
70 083	-	DB	2-4-0T	1Bn2t	1913	MR	Landshut (Longtime resident in Meiningen Works!)
74 231	-	DR	2-6-0T	1Ch2t	1908	M	Arnstadt
74 1192	-	DR	2-6-0T	1Ch2t	1915	M	DGEG Bochum Dahlhausen
74 1230	74 1230-7	DR	2-6-0T	1Ch2t	1916	MS	DBM Berlin Schöneweide
75 501	-	DR	2-6-2T	1C1h2t	1916	M	DDM. Neuenmarkt Wirsberg
75 515	-	DR	2-6-2T	1C1h2t	1911	M	VMD. SEM. Chemnitz Hilbersdorf
75 634	-	DB	2-6-2T	1C1h2t	1929	M	VVM. Aumühle
75 1118	-	DR	2-6-2T	1C1h2t	1921	MA	UEF. Gerstetten
78 009		DR	4-6-4T	2C2h2t	1912	M	VMD. Dresden Altstadt
78 192	078 192-6	DB	4-6-4T	2C2h2t	1920	M	Tuttlingen
78 246	078 246-6	DB	4-6-4T	2C2h2t	1922	M	DDM. Neuenmarkt Wirsberg
78 468	078 468-6	DB	4-6-4T	2C2h2t	1923	MA	Krefeld
78 510	078 510-5	DB	4-6-4T	2C2h2t	1924	M	DBM. Nürnberg
80 009	-	DR	0-6-0T	Ch2t	1928	P	Berlin Bohnsdorf
80 013	-	DB	0-6-0T	Ch2t	1928	M	DDM. Neuenmarkt Wirsberg
80 014	-	DB	0-6-0T	Ch2t	1928	M	SEH. Heilbronn
80 023	-	DR	0-6-0T	Ch2t	1928	M	VMD. Dresden Altstadt
80 030	-	DB	0-6-0T	Ch2t	1929	M	DGEG. Bochum Dahlhausen
80 036	-	DB	0-6-0T	Ch2t	1929	MR	VSM. Beekbergen, Netherlands
80 039	-	DB	0-6-0T	Ch2t	1929	MA	Hamm
81 004	-	DB	0-8-0T	DH2t	1928	MS	Naumberg
82 008	082-008-4	DB	0-10-0T	Eh2t	1950	M	DBM. Neumünster
85 007		DB	2-10-2T	1E1h3t	1932	P	DBM. Freiburg/Brsg.
86 001	86 1001-6	DR	2-8-2T	1D1h2t	1928	M	DBM, SEM Chemnitz Hilbersdorf
86 049	86 1049-5	DR	2-8-2T	1D1h2t	1932	M	VSE Schwarzenberg
86 056	86 1056-0	DR	2-8-2T	1D1h2t	1932	M	ÖGEG Ampflwang, Austria
86 283	086 283-9	DB	2-8-2T	1D1h2t	1937	M	DDM. Neuenmarkt Wirsberg
86 333	86 1333-3	DR	2-8-2T	1D1h2t	1939	MA	WTB. Futzen
86 346	086 346-4	DB	2-8-2T	1D1h2t	1939	MS	UEF. Menzingen
86 348	086 348-0	DB	2-8-2T	1D1h2t	1939	MS	Kornwestheim
86 457	086 457-9	DB	2-8-2T	1D1h2t	1942	M	DBM Nürnberg West
86 501	86 1501-5	DR	2-8-2T	1D1h2t	1942	MA	ÖGEG Ampflwang, Austria
86 607	86 1607-0	DR	2-8-2T	1D1h2t	1942	M	Adorf
86 744	86 1744-1	DR	2-8-2T	1D1h2t	1942	MR	MEM. Prussisch Oldendorf
88 7306		DB	0-4-0T	Bn2t	1892	M	DGEG. Neustadt/Weinstr.
88 7405		DB	0-4-0T	Bn2t	1899	M	DDM. Neuenmarkt Wirsberg

89 008		DR	0-6-0T	Ch2t	1938	M	VMD. Schwerin
89 312		DB	0-6-0T	Cn2t	1896	M	LTA. Mannheim
89 339		DB	0-6-0T	Cn2t	1901	M	DME. Darmstadt Kranichstein
89 357		DB	0-6-0T	Cn2t	1903	P	Kornwestheim
89 363		DB	0-6-0T	Cn2t	1905	MS	Stuttgart
89 407		DB	0-6-0T	Cn2t	1912	M	SEH. Heilbronn
89 801		DB	0-6-0T	Cn2t	1921	M	DBM. Nürnberg
89 837	(789.837)	ÖBB	0-6-0T	Cn2t	1921	M	BEM Nördlingen.
89 1004	89 1004-4	DR	0-6-0T	Ch2t	1906	M	DBM Halle P
89 6009	89 6009-8	DR	0-6-0T	Ch2t	1902	MA	DBM Dresden Altstadt
89 6024		DR	0-6-0T	Ch2t	1914	MA	DDM. Neuenmarkt Wirsberg
89 6237		DR	0-6-0T	Ch2t	1924	MA	MEM. Prussisch Oldendorf
"89 6311"	-	DR	0-6-0T	Ch2t		M	DBM Arnstadt
89 7005			0-6-0T	Ch2t	1882	M	Dahlhausen/Wupper
89 7077		DB	0-6-0T	Ch2t	1899	MS	Lübeck (Private)
89 7159			0-6-0T	Ch2t	1910	MA	DGEG. Neustadt/Weinstr.
89 7220			0-6-0T	Ch2t	1896	M	MBS. Haaksbergen, Netherlands
89 7296		DB	0-6-0T	Ch2t	1899	M	Gramzow
89 7462		DB	0-6-0T	Ch2t	1904	M	DBM. Koblenz
89 7513		DB	0-6-0T	Ch2t	1911	M	Loburg
89 7531		DB	0-6-0T	Ch2t	1898	M	SEH. Heilbronn
89 7538		DB	0-6-0T	Ch2t	1914	M	BLME. Braunschweig
90 009			0-6-2T	C1n2t	1893	M	DGEG. Bochum Dahlhausen
90 042			0-6-2T	C1n2t	1895	M	BLME. Braunschweig
91 134		DR	2-6-0T	1Cn2t	1898	M	DBM. Schwerin
91 319			2-6-0T	1Cn2t	1902	P	Münster-Gremmendorf (Westf)
91 896[II]		DR	2-6-0T	1Cn2t	1912	P	Dresden Friedrichstadt
91 936	(TKi3-112)	PKP	2-6-0T	1Cn2t	1903	M	DTM. Berlin
91 6580	-	DR	2-6-0T	1Ch2t	1939	M	DBM Arnstadt
92 011	-	DRG	0-8-0T	DH2t	1917	P	Rust/Lahr
92 442	-	DRG	0-8-0T	DH2t	1928	MA	Kornwestheim
92 503	-	DR	0-8-0T	DH2t	1910	M	VMD. Dresden Altstadt
92 638	-	DR	0-8-0T	DH2t	1912	M	MEM. Minden
92 739	-	DB	0-8-0T	DH2t	1914	M	DBM/DGEG. Neustadt/Weinstr.
93 230	-	DR	2-8-2T	1D1h2t	1917	M	VMD. Dresden Altstadt
93 526	093 526-2	DB	2-8-2T	1D1h2t	1918	M	DDM. Neuenmarkt Wirsberg
94 002	-	DRG	0-10-0T	Eh2t	1907	M	DGEG. Neustadt/Weinstr.
94 249	-	DR	0-10-0T	Eh2t	1908	M	Heiligenstadt
94 1184	094 184-9	DB	0-10-0T	Eh2t	1921	MR	Crailsheim or Ilmenau?
94 1292	94 1292-5	DR	0-10-0T	Eh2t	1922	MA	DBM. Ilmenau
94 1538	094 538-6	DB	0-10-0T	Eh2t	1922	MA	Krefeld
94 1640	094 640-0	DB	0-10-0T	Eh2t	1923	P	Gennep, Netherlands
94 1692	094 692-1	DB	0-10-0T	Eh2t	1924	M	DBM. Neumünster
94 1697	094 697-0	DB	0-10-0T	Eh2t	1924	M	BEM Nördlingen.
94 1730	094 730-9	DB	0-10-0T	Eh2t	1924	M	DDM. Neuenmarkt Wirsberg
94 2105	-	DR	0-10-0T	Eh2t	1923	M	VMD. Schwarzenberg
95 009	95 0009-1	DR	2-10-2T	1E1h2t	1922	M	Dieringhausen
95 016	95 1016-5	DR	2-10-2T	1E1h2t	1922	M	Neuenmarkt Wirsberg
95 020	95 0020-8	DR	2-10-2T	1E1h2t	1923	M	TM. Speyer
95 027	95 1027-2	DR	2-10-2T	1E1h2t	1923	M	DBM Arnstadt
95 028	95 0028-1	DR	2-10-2T	1E1h2t	1923	M	DGEG. Bochum Dahlhausen
95 6676	95 6676-9	DR	2-10-2T	1E1h2t	1919	MR	Blankenberg
97 501	-	DB	0-10-0RT	Ezzh2t	1923	MR	Reutlingen
97 502	-	DB	0-10-0RT	Ezzh2t	1923	M	DGEG. Bochum Dahlhausen
97 504	-	DB	0-10-0RT	Ezzh2t	1925	M	DTM. Berlin
98 001	-	DR	0-4-4-0T	BBn4vt	1910	M	VMD. Industrie Museum, Chemnitz
98 307	-	DB	0-4-0T	Bh2t	1909	M	DBM. Neuenmarkt Wirsberg
98 507	-	DB	0-6-2T	C1h2t	1903	P	DBM. Ingolstadt, Bhf.
98 727	-	DRG	0-4-4-0T	BBn4vt	1903	M	DME. Darmstadt Kranichstein
98 812	098 812-1	DB	0-8-0T	DH2t	1914	MA	UEF. Gerstetten
98 886	098 886-5	DB	0-8-0T	DH2t	1924	MA	Fladungen
98 7056	-	DR	0-4-0T	Bn2t	1886	M	VMD. Dresden Altstadt
98 7508	-	DRG	0-4-0T	Bn2t	1883	M	DGEG. Neustadt/Weinstr.
98 7658	-	DRG	0-6-0T	Cn2t	1892	M	Bayerische Eisenstein

99 162	-	DR	0-4-4-0T	BBn4vt	1902	M	Oberhainsdorf
99 193	-	DB	0-10-0T	Eh2t	1927	MA	Blonay Chamby, Switzerland
99 211	-	DB	0-6-0T	Ch2t	1929	P	Wangerooge
99 253	-	DB	0-6-2T	C1n2t	1908	P	Regensburg
99 516	99 1516-6	DR	0-4-4-0T	BBn4vt	1892	MA	Schöneheide Mitte
99 534	99 1534-9	DR	0-4-4-0T	BBn4vt	1898	P	Geyer
99 535	99 1535-6	DR	0-4-4-0T	BBn4vt	1898	M	VMD. Dresden
99 539	99 1539-8	DR	0-4-4-0T	BBn4vt	1899	MA	Radeburg
99 542	99 1542-2	DR	0-4-4-0T	BBn4vt	1899	MA	Jöhstadt
99 555	99 1555-4	DR	0-4-4-0T	BBn4vt	1908	MS	Bertsdorf
99 562	99 1562-0	DR	0-4-4-0T	BBn4vt	1909	M	DDM. Neuenmarkt Wirsberg
99 564	99 1564-6	DR	0-4-4-0T	BBn4vt	1909	MR	Freital Hainsberg
99 566	99 1566-1	DR	0-4-4-0T	BBn4vt	1909	M	SEM. Chemnitz Hilbersdorf
99 568	99 1568-7	DR	0-4-4-0T	BBn4vt	1910	MA	Jöhstadt
99 579	99 1579-4	DR	0-4-4-0T	BBn4vt	1912	P	Oberrittersgrün
99 582	99 1582-8	DR	0-4-4-0T	BBn4vt	1912	MA	Schöneheide Mitte
99 585	99 1585-1	DR	0-4-4-0T	BBn4vt	1913	MS	Schöneheide Mitte
99 586	99 1586-9	DR	0-4-4-0T	BBn4vt	1913	P	Radebeul Ost
99 590	99 1590-1	DR	0-4-4-0T	BBn4vt	1913	MA	Jöhstadt
99 594	99 1594-3	DR	0-4-4-0T	BBn4vt	1913	M	Straupitz
99 604	99 1604-0	DR	0-4-4-0T	BBn4vt	1914	M	DGEG. Bochum Dahlhausen
99 606	99 1606-5	DR	0-4-4-0T	BBn4vt	1916	M	DBM Nürnberg
99 633	-	DB	0-4-4-0T	BBn4vt	1899	MA	Ochsenhausen
99 637	-	DB	0-4-4-0T	BBn4vt	1904	P	Bad Buchau
99 651	-	DB	0-10-0T	Eh2t	1919	P	Steinheim
99 713	99 1713-9	DR	0-10-0T	Eh2t	1927	MA	Radeburg
99 715	99 1715-4	DR	0-10-0T	Eh2t	1927	MA	Dippoldiswalde
99 716	-	DB	0-10-0T	Eh2t	1927	MA	Ochsenhausen
99 750	99 1750-1	DR	2-10-2T	1E1h2t	1929	P	Trixipark, Zittau
99 759	99 1759-2	DR	2-10-2T	1E1h2t	1933	M	Oberrittersgrün
99 781	99 1781-6	DR	2-10-2T	1E1h2t	1953	M	DBM. Nürnberg
99 788	99 1788-1	DR	2-10-2T	1E1h2t	1955	MA	Ochsenhausen
99 790	99 1790-7	DR	2-10-2T	1E1h3	1957	P	Freital Hainsberg
99 3301	99 3301-1	DR	0-6-0T	Cn2t	1895	MA	Cottbus Park
99 3310	99 3310-0	DR	0-8-0T	Dn2t	1917	MA	Ohs Bruk Jvg. Sweden
99 3311	99 3311-8	DR	0-8-0T	Dn2t	1917	MR	Schinznach, Switzerland
99 3312	99 3312-6	DR	0-8-0T	Dn2t	1912	MA	Weisswasser
99 3313	99 3313-4	DR	0-8-0T	Dn2t	1914	MA	DRM. Frankfurt/M
99 3314	99 3314-1	DR	0-8-0T	Dn2t	1917	M	MPSF. Schwichtenberg
99 3315	99 3315-1	DR	0-8-0T	Dn2t	1917	MA	DKM. Muhlenstroth
99 3316	99 3316-9	DR	0-8-0T	Dn2t	1919	M	TM. Speyer
99 3317	99 3317-7	DR	0-8-0T	Dn2t	1918	MS	Weisswasser
99 3318	99 3318-5	DR	0-8-0T	Dn2t	1918	MR	DKM. Muhlenstroth
99 3351	99 3351	DR	0-6-2T	C1n2t	1906	MR	DRM. Frankfurt/M
99 3352	99 3352	DR	0-6-2TT	C1n2t	1907	P	Friedland
99 3353	99 3353	DR	0-6-2T	C1n2t	1908	MA	Brecon, UK
99 3361	99 3361	DR	0-8-0	Dn2t	1938	MA	Hesston, Indiana, USA
99 3461	99 3461	DR	0-8-0	Dn2t	1934	MA	Froissy, France
99 3462	99 3462	DR	0-8-0	Dn2t	1934	MA	DKM. Muhlenstroth
99 4301		DR	0-6-0T	Cn2t	1920	P	Gommern
99 4503		DR	0-6-0T	Cn2t	1920	P	Gramzow
99 4511		DR	0-6-2T	C1n2t	1899	M	Jöhstadt
99 4532	99 4532-0	DR	0-8-0T	Dn2t	1924	M	Bertsdorf
99 4631	99 4631-0	DR	0-8-0T	Dh2t	1913	M	Prora
99 4644	99 4644-3	DR	0-8-0T	Dh2t	1923	MR	Lindenberg
99 4652		DR	0-6-0TT	Cn2t	1941	MS	Putbus
99 4701		DR	0-6-0T	Cn2t	1914	P	Wollstein
99 5001		DR	0-4-0T	Bn2t	1922	MS	Portes la Valence, France
99 5605	99 5605-3	DR	0-4-0T	Bn2t	1925	MA	DEV. Bruchhausen Vilsen
99 5606	99 5606-1	DR	0-4-0T	Bn2t	1894	P	Nürnberg Langwasser
99 5611		DR	0-6-0T	Cn2t	1925	MS	Tence, France
99 5633		DR	2-6-0T	1Cn2t	1917	MA	DEV. Bruchhausen Vilsen
99 5703		DR	0-6-0T	Cn2t	1897	M	Lubbenau
99 7201		DB	0-6-0T	Cn2t	1904	P	Angl (Passau)

99 7202		DB	0-6-0T	Cn2t	1904	P	Mudau
99 7203		DB	0-6-0T	Cn2t	1904	MA	UEF. Amstetten
99 7204		DB	0-6-0T	Cn2t	1904	M	MME. Hersheid-Hünigshausen

5.2.2. ELECTRIC LOCOMOTIVES

Old No.	Computer No.	Co..	Wheel	Built	Status	Location
E03 001	103 001-4	DB	Co-Co	1965	MA	Frankfurt/M 1
E03 002	103 002-2	DB	Co-Co	1965	MS	DDM Neuenmarkt Wirsberg
E03 004	103 004-8	DB	Co-Co	1966	MS	DBM. Lichtenfels
	103 101-2	DB	Co-Co	1971	M	DME. Darmstadt
	103 113-7	DB	Co-Co	1970	M	DBM.
	103 132-7	DB	Co-Co	1971	MS	Garmisch Partenkirchen (Spares for 103 245)
	103 167-3	DB	Co-Co	1971	MS	Deutsches Museum, München
	103 184	DB	Co-Co	19	M	DBM.Frankfurt 1
	103 197-0	DB	Co-Co	1972	P	Köln Bickendorf
	103 220-0	DB	Co-Co	1973	M	DGEG. Neustadt (Weinstrasse)
	103 224-2	DB	Co-Co	1973	M	DBM. Lichtenfels
	103 226-7	DB	Co-Co	1973	M	Siegen
	103 233-3	DB	Co-Co	1973	M	DBM FF1
	103 245-7	DB	Co-Co	1974	M	DB Fernverkehr München
E04 01	204 001-2	DR	1Co1	1932	MA	Leipzig West
E04 07	204 007-9	DR	1Co1	1933	M	Stassfurt
E04 11	204 011-1	DR	1Co1	1934	M	Weimar
E04 20	104 020-3	DR	1Co1	1934	P	DB HQ Frankfurt/Main.
E10 002	110 002-3	DB	Bo-Bo	1952	MS	Lichtenfels
E10 005	110 005-6	DB	Bo-Bo	1952	M	BEM Nördlingen
E10 121	110 121-1	DB	Bo-Bo	1958	M	DBM/BSW. EOB/KK2
E10 228	110 228-4	DB	Bo-Bo	1961	MA	DBM TS
E10 348	110 348-0	DB	Bo-Bo	1964	MA	DBM. FF1
E10 1311	113 311	DB	Bo-Bo	1963	M	DBM Koblenz Lützel
E11 001	211 001-3	DR	Bo-Bo	1961	MS	Halle P
E11 030	211 030-2	DR	Bo-Bo	1963	M	Ferropolis
E11 049	109 049-7	DR	Bo-Bo	1970	MA	Schwerin
E11 061	109 061-2	DR	Bo-Bo	1973	MA	Rostock
E16 03	116 003-5	DB	1Do1	1926	M	DBM. Koblenz Lützel
E16 07	116 007-6	DB	1Do1	1926	M	Deutsches Museum, München
E16 08	116 008-4	DB	1Do1	1926	M	DME, Darmstadt Kranichstein
E16 09	116 009-2	DB	1Do1	1926	M	Garmisch Partenkirchen
E17 103	117 103-2	DB	1Do1	1929	MS	Lichtenfels
E17 113	117 113-1	DB	1Do1	1928	M	DGEG. Neustadt (Weinstr)
E18 03	118 003-3	DB	1Do1	1935	MS	DBM. Koblenz Lützel
E18 08	118 008-2	DB	1Do1	1936	MS	München
E18 19	218 019-9	DB	1Do1	1936	MS	Garmisch Partenkirchen (or Lichtenfels?)
E18 24	118 024-9	DR	1Do1	1936	M	Weimar
E18 31	218 031-3	DR	1Do1	1937	MA	Halle P
E18 047	118 047-0	DB	1Do1	1939	MR	Dessau Works
E19 01	119 001-6	DB	1Do1	1938	M	DTM. Berlin
E19 12	119 012-8	DB	1Do1	1939	M	DBM. Nürnberg
	120 003-9	DB	Bo-Bo	1979	M	DBM. Garmisch Partenkirchen (Latterly 752 003)
E32 27	132 027-4	DB	1C1	1925	M	DGEG. Bochum Dahlhausen
E41 001	141 001-8	DB	Bo-Bo	1956	M	DBM. Koblenz
E41 006	141 006-7	DB	Bo-Bo	1956	M	Dieringhausen
E41 011	141 011-7	DB	Bo-Bo	1956	MR	Private. NN1
E41 055	141 055-4	DB	Bo-Bo	1958	MS	Koblenz Lützel
E41 068	141 068-7	DB	Bo-Bo	1958	MS	Private. FF1
E41 228	141 228-7	DB	Bo-Bo	1962	M	DBM/DME. Darmstadt
E41 248	141 248-5	DB	Bo-Bo	1963	M	DBM/EFB. Siegen
E42 001	142 001-7	DR	Bo-Bo	1963	MA	Glauchau
E42 002	142 002-5	DR	Bo-Bo	1963	M	SEM. Chemnitz Hilbersdorf
E42 151	142 151-0	DR	Bo-Bo	1968	M	Weimar
E42 255	142 255-9	DR	Bo-Bo	1976	M	Weimar
E44 001	144 001-5	DB	Bo-Bo	1930	M	DBM/DDM. Neuenmarkt Wirsberg

101- 012   NEUSTADT

E44 002	144 002-3	DB	Bo-Bo	1933	MS	DBM. Koblenz
E44 039	144 039-5	DB	Bo-Bo	1936	P	Nordenhamm
E44 044	244 044-4	DR	Bo-Bo	1936	MA	Dessau Works
E44 045	244 045-1	DR	Bo-Bo	1936	M	SEM. Chemnitz Hilbersdorf
E44 046	244 046-9	DR	Bo-Bo	1936	MS	Leipzig West
E44 049	244 049-3	DR	Bo-Bo	1936	M	Falkenberg/Elster
E44 051	244 051-9	DR	Bo-Bo	1936	M	BEM Nördlingen
E44 059	144 059-3	DB	Bo-Bo	1937	MS	DBM/Pflazbahn, Worms
E44 084	144 084-1	DB	Bo-Bo	1938	MS	DBM/Plalzbahn, Worms
E44 103	244 103-8	DR	Bo-Bo	1940	M	Weimar
E44 105	244 105-3	DR	Bo-Bo	1940	M	Weimar
E44 108	244 108-7	DR	Bo-Bo	1939	M	DBM. Halle P
E44 119	144 119-5	DB	Bo-Bo	1941	MS	DBM. Lichtenfels
E44 131	244 131-9	DR	Bo-Bo	1942	M	DTM. Berlin
E44 137	244 137-6	DR	Bo-Bo	1942	MS	Fortezza (I)?
E44 139	244 139-2	DR	Bo-Bo	1942	M	ETM. Prora
E44 148	244 148-3	DR	Bo-Bo	1942	M	Hermeskeil
E44 150	144 150-0	DB	Bo-Bo	1942	M	DGEG. Neustadt (Weinstr)
E44 502	144 502-2	DB	Bo-Bo	1933	P	Freilassing
E44 507	144 507-1	DB	Bo-Bo	1934	M	Weimar
E44 508	144 508-9	DB	Bo-Bo	1934	M	Selb
E44 1170	145 170-7	DB	Bo-Bo	1944	M	Siegen
E44 1180	145 180-6	DB	Bo-Bo	1947	MS	DBM/Pfalzbahn, Worms
E50 091	150 091-7	DB	Co-Co	1963	M	DBM. Koblenz Lützel
150 186-5	150 186-5	DB	Co-Co	1972	M	DBM/SEH. Heilbronn.
E52 34	152 034-5	DB	2B-B2	1924	M	DBM. Nürnberg
E60 09	160 009-7	DB	1-C	1932	M	DME, Darmstadt Kranichstein
E60 10	160 010-5	DB	1-C	1932	M	DBM. Koblenz
E60 12	160 012-1	DB	1-C	1932	M	TM. Sinsheim
E63 01	163 001-1	DB	C	1935	P	Stuttgart, Bw Rosenstein (TS)
E63 02	163 002-9	DB	C	1935	MS	Kriegenbrunn
E63 05	163 005-2	DB	C	1936	M	Garmisch Partenkirchen
E63 08	163 008-6	DB	C	1938	M	Garmisch Partenkirchen
E69 01	-	DB	Bo	1905	M	Deutsches Museum, München
E69 02	169 002-3	DB	Bo	1909	M	Garmisch Partenkirchen
E69 03	169 003-1	DB	Bo	1922	M	BEM. Nördlingen
E69 04	169 004-9	DB	Bo	1922	P	Murnau
E69 05	169 005-6	DB	Bo	1922	M	BLM. Landshut
E71 19	-	DB	B-B	1921	M	DBM. Nürnberg
E71 28	-	DB	B-B	1922	M	DTM. Berlin
E71 30	-	DR	B-B	1922	M	VMD. Dresden
E75 09	175 009-0	DB	1B-B1	1928	MS	Bauhof Nürnberg Rbf.
E77 10	-	DR	1B-B1	1925	MS	VMD. Dresden Friedrichstadt
E91 99	191 099-1	DB	C-C	1929	M	Garmisch Partenkirchen
E93 07	193 007-2	DB	Co-Co	1936	MS	Kornwestheim
E93 08	193 008-0	DB	Co-Co	1936	P	AKW Neckarwestheim
E93 12	193 012-2	DB	Co-Co	1936	M	DGEG. Neustadt (Weinstr)
E94 040	254 040-9	DR	Co-Co	1942	M	Hermeskeil
E94 051	194 051-9	DB	Co-Co	1941	P	Singen (Now in traffic with PEG)
E94 052	254 052-4	DR	Co-Co	1941	M	Dieringhausen (Now in traffic with PEG)
E94 056	254 056-5	DR	Co-Co	1942	MS	Leipzig Engelsdorf
E94 058	254 058-1	DR	Co-Co	1941	M	Ferropolis
E94 059	254 059-9	DR	Co-Co	1942	M	SEM. Chemnitz Hilbersdorf
E94 066	254 066-4	DR	Co-Co	1942	M	Hermeskeil
E94 080	194 080-8	DB	Co-Co	1942	M	DGEG. Bochum Dahlhausen
E94 106	254 106-8	DR	Co-Co	1943	M	Arnstadt
E94 110	254 110-0	DR	Co-Co	1943	M	Hermeskeil
E94 135	1020 017-8	ÖBB	Co-Co	1945	MS	BEM. Nördlingen
E94 158	194 158-2	DB	Co-Co	1944	MR	Krefeld
E94 192	194 192-1	DB	Co-Co	1956	M	BEM Nördlingen
E94 279	194 579-9	DB	Co-Co	1955	MA	DBM. Kornwestheim
E94 580	194 580-7	DB	Co-Co	1955	MA	Glauchau
E95 02	-	DR	1Co-Co1	1910	MS	Halle P
E244 31	-	DB	Bo-Bo	1936	MS	LTA/HEM. Mannheim

E251 012	171 012-8	DR	Co-Co	1965	M	Weimar
E310 001	181 001-9	DB	Bo-Bo	1967	M	DBM. Koblenz
E320 01	182 001-8	DB	Bo-Bo	1959	M	DBM. Koblenz
E410 003	184 003-2	DB	Bo-Bo	1968	M	DBM Koblenz
E410 012	184 112-1	DB	Bo-Bo	1967	M	DTM. Berlin

5.2.3. DIESEL LOCOMOTIVES

Old No.	Computer No.	Co..	Wheel	Built	Status	Location
V15 002	-	DB	B DM	1935	M	Göteborg, Sweden
V15 005	-	DB	B DH	1943	M	Göteborg, Sweden
V16 100	-	DB	B DM	1936	M	ME Minden
V20 022	-	DB	B DM	1942	M	Almstedt
V20 035	270 035-9	DB	B DH	1943	M	BLME
V20 036	270 036-7	DB	B DH	1943	M	DBM. Neumünster
V20 039	270 039-1	DB	B DH	1943	M	VVM. Schonberger Strand
V20 051	270 051-6	DB	B DH	1943	M	EKF. Bhf Sinsheim
V20 058	-	DB	B DH	1943	M	BLME
V29 952	-	DB	B-B DH	1952	MA	Bruchhausen Vilsen
V36 027	103 027-9	DR	C DH	1939	M	DB Museum, Schwerin
V36 102	236 102-0	DB	C DH	1945	M	DME Darmstadt
V36 107	236 107-9	DB	C DH	1940	P	AW Bremen
V36 108	236 108-7	DB	C DH	1940	MS	DBM. Lichtenfels
V36 114	236 114-5	DB	C DH	1945	M	Oberhausen
V36 116	236 116-0	DB	C DH	1941	M	DGEG. Neustadt (Weinstr)
V36 123	236 123-6	DB	C DH	1940	MA	Ebermannstadt
V36 211	236 211-9	DB	C DH	1942	MA	BEM. Nördlingen
V36 222	236 222-6	DB	C DH	1945	M	Bruchhausen Vilsen?
V36 225	236 225-9	DB	C DH	1944	MA	BLME
V36 231	236 231-7	DB	C DH	1939	MA	DGEG. Bochum Dahlhausen
V36 237	236 237-4	DB	C DH	1947	M	Bruchhausen Vilsen?
V36 262	236 262-2	DB	C DH	1948	M	Bodenwerder
V36 311	-	DB	C DM	1940	M	BLME
V36 314	-	DB	C DM	1941	M	ME Minden
V36 316	-	DB	C DM	1942	M	Dieringhausen
V36 401	236 401-6	DB	C DH	1950	MA	DME. Darmstadt Kranichstein
V36 405	236 405-7	DB	C DH	1950	MA	HE Frankfurt/M
V36 406	236 406-5	DB	C DH	1950	M	HE Frankfurt/M
V36 411	236 411-5	DB	C DH	1950	M	DME. Darmstadt Kranichstein
V36 412	236 412-3	DB	C DH	1950	MR	ET. Lengerich
V45 009	245 009-6	DB	B DH	1956	M	DDM. Neuenmarkt Wirsberg
V45 010	245 010-4	DB	B DH	1956	P	Paderborn Works (? Scrapped)
V51 902	251 902-3	DB	B-B DH	1964	MS	Biberach
V60 1001	-	DR	D DH	1959	M	SEM. Chemnitz Hilbersdorf
V60 1016	346 016-9	DR	D DH	1962	M	Lutherstadt Wittenberg
V60 1050	346 050-8	DR	D DH	1962	M	Dieringhausen
V60 1067	346 067-2	DR	D DH	1962	M	Belzig
V60 1068	346 068-0	DR	D DH	1962	M	Aschersleben
V60 1078	346 078-9	DR	D DH	1963	M	Falkenberg/Elster
V60 1095	346 095-3	DR	D DH	1963	M	Heilgenstadt
V60 1100	346 100-1	DR	D DH	1963	M	Arnstadt
V60 1120	346 120-9	DR	D DH	1963	M	SEM Chemnitz
106 182-9	346 182-9	DR	D DH	1981	M	Falkenberg/Elster
106 521-8	346 521-8	DR	D DH	1968	M	Oelsnitz
106 660-4	346 660-4	DR	D DH	1970	M	Falkenberg/Elster
260 303-3	360 303-2	DB	C DH	1957	M	DBM. Neumünster
260 150-8	360 150-7	DB	C DH	1957	M	DBM. Nürnberg West
V65 001	265 001-8	DB	D DH	1956	MA	Osnabrück
V65 011	265 011-7	DB	D DH	1956	M	DGEG. Bochum Dahlhausen
V75 004	107 004-4	DR	Bo-Bo DE	1962	MS	Klingenthal/Falkenstein
V80 002	280 002-7	DB	B-B DH	1952	M	DBM. Lichtenfels
V100 003	201 003-1	DR	B-B DH	1968	MA	Lutherstadt Wittenberg
V100 019	201 019-7	DR	B-B DH	1967	M	Röbel

V100 025	201 025-4	DR	B-B DH	1967	M	SEM Chemnitz
V100 093	201 093-2	DR	B-B DH	1968	MA	VSM Beekbergen, Netherlands
V100 101	201 101-3	DR	B-B DH	1968	M	Nossen
DE 2500	202 002-2	DB	Co-Co DE	1971	P	Bombardier Transportation, Kassel
-	202 003-0	DB	Bo-Bo DE	1973	M	DTM Berlin
-	202 004-8	DB	Co-Co DE	1983	M	LTA. Mannheim
110 228-4	201 228-4	DR	B-B DH	1970	M	Belzig
V100 1023	211 023-7	DB	B-B DH	1961	MA	DBM. Lichtenfels
V100 1054	211 054-2	DB	B-B DH	1962	P	Eschenau
V100 1200	211 200-1	DB	B-B DH	1962	MA	DGEG Bochum Dahlhausen
V100 1357	211 357-9	DB	B-B DH	1962	MA	GES Kornwestheim
V100 2001	212 001-2	DB	B-B DH	1959	M	DBM. Frankfurt/M or Nürnberg?
V100 2007	212 007-9	DB	B-B DH	1962	M	DGEG. Bochum Dahlhausen
V100 2062	212 062-4	DB	B-B DH	1963	M	DB FF1
V100 2203	212 203-4	DB	B-B DH	1963	M	BSW. Giessen
V140 001	-	DB	1-C-1 DH	1935	M	Deutsches Museum, München
	215 049-8	DB	B-B DH	1970	M	DB Nostalgie Neumünster
	215 122-3	DB	B-B DH	1970	M	DB Nostalgie Neumünster
V160 003	216 003-4	DB	B-B DH	1960	MA	DBM Lübeck
V160 221	216 221-2	DB	B-B DH	1968	M	DBM. Neumünster
119 003-2	219 003-1	DR	B-B DH	1978	M	SEM. Chemnitz Hilbersdorf
119 029-7	219 029-6	DR	B-B DH	1981	M	DBM. Weimar?
119 059-4	219 059-3	DR	B-B DH	1981	M	DBM. Weimar?
119 084-2	219 084-1	DR	B-B DH	1981	M	Weimar
119 158-4	219-158-3	DR	B-B DH	1983	MA	DBM. Berlin Grünewald
	229 188-8	DB	B-B DH	1992	M	Weimar
V180 005	228 505-4	DR	B-B DH	1963	M	Arnstadt
V180 075	118 075-1	DR	B-B DH	1965	M	DTM. Berlin
V180 118	228 118-6	DR	B-B DH	1965	MS	Schwerin
V180 141	228 141-8	DR	B-B DH	1965	MA	SEM Chemnitz
V180 175	228 175-6	DR	B-B DH	1966	M	LDC Cottbus
V240 001	228 202-8	DR	C-C DH	1971	M	Dresden
V180 372	228 372-9	DR	C-C DH	1969	MA	Magdeburg
V180 078	228 578-1	DR	B-B DH	1965	M	Falkenberg/Elster
V180 086	228 586-4	DR	B-B DH	1965	M	Stassfurt
V180 217	228 617-7	DR	C-C DH	1967	M	Tuttlingen
V180 283	228 683-9	DR	C-C DH	1968	M	Löbau
V180 292	228 692-0	DR	C-C DH	1968	M	Salzwedel
V180 314	228 714-2	DR	C-C DH	1968	M	Krefeld
V180 342	228 742-3	DR	C-C DH	1968	M	Dieringhausen
V180 349	228 749-8	DR	C-C DH	1968	MA	Arnstadt
V180 350	228 750-6	DR	C-C DH	1968	MS	Chemnitz Works?
V180 376	228 776-1	DR	C-C DH	1969	M	VSE Schwarzenberg
V180 382	228 782-9	DR	C-C DH	1969	M	SEM Chemnitz
V180 402	228 802-5	DR	C-C DH	1970	M	Dresden
130 002-9	230 002-8	DR	Co-Co DE	1971	M	Dresden
130 101-9	754 101-4	DR	Co-Co DE	1973	M	DBM. Halle P
131 001-0	231 001-9	DR	Co-Co DE	1973	M	DBM. Halle P
131 060-6	231 060-5	DR	Co-Co DE	1973	M	SEM Chemnitz
131 072-0	231 072-0	DR	Co-Co DE	1973	M	Arnstadt
132 387-2	232 387-1	DR	Co-Co DE	1976	P	Kratzenberg
232 304-6	234 304-4	DR	Co-Co DE	1976	M	Nossen
V200 001	220 001-2	DB	B-B DH	1953	MR	FME. Nürnberg
V200 002	220 002-0	DB	B-B DH	1954	MA	DBM Nürnberg West
V200 007	220 007-9	DB	B-B DH	1956	MA	Lübeck
V200 009	220 009-5	DB	B-B DH	1956	M	TM. ETM Prora
V200 015	220 015-2	DB	B-B DH	1957	MS	GES Kornwestheim
V200 016	220 016-0	DB	B-B DH	1957	MS	GES Kornwestheim
V200 017	220 017-8	DB	B-B DH	1957	S	Düsseldorf (Classic Train Tours)
V200 018	220 018-6	DB	B-B DH	1957	M	DTM. Berlin
V200 033	220 033-5	DB	B-B DH	1956	MA	HEF. Hamm
V200 058	220 058-2	DB	B-B DH	1959	M	TM. Speyer
V200 071	220 071-5	DB	B-B DH	1959	M	TM. Speyer

V200 077	220 077-2	DB	B-B DH	1959	S	Düsseldorf (Classic Train Tours)
V200 001	220 001-2	DR	Co-Co DE	1966	MS	Dieringehausen
120 198-7	220 198-6	DR	Co-Co DE	1969	MS	Dieringehausen
V200 269	220 269-5	DR	Co-Co DE	1969	M	SEM Chemnitz
120 274-6	220 274-5	DR	Co-Co DE	1969	M	Arnstadt
	120 338-9	DR	Co-Co DE	1973	M	VMD. Dresden Altstadt
120 355-3	220 355-2	DR	Co-Co DE	1975	MA	Hermeskeil
120 366-0	220 366-9	DR	Co-Co DE	1975	M	Stassfurt
V200 101	221 101-9	DB	B-B DH	1962	M	SEH. Heilbronn
V200 104	221 104-3	DB	B-B DH	1963	MS	EOB (Spares)
V200 116	221 116-7	DB	B-B DH	1963	MS	DBM. Lübeck
V200 120	221 120-9	DB	B-B DH	1963	M	SEH. Heilbronn
V200 135	221 135-5	DB	B-B DH	1965	MA	Krefeld
Kö 0049	-	DR	B DM	1933	M	VSE Schwarzenberg
Kö 0073	-	DB	B DM	1933	M	Dresden Altstadt
Kö 0082	-	DB	B DM	1934	MS	Heiligenstadt
Kö 0099	-	DB	B DM	1934	M	ETM Prora
Kö 0110	-	DB	B DM	1935	MS	Sinsheim
Kö 0116	-	DB	B DM	1935	MS	BEM Nördlingen
Kö 0128	-	DB	B DM	1935	MA	Berlin
Kö 0181	-	DB	B DM	1935	M	Selb
Kö 0186	311 186-1	DB	B DM	1936	M	Crailsheim
Kö 0188	311 188-7	DB	B DM	1936	M	Siegen
Kö 0203	-	DB	B DM	1936	M	RIM Koln
Kö 0204	311 204-2	DB	B DM	1936	MS	EF. Regensburg
Kö 0206		DB	B DM	1936	M	Herborn
Kö 0210	100 010-8	DR	B DM	1936	M	LDC Cottbus
Kö 0221	311 221-6	DB	B DM	1936	MS	Gerolstein
Kö 0225	311 225-7	DB	B DM	1936	MS	DBM. Walburg
Kö 0227	311 227-3	DB	B DM	1936	M	ETM Prora
Kö 0229	311 229-9	DB	B DM	1936	MA	Krefeld Oppum
Kö 0242	100 042-1	DB	B DM	1936	MA	Berlin Schöneweide
Kö 0245	100 045-4	DR	B DM	1936	MS	SEM Chemnitz Hilbersdorf
Kö 0247	311 247-1	DB	B DM	1936	MS	EFZ Tübingen
Kö 0255	311 255-4	DB	B DM	1936	MS	Klein Mahner
Kö 0258	311 258-8	DB	B DM	1936	MS	DBM. Walburg
Kö 0260	311 260-4	DB	B DM	1936	M	Nürnberg
Kö 0262	311 262-0	DB	B DM	1936	MS	Ochsenhausen
Kö 0265	311 265-3	DB	B DM	1936	MS	EFZ Tübingen
Kö 0274	311 274-5	DB	B DM	1936	MS	Almstedt
Kö 0278	311 278-6	DB	B DM	1936	P	Neustadt/Aisch
Kö 0281	311 281-0	DB	B DM	1936	MA	Essen
Kö 0289	100 089-2	DR	B DM	1936	MA	Torgau
Kö 1002	-	DRG	B DM	1940	MA	DME Darmstadt
Kö 4002	310 102-9	DR	B DM	1961	M	Tuttlingen
Kö 4006	310 106-0	DR	B DN	1961	P	Bad Langelsalza-Merxleben
Kö 4009	310 109-4	DR	B DM	1940	M	Wismar
Ks 4013	-	DB	Bo DE	1930	M	DGEG Bochum Dahlhausen
Ks 4015	381 101-5	DB	Bo DE	1930	M	BEM Nördlingen
Kö 4024	310 124-7	DR	B DM	1961	MS	Blumberg
Kb 4026	310 126-2	DR	B DM	1962	MA	Glauchau
Kb 4031	310 131-2	DR	B DM	1962	M	Hermeskeil
Ks 4071	381 201-3	DB	Bo DE	1932	P	DBM Limburg
Kbe 4096	310 196-1	DR	B DM	1934	M	Magdeburg
Kb 4102	323 002-6	DB	B DH	1933	MS	Wuppertal
Kb 4103	323 906-9	DB	B DH	1933	P	Oberthingau
Kb 4117	310 217-5	DR	B DM	1933	MA	Torgau
Kb 4118	310 218-3	DR	B DM	1933	MA	Torgau
Kb 4140	323 004-2	DB	B DH	1934	MA	MEM. Prussisch Oldendorf
Kb 4146	322 128-0	DB	B DH	1934	MA	Hanau
Kö 4150	322 174-4	DB	B DM	1934	P	Reichelshofen
Kö 4175	310 275-3	DR	B DM	1933	MS	Worms
Kö 4178	310 278-7	DR	B DM	1933	MS	Worms
Kö 4180	310 280-3	DR	B DM	1933	P	Wetzlar

Kö 4181	310 281-1	DR	B DM	1933	P	Rostock Seehafen
Kö 4201	310 201-9	DR	B DM	1933	MA	Arnstadt
Kö 4202	322 656-0	DB	B DH	1933	MA	Hamm
Kö 4210	310 210-0	DR	B DM	1933	P	Weisswasser
Kö 4211	310 211-8	DR	B DM	1934	M	SEM Chemnitz Hilbersdorf
Kö 4228	310 228-2	DR	B DM	1934	MS	Röbel
Kö 4240	323 502-5	DB	B DH	1933	M	München
Kö 4270	323 903-5	DB	B DH	1933	M	OEF. Giessen
Kö 4274	322 141-3	DB	B DM	1934	M	DBG. Bodenwerder
Kö 4280	323 605-7	DB	B DH	1934	M	BEF. Basdorf
Kö 4285	322 137-1	DB	B DH	1934	M	Hermeskeil
Kö 4287	322 613-1	DB	B DH	1934	M	Fladungen
Kö 4290	322 143-9	DB	B DH	1934	MA	DME Darmstadt
Kö 4293	322 607-3	DB	B DH	1934	M	NTB. Wiesbaden
Kö 4294	322 635-4	DB	B DH	1934	MS	Reutlingen
Kö 4309	310 309-0	DR	B DM	1934	M	Hermeskeil
Kb 4323	322 636-2	DB	B DH	1934	M	DDM Neuenmarkt Wirsberg
Kb 4324	310 324-9	DR	B DM	1934	P	Bad Segeberg
Kb 4326	310 326-4	DR	B DM	1934	P	Bad Segeberg
Kö 4350	322 628-9	DB	B DH	1934	M	Petite Roselle, France
Kö 4353	310 353-8	DR	B DM	1934	M	Falkenberg/Elster
Kö 4371	310 371-0	DR	B DM	1934	M	Falkenberg/Elster
Kö 4375	322 106-6	DB	B DH	1934	M	Braunschweig
Kö 4412	310 412-2	DR	B DM	19345	P	Potsdam
Kö 4418	310 418-9	DR	B DM	1934	P	Berlin Templehof
Kö 4430	310 430-4	DR	B DM	1934	M	ETM Prora
Kö 4439	310 439-5	DR	B DM	1934	MS	Arnstadt
Kö 4445	310 445-5	DR	B DM	1935	M	Eschwege
Kö 4492	100 492-8	DR	B DM	1934	M	Haselbach
Kö 4498	310 498-1	DR	B DM	1934	MA	Nossen
Kö 4500	310 500-4	DR	B DM	1934	MA	Dresden
Kö 4501	310 501-2	DR	B DM	1934	P	Cottbus Park
Kö 4528	310 528-5	DR	B DM	1934	M	Falkenberg/Elster
Kö 4537	310 537-6	DR	B DM	1935	MA	VSE Schwarzenberg
Kö 4572	322 618-0	DB	B DH	1934	MS	Gerolstein
Kö 4573	310 573-1	DR	B DM	1934	P	Prerow
Kö 4579	310 579-8	DR	B DM	1934	M	Walburg
Kö 4594	310 594-7	DR	B DM	1934	P	Neumarkt (Sachs)
Kö 4604	310 604-4	DR	B DM	1934	MS	Oebisfelde
Kö 4610	322 109-0	DB	B DH	1934	M	SEH. Heilbronn
Kö 4617	310 617-6	DR	B DM	1934	M	Stassfurt
Kb 4630	310 630-9	DR	B DM	1934	MA	Löbau
Kö 4632	100 632-9	DR	B DM	1934	P	Wolkenstein
Kb 4634	100 634-5	DR	B DM	1934	MA	Buckow
Kö 4642	X112.02	ÖBB	B DM	1935	M	TM Berlin
Kö 4646	100 646-9	DR	B DM	1935	MA	Finsterwalde
Kö 4667	323 016-6	DB	B DH	1935	MA	FME. Nürnberg
Kö 4669	323 508-2	DB	B DH	1935	P	Berlin-Kreuzberg
Kö 4696	323 510-8	DB	B DH	1934	M	Bochholt
Kö 4701	310 701-8	DR	B DM	1934	P	Rostock Seehafen
Kö 4706	323 922-5	DB	B DH	1934	P	Hofheim
Kö 4714	322 602-4	DB	B DH	1934	MA	Sinsheim
Kö 4731	-	DRG	B DM	1934	MS	Verden
Kbf 4736	100 736-8	DR	B DM	1935	P	Sachsendorf
Kö 4737	323 482-0	DB	B DH	1935	M	Bochhum Dahlhausen
Köe 4744	310 744-8	DR	B DM	1934	MA	Belzig
Köe 4751	310 751-3	DR	B DM	1935	P	Bitterfeld
Köe 4755	310 755-4	DR	B DM	1935	M	Stassfurt
Kb 4757	310 757-0	DR	B DM	1935	M	Falkenberg/Elster
Kö 4772	322 121-5	DB	B DH	1935	MA	Treysa
Kö 4788	310 788-5	DR	B DM	1935	P	Berlin Köpenick
Kö 4796	310 796-8	DR	B DM	1935	MS	Eisenach
Kö 4798	310 798-4	DR	B DM	1935	M	Tuttlingen
Kö 4800	310 700-0	DR	B DM	1935	M	Neuf Brisach, France

Kö 4809	322 646-1	DB	B DM	1935	MR	Mannheim
Kö 4812	323 927-4'	DB	B DM	1935	M	Mannheim
Kö 4822	310 722-4	DR	B DM	1936	M	Giessen
Kö 4825	100 725-1	DR	B DM	1936	M	SEH. Heilbronn
Kö 4842	323 017-4	DB	B DH	1936	M	Hanau
Kö 4853	310 773-7	DR	B DH	1937	M	Meuselwitz
Kbf 4858	310 758-8	DR	B DM	1935	M	Rostock
Ks 4862	381 005-8	DB	Bo DE	1936	MA	Köln Deutzerfeld
Kö 4872	310 774-5	DR	B DM	1936	MS	EFZ Tübingen
Kö 4879	323 484-6	DB	B DH	1936	P	Hallstadt
Kö 4880	322 157-9	DB	B DH	1936	MA	BEM Nördlingen
Kö 4900	310 703-4	DR	B DM	1936	M	Bad Segeburg
Kö 4902	310 704-2	DR	B DM	1936	P	Berlin Bohnsdorf
Ks 4909	381 011-6	DB	Bo DE	1937	MS	BEM Nördlingen
Ks 4910	381 012-4	DB	Bo DE	1937	P	Dorfen
Kö 4923	322 009-2	DB	B DH	1938	P	Mönchengladbach
Kö 4934	310 735-6	DR	B DM	1938	MA	Belzig
Kö 4936	310 738-0	DR	B DM	1937	MA	Oelsnitz
Köf 4959	310 759-6	DR	B DM	1937	P	Erfurt Mittelhausen
Köf 4962	310 765-3	DR	B DM	1938	MS	Adorf
Kö 4963	310 763-8	DR	B DM	1938	P	Ebeleben
Köf 4978	310 778-6	DR	B DM	1939	P	Lontzen, Belgium
Ks 4984	381 018-1	DB	Bo DE	1938	MS	BEM Nördlingen
Ks 4986	381 013-3	DB	Bo DE	1938	MS	Rottau
Köf 4999	310 789-3	DR	B DM	1942	M	Tuttlingen
Köf 5009	310 809-9	DR	B DH	1941	M	Belzig
Kö 5033	323 032-3	DB	B DM	1943	MS	Bocholt
Kö 5044	323 442-4	DB	B DH	1943	P	Merzen
Köf 5046	310 846-1	DR	B DH	1937	MS	Cottbus
Kö 5048	322 150-4	DB	B DH	1938	MS	Reutlingen
Kö 5049	310 849-5	DR	B DH	1939	M	Gramzow
Kbf 5057	323 036-4	DB	B DH	1943	M	Stadskanal, Netherlands
Kbf 5063	310 863-6	DR	B DH	1943	M	Dresden
Kbf 5064	310 864-4	DR	B DH	1943	MA	EFZ Tübingen
Kbf 5065	310 865-1	DR	B DH	1943	M	Selb
Kbf 5067	310 867-7	DR	B DH	1943	M	ETM Prora
Kbf 5068	310 868-5	DR	B DH	1943	P	Karow
Kbf 5072	100 872-1	DR	B DH	1943	MS	Kalbe (Milde)
Kbf 5116	323 044-8	DB	B DH	1943	M	Berlin
Kb 5142	310 842-0	DR	B DH	1944	M	DBM. Halle P
Kb 5159	X111.04	ÖBB	B DH	1944	M	Strasshof, Austria
Köf 5182	310 882-6	DR	B DH	1941	P	Erfurt
Kö 5186	324 043-9	DB	B DH	1938	M	Treysa
Köf 5193	310 892-5	DR	B DH	1942	MA	Neuoffingen
Köf 5226	100 826-7	DR	B DH	1944	M	SEM. Chemnitz Hilbersdorf (or Aschersleben?)
Kbf 5231	323 049-7	DB	B DH	1944	M	Verden
Kbf 5242	100 832-5	DR	B DH	1944	P	Ziegenruck
Kbf 5261	310 881-8	DR	B DH	1944	M	Hermeskeil
Kbf 5262	310 822-2	DR	B DH	1944	P	Erfurt
Kbf 5266	100 886-1	DR	B DH	1944	MA	Weimar
Kbf 5271	323 463-0	DB	B DH	1944	MS	Hamburg Wilhelmsburg
Köf 5274	323 470-5	DB	B DH	1944	M	Siegen
Kbf 5290	-	DRG	B DH	1946	MA	DGEG Bochum Dahlhausen
Köf 5712	310 912-1	DR	B DH	1942	MA	Frankfurt/M
Köf 5714	310 914-7	DR	B DH	1942	MA	Munchberg
Kö 5722	-	DR	B DH	1935	P	Wittenberge
Köf 5727	310 927-9	DR	B DH	1936	M	Röbel
Kö 5729	310 929-5	DR	B DH	1939	M	Röbel
Kö 5730	310 930-3	DR	B DH	1934	MS	Worms
Kö 5731	100 931-5	DR	B DH	1934	MA	Putlitz
Köf 5736	100 936-4	DR	B DH	1939	M	ETM Prora
Kö 5742	310 942-8	DR	B DH	1941	P	Espenhain
Kö 5743	-	DR	B DH	1935	MA	Magdeburg
Kö 5746	310 946-9	DR	B DH	1943	M	Quadenschonfeld

Köf 5750	310 950-1	DR	B DH	1939	MA	Klütz
Kö 5752	310 952-7	DR	B DH	1938	M	Schwerin
Köf 5753	310 953-5	DR	B DH	1943	MA	VSE Schwarzenberg
Kö 5755	310 955-0	DR	B DH	1952	M	Weimar
Köf 6007	322 609-9	DB	B DH	1937	MA	Bad Salzdetfurth
Kö 6020	-	DB	B DH	1937	M	Dieringhausen
Köe 6042	-	DB	Bo DE	1938	MS	DBM Gluckstadt
Köf 6046	322 173-6	DB	B DH	1941	M	Treysa
Köf 6119	324 044-7	DB	B DH	1951	MA	Oberhausen
Köf 6124	322 036-5	DB	B DH	1951	M	DBM. Walburg
Köf 6136	322 039-9	DB	B DH	1952	M	Fladungen
Köf 6139	322 172-8	DB	B DH	1952	M	Gemünden
Köf 6140	324 057-9	DB	B DH	1950	P	Hohenstadt
Köf 6152	322 041-5	DB	B DH	1953	MA	Norden
Köf 6157	323 440-8	DB	B DH	1953	MS	DB (current situation not known)
Köf 6158	322 147-0	DB	B DH	1953	P	Nürnberg Langwasser
Köf 6168	323 525-6	DB	B DH	1954	MA	Neumünster
Köf 6169	323 526-4	DB	B DH	1954	MA	GES. Kornwestheim
Köf 6170	322 510-9	DB	B DH	1954	M	DGEG Neustadt/Weinstr
Köf 6182	322 640-4	DB	B DH	1954	MR	Mannheim
Köf 6183	323 958-9	DB	B DH	1954	M	FME. Nürnberg
Köf 6190	322 614-9	DB	B DH	1954	M	FME. Nürnberg
Köf 6203	322 043-1	DB	B DH	1954	M	Darmstadt
Köf 6204	322 044-9	DB	B DH	1954	MA	Ebermannstadt
Köf 6265	323 582-7	DB	B DH	1956	M	Treysa
Köf 6276	323 593-4	DB	B DH	1957	M	Haltingen
Köf 6277	323 597-5	DB	B DH	1956	P	Duingen
Köf 6286	323 602-3	DB	B DH	1957	M	NTB. Wiesbaden
Köf 6306	323 617-1	DB	B DH	1957	M	BSW Krefeld
Köf 6311	323 626-2	DB	B DH	1958	M	Bahnpark, Augsburg
Köf 6315	323 627-0	DB	B DH	1958	MA	Blumberg
Köf 6325	323 637-9	DB	B DH	1958	M	BSW Oberhausen Osterfeld Süd
Köf 6330	323-642-9	DB	B DH	1958	M	HEM. Mannheim
Köf 6334	323 646-0	DB	B DH	1958	M	BSW. Regensburg
Köf 6359	322 058-9	DB	B DH	1959	MA	Neustadt/Weinstr
Köf 6372	323 102-4	DB	B DH	1959	M	Aumühle
Köf 6382	322 520-8	DB	B DH	1959	M	SHE. Heilbronn
Köf 6383	322 521-6	DB	B DH	1959	P	Osnabrück, Hafen Strasse.
Köf 6424	323 137-0	DB	B DH	1959	M	Walburg
Köf 6433	323 146-1	DB	B DH	1959	M	Schwaben Dampf, Neuoffingen
Köf 6436	323 149-5	DB	B DH	1959	MA	Linz/Rhein
Köf 6449	323 156-0	DB	B DH	1960	M	Hermeskeil
Köf 6463	323 219-6	DB	B DH	1960	M	EF Wetterau
Köf 6472	323 227-9	DB	B DH	1960	MA	Kassel
Köf 6482	323 237-8	DB	B DH	1960	MA	Rahden
Köf 6498	323 680-9	DB	B DH	1959	MA	BEM München Neuaubing
Köf 6499	323 681-7	DB	B DH	1959	M	Walburg
Köf 6501	323 683-5	DB	B DH	1959	MA	BEM Nördlingen
Köf 6510	323 710-4	DB	B DH	1960	M	Vienenburg
Köf 6519	323 719-5	DB	B DH	1960	MA	Neuoffingen
Köf 6524	323 724-5	DB	B DH	1960	M	GES Kornwestheim
Köf 6525	323 725-2	DB	B DH	1960	M	SHE. Heilbronn
Köf 6526	323 726-0	DB	B DH	1960	M	MEC Losheim
Köf 6528	323 728-6	DB	B DH	1960	M	Azpeitia, Spain.
Köf 6533	323 733-6	DB	B DH	1960	MA	FME. Nürnberg
Köf 6546	323 746-8	DB	B DH	1960	P	St. Englmar
Köf 6547	323 747-6	DB	B DH	1960	M	Petite Roselle, France
Köf 6551	323 751-8	DB	B DH	1960	M	DEW Rinteln
Köf 6557	323 757-5	DB	B DH	1960	M	DBM. Lichtenfels
Köf 6571	323 771-6	DB	B DH	1960	MR	Schwaben Dampf, Neuoffingen
Köf 6579	323 871-4	DB	B DH	1961	M	Münchberg
Köf 6580	323 872-2	DB	B DH	1961	M	SHE. Heilbronn
Köf 6606	323 174-3	DB	B DH	1959	MA	Hamm
Köf 6617	323 185-9	DB	B DH	1959	M	Losheim

Köf 6624	323 250-1	DB	B DH	1959	MA	DEW Rinteln
Köf 6642	323 268-3	DB	B DH	1960	M	ET Lengerich
Köf 6648	323 274-1	DB	B DH	1960	MA	Oberhausen
Köf 6705	323 703-9	DB	B DH	1959	MA	BEM. München
Köf 6712	323 782-3	DB	B DH	1959	M	St. Sulpice, Switzerland
Köf 6732	323 802-9	DB	B DH	1960	MA	BEM. München Neuaubing
Köf 6741	323 811-0	DB	B DH	1960	M	Aschaffenburg
Köf 6759	323 829-2	DB	B DH	1960	MS	Viechtach
Köf 6767	323 837-5	DB	B DH	1960	M	Schwarzenden
Köf 6772	323 842-5	DB	B DH	1960	MA	Siershahn
Köf 6782	323 852-4	DB	B DH	1960	M	DBM. Koblenz
Köf 6791	323 861-5	DB	B DH	1960	M	Hermeskeil
Köf 6796	323 866-4	DB	B DH	1960	P	Gerwisch, Magdeburg
Köf 6797	323 867-2	DB	B DH	1960	P	Dransfeld
Köf 6803	323 323 -6	DB	B DH	1965	MA	DEW Rinteln
Köf 6808	323 328-5	DB	B DH	1965	M	Crailsheim
Köf 6815	323 335-0	DB	B DH	1965	MA	Bösingfeld
Köf 6816	323 336-8	DB	B DH	1965	M	Herborn
Köf 6817	323 337-6	DB	B DH	1965	P	Bischofsmais
Köf 6833	323 353-3	DB	B DH	1965	M	Braunschweig
Köf 11 093	332 093-4	DB	B DH	1964	M	Siegen
Köf 11 098	332 098-3	DB	B DH	1964	MA	Schwarzenden
Köf 11 187	332 187-4	DB	B DH	1964	MS	Simpelveld, Netherlands
Köf 11 204	332 204-7	DB	B DH	1964	M	Siegen
Köf 11 227	332 227-8	DB	B DH	1966	M	Treysa
Köf 11 238	332 238-5	DB	B DH	1966	M	Frankfurt/M
-	335 039-4	DB	B DH	1968	M	Schwarzenden
-	335 059-2	DB	B DH	1969	M	Schwarzenden
-	333 068-5	DB	B DH	1969	M	DBM. Koblenz
-	335 200-2	DB	B DH	1976	P	DB Systems, Frankfurt/M
V15 1001	-	DR	B DH	1959	MA	Dresden Altstadt
V15 1002	-	DR	B DH	1959	M	Magdeburg
V15 1009	311 009-5	DR	B DH	1960	M	Falkenberg/Elster
V15 1012	311 012-9	DR	B DH	1960	M	Röbel
V15 2020	311 020-2	DR	B DH	1961	M	Löbau
V15 2035	311 705-8	DR	B DH	1961	M	Falkenberg/Elster
V15 2082	311 559-9	DR	B DH	1962	M	BEF. Basdorf
V15 2232	311 544-1	DR	B DH	1962	M	Salzwedel
V15 2289	311 569-8	DR	B DH	1963	M	Dresden
V15 2299	311 535-9	DR	B DH	1963	MA	Salzwedel
V23 001	312 001-1	DR	B DH	1967	M	DBM. Halle P
V23 009	312 009-4	DR	B DH	1968	M	Falkenberg/Elster
V23 046	102 046-0	DR	B DH	1968	M	SEM Chemnitz
V23 072	312 072-2	DR	B DH	1968	M	Falkenberg/Elster
102 140-1	312 140-1	DR	B DH	1970	M	SEM. Chemnitz Hilbersdorf
102 125-8	312 125-8	DR	B DH	1970	M	Weimar
102 172-0	312 172-0	DR	B DH	1970	MA	Oelsnitz
102 182-3	312 182-3	DR	B DH	1970	M	Glauchau
102 187-2	312 187-2	DR	B DH	1970	M	SEM. Chemnitz Hilbersdorf
329 501-1	399 101-5	DB	C DH	1952	MS	TM Prora
329 502-9	399 102-3	DB	C DH	1957	MS	TM Prora
329 503-7	399 103-1	DB	C DH	1957	MS	TM Prora
329 504-5	399 104-9	DB	B DH	1957	MS	TM Prora
199 007-6	399 701-2	DR	C DH	1972	MA	Jöhstadt
199 101-7	399 601-4	DR	C DM	1980	MA	Berlin Park Railway
199 102-5	399 602-2	DR	C DM	1980	MA	Berlin Park Railway
199 103-3	399 603-0	DR	C DM	1980	MA	Berlin Park Railway
Kdl 91-0001		DB	B DM	1953	M	Gerolstein
Kdl 91-0005		DB	B DM	1958	P	Hemmor
Kdl 91-0006		DB	B DM	1958	M	DBM. Walburg
Kdl 91-0012		DB	B DM	1958	M	Fredesdorf
ASF 1		DR	Bo BE	1982	MA	Arnstadt
ASF 2		DR	Bo BE	1983	MA	Weimar

ASF 01		DR	Bo BE	1964	MA	SEM. Chemnitz Hilbersdorf
ASF 8		DR	Bo BE	1966	MA	SEM. Chemnitz Hilbersdorf
ASF 45		DR	Bo BE	1971	M	Pasewalk
ASF 75		DR	Bo BE	1974	MA	Arnstadt
ASF 94^{II}		DR	Bo BE	1979	M	Nossen
ASF 114		DR	Bo BE	1981	M	SEM. Chemnitz Hilbersdorf
ASF 122^{I}		DR	Bo BE	1977	M	Schwerin
ASF 122^{II}		DR	Bo BE	1983	M	SEM. Chemnitz Hilbersdorf
ASF 14271			Bo BE	1974	M	Arnstadt
ASF 17762	ASF 1		Bo BE	1982	M	Arnstadt

EMUS

Old No.	Computer No.	Co..	Type	Built	Status	Location
1624ab		DB	2-car	1927	M	VVM. Aumuhle
ET 11 01		DB	2-car	1935	M	DGEG. Neustadt (Weinstr)
-	410 001-2	DB	Bo-Bo	1985	P	ST Minden
-	420 001-0	DB	3-car	1969	MA	S-Bahn München
	420 117-4	DB	3-car	1972	MA	IG S-Bahn München
-	420 250-3	DB	3-car	1978	MA	DB Frankfurt
ET25 015	425 115-3	DB	2/3/4-car	1935	MR	Haltingen
ET25 020	425 120-3	DB	2/3/4-car	1935	MA	Stuttgart
ET26 002	426 002-2	DB	2-car	1941	M	Peenemünde
ET27 005	427 105-2	DB	3-car	1965	MR	Stuttgart
ET30 114	430 114-9	DB	3-car	1956	MS	DBM. Koblenz Lützel
ET 32 201 a	432 201-2	DB	}			
EM 32 201	831 201-8	DB	} 3-car	1936	MR	Stuttgart
ET 32 201b	432 501-5	DB	}			
ET 65 005	465 005-7	DB	Bo-Bo	1933	MS	Stuttgart
ET 65 006	465 006-5	DB	Bo-Bo	1933	MS	Freiburg
ET183 05	-	DB	1Ao-Ao1	1899	M	DTM. Berlin
ET188 511	-	DR	Bo	1930	MS	Dresden Altstadt
ET188 521	-	DR	Bo	1930	MS	Dresden Altstadt
-	470 136-3	DB	3-car	1969	M	Kulturbahnhof Schmilau
ET171 014	471 114-9	DB	3-car	1940	MS	S-Bahn Exner Althüttendorf
ET171 039	471 139-6	DB	3-car	1943	MS	Schönberger Strand
ET171 044	471 144-6	DB	3-car	1942	M	LHB Salzgitter
ET171 075	471 175-0	DB	3-car	1955	MS	S-Bahn Exner Althüttendorf
ET171 080	471 180-0	DB	3-car	1955	MS	S-Bahn Exner Althüttendorf
ET171 018	471 181-8	DB	2-car	1955	MS	S-Bahn Exner Althüttendorf
ET171 082	471 182-6	DB	2-car	1958	MR	S-Bahn Hamburg
270 001-1	-	DR	2-car	1985	MS	HSB Berlin
275 003-2	475 001-4	BVG	2-car	1929	P	B-Kleistpark (Bar)
275 031-3	475 003-0	BVG	2-car	1928	M	Bochum Dahlhausen
275 045-3	475 005-5	BVG	2-car	1928	MA	HSB Berlin
275 061-0	475 008-9	BVG	2-car	1928	P	Dresdener Tor on A4 road
275 081-8	475 009-7	BVG	2-car	1928	P	Beelitz Süd
275 085-9	475 011-3	BVG	2-car	1928	P	Herzhausen (34516)
275 109-7	475 013-9	BVG	2-car	1928	P	Gaststätte, Breitenbrunn
275 169-1	475 017-0	BVG	2-car	1928	MS	Walburg
275 247-5	475 024-6	BVG	2-car	1929	MS	Beelitz
275 313-5	475 031-1	BVG	2-car	1929	MS	S-Bahn Exner Althüttendorf
275 319-2	475 601-1	BVG	2-car	1929	MS	Walburg
275 343-2	475 037-8	BVG	2-car	1928	P	Luckenwalde
275 357-2	475 040-2	BVG	2-car	1928	MS	S-Bahn Exner Althüttendorf
275 407-5	475 049-3	BVG	2-car	1928	MS	Walburg
275 411-7	475 050-1	BVG	2-car	1928	P	B-Falkensee, Bar
275 415-8	475 052-7	BVG	2-car	1928	MS	Klutz
275 417-4	475 053-5	BVG	2-car	1928	P	B-Falkensee, Bar
275 421-6	475 055-0	BVG	2-car	1928	P	Autohaus Albrecht, Eggersdorf
275 429-3	475 057-6	BVG	2-car	1928	M	ETM. Prora
275 517-1	475 075-8	BVG	2-car	1929	P	Gaststätte, Dabendorf
275 519-7	475 076-6	BVG	2-car	1928	P	Hohenschonhausen Bhf.

275 625-2	475 161-6	BVG	2-car	1927	M	HSB Berlin
275 641-9	475 605-2	BVG	2-car	1928	MA	S-Bahn Berlin
275 659-1	488 165-2	DR	2-car	1928	MA	HSB Berlin
275 683-1	475 60-68	BVG	2-car	1928	MS	Berlin Schöneweide
275 693-0	488 166-0	DR	2-car	1928	MA	S-Bahn Berlin
275 701-1	475 612-8	BVG	2-car	1928	P	Lübars
275 737-5	475 162-4	DR	2-car	1928	M	DBM. Nürnberg
275 747-4	488 167-8	BVG	2-car	1928	M	DTM Berlin
275 783-0	488 168-6	DR	2-car	1928	MA	S-Bahn Berlin
275 815-9	488 169-4	DR	2-car	1929	MA	S-Bahn Berlin
275 959-5	475 126-9	DR	2-car	1932	MA	S-Bahn Berlin
276 035-3	-	DR	2-car	1949	MS	DTM Berlin
276 069-2	-	DR	2-car	1938	M	HSB Berlin
276 075-9	476 602-8	DR	2-car	1928	P	Falkensee
276 243-3	476 033-6	DR	2-car	1928	M	DME. Darmstadt
276 279-7	476 061-7	DR	2-car	1928	MS	S-Bahn Exner Althüttendorf
276 301-9	476 352-0	DR	2-car	1930	MS	Private, Berlin.
276 347-2	476 372-8	DR	2-car	1930	P	Stadthalle, Kirchberg (55481)
276 415-7	476 396-7	DR	2-car	1928	P	Tiroler Stadl, Seftenberg
276 469-4	476 418-9	DR	2-car	1928	P	Schildow
276 495-9	476 074-0	DR	2-car	1928	MS	S-Bahn Exner Althüttendorf
276 503-0	476 432-0	DR	2-car	1928	P	Schildow
276 513-9	476 002-1	DR	2-car	1928	P	HSB Berlin
276 519-6	476 005-4	DR	2-car	1928	P	Bornholmerstrasse, Berlin
276 523-8	476 007-0	DR	2-car	1929	MS	S-Bahn Exner Althüttendorf
276 535-2	476 013-8	DR	2-car	1928	P	School, Berlin Spandau
276 555-0	476 023-7	DR	2-car	1930	MS	S-Bahn Exner Althüttendorf
277 003-0	477 197-8	DR	2-car	1938	M	HSB Berlin
277 087-3	477 206-7	DR	2-car	1939	M	HSB Berlin
277 129-3	477 053-3	DR	2-car	1939	P	Töpchin
277 163-2	477 070-7	DR	2-car	1940	M	Private
277 195-4	477 085-5	DR	2-car	1940	M	Ziesar-Bucknitzer Eisenbahn
277 263-0	477 117-6	DR	2-car	1943	P	Töpchin
277 267-1	477 119-2	DR	2-car	1943	P	Berlin-Schönefeld
277 403-2[II]	477 601-9	DR	2-car	1940	M	S-Bahn Exner Althüttendorf
277 407-3	477 602-7	DR	2-car	1940	M	HSB Berlin
277 407-3	477 603-5	DR	2-car	1936	M	Ziesar-Bucknitzer Eisenbahn
277 409-9	477 604-3	DR	2-car	1941	M	Pennemünde
277 415-6[II]	477 606-8	DR	2-car	1936	P	Berlin school.
277 427-1	477 184-6	DR	2-car	1935	MS	S-Bahn Exner Althüttendorf
277 449-5	477 194-5	DR	2-car	1935	MS	S-Bahn Exner Althüttendorf
278 005-4	478 004-5	DR	2-car	1925	M	S-Bahn Berlin
278 007-0	478 005-2	DR	2-car	1925	M	S-Bahn Berlin
278 101-1[II]	478 006-0	DR	2-car	1928	MS	S-Bahn Exner, Alhüttendorf
278 103-7[II]	478 007-8	DR	2-car	1928	MS	S-Bahn Exner, Alhüttendorf
278 107-8	-	DR	2-car	1928	MS	HSB Berlin
279 001-2	479 601-7	DR	Bo	1930	MS	Buckow
279 003-8	479 602-5	DR	Bo	1930	MS	Buckow
279 005-3	479 603-3	DR	Bo	1930	MS	Buckow
475 602-1	478 801-4	BVG	2-car	1928	MS	S-Bahn Exner, Althüttendorf
476 432-8	477 803-0	DR	2-car	1928	P	Berlin Schildow as imbiss/bar
476 418-9	477 803-5	DR	2-car	1928	P	Berlin Schildow as imbiss/bar
ET91 01	491 001-4	DB		1936	MR	BSW Gruppe 491, München Neuaubing
ETA150 011	515 011-5	DB	Bo BE	1955	M	BEM Nördlingen
ETA150 556	515 556-9	DB	Bo BE	1960	M	Bochum Dahlhausen
ETA176 001	517 001-4	DB	Bo-Bo BE	1956	MS	DBM. Lübeck
AT 589/590	-	DR	2A-A2 DE	1927	MR	VMD. Weimar

DMUs

Old No.	Computer No.	Co..	Type	Built	Status	Location
VT 4.12.01	173 001-9	DR	1A-A1dm	1964	MR	Hoyerswerda
VT 4.12.02	173 002-7	DR	1A-A1dm	1964	MR	Dessau

VT 06 104ab		DB	2-car	1938	M	LHB Salzgitter
VT 06 106a		DB	1/3 3-car	1938	P	Lübeck Travemünde Hafen
VT 06 106bc		DB	2/3 3-car	1938	P	Konstanz
VT 137 856a	182 009-1	DR	2-car	1938	MS	LL1
VT 137 856 b	182 010-9	DR	2-car	1938	MS	LL1
VT 08 503	613 603-0	DB	B-2 DH	1952	MA	DBM Braunschweig
VT 08 520	613 620-4	DB	B-2 DH	1954	MA	DBM Braunschweig
VT 11 5002	601 002-9	DB	B-2 DH	1957	M	Gemünden
VT 11 5008	601 008-6	DB	B-2 DH	1957	MR	DBM Lübeck
VT 11 5012	602 012-7	DB	B-2 GTH	1957	M	DBM. Nürnberg
VT 11 5013	601 013-6	DB	B-2 DH	1957	MR	DBM Lübeck
VT 11 5014	601 014-4	DB	B-2 DH	1957	MR	DBM Lübeck
VT 11 5018	601 018-5	DB	B-2 DH	1957	MR	DBM Lübeck
VT 11 5019	601 019-3	DB	B-2 DH	1957	MR	DBM Lübeck
VT 12 506	612 506-6	DB	B-2 DH	1957	MA	DBM Stuttgart
VT 12 507	612 507-4	DB	B-2 DH	1957	MA	DBM Stuttgart
VT 18.16.02a	175 003-3	DR	B-2 DH	1965	M	SEM Chemnitz Hilbersdorf
VT 18.16.02b	175 004-1	DR	B-2 DH	1965	M	SEM Chemnitz Hilbersdorf
VT 18.16.03a	175 005-8	DR	B-2 DH	1966	P	Chemnitz, Solaris
VT 18.16.03b	175 006-6	DR	B-2 DH	1966	P	Chemnitz, Solaris
VT 18.16.07b	175 014-0	DR	B-2 DH	1968	MA	Berlin Lichtenberg
VT 18.16.08a	175 015-7	DR	B-2 DH	1968	MS	Berlin Lichtenberg
VT 18.16.08b	175 016-5	DR	B-2 DH	1968	MS	Berlin Lichtenberg
VT 18.1610a	175 019-9	DR	B-2 DH	1968	MA	Berlin Lichtenberg
VT 36 519	-	DB	B-2 DH	1936	M	VEFS Bochholt
VT 60 531	723 003-0	DB	1A-2 DH	1940	MR	Aschersleben
VT 63 902	-	DB	B-2 DH	1935	M	Hamburg Wilhelmsburg
VT 66 904	-	DB	1A-A1 DM	1927	MA	Harsefeld
VT 66 906	-	DB	B-B DM	1928	MR	UEF. Gerstetten (WEG T401)
VT 70 919	-	DB	A-1 DM	1937	MA	Ebermannstadt
VT 70 921	-	DB	A-1 DM	1937	MR	DME. Darmstadt
VT 78 901	-	DB	A-1 DM	1932	M	Ebermannstadt
VT 79 902	-	DB	A-1 DM	1932	MA	VEFS Bochholt
VT 88 902	-	DB	A-1 DM	1934	M	HIS
VT 92 501	692 501-0	DB	B-2 DH	1932	MS	BEM. Nördlingen
VT 95 9122	795 122-1	DB	A-1 DM	1953	MA	HEF. Hamm
VT 95 9240	795 240-1	DB	A-1 DM	1952	MS	Worms
VT 95 9256	795 256-7	DB	A-1 DM	1952	MA	Gerolstein
VT 95 9286	795 286-4	DB	A-1 DM	1955	MA	HEF. Hamm
VT 95 9326	795 326-8	DB	A-1 DM	1957	P	Rehlingen. Clubhouse.
VT 95 9396	795 396-1	DB	A-1 DM	1954	MA	Basdorf
VT 95 9414	795 414-2	DB	A-1 DM	1954	M	Dieringhausen
VT 95 9445	795 445-6	DB	A-1 DM	1954	M	Wesseling
VT 95 9465	795 465-4	DB	A-1 DM	1954	M	DTM. Berlin
VT 95 9497	795 497-7	DB	A-1 DM	1954	MR	Wesseling
VT 95 9626	795 626-1	DB	A-1 DM	1955	M	DGEG. Bochum Dahlhausen
VT 95 9627	795 627-9	DB	A-1 DM	1955	M	Wesseling
VT 95 9662	795 662-6	DB	A-1 DM	1955	MA	CFV3V, Mariembourg, Belgium
VT 95 9669	795 669-1	DB	A-1 DM	1955	MA	CFV3V, Mariembourg, Belgium
VT 98 9597	796 597-3	DB	A-A DM	1956	MA	Giessen
VT 98 9683	796 683-1	DB	A-A DM	1960	M	Nürnberg
VT 98 9690	796 690-6	DB	A-A DM	1960	MA	Menden
VT 98 9739	796 739-1	DB	A-A DM	1960	MA	DDM. Neuenmarkt Wirsberg
VT 98 9744	796 744-1	DB	A-A DM	1960	MS	Schenklengsfeld?
VT 98 9760	796 760-7	DB	A-A DM	1960	MA	Klütz
VT 98 9761	796 761-5	DB	A-A DM	1960	M	Walburg
VT 98 9784	796 784-7	DB	A-A DM	1961	MA	Gerolstein
VT 98 9790	796 790-4	DB	A-A DM	1961	MR	Reutlingen
VT 98 9796	796 796-2	DB	A-A DM	1961	MA	Haselünne
VT 98 9802	796 802-7	DB	A-A DM	1961	MA	Menden
VT 97 902	797 502-2	DB	A-A DM	1962	MR	Reutlingen
VT 97 903	797 503-0	DB	A-A DM	1962	MR	Reutlingen
VT 97 904	797 504-8	DB	A-A DM	1962	MS	Wuppertal
VT 97 905	797 505-5	DB	A-A DM	1962	MR	Reutlingen

VT 98 9516	798 516-1	DB	A-A DM	1955	S	Neumünster
VT 98 9522	798 522-9	DB	A-A DM	1955	MA	BEM. Nördlingen
VT 98 9554	798 554-2	DB	A-A DM	1955	MS	Krefeld
VT 98 9585	798 585-6	DB	A-A DM	1956	MR	Wesseling
VT 98 9589	798 589-8	DB	A-A DM	1956	MA	Giessen
VT 98 9598	798 598-9	DB	A-A DM	1956	MA	EVG. Gerolstein
VT 98 9622	798 622-7	DB	A-A DM	1956	MA	Worms
VT 98 9623	798 623-5	DB	A-A DM	1956	MA	Stuttgart
VT 98 9625	798 625-2	DB	A-A DM	1956	MR	EFZ. Tübingen
VT 98 9629	798 629-2	DB	A-A DM	1956	MA	Frankfurt/M
VT 98 9632	798 632-6	DB	A-A DM	1956	MS	BEM. Nördlingen. (Or Private?)
VT 98 9647	798 647-4	DB	A-A DM	1956	MA	Simpelveld, Netherlands
VT 98 9652	798 652-4	DB	A-A DM	1959	MA	Ulm
VT 98 9653	798 653-2	DB	A-A DM	1959	MA	Ulm
VT 98 9659	798 659-9	DB	A-A DM	1959	MS	Ocholt
VT 98 9668	798 668-8	DB	A-A DM	1959	MR	ZSLM. Simpelveld, Netherlands
VT 98 9670	798 670-6	DB	A-A DM	1959	MR	Gerolstein
VT 98 9675	798 675-5	DB	A-A DM	1959	MA	BEM. Nördlingen
VT 98 9677	798 677-1	DB	A-A DM	1959	MS	Dorsten
VT 98 9706	798 706-8	DB	A-A DM	1960	MA	Passau
VT 98 9726	798 726-6	DB	A-A DM	1960	M	Schiltach
VT 98 9731	798 731-6	DB	A-A DM	1960	MA	Darmstadt
VT 98 9751	798 751-4	DB	A-A DM	1960	MR	Gerolstein
VT 98 9752	798 752-2	DB	A-A DM	1960	MA	Stuttgart
VT 98 9766	798 766-2	DB	A-A DM	1960	MA	Treysa
VT 98 9776	798 776-1	DB	A-A DM	1960	MR	Passau
VT 98 9777	798 777-9	DB	A-A DM	1960	S	Neumünster
VT 98 9778	798 778-7	DB	A-A DM	1960	S	Neumünster
VT 98 7979	798 794-4	DB	A-A DM	1961	MS	Seelze
VT 98 9818	798 818-1	DB	A-A DM	1962	MS	Pfalzbahn, Worms
VT 98 9823	798 823-1	DB	A-A DM	1962	M	Minden
VT 98 9825	798 825-8	DB	A-A DM	1962	MS	EfW Tours. (Now?)
VT 98 9828	798 828-2	DB	A-A DM	1962	MS	EfW Tours. (Now?)
VT 98 9829	798 829-8	DB	A-A DM	1962	MR	Giessen
VT 133 522	187 001-3	DR	A-1 DM	1933	MA	Wernigerode HSB
VT 135 054	186 257-2	DR	A-1 DM	1935	M	Stassfurt
VT 135 057		DB	A-1 DM	1935	M	ME. Minden
VT 135 060		DB	A-1 DM	1935	M	ME. Minden (Pr. Oldendorf)
VT 137 063	723 101-2	DR	2-Bo DE	1934	MR	Berlin-Schöneweide
VT 137 099	185 254-0	DR	2-Bo DE	1935	MS	DBM. Schwerin
VT 137 110	786 258-4	DR	A-1 DM	1935	MS	DBM. Halle P
VT137 225ab	183 252-6	DR	2-car	1935	P	Leipzig Hbf.
VT 137 234	183 251-8	DR	2-car	1935	MR	Eisenbahn Kurier, Leipzig?
VT 137 322	-	DR	B-2 DM	1938	MS	Bertsdorf
VT 137 527	185 256-5	DR	1A-A1 DM	1939	M	Gramzow
VT 137 532	187 101-1	DR	1A-A1 DM	1939	MA	DEV. Bruchhausen Vilsen
VT 137 566	187 025-2	DR	1A-A1 DM	1940	MA	HSB Wernigerode
188 001-2	708 001-3	DR	A-1 DM	1956	M	Stassfurt
188 005-3	708 005-4	DR	A-1 DM	1959	M	Finsterwalde
188 006-1	708 006-2	DR	A-1 DM	1959	MA	DB Leipzig
188 201-8	708 201-9	DR	2-Bo DE	1968	MR	Weimar
188 202-6	708 202-7	DR	2-Bo DE	1968	M	Dresden
188 203-4	708 203-5	DR	2-Bo DE	1968	M	SEM. Chemnitz Hilbersdorf
699 001-4	699 101-2	DB	B-2 DH	1933	MA	DEV. Bruchhausen Vilsen
Köl 6204	701 018-4	DB	A-A DM	1955	MA	Wesseling
VT38 002	712 001-7	DB	Bo-2 DE	1936	MA	Bochum Dahlhausen
VT2.09 003	771 003-1	DR	A-1 DM	1962	MA	Gramzow
VT2.09 101	772 101-4	DR	A-1 DM	1965	M	BSW. Neustrelitz
VT2.09 103	772 103-0	DR	A-1 DM	1965	MA	Oelsnitz
VT2.09 131	772 131-9	DR	A-1 DM	1968	MA	Belzig
SVT 877		DB	Part only	1932	M	DBM. Nürnberg

PRESERVED LOCOS & MUs of PRIVATE RAILWAYS

Steam

Gauge	Railway	No.	Type	Built	Status	Location etc.
1000	AVG	7s	0-4-4-0T	1898	MR	Bruchhausen Vilsen
900	Borkumer Kleinbahn	I	0-4-0WT	1938	MA	Borkum
900	Borkumer Kleinbahn	II	0-4-0WT	1937	P	Bevern
1000	Klb. Bremen - Turmstedt	1	0-6-0T	1899	P	Bremen
1435	BE	22	0-6-0WT	1925	P	Nordhorn
1435	BLE	146	2-6-0T	1941	MA	Bochum Dahlhausen
1000	Brohltalbahn	Sm 11	0-4-4-0T	1906	MS	Brohl
1435	DEG	184	0-8-0T	1946	MR	Darmstadt
1435	DHE	4	0-6-0T	1925	MS	Haaksbergen, Netherlands
1435	FK	262	2-8-2T	1954	MR	Huttwil, Switzerland
1435	HzL	11	0-8-0T	1911	MA	Neuffen
1435	HzL	16	0-8-0T	1928	MR	Kornwestheim
1435	Julicher Kreisbahn	152	2-6-0T	1927	MA	Haaksbergen, Netherlands
1000	Klb. Hoya-Syke-Asendorf	31	0-6-0T	1899	MS	Asendorf
1000	Klb. Hoya-Syke-Asendorf	33	0-6-0T	1899	P	Bruchhausen Vilsen
1000	KAE	13	0-6-0T	1907	P	Altena
1000	KAE	15	0-6-0T	1911	MA	Bruchhausen Vilsen
1000	KAE	22	0-6-0T	1930	M	Ludenscheid
1435	KFBE	21	0-8-0T	1915	M	Dieringhausen
1435	KNE	206	0-10-0T	1941	MR	Kassel
1435	Lb. Lam - Kotzting/Schwarzeck		0-8-0T	1928	M	Bayerisch Eisenstein
1000	MEG	46	0-4-0T	1897	MS	Schierwaldenrath
1000	MEG	101	0-4-0T	1949	MA	Worblaufen, Switzerland
1000	OEG	56	0-4-0T	1886	M	Mannheim
1000	OEG	102	0-4-0Tm	1891	M	Mannheim
1435	Marburger Kreisbahn	1	0-6-0T	1904	MA	Bad Nauheim
1435	RAG	01	0-6-0WT	1890	M	Bayerisch Eisenstein
1435	RAG	03	0-6-0T	1923	M	Bayerisch Eisenstein
1435	RAG	04	0-8-0T	1927	M	Bayerisch Eisenstein
1435	RAG	05	0-8-0T	1927	M	Bayerisch Eisenstein
785	RSE	53	2-8-2T	1944	M	Asbach
1435	SWEG	7	0-4-0T	1907	P	Staufen
1435	SWEG	14	0-6-0T	1902	MS	Offenbach
1435	SWEG	20	0-6-0WT	1928	MS	Ottenhofen
1435	SWEG	23	0-6-0WT	1897	P	Zell Unterharmersbach
750	SWEG	24	0-6-0T	1929	MR	Dörzbach
1435	SWEG	28	0-6-0WT	1900	MA	Ottenhöfen
1435	SWEG	30	0-6-0T	1904	MA	Kandern
1435	SWEG	394	0-8-0T	1917	P	Rust/Lahr
1435	TAG	7	2-8-2T	1936	MR	Landshut
1435	TAG	8	2-6-4T	1942	M	Nördlingen
1435	TWE	154	2-6-0T	1940	MA	Mariembourg, Belgium
1000	WEG (AL)	2s	0-6-0T	1901	M	Amstetten
1000	WNB	11	0-4-0T	1913	MS	Neresheim
1000	WNB	12	0-4-0T	1913	MA	Neresheim
1000	Zell-Todtnau	74	0-6-0T	1888	M	Bochum Dahlhausen
1000	Zell-Todtnau	104	0-6-6-0T	1925	M	Chaulin, Switzerland
1000	Zell-Todtnau	105	0-4-4-0T	1918	M	Chaulin, Switzerland

Diesel

Gauge	Railway	No.	Type	Built	Status	Location etc.
1435	AKN	V2.003	0-8-0DH	1953	MA	Wiesbaden
1435	AKN	V2.004	0-8-0 DH	1953	MS	Almstedt
1435	AKN	V2.011	B DM	1935	MA	Sch"nberg
1435	BE	D 10	B DM	1941	MS	Stadskanal, Netherlands
1000	Borkumer Kleinbahn.	Emden	Bo DE	1942	MA	Bruchhausen Vilsen